The Police of Paris
1718–1789

The
POLICE
of PARIS

1718-1789

ALAN WILLIAMS

Louisiana State University Press
Baton Rouge and London

Designer: Albert Crochet
Typeface: VIP Trump Medieval
Typesetter: G&S Typesetters, Inc.
Printer: Thomson Shore, Inc.
Binder: John Dekker & Sons, Inc.

LIBRARY OF CONGRESS CATALOGING IN PUBLICATION DATA

Williams, Alan, 1944–
    The police of Paris, 1718–1789.

    Bibliography: p.
    Includes index.
    1. Paris—Police—History.   2. Police
administration—France—Paris—History.   I. Title.
HV8206.P3W54   363.2'0944'361   78–24189
ISBN 0–8071–0491–4

For my parents

Contents

Tables

Maps

Abbreviations

For the sake of brevity, I have employed the following abbreviations in footnotes:

AN   Archives Nationales

APP   Archives de la Préfecture de Police

BA   Bibliothèque de l'Arsenal

BHVP Bibliothèque Historique de la Ville de Paris

BN   Bibliothèque Nationale

BO   Bibliothèque Municipale d'Orléans

c.p.   *cote provisoire* (provisional classification)

JF   Collection Joly de Fleury at the Bibliothèque Nationale

MS(S) fr. *manuscrit(s) français* (French manuscripts—manuscripts in French rather than another language such as Latin or Greek) at the Bibliothèque Nationale

n.a.   *nouvelles acquisitions* (new acquisitions)

Preface

This study of what was initially an urban institution—the police—began ironically in a barn. Well, in what once had been a barn, though by the time I first saw the place it was full of books, not hay or cows. It was here, while going through a worn old set of encyclopedias, that I initially found allusion to the lieutenancy of police, here that I first encountered the claim that this official had been one of the most interesting and powerful figures in prerevolutionary France. Intrigued, I began to look for more information. Books about the police of Paris during the seventeenth and eighteenth centuries did not prove hard to find; but as I made my way through them, I found that many questions remained unanswered. Despite the work that had been done, much of it unfortunately no more than anecdotal, I could only concur with Olwen Hufton's description of the police as "perhaps the most neglected element of *ancien régime* society." Anyone interested in details about their structure and work does, in the end, find himself, as she put it, "confronted with an almost impenetrable blanket of ignorance."

There was no alternative, given my persistent curiosity, but to set about studying the police myself. How, indeed, were they organized? How many of them were there? What did they actually spend most of their time doing? How did they or their activity change across time, and what impact did their work or changes in it have on the lives of Parisians and on the regime that the police served? These were the principal questions I put to myself; what follows is an attempt to answer them.

But why bother? What makes the police worth such attention? In all societies, it is part of the business of the police to observe carefully what goes on about them. They are, in a sense, a society's eyes permanently fixed on itself, and through them—through these eyes—we obtain as complete a panorama of that society as we are likely to find. Whichever level of society attracts our attention, whatever our particular preoccupation, we can turn, if we have access, to the files of the police, reasonably confident that their curiosity has preceded us, that from them we can obtain some of the information we seek. But it is not only the unblinking sweep of their view that makes the police interesting; it is also their occasional encounter with the extraordinary. In their company we may hope to escape mundane circumstance for a time, to pass beyond the familiar and satisfy our timid but powerful curiosity about the bizarre, the deviant, the unusual. Indeed, by following the activity of another society's police, we may not only observe conduct we consider strange but also determine the contour of that other culture's boundary between normal and deviant behavior. And, through the police, we may find our ordinary emotional states altered by vicarious contact with danger and tragedy, or we may gratify our desire to become party to the secrets of whatever world intrigues us.

For what they permit us to know and experience, the police of any society might well merit our attention. But there are additional, specific reasons for studying the police of eighteenth-century Paris. To begin with, this company of men constituted, by virtue of its size, tasks, and structure, the first modern police force to evolve in Europe. As such, and because of its reputation for efficiency, it served as a model to many of France's neighbors—to the English as they experimented in Ireland during the 1790s; to Maria Theresa and Vienna; to Scandinavian monarchs in the 1770s; to at least one state in northern Italy; and, following the Revolution, to Napoleon in France itself as he reconstructed the police of Paris. The urban police forces of Europe developed in the light of what had been achieved in Paris, choosing sometimes to imitate, sometimes to alter forms and procedures they could do anything with but ignore. To understand fully their development, one must know something about the institution that preceded them.

In addition, if significant portions of the French past must remain incomprehensible unless one knows something about the history of Paris, so, too, must developments in that city at times confound those who have no understanding of its police. The person who headed the Parisian police prior to 1789, the lieutenant of police, was one of the ten most powerful figures in France—a veritable minister, Roland Mousnier has called him. During the last century of the Old Regime, the lieutenant of police served as the crown's principal representative

in Paris, finding time to intervene in matters as diverse as the machina-
tions of high politics and the domestic squabbles of the poor. Inevitably, this individual and those who served him played a significant part
in shaping the course of events in Paris, a course that more than once
dictated what happened elsewhere in France.

Study of the Parisian police is important, then, to the history of
police forces elsewhere in Europe and to the history of an imposing
city. But it is also important, I would argue, to our understanding of the
state and its evolution; for the creation of the lieutenancy of police in
1667 represents for the French crown—for the French state—an important departure, a decision to reach beyond its traditional functions of
defense and justice to assume, in one city at least, extensive new responsibilities for public order and public welfare. The word "police"
was, in the seventeenth century, a rough synonym for control or administration, a way of referring (as in the full title given the royal
provincial administrators who were properly known as intendants of
justice, police, and finances) to all that government might do in addition to making war, settling legal disputes, and collecting taxes. In
naming a lieutenant of police for Paris, the crown was declaring its
intention to venture into a vast new domain of potential activity. To
discover how far it went, to determine the precise extent of its new
endeavor, one must examine the work of those in Paris who, for the
first time, began seriously to exercise those police powers the crown
had long claimed but only occasionally used and never defined. Study
of the police permits us to track the progress of the French state as
it moved from its long-standing, relatively passive, domestic role of
adjudicator toward an expanded definition of its competence, a definition that involved it in efforts to direct and control dimensions of life
it had formerly neglected, or whose management it had been content
to leave to others.

The new royal ambitions in Paris, manifest after 1667, constituted
both a threat and a promise to those who inhabited the city: a threat to
established institutions like the Church and the Parlement whose ancient prerogatives were increasingly infringed; a promise to all who
suffered from the insalubrity, inconvenience, and insecurity of life in
seventeenth-century Paris. When it created the lieutenancy of police,
the French monarchy marked out a sphere of ambition and activity
that enhanced its resemblance to a modern state; but in so doing it
generated or exacerbated hostilities that would haunt it until the Rev-

olution; and it assumed responsibilities that would make it, rather than a congeries of other social institutions, accountable for the quality of life in Paris.

Despite real progress, which we shall chart, the French crown with its limited resources and proclivity for war could not fulfill its implicit promise to cure the ills of urban life. But the undertaking, apparent above all in the work of the police, was in many ways a worthy one; for the new tasks the police assumed in Paris on behalf of the state represent an early and limited experiment in what we might be inclined to call "modernization," an attempt to purge at least one European city of all that was primitive in it. Eighteenth-century usage equated "police" with the existence of civilization itself: where there was policing, there was civilized, modern society; where there was not, there was only barbarism. To take seriously the work of policing Paris, as the crown did after 1667, was to admit the rudeness that remained in France's most important city and to undertake at home the mission of modernizing, of civilizing, that Frenchmen, like other Europeans, had begun to arrogate to themselves abroad.

But if the police of prerevolutionary Paris are important as a model to other European states, as a prominent force in the history of an influential city, and as an embodiment of the French government's new domestic pretensions and its desire to civilize—to modernize—a significant portion of its own society, why consider only a part of that police's past, why choose to begin their study in 1718 rather than in 1667 when tradition has it they were established? For two reasons: first, in order not to duplicate the extensive and decent work that has been done on the early history of the police, especially on the first lieutenant of police, Nicolas de la Reynie, who has served as the subject for several books; and second, because my own research has led me to conclude that the significant history of the Old Regime's police lies not in the seventeenth century, where most attention has thus far been directed, but in the eighteenth.

To be sure it was Jean Baptiste Colbert and Louis XIV who gave Paris its first lieutenant of police, but it was their successors who furnished this single new official with subordinates; and though it was also Colbert and Louis who formally delineated a broad new sphere of responsibility and activity for the state, it was again those who followed them to power after 1715 who created an agency of sufficient size to make the state's new pretensions something more than ludicrous. While neither of Louis XIV's lieutenants of police ever had to complain (as did the officer who before them had borne principal responsibility for order in the city) that he had only two or three men on whom he could count to execute the king's will, neither of these individuals possessed anything approaching a force adequate to their responsibilities. If the seventeenth century did, indeed, establish an important new royal post in Paris, it was really the eighteenth century—the century we shall consider here—that created the city's police.

Having too many times felt the frustration that goes with encountering words or passages in a language that one does not read, I have tried in what follows to translate as much as possible. But, as everyone who has acquired some second language knows, there is a point at which translation becomes deception. As long as cultures remain distinct, many—perhaps most—words in one language will have no precise equivalent in another. A French boy who learns to use the word *église* in the midst of Catholic masses and Gothic spires will never mean the same thing when he pronounces or writes this word as does an American boy who learns to say "church" in a New England town.

The subject of this book is one aspect of a culture that was different from our own, a culture that lies distant from us not only in space but in time; so I ask the reader simply to accept the fact that a number of terms essential to any work on the police of eighteenth-century Paris have no good equivalents in English. Hence, except where custom or elaborate description of function in the text justifies use of translation, I have left in French the names of most offices and institutions, often providing in parentheses a rough English translation or equivalent on the first occasion of their use.

Noble titles appear in their English form for the convenience of the general reader; but with this practice must go the warning that here, too, translation can be misleading, for the attributes and prerogatives of a French *duc* or *marquis* or *comte* were not the same as those of a man bearing one of these titles in eighteenth-century England. Ordinary citations from French sources I have given in English; the translations are my own unless otherwise noted.

In preparing this work, I have encountered many forms of generosity and assistance. These range from the financial support provided by Yale University and the Alliance Française de New York—support which made possible and more pleasurable the research I did in France —to the helpful questions of colleagues who took time from their own inquiry to further mine. Both Chief Dilieto of the New Haven police and Police Commissioner Robert J. diGrazia of Boston found time in the midst of busy schedules to answer questions I addressed to them. For their help and their openness I am truly grateful, as I am to Professor Raymond Kierstead for the kind assistance he offered me years ago as I first began to talk about working on the police.

Celia Sparger has given many hours of her time and much care to helping me prepare the manuscript for this book; Marty Lentz, Douglas Barger, and Charles Church have all had a hand in the exacting task of doing the maps; and, to help cover the cost of all this work, Wake Forest University has provided generous assistance. Finally, I am pleased to have a chance to thank Professor R. R. Palmer for the wise counsel and patient commentary he has offered me during the whole course of this project.

Any individual inquiry has its limits. Some of these boundaries we can alter, some we cannot; some yield before the application of money and the exercise of discipline, some do not. Others will note in what follows the deficiencies that were not inevitable and rightly, I suppose, censure me for them. Still, my own inclination is to shirk responsibility for these shortcomings and blame them instead on good friends, whose company was often too rich to quit, and on all the distractions of Paris.

But Paris is a veritable ocean. Sound it; you
will never know its depth. Examine it, describe
it! Whatever care you take in examining it, in
describing it; however numerous and committed may
be the explorers of this sea, there will always
remain a virgin place, an unknown grotto, flowers,
pearls, monsters—something extraordinary—overlooked
by literary divers.

Balzac, *Père Goriot*

The history of the Parisian police . . . would be
the history of the city itself.

Maurice Bloch and Henride Pontich,
*Administration de la ville de Paris
et du departement de la Seine*

Part I

The Power of the Police

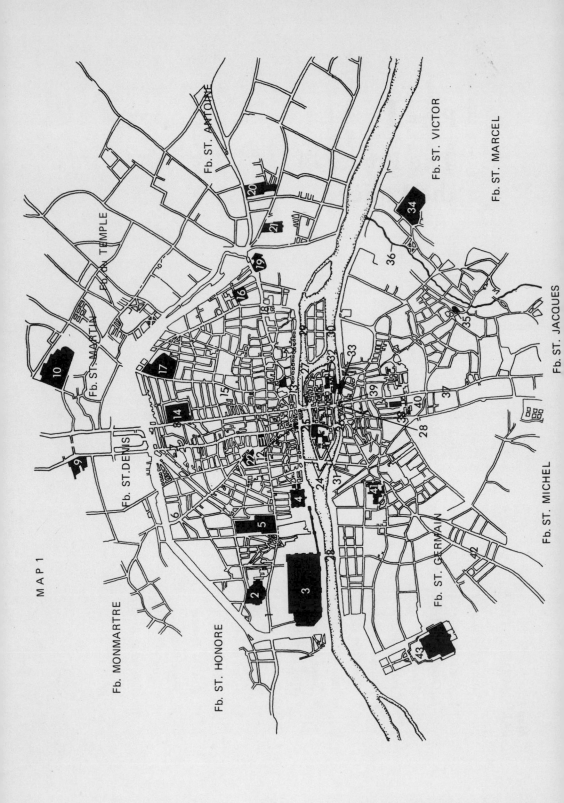

MAP 1

Fb. MONMARTRE

Fb. ST. HONORE

Fb. ST. DENIS

Fb. ST. MARTIN

Fb. DU TEMPLE

Fb. ST. ANTOINE

Fb. ST. VICTOR

Fb. ST. MARCEL

Fb. ST. JACQUES

Fb. ST. MICHEL

Fb. ST. GERMAIN

Map 1
PARIS, MID-CENTURY

1 Rue Saint Honoré
2 Place Louis le Grand (Place Vendôme)
3 Garden and Palace of the Tuileries
4 Louvre
5 Palais-Royal
6 Rue Montmartre
7 Rue Saint Denis
8 Rue Saint Martin
9 Saint Lazare
10 Hôpital Saint Louis
11 Cemetery of the Innocents
12 Châtelet
13 Hôtel de Ville
14 Saint Martin
15 Rue du Temple
16 Place Royale
17 Temple
18 Rue Saint Antoine

19 Bastille
20 Enfants Trouvés (Foundling Hospital)
21 Hôtel des Mousquetaires (Musketeers barracks)
22 Halle au Blé (Grain market)
23 Pont Royal
24 Pont Neuf
25 Pont au Change
26 Pont Saint Michel
27 Pont Notre-Dame
28 Petit Pont
29 Pont Marie
30 Pont de la Tournelle
31 Palais
32 Notre-Dame
33 Hôtel-Dieu
34 Salpêtrière
35 Saint Médard

36 Bièvre or Gobelins stream
37 Rue Saint Jacques
38 Rue de la Harpe
39 Petit Châtelet
40 Sorbonne
41 Saint Germain des Prés
42 Rue de Sèvres
43 Les Invalides

1

Toward Definition

Study of the past is enough, sometimes, to make one believe in ghosts; for now and then, in accounts of the centuries that lie behind us, there are tales of strange creatures that do not perish as would a man or woman, that instead live on through successive generations and, yet, manage to leave no trace of themselves. The police of eighteenth-century Paris are, in a way, one of these creatures. Examine any text on the history of France, and you are likely to learn that the police came into being in 1667. Go further and you can, if you are interested, find books devoted to their establishment and subsequent activity. And yet, relevant documents of the late seventeenth and early eighteenth centuries make no mention of them. Viewed from the perspective these materials afford, Paris seems not to have known it had a police force prior to the Revolution. It is embarrassing and disturbing, but one begins to wonder whether such an entity really existed.

There is, then, a mystery of sorts about the police. Earnest and able historians casually include them in their discussions of Paris and France, but men and women alive at the time seem not to have been able to see them. Reluctantly one concludes that the first step in any study of the police is going to be that of finding them.

Doing this, however, turns out to be less a matter of detection than of semantic clarification and arbitrary decision. Though sources prior to 1750 refer to no body of men as the police, the word itself appears frequently in unexpected contexts; and comprehending this presence, deciphering usage that is unfamiliar, becomes the first step anyone interested in locating the police must take. To track those who initially appear so elusive, one must begin here—with a word, and with an effort to shake from it the sense it had for eighteenth-century Parisians.

The task is by no means an easy one. Writing from exile several years

5

after revolution had forced him from Paris, Jean Charles Lenoir, a former lieutenant of police, spoke of the abundant and careless use his countrymen made of the word "police": "Formerly in society, that which is a part of police and that which is a part of discipline were confounded as are today the many and diverse usages of the word *police*. These meanings, poorly understood, give rise to arbitrary and contradictory interpretations. High police, ordinary police, military police, inspectorial police, police of the streets, police of buildings, police of governmental properties—it is without end."[1]

Revolution had not sufficed to remedy all the ills of the Old Regime; for the conceptual confusion of which Lenoir complained in the 1790s had, as he implied, preceded the events of 1789. Throughout the seventeenth and eighteenth centuries the French wrote the word "police" readily and in what appears to us, no less than to Lenoir, an overwhelming variety of contexts: the statutes of a guild announced that its officers "will make . . . the visits and inspections necessary for the well-being and the Police of their Community"; a commissioner of the Châtelet, the busiest of the royal courts in Paris, was required to draw up "in each of [his] Polices an exact list of the violations he will have observed"; an official of the municipal government spoke of "those regulations which have been made for the maintenance of the Police"; and in 1770 appeared a statute "to fix for all time the limits of the police between the *bureau de ville* and the Châtelet."[2] One finds that there were "judicial officers having police," "troubles and accidents that could interrupt good order and police," "police sentences," "assemblies of Police," and a "chamber of Police"; indeed, one finds the word police, as did Lenoir, in what first seems an inexhaustible number of confusing contexts.

Converting this confusion into comprehension requires above all stifling one's initial impulse to equate police with the image of a group of men in uniform. This ready association confounds all effort to appreciate seventeenth- and eighteenth-century usage, usage in which the word designated no identifiable body of men and no administrative agency—in which, in fact, it referred to no entity whatsoever.

1. MS 477, fol. 23 in the *nouvelles acquisitions* (new acquisitions) of the Bibliothèque Historique de la Ville de Paris (hereinafter cited as BHVP, MS n.a. 477, fol. 23).
2. These brief citations and those that follow I draw from documents scattered throughout MS 1333 of the Collection Joly de Fleury in the Bibliothèque Nationale (hereinafter cited as BN, MS JF 1333), and from MS 13728 in Series Y of the Archives Nationales (hereinafter cited as AN, Y 13728).

Where are the police of Paris? The initial, awkward response to this question is that they are nowhere, that they do not exist. To what, then, did the word police refer? A different question and yet an important one; for by answering it, one begins to discover a way out of confusion. Prior to 1750, police designated not an entity but an act, or rather, a group of actions. Comprehending a sixteenth-, seventeenth-, or eighteenth-century passage in which the word police appears requires that one begin by equating it not with a company of men but with a set of functions. What is needed is the mentality of an army sergeant or a Boy Scout leader who, bent on bringing order to a small universe, insists that a barracks or campsite be properly policed. This usage in English is generically similar to that one encounters everywhere in French during the seventeenth and eighteenth centuries. Like residents of Paris under the Old Regime, the sergeant and the scout leader treat police as an activity; and if we do the same, we can begin to make sense of our materials. Viewing police as a function rather than an entity, it is no longer puzzling to find a public officer engaged "doing his police" or to discover that an edict of 1699 has "removed the functions of police from those of the senior Officers of [royal] courts." Nor does a judicial decision of 1707 that speaks of "the . . . functions of the commissioners at the Châtelet, of which Police is one of the principal" require anything more than a single reading.

Having discovered before about 1750 no contemporary designation of a body of men as the police, we are left to devise our own limits for the term as we ordinarily employ it.[3] Anachronism this may be, but there is no alternative for a study of the police that presumes to begin in 1718. Locating the police of Paris becomes a matter of creating them conceptually, of deciding upon and indicating those one intends in using this difficult word. Two ways of proceeding suggest themselves. Having determined that police is a set of functions, we might attempt to specify the nature of these activities and designate as the police those engaged in performing them. Or, after 1667 when a single man, the lieutenant of police, is given considerable authority over police activity in Paris, we might use this individual as a point of reference and name all those subordinate to him the police. While neither ap-

3. As late as 1779 the lieutenant of police himself, in referring to those charged with police functions, spoke of them not as the police but as "judicial officers having police"; and not until the fifth edition of its dictionary (largely complete in 1789, but not published until 1798) did the Académie Française sanction application of the term to those who acted as well as to the act itself.

proach is without its problems and neither permits the elimination of a certain arbitrariness, both appear to promise a way out of difficulty, a way of locating the Parisian police.

One course, then, seems to begin with an identification of those activities the seventeenth and eighteenth centuries associated with the word police. Despite the ring of paradox, one may well say that though Paris lacked a police force in 1650 and 1720, it did not want for policing. Numbers of men performed police functions without bearing what we would judge the appropriate title. Is it not reasonable to consider these men the police force we are hunting? But what, then, were the functions they performed? Was the term "police," as we might initially suspect, a means of denoting that part of public administration concerned with the enforcement of law and the prevention of crime? To this question there is no simple reply; for, in exploring usage of the word throughout the duration of the Old Regime, one is trying to lay hands on something in flight, on meaning in the process of change.

"Police" did not in 1750 designate the same activities it had two hundred years before. With the flow of time, usage changed, shifting slowly from broad to narrow denotation, from the designation of general and extensive powers to more specific, more limited functions. Consider a sixteenth-century equivalent of the term, that offered by Robert Estienne in his *Dictionnaire françois-latin* of 1539: police he defines simply as "the . . . government of a republic." Far from describing some limited administrative activity, the word is equated with the act of governance itself. This equation continues throughout the sixteenth century and on into the seventeenth. In the first edition of his *Dictionarie of the French and English Tongues* (1611), Randle Cotgrave offers "to order, govern, rule advisedly" as synonyms for the verb *policier* and defines police as "civill government." Nicolas Delamare, writing as late as 1720, claims in his *Traité de la police* that the word is still often understood to mean government; hence, he continues, there may be a police that is monarchical, another that is aristocratic, and yet a third that is democratic.[4] In each of these definitions—one from the sixteenth century, one from the seventeenth, and one from the eighteenth—police stands as a synonym for governance or, one might say, for the act of control: control over an area as extensive as the state itself; control of all activity, all dimensions of experience, deemed

4. Nicolas Delamare and Le Clerc du Brillet, *Traité de la police* (2nd ed., rev., 3 vols.; Amsterdam, 1729), I, 2.

properly subject to public authority; control unqualified by adjectives like administrative or judicial.

Though police might be used as late as 1720 as an equivalent for governance, this was, by then, no longer its most common denotation. It had, during the seventeenth century, begun to assume a more limited sense, one that came gradually to predominate. While the word remained roughly synonymous with regulation or control, both the space over which such control was exercised and the range of activities subject to it narrowed. Appropriately, given its etymology (from the Greek *polis*, for city), police came to mean regulation not of an entire state but of a city. As early as 1611, Cotgrave, after defining police as civil government, quoted a lawyer who claimed the word properly referred to "the regulation of the city." He continued his discussion by noting that the "right of police" was the "power to make particular orders for the government of all the inhabitants of a Towne or Territorie." By the end of the first quarter of the eighteenth century the link between police and city was firmly established. Pierre Richelet, in his *Nouveau Dictionnaire françois* (1719), says nothing about state or republic, defining the word simply as "regulation of the city." The same definition, once again without reference to the state, appears in François Chasles's *Dictionnaire universel, chronologique et historique de justice, police et finance*, which appeared in 1725. More importantly, given the influence of his work, Delamare, having indicated that police may serve as a synonym for government, goes on to say that ordinarily its sense is more restricted, designating not the governance of a state but the administration of a city, the "public order of every town."[5]

By extension police is sometimes used to refer not simply to a form of control but to the results of this control—not only to various acts of regulation but to the consequent harmony and order these acts were thought to produce. It is in this sense that Delamare uses the word here. One meets it elsewhere, as in a royal declaration posted in Paris in 1729 which proclaims that it had "for its object to maintain the Police in the enclosed and open markets of this city"; and it is in this extended sense that the *Dictionnaire de Trévoux* treats police together with religion as equivalent to civilization itself: "in general it [the word "police"] is the opposite of barbarism. The savages of America had neither faith nor police when they were discovered." In contrast

5. The prefatory remarks to the *Traité de la police* served as the basis for the article on police which appears in the famous *Encyclopédie* of Diderot and d'Alembert.

to the unregulated life of the American Indians who lack all police and live consequently "like beasts" stands the Jesuits' portrayal of China as the best policed and hence the most harmonious, most civilized of eighteenth-century societies.[6]

As police becomes increasingly associated with the city during the seventeenth and eighteenth centuries, the number of functions encompassed by the term diminishes. Gradually, it ceases to be an adequate substitute for the act of governance, taking on a more restricted sense, though one that is not easy to delineate. An attempt at such delineation might begin by indicating that the term encompassed what today would be considered both judicial and administrative functions. Under each of these rubrics it is easier to indicate what the word did not designate than to give it a coherent positive content.

Comprehending police as a judicial function involves distinguishing a kind of case, which, under the Old Regime, was considered neither criminal nor civil, but which lay between these two familiar forms of jurisdiction. In common with criminal justice, *police judiciaire*, or judicial police, treated incidents of behavior viewed as having import for the community as a whole, conduct in whose detection and prosecution the community took an immediate interest. It differed from criminal jurisdictions only in that the behavior judged, while perceived as antisocial, did not warrant the extreme disapprobation expressed by the word "criminal." The inhabitant of a city who, in the heat of summer, permitted refuse to collect on his property warranted public prosecution; but his behavior, while meriting censure of some kind, was not, in the eyes of his contemporaries, criminal. Those deciding this kind of affair performed the function known as *police judiciaire*, and it was to the rendering of such judgments that one referred in speaking of police as a judicial activity. Montesquieu used the word in this sense when he wrote in *Spirit of the Laws* (Book XXVI, chapter xxiv): "Matters of police are affairs of the moment in which little is ordinarily involved; hence, formalities are hardly necessary. Police judgments are prompt, and they concern themselves with everyday matters; heavy punishments are, therefore, inappropriate here. . . . Thus, one must not confound major violations of the law with a simple police violation; these things are of a different order."

That police should designate certain administrative functions is in-

6. BN, MS JF 1322, fol. 47; *Dictionnaire universel françois et latin, vulgairement appelé Dictionnaire de Trévoux* (7th ed., 8 vols.; Paris, 1771).

tuitively less surprising for us than its use to describe a form of justice; but the administrative functions to which it refers, we quickly discover, do not readily correspond to our notion of appropriate police activity. Most significantly, these functions are more extensive than those we are accustomed to associating with modern police forces. While no longer coextensive with governance itself, police remains a way of designating much more than the detection of crime and the guarantee of personal and proprietary security. The title the crown gave its omnicompetent representatives in the provinces during the seventeenth and eighteenth centuries—intendant of justice, police, and finances—suggests the broad compass of the term. In this context police appears to be a way of describing all administrative acts of government but the assessment and collection of taxes; and, if one excepts as well provisions for defense, this is what it was: an omnibus term, a handy, flexible device for referring to activities as disparate as censorship and poor relief.

If the reach of the term made it useful to eighteenth-century administrators, this same characteristic discourages efforts to locate the police by reference to function. Such an approach, given the variety and number of activities the word encompassed, can only produce a delineation of the police that is of extraordinary and unconvincing proportions. Most contemporary attempts to give the term precision only underscore its unmanageable extent. Equating police with control or regulation, the *Dictionnaire* of the French Academy (4th ed., 1762) seeks to distinguish police activity from other forms of control by referring to its purpose. Police, it asserts, is regulation "established in a city for all that affects the security and comfort of the inhabitants." The article in the *Encyclopédie* employs the same technique in its effort to define police. Men, the article contends, seek two things from social existence: comfort and order. Ironically, a social context brings to the surface more of the evil in man than does isolation; hence, one finds among individuals gathered together more error, more selfishness and egotism, more passion than one would observe among the same number of human beings living separately. Paradoxically, the very ends that initially brought men to live in one another's presence prove harder to attain as a consequence of their assembly. Police activity is the community's response to this dilemma, its effort to resolve the paradox confronting it. Regardless of the particular forms it may take under varying circumstances, it is regulation whose peculiar preoccupation is

procuring "for the residents of a city, of the Capital for example, a comfortable and tranquil life, despite the work of error and the disturbances
of selfishness and passion." It is hard to see how these efforts at definition permit one to distinguish functions properly described by the
word "police" from other activities of government. What act of government may not be said to aim at either the preservation of public order
or the promotion of public well-being?

Other attempts at definition, while also implicitly equating police
with control, seek to narrow the conception by specifying not simply
the purpose of such control but the areas over which it is exercised. In
his *Thresor de la langue françoise* (1606), Jean Nicot defined police as
regulation of "supplies, clothing, commerce and other things affecting
the good of all." More than a century later Pierre Richelet offered a
similar definition in his *Nouveau Dictionnaire françois* (1719): "police
consists in making various regulations for the well-being of a city, and
these diverse regulations ought to concern themselves with supplies,
occupations, streets, and roads." While these definitions, especially
the latter, are indeed more precise, few would have regarded them as
sufficiently extensive. In the eyes of most, police—though it included
control over artisanal activity, city streets, and essential commodities
—had a broader compass. But because its extent remains without clear
perimeters, because the nature and number of activities it designates
are finally indeterminate, hunting the police by way of function leads
only to frustration.

To embark on this course, to use function as a means of identification, is to lose oneself amid the myriad forms of control to which the
word police was applied; it is to seek conceptual precision where none
exists. A few makers of dictionaries might agree that certain functions
were clearly part of police activity; but beyond the quintessential lay
vast stretches of ambiguity, and anyone who has ventured into them
can only sympathize with the eighteenth-century lexicographer's reluctance to do so. Proceeding to the limits prescribed by these functions and having found no boundary to police, one goes on without a
chart hoping to stumble against some tangible frontier. But, in the end,
none exists. Police activity and other governmental functions shade
into and out of one another in an elaborate chiaroscuro.

Conceptual ambiguity is not the only obstacle to using functional
criteria to locate the police. Eliminate this ambiguity insofar as possible; confine oneself to those activities that lexicographers concur in

placing within the province of police power; and, still, the result is
unsatisfactory. While the number of individuals within Paris claiming
some voice in the regulation of craft and commerce or the control of
construction and city streets may not have quite equalled the city's
population, it was certainly large. A police force delineated using these
activities as touchstones would include, among others, the members of
the Parisian Parlement, the officers of the Hôtel de Ville, the treasurers of France for the *généralité* of Paris, and an assortment of baillis,
abbots, and public prosecutors. In the end, functional criteria simply
do not permit one to distinguish something called the police from the
whole complicated apparatus of eighteenth-century urban administration.

Yet, an effort at their enumeration is not without value, suggesting,
as it does, some of the themes to which study of the police must lead.
Clearly a work on the police must be, in part, a work on governance,
and, as such, to some extent a reiteration of tales told elsewhere concerning the Old Regime—tales of expansion, of growing specialization
and consequent problems of coordination, of rival claims to authority
and ensuing struggle. If public order and communal well-being are conceived to be the characteristic objectives of police activity, then such a
study cannot neglect the relationship between these two aspirations
and their relative importance in determining lines of policy and the
allocation of resources. Nor, given the increasing association of police
activity with urban areas, can interest in the police of the eighteenth
century fail to become, at least in part, interest in the city, in its prob-
blems, and in efforts to resolve them.

But the immediate difficulty remains that of locating the police. If
functional criteria are inadequate, there yet remains a structural device, one afforded by the creation in 1667 of what initially seems a
minor magistracy. Charged in theory with supervising police activity
in the city, the new magistrate—the lieutenant of police—provides an
alternative means of identifying the elusive police of the capital, a
means before unavailable. Where are the police of Paris? They lie at the
end of each line of authority linking the new magistrate to those who
served him as agents. Locating the Parisian police becomes a matter of
discovering and naming those who assisted the lieutenant of police in
the performance of his duties.

Though this procedure is more fruitful than one based on an effort to
enumerate police functions, it is not without its own difficulties. Lines

of authority reaching downward from the lieutenancy of police are sometimes tenuous and difficult to trace; and, in seeking to reconstruct them, one cannot always be sure that the finished work is exact. Authority over another individual assumes various forms and is not always easy to document. Under the Old Regime it depended on more than the position a man occupied. Personal status, the "protection" one could enlist, and a number of other circumstances that varied with the individual had more than a negligible share in determining its extent. In addition, the lines of command descending from the lieutenancy of police did not remain free from confusing entanglement with other bonds of authority. Unraveling the confusion, one finds agents of the lieutenant of police tied at times to other officials in the city—the prévôt des marchands (provost of merchants), for example. Should one call these individuals policemen, or instead consider them subordinates of this older municipal authority?

Beyond the difficulty of determining what constituted subordination to the lieutenant of police lies another problem. Relying on a structural criterion to define the police and using the new magistrate as a point of reference, one finds that each of those who acted as lieutenant of police had other responsibilities as well; and it is not always easy to decide which subordinates served him as lieutenant of police and which, for example, as a commissioner of the Council of State or as director of the Librairie (booktrade).

When the latter post fell vacant in 1763 following the resignation of Lamoignon de Malesherbes, the crown named Antoine de Sartine, already lieutenant of police, to fill it. Uniting in his own hands two positions long separate, Sartine gained control over 130 men—the regime's censors—who had not worked for him a year before. Are we to designate these new subordinates members of the police force in accord with our criterion; or are we to say that subordination to Sartine was not necessarily subordination to the lieutenant of police, thereby leaving the censors, for purposes of classification, what they were before—employees of the Chancellory?

Consider another case posing a similar problem—that of Louis Charles de Machault, lieutenant of police for two years (1718–1720). While lieutenant of police, Machault also sat on four commissions of the Council of State. Three of these worked on matters relating to the capital, matters that might understandably engage his services as lieutenant of police; but the fourth existed to try disputes arising through-

out France as a result of a governmental effort to reduce the vast number of offices created under Louis XIV. Nor did service on this last
commission exhaust Machault's involvement with the royal councils
and with work that appears unrelated to his position as lieutenant of
police in Paris. Coupled with the judicial duties the four commissions
imposed was the administrative labor deriving from his seat on the
Council of Commerce. Meeting weekly with this body at the Louvre,
Machault assumed a burden that was, for the most part, defined geographically. Not surprisingly, as lieutenant of police, he did work for
the council that concerned the commercial and industrial affairs of
Paris; but the boundaries of his responsibility reached beyond those of
the city: in addition to Paris, Machault was charged with authority
over all of southeastern France—the provinces of Languedoc, Dauphi-
né, Provence, and Lyonnais.[7] Several subsequent lieutenants of police,
while not holding a place on the Council of Commerce, were still more
deeply involved in the work of the Council of State. Taschereau de
Baudry sat on ten of its commissions or *bureaux* (only two of which
treated Parisian affairs), and Feydeau de Marville on nine.[8]

Given this range of activity and the difficulty involved in deciding
what is done as lieutenant of police and what in some other capacity,
one is reluctant to list as part of the Parisian police all those who
assisted its chief officer in the exercise of his numerous functions.
Without resort to discretion, we could find ourselves impressing half
the Council of State into police service; but having invoked discretion
to avoid this awkward gesture, we cannot then pretend that the structural criterion employed to distinguish the police produces precise,
unequivocal results. We can only argue that of the devices available for
locating the police it is the more sensitive, the more discriminating.
Imperfect it may be, but to it there is no viable alternative.

Where then are the police of Paris? Recalling that the question is
ours and that to an eighteenth-century Parisian, who conceived of
police as function rather than substance, it would have been nonsensi-
cal, we may say that they are to be found not in uniform and neat
array but rather scattered about at the far end of many lines emanating
downward from the lieutenancy of police. But having located the police in this way, we cannot with finality map their compass; for the
police of Paris did not yet constitute an entity long extant, whose con-

7. *Almanach royal, 1720* (Paris, 1720), 65–87.
8. *Almanach royal, 1721*, 66–88; *Almanach royal, 1747*, 124–46.

figuration time had made precise. They were, during the eighteenth century, a loose amalgamation, a coalescence in process, whose periphery is not always distinguishable amid the intricate and uncharted patterns of institutionalized authority that characterized the Old Regime. Perimeters we must try to draw; but in doing so, let us admit that the precise location of some of these boundaries must remain a matter over which there can and will be honest difference.

2

The Lieutenancy
of Police

Once each week, usually on Sunday or Monday, the lieutenant of police journeyed to Versailles to confer with the king's ministers and, on occasion, with the king himself; once each week, on a day he found convenient, the same man opened the doors of his *hôtel* in Paris to throngs of aggrieved and powerless men, each seeking a form of aid or redress that he alone, they believed, was capable of granting them.[1] The lieutenancy of police was a social and political nexus, a junction of the Old Regime, a point from which lines radiated in many directions: upward to the glitter and power of Versailles, to its ministries, to the royal family and the king himself; down to the dim retreats of Paris, to its rooming houses, brothels, and cafes, to lives ruled not by mirrors but by want, lives unsplendid, grim, and mute. Few men were better placed than the lieutenant of police to survey the manifold forms existence assumed under the Old Regime; few had greater occasion to touch both its magnificence and its squalor or to converse more frequently with both its proud and its impotent.

ORIGIN AND TITLE

On first view, that afforded by his title, the lieutenant of police appears as a judge, a magistrate of secondary importance in a city that boasted not only the most powerful *parlement* in France, but a handful of other sovereign courts as well. The full title he bore—that of *lieutenant général de police de la ville, prévôté et vicomté de Paris*—derived from the position he occupied in the judicial hierarchy of the Old Regime and suggests a place even humbler than that he in fact held.

1. MS 1424, p. 34 in the Bibliothèque Municipale d'Orléans (hereinafter cited as BO, MS 1424, p. 34). The manuscript bears the title "Mémoire sur l'administration de la police" and is a copy of that initially written in 1770 by Jean Charles Lemaire, a commissioner of police.

17

The *prévôtés* had, under the Old Regime, been the lowest of royal jurisdictions, ranking beneath what were called bailliages in the north of France and *sénéchaussées* in the south. By the middle of the eighteenth century all of these minor courts had disappeared, all, that is, but one: the *prévôté* of Paris, better known as the Châtelet. Because the city of Paris never had a bailliage, the *prévôté* had managed to root itself firmly, becoming the principal royal jurisdiction in the capital, the immediate subordinate of the Parlement. It was at once the city's *prévôté*, its bailliage, and after 1552, when the crown added another level to the judicial hierarchy, its presidial court.

At its head stood the *prévôt* of Paris, a venal officer, who, while yet bearing rights of precedence, had by the eighteenth century long been without function or power. As early as the thirteenth century, the *prévôt* had begun to name assistants, or lieutenants, to aid him in his work; and by 1320, there were complaints that it was no longer the *prévôt* but instead these lieutenants who actually decided cases brought before the Châtelet.[2] Content with honor and formal precedence, the *prévôts* of Paris gradually surrendered their judicial power into the hands of two principal assistants: one, the lieutenant civil, actual head of the Châtelet by the sixteenth century, responsible for deciding civil disputes among corporations and individuals; the other, the lieutenant criminal, charged with initial jurisdiction over most crimes committed in the city.

The line dividing these two jurisdictions was not a clear one. Between civil affairs, involving contracts or quarrels among individuals, and criminal cases, to which the state was always a party, lay an area— a range of behavior—that both jurisdictions claimed was properly theirs to regulate. Certain kinds of conduct, while not warranting the adjective criminal, were clearly harmful to the community as a whole. Jurisdiction over such conduct was considered neither civil nor criminal, bearing instead its own appellation—that of "la police." Within its range fell, for example, the behavior of a grain merchant who sought to convert public shortage and hunger into personal profit or the negligence of a neighbor who, in refusing to see that his chimney was properly cared for, augmented the community's vulnerability to fire.

In a city the size of Paris, physical proximity no longer coincided with affective distance, with mutual acquaintance and concern. Men and women whose conduct was of inevitable consequence to those

2. Michel Antoine *et al.*, *Guide des recherches dans les fonds judiciaires de l'ancien régime* (Paris, 1958), 167.

who lived only a few feet above, beneath, and beside them were increasingly ignorant of the sensitivities amid which they lived: ignorant and, in the absence of affection and familial bonds, unconcerned over the offense they gave. The more highly concentrated the population became, the more numerous became those whom one might unknowingly or carelessly offend; and as the number of injured parties increased, the offense lost its private character and became a matter of concern to the community as a whole. Neighbors to whom were unavailable the subtle sanctions that operate effectively within a family, within a context of mutual need and affection, demanded the support and sanction of public authority. As population grew, so did the list of cases that could not be construed simply as private disputes among individuals, cases that clearly impinged on public well-being and that, as such, obliged the community to intervene as regulator and plaintiff.

But who was to act on behalf of the community in such affairs—affairs that were neither wholly civil nor purely criminal? Throughout the sixteenth and part of the seventeenth centuries the two lieutenants of the Châtelet struggled for clear title to the right of exercising this authority, the authority known as "la police." Administrative and judicial inconvenience arising from this struggle at last prompted the intervention of a higher authority—the Parisian Parlement. In a decision issued March 12, 1630, it declared that, henceforth, police jurisdiction would lie solely in the hands of the lieutenant civil; but this determination on the part of the Parlement did not silence the pretensions of the lieutenant criminal or end his involvement in police affairs.[3]

More important than the action of Parlement in 1630 was the intervention of the crown thirty-six years later. In October, 1666, it created a special Conseil de Police, comprising a core of fourteen men, among them the new controller general of finances, Jean Baptiste Colbert, and the chancellor, Pierre Séguier. The stated objective of the new *ad hoc* council was a reformation of "la police" in Paris;[4] and given the meaning contemporaries attached to this word, the aspiration was one of

3. Delamare, *Traité de la police*, I, 115.
4. MSS 8118 and 16847 in the *fonds français* (that collection of documents in French as opposed to other collections in other languages) of the Bibliothèque Nationale (hereinafter cited as BN, MSS fr. 8118 and 16847). Both manuscripts contain a complete list of those sitting on the council. They also contain minutes of the council's meetings and serve as the basis for my discussion of its activity. See especially fols. 1–40 of MS fr. 8118 and fols. 104–105 of MS fr. 16847, the former being minutes of the group's first three meetings and the latter, a working paper drafted by Séguier and designed to guide the deliberations of the council.

considerable magnitude. At its almost weekly meetings between October, 1666, and February, 1667, the council sought to accomplish far more than the resolution of a single dispute over judicial and administrative competence. Its aim was nothing less than to define and resolve the most serious problems afflicting what had become a great city—problems long the concomitants of urban life but amplified in Paris by rapid growth during the first half of the seventeenth century.

Although the first official census of the French capital was not conducted until 1801 and though indisputable figures on the city's population during the seventeenth century do not exist, there is considerable circumstantial evidence that, as the Wars of Religion drew to a close, Paris began to grow at, what was for some, an alarming rate. Not least among the anxious witnesses of this expansion was Louis XIII, who, in acts of 1627 and 1638, declared further development of the city undesirable and illegal. But what was illegal under the Old Regime was only rarely impossible. Despite the royal proscription, immigration into Paris and construction there apparently proceeded as they had before, forcing Louis XIV to try again in 1674 to halt the increase in population.[5]

If these royal attempts to restrain growth are testimony that it was, in fact, occurring at a disturbing pace, we have other evidence as well. After study of his city's past and on the basis of his own observation, Nicolas Delamare (1639–1723) asserted that the number of Parisians had increased by a third in little more than a century; and having made this assertion, he proceeded to substantiate it by describing in some detail the changes that had occurred in Paris between 1580 and 1700. Like a drop of oil spilled on a piece of cloth, the city had reached out in all directions. Expansion to the west, in the Faubourg Saint-Honoré and out beyond the abbey Saint-Germain-des-Prés, began shortly before Henry IV's accession to the throne in 1589 and continued at an accelerated rate under this first Bourbon king and his successors. By 1642, the new population south of the river and west of the abbey had become so considerable that the section of the city in which it lay, the quarter of Saint-André-des-Arts, had to be divided in half to facilitate administration; and despite this division, the newly formed quarter, Saint-Germain-des-Prés, remained the city's largest, larger than four of the other sixteen taken together.

5. Royal declaration of July 29, 1627, and decrees by the Conseil d'État of January 15, 1638, and April 28, 1674, cited in Jeanne Pronteau, *Les Numérotages des maisons de Paris du XVe siècle à nos jours* (Paris, 1966), 71–72.

Growth had proceeded in other directions as well, according to Delamare. On the east the Faubourg Saint-Antoine grew to encompass what had been the villages of Reuilly and Pincourt; along the northern perimeter of the city new faubourgs sprang up beyond the gates of the Temple, of Richelieu and of Montmartre, while the already extant faubourgs of Saint-Denis and Saint-Martin each increased in size by 50 percent. Expansion southward began later than it had elsewhere; but between 1684 and 1686, the gates of Saint-Michel, Saint-Jacques, Saint-Victor, and Saint-Marcel disappeared from the southern edge of the city, and the faubourgs bearing these names that had stood outside the gates became, in fact if not in principle, part of Paris. Under Louis XIV, eighty-two new streets with buildings to line them appeared in the capital. Four new ports and fifteen new public fountains had to be built to provide food and water sufficient to meet the city's augmented demand.[6]

Inexact though they may be, maps of the city, drawn at various intervals between 1530 and 1697, corroborate Delamare's testimony. Of particular use in verifying the changes he describes is a map known as the *Plan des trois personnages*, sketched in 1538. On this map dating from the mid-sixteenth century only the faubourgs of Saint-Germain-des-Prés and Saint-Marcel are anything more than a few houses lining a prinicpal access to the city. There is here no faubourg of the Temple or of Montmartre; no Faubourg Saint-Michel or Saint-Antoine. Even within the walls of the city itself considerable space lies open and apparently unused, particularly to the east of the city's center. By 1676, when Jouvin de Rochefort produced his second map of Paris, or 1697, when the map of Nicolas de Fer appeared, the city had become a much larger place, acquiring many of the new elements—streets and whole faubourgs—that Delamare tells us came into being during the reigns of the first three Bourbons.[7]

Further evidence of the city's growth in the seventeenth century exists in the form of several attempts to count the number of houses in Paris. The first of these efforts, undertaken in 1637, put the number of houses at 20,000 and estimated the population at 415,000 persons; fifty years later, in 1684, a second enumeration produced a count of

6. Delamare, *Traité de la police*, I, 80–91. Pons Augustin Alletz, writing under the pseudonym of Le Sage, confirms most of what Delamare reports and provides further details. See Alletz, *Le Géographe parisien, ou le conducteur chronologique et historique des rues de Paris* (2 vols.; Paris, 1769), I, 40–49.

7. Howard Saalman, *Medieval Cities* (New York, 1968), fig. 7; Adolphe Alphand (ed.), *Atlas des anciens plans de Paris* (2 vols.; Paris, 1880).

23,086 houses, while the map of Nicolas de Fer states that by 1697 Paris contained 24,000 residential structures, not counting its 268 hôtels, 30 hospitals, 52 monasteries, 78 convents, and 55 colleges.[8] Estimates of the average number of persons inhabiting each of these so-called houses vary. Some eighteenth-century demographers and twentieth-century historians suggest the figure twenty-five, while other scholars in both centuries prefer twenty-one or twenty.[9] Whichever figure one chooses, if there was, indeed, an increase of 3,000 or 4,000 houses in Paris between 1637 and the last years of the century, then there would have been, in little more than fifty years, an increase in population amounting to between 60,000 and 100,000 persons. This is not the increase by one-third of which Delamare speaks, but it is an augmentation approaching 20 percent in a relatively brief period, an increase that would undoubtedly have caused considerable difficulty and readjustment.

Settling the jurisdictional dispute between the lieutenant civil and the lieutenant criminal of the Châtelet was, then, but one of the tasks the Conseil de Police had before it when it met for the first time in October, 1666. Beyond this work there lay the need to find solutions to all the problems of a city that had grown too fast. If in 1666 it was time for the crown to resolve a long-standing conflict between two important royal magistrates in Paris, it was also time for it to face the physical and social problems in that city that recent expansion had exacerbated.

A working paper, apparently drafted by the chancellor, Séguier, and designed to guide the Conseil de Police in its deliberations, reflected this broad concern with urban difficulties. Specifying those problems the crown deemed most pressing, it gave each of the six subcommittees into which the council had been divided responsibility for grappling with one or more of these dilemmas. One of the subcommittees —that on which Colbert served—was to concern itself with the city's streets and their deficiencies in lighting, paving, and cleanliness, as well as with the many inconveniences resulting from the multiple jurisdictions in the city and the consequent fragmentation of authority; another was to examine the problem of security and suggest ways of guaranteeing personal and proprietary safety; a third took up the

8. BN, MS JF 1428, fols. 1–4; BN, MSS fr. 8633–34.
9. Marcel Reinhard, *Paris pendant la Révolution* (2 vols.; Paris, 1966), I, 32; Roland Mousnier, *Paris au XVIIe siècle* (Paris, 1969), 22.

difficulties involved in provisioning so numerous an assemblage of persons, of providing them not only with food and fuel but of seeing that these necessities were furnished at a "just" price; a fourth sub-committee began study of the city's water supply and its facilities for the disposal of waste; a fifth sought to formulate measures for purging Paris of increasing offense to public morality—brothels, gambling houses, and tobacco merchants; and the sixth and last subcommittee concerned itself with the Parisian prisons, while simultaneously seeking information about other cities it considered well-administered, among them Lyon, Rouen, Amsterdam, Venice, Rome, and Hamburg. [10]

As part of their effort to articulate with some precision the problems of Paris, each of these subcommittees sought the testimony of the city's inhabitants—not directly, but by way of the commissioners of the Châtelet. Dispersed throughout the city, the commissioners were well-placed to provide information on the character and difficulties of particular neighborhoods; but to enhance the utility of the reports it received, the Conseil de Police ordered these officials to convoke special meetings with the prominent residents of their districts and to elicit from those who attended a statement of local concerns and a list of suggestions for the remedy of local problems. This data, together with their own commentary on it, the commissioners then carried before each of the subcommittees responsible for some aspect of urban reform. [11]

Having heard and examined this material in small groups, the council as a whole set to work on October 28, 1666. Its first meeting was devoted to ways of establishing security within the city, of ending the violence and disorder that seemed to plague all Parisians, regardless of neighborhood. At its second session it considered the sometimes impassable, always imperfect streets of the city, seeking ways to maintain them free from obstruction and filth. In its attempt to remedy this latter inconvenience and hazard, the council inadvertently brought itself face to face with a problem more primitive and more important than the others with which it had so far wrestled.

By naming one commissioner of the Châtelet—a man named Galliot —to supervise efforts at improving city streets, the council provoked revolt among Galliot's colleagues—the forty-seven other commissioners in Paris, who saw in this special assignment an "elevation" of one

10. BN, MS fr. 16847, fols. 104–105.
11. BO, MS 1424, p. 27.

of their number and a dangerous infringement upon their own independent exercise of authority. Of necessity, the attention of the council turned from substantive urban problems to problems of governance and to the difficulty of exacting obedience from men who guarded jealously the power confided to them. Colbert labeled the resistance of the commissioners a "cabal" and raged against those involved, telling members of the council that "the public would be served" and that if these recalcitrant officials refused to accept Galliot's authority, "there was enough money in the treasury to reimburse and dismiss them."[12]

Though at times in the course of the three months it met the council returned to such matters as provisionment and water supply, the conduct of the Châtelet's commissioners and the ramifications of this conduct consumed increasing quantities of its energy. In the recalcitrance of these men the council began to see a single explanation for the manifold specific difficulties afflicting Paris. Behind their resistance it glimpsed and disapproved the habit of independent control, of authority and command exercised without regard for the advantage— indeed the necessity—of coordination. What Paris required, what it lacked above all else, was competent, unified authority.

Power to cope with urban problems lay scattered about the city, each fragment defended with a zeal appropriate to an ancient and holy relic. A legion of individuals and corporations stood perpetually ready to dispute any encroachment on their small dominions. While the commissioners were refusing to accept Galliot's authority, archers of the city's watch (guet) contested the right of anyone but their own commanders to issue valid orders, refusing to obey those they received from the prévôt's lieutenants at the Châtelet;[13] and these lieutenants, as we have seen, quarreled over the right to issue such orders.

The special Conseil de Police had been empowered to legislate those reforms for the city it found necessary, and among its first acts was a decree giving the Châtelet precedence in police affairs over all other jurisdictions in Paris. This order was an initial step toward effective, central authority in the capital.[14] The council soon took another. Having authorized the Châtelet to exercise an essential form of jurisdiction over the fragmented capital—one that encompassed most of the sub-

12. BN, MS fr. 8118, fols. 42–43. The position of commissioner at the Châtelet was a venal office.
13. *Ibid.*, fol. 95.
14. For the text of this decree, issued November 5, 1666, see Delamare, *Traité de la police*, I, 120–22.

stantive problems facing the city—it remained to terminate the quarrel within the Châtelet itself over the right to exercise this police power. The Parlement's decree of 1630 granting this prerogative to the lieutenant civil had not ended the involvement of the lieutenant criminal in police affairs; nor had it ended the confusion and paralysis this continuing involvement occasioned. In March, 1667, the crown moved to stop once and for all the long-standing quarrel within the Châtelet. The office of lieutenant civil lay vacant, its previous occupant—Dreux d'Aubray—having died during the fall of 1666, after being slowly poisoned by his eldest daughter whose lover he had sent to the Bastille. Availing itself of the opportunity occasioned by d'Aubray's death, the crown stripped the vacant office of its police powers and invested them in a newly created official—the lieutenant general of police.[15]

Henceforth, the bulk of police power in Paris was to lie in the hands of a single jurisdiction, and within this jurisdiction in the hands of a single official. To underscore its intention of making the new post an effective source of authority, one capable of coping with the city's problems, the crown selected the first lieutenant of police and all his successors from the ranks of the maîtres des requêtes—the same body from which it drew the provincial intendants and most other important administrators.

FUNCTIONS

The new lieutenant of police became the third of the principal lieutenants at the Châtelet. As such, as a magistrate within this jurisdiction, he stood second in precedence to the lieutenant civil, but his actual power in the city far exceeded that of any colleague at the Châtelet.

The edict of March, 1667, creating the lieutenancy of police attempted to define those areas of urban life over which the new officer was to have control. It was, necessarily, an effort to sharpen conceptions of

15. The edict creating the lieutenancy of police is dated March 15, 1667, and may be found reproduced in either Delamare, *Traité de la police*, I, 122–24, or Francois Isambert, Athanase Jourdan, and Decrusy, *Recueil général des anciennes lois françaises depuis l'an 420 jusqu'à la révolution* (29 vols.; Paris, 1821–33), XVIII, 100–103. What role the special Conseil de Police played in bringing about the creation of this post remains unclear. I assume, given the date of the edict, that it was either drafted by the council or issued in accord with its recommendations; but, surprisingly, the minutes of the council's meetings (BN, MS fr. 8118) contain no discussion regarding the need of a new, more specialized magistrate. See Jacques Saint-Germain, *La Reynie et la police au grand siècle* (Paris, 1962), 25–26, for an alternative account of how the lieutenant of police came into being.

police power and to distinguish it from authority exercised by the civil
and criminal magistrates of the Châtelet. The extent of the responsibility it bestowed on the newly created official will not surprise anyone familiar with the encompassing sense contemporaries gave to the
word police. Security, fire, flood, provisionment, mendicancy, manufacture, commerce, illicit publications, price control, filth and rubbish
—the list could hardly be more various; and while its compass may
have resulted simply from the meaning of a word, it may also have
sprung from a sense that Paris was in the grip of a hydra-headed crisis,
one that required a general mandate of authority assuring continuation
of the remedial labor begun by the special Conseil de Police.

The existence of such a crisis in the latter half of the seventeenth
century is problematic. It is an inference founded primarily on other
inference, an assertion that becomes credible only if one accepts
the earlier argument that Paris grew considerably during the first half
of the century. Belief in a disruptive expansion of the city is shared by
at least one other historian. Leon Bernard has founded his study of
seventeenth-century Paris on this hypothesis and is inclined, as I am,
to speak of what the city experienced during the reigns of Louis XIII
and Louis XIV as an urban crisis. In support of this view Bernard points
out that the laws of 1627 and 1638, which I have already mentioned, as
well as another of 1633, all remark upon the "extraordinary disorder"
resulting from the recent growth of Paris; and he cites Louis XIII's
complaint that this expansion had fouled the air, made difficult the disposal of filth, undermined efforts at provisionment, and brought to
Paris the evils of uncontrolled larceny, robbery, and murder.[16]

The sudden growth of Paris would surely have created a number of
problems regardless of the character of the new population. A larger
city required more grain, men to organize commerce across greater distances, administrators to improve means of conveyance, and new
structures in which to store greater quantities of provisions. Large
numbers of new inhabitants produced overwhelming quantities of refuse and waste. The newcomers died and, even in dying, burdened their
neighbors and the city with the problems of putrefaction and burial.
More inhabitants meant more civil disputes, requiring the appointment of new judges and the hiring of men to enforce their decisions.

But if Bernard is right and if the growth of Paris resulted from "the

16. Leon Bernard, *The Emerging City: Paris in the Age of Louis XIV* (Durham, N.C.,
1970), 30.

dislocation and pauperization of large segments of rural society in France," then those who came to Paris were not drawn to the city by a significant economic expansion there, one requiring unskilled labor and able to reward it.[17] They were instead pushed from their homes by local circumstance and turned to Paris for want of an alternative. If such were the case, these immigrants would have come to a city unready to absorb them and without the money or the skills that supported men in an urban community. To survive they would have taken up begging or learned to use craft and the night to take what they needed. If Bernard is right, then it was not simply the arrival of new persons in the city that created an urban crisis, but the conditions and circumstances of those who came.

Still, one may wonder why the problems these newcomers created in Paris suddenly seemed acute in 1666. Why was it in this year that the crown chose to make a major effort at remedying the ills of France's largest city? Why not 1665, or 1664, or 1668? It is possible that the answer lies not in Paris but elsewhere, not in the labor of a dedicated minister but in the conduct of insects and rats; for in 1666, plague, which had decimated England the previous year, leapt the Channel and began to make its way south and east. It raged in Dunkerque, then in Lille, Amiens, and Beauvais. Nothing generated more fear in a city than the approach of this disease; and though the epidemic abated this time and never reached Paris, its march toward the capital must have created considerable apprehension, always a strong stimulus to reform. If recent and relatively rapid immigration had created the problems Paris was experiencing by the middle of the seventeenth century, it may well have been plague that opened the crown's eyes to these problems and stimulated the efforts at reform embodied in and undertaken by the Conseil de Police, efforts which seem, in turn, to have produced the lieutenancy of police.[18]

No doubt a number of Parisians who dealt with the lieutenant of police in subsequent years would have been more than ready to attribute his existence entirely to the plague, but it is important here for us to remember the part played by human agents. Whatever the role of disease in producing a third lieutenant at the Châtelet, it was, in all

17. *Ibid.*, 133.

18. On the plague of 1666–1667, see Jean Meuvret, "Demographic Crisis in France from the Sixteenth to the Eighteenth Century" in David Victor Glass and David Edward Charles Eversley (eds.), *Population in History* (Chicago, 1965), 515.

likelihood, the members of the Conseil de Police who decided what the powers and duties of the new official would be. The lieutenant of police was above all their permanent successor; and his functions derived not only from the extensive sense members of the council, like their contemporaries, gave the word police, but also from this body's initial definition of its own competence, a definition founded on its perception of what actually and urgently needed to be done in Paris. If the powers of the lieutenant of police were broad, it is, in part, because the difficulties urban expansion had brought were numerous; if the work the lieutenant of police was asked to do did not always seem of one piece, it is because the description of his functions was as much an empirical definition of the problems Paris faced as it was an attempt to distinguish logically among the civil, criminal, and police jurisdictions of the Châtelet.

Long citations from the edict of 1667 which created the lieutenancy of police are useful in conveying an impression of the position's extensive and varied responsibilities, but it is important at the outset not to become lost in the details of this edict, details that can obscure the essential character of the new post. Indeed, it is helpful initially to note what the edict of March, 1667, omits rather than what it asserts, remarking that it does not distinguish between judicial and administrative functions. One begins to appreciate both the character and the ambiguity of the lieutenancy of police when one realizes that the man who filled it, like many other men bearing the title of magistrate, was simultaneously judge and executive agent.

The Judge

By title the lieutenant of police was a magistrate. The post he held, like other judicial offices under the Old Regime, required an initial investment of capital; and, in theory, each of the fourteen lieutenants of police who succeeded one another in office between 1667 and 1789 was to pay 150,000 livres into the fund known as the *parties casuelles*.[19] Each of the first seven of these men, like other magistrates, collected fees from those who appeared before them. Only the eighth individual to hold this office, Nicolas René Berryer, managed to obtain

19. MS 69, fols. 243–44 from subseries 1 of Series 0 at the Archives Nationales (hereinafter cited as AN, 0-1 69, pp. 243–44). The *parties casuelles* (literally "contingent" or "eventual revenues") was that part of the royal financial administration which collected and managed revenues derived from the sale of offices.

from the crown an annual income that permitted him to render justice without charge.[20]

To receive hearing and judgment before the lieutenant of police an affair had to be formally attested to in an official report (*procès verbal*) drafted most often by a commissioner of the Châtelet. Should initial information regarding some infraction come not from a public official but from a private individual, the lieutenant of police again called for the intervention of a commissioner, ordering that the man from whose section of the city the information had come conduct a preliminary inquiry. This inquiry, which preceded any action on the part of the lieutenant of police, was hardly an elaborate affair. The commissioner assembled before him those allegedly involved and, having collected their testimony, sent it on to the clerk of the police court. Here the material received the scrutiny of the crown's prosecutor at the Châtelet, the *procureur du roi*, who decided whether or not it warranted action before the lieutenant of police.[21]

Those called into police court under the Old Regime would have made their way to the Châtelet on a Friday afternoon; for it was then, between three o'clock and six, that most affairs were decided. Inside the old fortress the court convened in a room, which, when occupied by the lieutenant of police, was known as the *chambre de police*, but which seems to have been the same room used by the lieutenant civil the remainder of the week.

The cases heard here on Fridays fell into two categories. Matters which might result in a simple fine were classified under the rubric of *police ordinaire*, while those to which a more severe penalty (prison or banishment) was attached constituted what was known as *police extraordinaire* or *grande police*. Each of these categories of cases was further subdivided. A session of the *police ordinaire*, held on Friday afternoon, comprised, in theory though not always in fact, two parts. The first of these went by a variety of names—*police civile*, *police contentieuse*, or *police délibérée*. Here two corporations of merchants or artisans, each claiming exclusive right to manufacture or sell some product, argued their cases; here officers of a guild sought the condemnation of some recalcitrant master charged with violating provisions of

20. MS 1422, p. 965, of the Bibliothèque Municipale d'Orléans. This manuscript, together with those numbered 1421 and 1423, bears the title "Memoires de J. P. Lenoir." Hereinafter these documents will be cited simply as BO, MS 1421, 1422, or 1423.

21. BO, MS 1424, p. 4.

the group's charter; here an individual who had suffered certain kinds of injury at the hands of someone else might seek recompense, as did a prominent surgeon whose clothes and wig had been ruined when a man named Cottet poured wine on him. The second part of the *police ordinaire*, usually called the *police simple*, required the lieutenant of police to pass judgment on routine infractions of police regulations, matters reported by the commissioners of the Châtelet and those observed by the city's guard during its rounds. No doubt this was one of the more boring parts of the afternoon, involving long lists of those who had left doors unlocked at night, served drink after hours, blocked the street, failed to clean in front of their shops, or thrown excrement on the guard.[22]

Once or twice a month, not every Friday, a session of *police extraordinaire* or *grande police* preceded the *police ordinaire*. On these occasions the lieutenant of police pronounced sentence against individuals guilty of offenses deemed serious enough to warrant arrest and confinement, offenses like vagrancy and prostitution, both of which fell within his purview rather than that of the lieutenant criminal.[23] Because men and women were brought before the court in separate groups, the portions of the session devoted to the two sexes were sometimes distinguished, one being called *police des hommes*, the other, *police des femmes*.[24] Also considered part of the *grande police* were those cases—increasingly numerous as the century progressed—involving parents who had defaulted on payments to a wet nurse whom they had employed. While the lieutenant of police's judgment in these cases was invariably that the sum owed should be paid, a considerable number of parents were unable or unwilling to comply and so went to prison.[25]

During the *police simple*—a regular feature of every Friday after-

22. This classification of the lieutenant of police's activity as a judge and the specific instances alluded to derive from BO, MS 1424, pp. 19–22, and from an examination of police court records contained in BN, MS JF 1323, and in AN, Y 9410, 9467, 9490, 9510, 9539, 9625, and 9631.

23. In a letter to the commissioners of the Châtelet dated April 9, 1760 (in AN, Y 13728), the chief prosecutor of this institution listed those cases that were to be heard by the lieutenant of police rather than the lieutenant criminal: begging and vagrancy; pimping and prostitution; resistance to the archers of the Hôpital Général, to the guard at dramatic presentations, or to the officers of the city's mercantile and industrial guilds; the carrying of proscribed weapons; forcible recruitment into the military; illegal confinement; gambling; insolent or violent cab-drivers; and illegal assembly on the part of journeymen or apprentices.

24. Rolls of defendants, May 25, 1759, in AN, Y 9539.

25. Sentences pronounced against parents not paying wetnurses, 1723–1757, in AN, Y 9510.

noon—and whatever else was scheduled for that day, the lieutenant of police acted alone in his capacity as judge. Legal representation was permitted those appearing at the *police contentieuse*, but attorneys played no part elsewhere in the afternoon's proceedings. Procedure was kept deliberately routine and uncomplicated in order to expedite the process of judgment. At the *police simple*, for example, the commissioner who had witnessed an infraction, or to whom it had been reported, succinctly presented what he took to be the facts of the case, after which the accused—if he had bothered to appear—had a moment or two to speak. Following the statement by the defendant, assuming that he had, indeed, come to court to contest the charge against him, there came the turn of one of the royal prosecutors at the Châtelet, who, after calling the court's attention to a relevant legal principle or a concrete piece of evidence, recommended the decision he thought appropriate.

It would be wrong to imagine lengthy accusations, eloquent replies, or elaborate and learned summaries as even occasional features of these Friday afternoons. Given the number of cases heard, each part of the proceedings could have consisted of no more than a few sentences; and the affairs tried here were remarkable not for the legal forms or brilliance that attended them but for the celerity with which they were decided. Whatever the delays suffered in adjudicating a matter before other tribunals, cases appearing before the lieutenant of police were quickly settled. Those charged with some routine infraction of regulations usually waited no longer than the approaching Friday to have their say and to hear a verdict. Persons whose offense had led to confinement received attention that was less prompt, but only rarely did they wait longer than four weeks. Amid the proliferation of specialized courts in Paris, that presided over by the lieutenant of police became known for its quick and, after 1750, gratuitous justice. To be sure, all sentences imposed by the lieutenant of police, except those against vagrants and vagabonds, were subject to appeal before the Parlement of Paris; but such appeals were not ordinarily numerous, and when one was undertaken, a definitive verdict from this body was not long delayed.

Take, for example, the case of three grocers—Pelletier, Girard, and Castellant—who appeared at the *police ordinaire* of May 4, 1759. Two days before, they had been charged by Commissioner Machurin with selling butter above the prescribed price. In court, on the fourth, the lieutenant of police, Henri Baptiste Bertin, fined each of them 100 livres. This action came, of course, on a Friday. On Monday, May 7, the grocers appealed Bertin's decision to Parlement, which on the following day agreed to hear their case. On May 12, the grocers obtained a final verdict from the higher court.[26] Only eight days had elapsed since the initial judgment of their case and only ten since the alleged violations had occurred.

Under the Old Regime delays in obtaining justice did not result from the speed with which individual courts acted; nor, it would seem, did they result from the appellate process, so long as the lines of jurisdiction were clear. Rather delay and consequent frustration with the judicial apparatus derived from the indefinite boundaries separating jurisdictions. Given the number of courts and an inadequate definition of their responsibilities, few decisions could be contained within a single ladder of judicial authority. Invariably, there were alternative, collateral systems willing to claim both jurisdiction and the resultant fees. Under these circumstances, definitive verdicts were often difficult to obtain. Defeated in one arena, a litigant might claim the right to a second or third contest elsewhere before submitting.

Penalties inflicted by the lieutenant of police consisted most often of warnings, fines, and periods of confinement. In the case of civil matters—those constituting a part of the form of jurisdiction known as *police contentieuse*—punishment was not an important issue. Such cases obliged the lieutenant of police to decide between the claims of two private parties. They rarely engaged the public interest, giving the crown no reason to consider the relevance of retribution or deterrence.

Other cases, however, educed these considerations, particularly that of deterrence. Such affairs constrained the lieutenant of police to decide which of the penalties prescribed by statute was most likely to insure future compliance. Those for which he opted were rarely severe or exotic. Persons charged at the *police simple* with routine infraction of police regulations received warnings or fines. The sums imposed, paid not to the lieutenant of police or his clerk but to a specialized officer of the Châtelet known appropriately as the *receveur des amendes* (receiver of fines), ranged generally between two and five livres, well beneath the maximums permitted by law. Heavy fines

26. BN, MS JF 1323, fols. 5–9.

the court reserved for those it deemed guilty of willful, flagrant, and rebellious offense.[27]

More often, if a harsher penalty seemed necessary to deter imitation of a particular infraction, the lieutenant of police ordered that the verdict he handed down be printed, read, and posted throughout the city. Most of those summoned to police court were anxious to avoid such public proclamation of their guilt. Especially sensitive to this form of punishment were merchants, who, having exceeded established prices and been summoned before the *police deliberée*, hoped to forestall any consequent communal aversion or wrath. Printed sentences were invariably intended as exemplary punishment and must not, in their severity, be mistaken for the ordinary acts of the court. These sentences indicate a special sensitivity on the part of public authority and an earnest desire to prevent repetition of an offense. In a letter to the secretary of state for the king's household, Lenoir noted popular reaction to a published verdict and its consequent utility to government: "this printed sentence," he said, "is regarded as a more severe punishment than a fine and always has a greater effect."[28]

The number of individuals summoned to the *chambre de police* was considerable. On those Fridays when the lieutenant of police conducted a session of *police extraordinaire* as well as one or both parts of the *police ordinaire* (and this he seems to have done once or twice a month), he might in the course of three hours dispose of as many as two hundred cases.[29] At other times, when there was only the usual session of *police ordinaire*, he rarely made decisions affecting fewer than a hundred persons. If one assumes that the inhabitants of the city numbered between 500,000 and 600,000 and that the lieutenant of police averaged a hundred verdicts a week, it would appear that each year approximately one of every hundred Parisians found his life touched in some large or small way by the judicial action of this magistrate.

Consider the first session of the proceedings before him on May 25, 1759, a session of the *police extraordinaire*. Forty-five women and sixteen men, charged with a variety of violations, appeared at this

27. See penalties imposed on February 10, 1764, or any other Friday in AN, Y 9631. BO, MS 1424, pp. 3, 21–22.

28. AN, 0-1 361, no. 263. For a baker's apprehension about having a sentence against him printed and posted, see Jean Charles Lenoir to Commissioner Dupuy, July 20, 1776, in AN, Y 12830.

29. Entry for January 31, 1749, in AN, Y 9625.

initial sitting of the court. Most of the women, confined until their appearance before the lieutenant of police in the prisons of Saint-Martin and the Petit Châtelet, had been arrested for overt prostitution, various forms of insult, or petty theft. Thirty-three of them Bertin ordered sent to the *maison de force*, or prison, at Salpêtrière for indefinite periods of detention and labor; twelve he banished from the city. The men who appeared that day had, as was customary, been detained either in the prisons of the Châtelet itself or at For l'Évêque. The charges against them—vagrancy, assault, and cozenage of various sorts —resulted in further confinement at Bicêtre for fifteen of these individuals and banishment from Paris for the last.[30]

Having concluded this opening session of *police extraordinaire*, the court often proceeded to civil affairs, to matters falling within the scope of *police contentieuse*. On January 31, 1749, thirty such cases required a decision from the lieutenant of police, who, in rendering judgment, relied heavily on the recommendations of the *procureur du roi*.[31]

Yet the majority of decisions on any given Friday came during the second half of the *police ordinaire*, that is to say, during the course of the *police simple*. Here a number of commissioners reported those infractions of police regulations that had come to their attention during the previous week. While these reports might vary to some extent with the character of the neighborhood for which the commissioner was responsible, most of them were much alike. On September 22, 1758, Commissioner Leblanc reported sixteen infractions in his quarter. Half of these involved persons who had neglected to lock up at night as police regulations required. Against these individuals Bertin imposed no penalty—permitting them to leave after warning them against a repetition of such oversight. Severity on this particular Friday he reserved for five wine merchants who, according to Leblanc, had not closed their shops at the prescribed hour. The commissioner had found each of them still serving drinks well after 11:00 P.M.; and on the basis of his report, Bertin fined these men sums ranging between twelve and twenty-four livres. At the same time he imposed a penalty of only ten livres on an individual who, two days in succession, had fired shots into the courtyard of his neighbor; and another man forfeited the same sum for having poured urine from his fourth- or fifth-story window on-

30. Entry for May 25, 1759, in AN, Y 9539.
31. Entry for January 31, 1749, in AN, Y 9625.

to the street below. Had the liquid missed two passing horsemen of the city's guard, this last culprit might have escaped with a warning.[32]

Such were the more ordinary affairs that occupied the lieutenant of police in his capacity as judge: few were of great consequence; few involved serious deliberation or grave punishment. But in addition to the two jurisdictions of *police extraordinaire* and *police ordinaire*, the lieutenant of police had responsibility for a third. This—known variously as *police criminelle*, *police mixte*, and sometimes, confusingly, also as *police extraordinaire*, or *grande police*—he exercised not by virtue of his post as an officer of the Châtelet, but rather as a representative of the royal council. Throughout the eighteenth century, the Conseil d'État regularly delegated to the lieutenant of police a portion of the judicial authority it was called upon to discharge in the capital. Authorization to act on its behalf took the form of conciliar decrees (*arrêts*) and consequent letters patent. These sometimes directed the lieutenant of police to adjudicate an affair alone as agent or commissioner of the council and sometimes ordered him to act in conjunction with six other officers (*conseillers*) of the Châtelet. Known as the *conseil de police* (not to be confused with the special Conseil de Police of 1666–1667), this group assembled twenty-four times during 1726. Most of the several hundred cases it heard involved acts of mendicancy and theft; but the court also tried a number of persons charged with murder or with behavior that offended public notions of propriety.[33]

Sodomy was the accusation that brought forty-five-year-old Benjamin Dechauffour before this body on May 24, 1726. When Dechauffour denied the charge, the crown countered by producing a number of Dechauffour's partners as witnesses against him. First came a fifteen-year-old boy, Louis Danin, known to his friends, it seems, as "Little Louis." He had had intercourse with Dechauffour on four occasions, he said, beginning the day chance had made him the bearer of a letter to Dechauffour. Once the older man had given him twenty-six sous afterwards. Another fifteen-year-old spoke of his first encounter with Dechauffour. The defendant had visited his family one day; and while both parents were out of the room, the boy explained, "he put his hand inside my pants."

Each boy, asked to describe his relationship with Dechauffour, did

---

32. Entry for September 22, 1758, in AN, Y 9539.
33. Entry for January 31, 1749, in AN, Y 9625; entries for 1725 and 1726, in AN, Y 9623; BN, MS fr. 8058, fols. 160–64.

so in detail, and the clerk of the court faithfully recorded even the minutiae of what they said. If much in these accounts is amusing and more than a trifle sad, their consequence was cruel. With little apparent hesitation, the court found Dechauffour guilty and sentenced him to die the following day. Fire, set in the Place de Grève, was to purge the city of its corruption; a gentle wind was to scatter all trace of its shame. Dechauffour died the next morning, in agony, before a crowd.

A month earlier the same tribunal that ordered this execution had heard a case involving the bribery of several minor public officials. Nicolas Levesque, a sergeant in one of the units that patrolled the city, was charged with permitting persons arrested for mendicancy to buy their release from the Petit Châtelet. Twenty-six former prisoners testified that they had purchased their liberty for ten or twelve livres. Though none had dealt directly with Levesque, the court found him guilty and ordered that he be chained for two hours to a post in the Place de Grève. He was to wear a sign labeling him "corporal in the archers of the Hôpital [Général], convict and extortionist." Following this public humiliation, he was to be branded on the right shoulder with the letters GAL (for *galérien*—a rower on a galley) and sent to work for nine years in Toulon, the port of the Mediterranean fleet. Sitting with the *conseil de police*, the lieutenant of police appears as anything but a forgiving and lenient judge.[34]

Most of the matters which the lieutenant of police adjudicated on behalf of the Conseil d'État were more mundane; and in resolving many of these affairs, he acted alone. Every two weeks he presided at the drawings for the royal lottery, and at other times during the month he was obliged to judge the many disputes arising from this institution. Several times a week he held sessions at his *hôtel* where he handed down decisions known as *jugements de commission*, most of which seem to have concerned various forms of smuggling.

Finally, he headed a commission composed of judges from the Cour des Aides, a commission whose precise functions are unclear. Armand de Miromesnil, the keeper of the seals, says simply that to this commission the royal council sent "important matters like those of M. the prince de Guémenée, M. de Boynes, and others."[35]

34. For material on the cases of Dechauffour and Levesque, see AN, Y 9643, fols. 16–25.

35. MS 1021, pieces 1 and 2, of Series K at the Archives Nationales (hereinafter cited as AN, K 1021, nos. 1–2).

The Administrator

Despite the many cases like these, heard on commission from the Conseil d'État, despite the large number of matters he decided each Friday as an officer and magistrate of the Châtelet, it would be wrong to represent the lieutenant of police as primarily a judge. Judicial decision was an inescapable part of his function; but, as the eighteenth century wore on, it became an activity far less important to those who headed the police than the administrative responsibilities with which they were also charged. As early as the first decade of the century, Nicolas Delamare, a commissioner of the Châtelet, had contended that police activity was principally a matter of administration: "In effect, that which is called Police, having as its only object service to King and to public order, is incompatible with the obstacles and subtleties of litigated affairs and derives its functions far more from the Government than from the Bar."[36]

By 1780 the lieutenant of police was working to divest himself entirely of his judicial functions. Having shouldered the burdens of his office for six years, Lenoir argued that the proper work of the police was not judging violations of the law but rather preventing them, or—failing in this—locating and arresting the probable offenders. With encouragement from Louis XVI's principal minister, the Count of Maurepas, he went so far as to draft a proposal that would have created a new administrator of police for the city, an official free from judicial responsibilities; but, due perhaps to the death·of Maurepas in 1781, the plan produced no reformatory action.[37]

Until the collapse of the regime, the lieutenant of police remained both administrator and judge, but increasingly with the years he became more one than the other. Speaking of the late 1740s, Lenoir says that "in effect the functions of the lieutenant general of police, as judge, were, from this time on, of little consequence compared to his duties as administrator." Lenoir testifies that by the time he entered office (1774), the number of administrative tasks had become so considerable that it was almost impossible to fulfill both the obligations they imposed and those incumbent upon him as judge.[38] Given this increasing administrative burden, lieutenants of police appeared less fre-

36. Delamare, *Traité de la police,* I, 120.
37. BO, MS 1423, pp. 119, 121.
38. BO, MS 1422, p. 716; MS 1423, p. 119.

quently in their court on Friday afternoons, permitting one of the two *lieutenants particuliers* at the Châtelet to act on their behalf. With each year that passed, the title lieutenant of police—suggesting as it did the position and labor of a relatively minor judge—became more and more misleading.

Another appellation, grander and more accurate, might well have affixed itself publicly to this post had it not been for the sensitivity of the Parisian Parlement. *Intendant* was a title for which magistrates all over France had long felt considerable aversion, and the government did not insist on its application to the lieutenant of police. Nonetheless, it was apparent to many that this designation would have been more accurate. If one examines the correspondence of the secretary of state for the king's household, one notes separate listings of those to whom he addressed letters. Recipients of like position are grouped together. There is a list of cardinals and one of ministers. There is also a list of the intendants over whom he exercised authority; and here, among eighteen other names, is that of Lenoir—the lieutenant of police in Paris.[39] After revolution had made concern for the sensitivity of the Parlement anachronistic, Lenoir did not hesitate to state that, as lieutenant of police, he had been "intendant of the Capital," performing there the functions appropriate to that title; and it is as such that the keeper of the seals described him in a memorandum of 1785 which he presented to Louis XVI.[40] To say that the lieutenant of police was the intendant of the city of Paris—in fact, if not in name—is to say that he was more than one magistrate among many in the capital; it is to say that he was the city's chief administrator, the principal executor of the royal will in Paris.

Though the lieutenancy of police had a price of 150,000 livres affixed to it, the charge was not truly a venal one. Rather, it was held in the same way that one held the post of secretary of state. While requiring the payment of a considerable sum, the lieutenancy of police resembled a commission in that it was revocable at any time without resort to legal proceedings. The money one surrendered was far more a kind of bond than a price which, once paid, gave one proprietary rights.[41] A

39. AN, 0-1 480 (folios unnumbered).

40. BHVP, MS n. a. 477, fol. 20; AN, K 1021, nos. 1–2.

41. BO, MS 1422, p. 967; AN, 0-1 69, fols. 243–44; and a manuscript provisionally classified as no. 4725, fols. 2–3, in the Bibliothèque Historique de la Ville de Paris (hereinafter cited as BHVP, c.p.—for *cote provisoire* or provisional classification—4725, fols. 2–3).

lieutenant of police held his post on terms appropriate under the Old Regime to an administrator, not a magistrate—terms applicable to a secretary of state, not a member of a *parlement* or some lesser judicial body.

The administrative character of his position becomes clearer if one realizes that each lieutenant of police was simultaneously and explicitly a royal *commissaire.* Like a provincial intendant he received from the crown an initial encompassing commission specifying the functions he was to perform.[42]

This commission empowered him to act not only as lieutenant of police but as a representative of the royal council; and it was this latter designation, that of commissioner of the council, that accounted in large part for both the scope of his administrative labor and the magnitude of his power. Regarding the functions of the lieutenant of police, Lenoir remarks that "the extent of the powers attached to his administration and outside his judicial competence was large not by virtue of his formal authority (*pouvoirs directs*) but as a consequence of those [tasks] delegated to him haphazardly, temporarily, or otherwise by the king, his Council, and his ministers."[43] Because each lieutenant of police, as a commissioner of the council, received numerous *ad hoc* assignments—responsibilities that were by their very nature unique and ephemeral—it is impossible to give a description of the functions attaching to this post that is both complete and universally valid. Nonetheless, many of the duties it imposed remained constant from term to term, and these may be summarized.[44]

The administrative tasks of a lieutenant of police were sufficiently various to require that he report to each of the six great officers of state: the chancellor or keeper of the seals, the four secretaries of state, and the controller general. It was to the lieutenant of police, more than any other, that these powerful personages turned for action on their behalf in the capital.

42. For several such commissions see BN, MS fr. 22063, fols. 191 (to Lenoir), 196 (to Albert), 290 (to Crosne).

43. BO, MS 1422, p. 889. For an example of one of these temporary commissions, in this case to Sartine, see BN, MS fr. 22177, fols. 236.

44. Principal sources for information on the responsibilities of the lieutenant of police are the edict of March 15, 1667, creating the position (Delamare, *Traité de la police*, I, 120–22); the account in Lemaire's "Mémoire sur l'administration de la police" (BO, MS 1424, pp. 26–37); Miromesnil's memorandum to Louis XVI (AN, K 1021, pieces 1 and 2); and Lenoir's recollection of a paper prepared about 1750 and presented to each new lieutenant of police as a means of familiarizing him with his duties (BO, MS 1422, pp. 717–18). What follows I have drawn from these four sources, especially the latter two.

The chancellor or, more often, the keeper of the seals demanded that the police keep watch over the unruly magistrature of the city; and while no lieutenant of police assumed actual direction of the book trade until 1763 when Sartine replaced Lamoignon de Malesherbes as director of the Librairie, the Chancellory had long relied on Sartine's predecessors to enforce its efforts at censorship.

During his stay at Versailles each Sunday, the lieutenant of police found himself at times called into conference with the secretary of state for war to whom he was responsible for the militia of the capital. In addition to administering the funds provided by the War Department to equip and maintain this force, the lieutenant of police had responsibility for conscripting the five thousand men it comprised, and this task was something more than a routine administrative assignment. Conscription—like taxation—is initially always a provocative act, one of the more dangerous demands a government can make of its people; and those responsible for it rarely endear themselves to the public. It is unlikely that there was a single young man in Paris who wanted to see his name inscribed on the regimental rolls of the militia. Indeed, resistance in the capital to this kind of service had been such that, until 1743, the city had managed to avoid raising auxiliary troops for the army, even though most other parts of France had been doing so since 1688. To raise the requisite number of men and to forestall any resistance, Feydeau de Marville, the lieutenant of police called upon to initiate conscription, devised a series of carefully planned lotteries over which he and those who succeeded him presided on behalf of the Department of War.

Though the lotteries themselves occupied less than a month, they brought additional labor in their train. The conscription produced many evaders, known as *fuyards*, whom it was the business of the police to apprehend; and to gain dedicated assistance in this effort, Marville—and presumably his successors—offered release from the militia to any member who joined in the discovery and capture of someone who had fled service.[45]

Supervision of the militia was not the only responsibility that brought the lieutenant of police into regular contact with the secretary of state for war. This same secretary employed the police to maintain

45. Marville's successors went on managing this conscription for another thirty years, until popular discontent at last crystallized into resistance. At the urging of the lieutenant of police, the minister of war first suspended the lotteries and later, at the insistence of Lenoir, gave them up altogether. BO, MS 1422, p. 729.

a general surveillance over regular army personnel in the capital; and it was through the police that the Ministry of War sought both to regulate recruitment and to uncover deserters.

The police performed similar services for the secretary of the navy; it was through the lieutenant of police that this minister exercised his authority over blacks in the capital and through him, too, that careful watch was kept over persons traveling between England and Paris.

To the secretary of state for foreign affairs the lieutenant of police sent weekly reports on all foreigners who entered or left Paris. Another series of reports to this secretary described the activities of foreign ambassadors in France. These are no more than long catalogues of receptions, meals, and carriage rides; but from them, the government hoped, some significant patterns might eventually emerge. The Department of Foreign Affairs seems also to have used the police to watch its own independently employed agents in the capital—men whose true loyalties it apparently had occasion to doubt.[46]

Passports fell within the province of the Parisian police; and it was they, rather than the Department of Foreign Affairs, who decided upon most requests to leave the country, whether these requests came from those planning emigration or from persons interested only in travel.

Despite these obligations to the Departments of War, Navy, and Foreign Affairs—as well as to the Chancellory—the lieutenant of police dealt more frequently with two other sections of the government. Responsibility for provisioning Paris meant frequent intercourse with the controller general of finances, and it was largely through the police that this powerful figure sought to implement the government's commercial and industrial policy in Paris. Like intendants elsewhere, the lieutenant of police had a hand, under the authority of the controller general, in apportioning taxes exacted from the city or in granting exemption from them.[47] After the founding in 1724 of the Parisian money market and stock exchange, the lieutenant of police assumed responsibility for informing the government's chief financial officer of its pro-

46. BA, MSS 10283–84, *passim.*
47. BA, MS 10321. See the printed "Commandement pour la capitation" ("order to pay the *capitation*"—a head tax, first instituted in 1695, to which corporations as well as individuals were subject) dated October 15, 1720, which declares that the lieutenant of police has issued a statement indicating how much of the total sum owed by the corporations of Paris will be assessed against each of them. In an ordinance of September 4, 1721—MS 1880(6), fol. 108, in subseries 2 of Series H at the Archives Nationales (hereinafter cited as AN, H-2 1880(6), fol. 108)—he exempted a messenger of the university from a tax collected to clean and light city streets.

ceedings; and it was, of course, to the controller general that the lieutenant of police answered for his administration of funds allocated to the police.

For his general stewardship of Paris, the head of the police was responsible to the secretary of state for the king's household. It was through this figure—often called the minister of Paris—that the lieutenant of police derived a delegated authority over the prisons of the capital and its guard, over the basic services performed there, and over the mounted constabulary (maréchaussée) of the Île-de-France. Though lettres de cachet dispatched to the city bore only the signatures of the king and the minister of Paris, another hand had done the drafting. More often than not, the lieutenant of police determined when this intervention of royal authority was required, against whom it should be directed, and what form it should take.

In addition to the six great officers of state, the lieutenant of police met regularly with a host of other individuals. Responsibility for funds raised by various lotteries in the city brought contact with those who used these funds, principally the heads of parishes and religious communities in the capital. From time to time he met with the director general of buildings to discuss construction in the city, and with this same individual he shared control over all quarries within fifteen miles of Paris. As one of the principal administrators of the Hôpital Général and the Hôtel-Dieu, the lieutenant of police had frequent contact with the prévôt des marchands, the first president of the Parlement, the procureur general of the Parlement, the archbishop of Paris, and the first president of the Chambre des Comptes—all of whom shared this responsibility and who together constituted what amounted to a board of governors for the two institutions. Inspection of hospices and other charitable institutions in the city, administration of the Mont-de-Piété after its founding in 1777, and charge of a spinning enterprise operated on behalf of the city's poor brought administrative involvement with a yet larger circle of public and private persons.

CONTROL OF THE POLICE

If toward the end of the eighteenth century the lieutenant of police sought to divest himself of judicial responsibilities, he remained until the Revolution simultaneously judge and administrator. As one of the principal magistrates of the Châtelet, he was accountable to the Parlement of Paris, while as untitled intendant of the capital he was subordinate to the crown. None has doubted that the lieutenant of police loyally obeyed the king who appointed and paid him, but a number of historians have not taken seriously the notion that he was also accountable to the Parlement and bound to court its favor. They have claimed that dual subordination existed in form only and that, in fact, the Parlement was an impotent master, safely ignored.[48]

Contemporaries found it more difficult to dismiss the claim and power of the Parlement. In a letter to the king dated June 30, 1785, and written while the crown searched for a successor to Lenoir, Miromesnil reported his conversation with one of the candidates, Antoine de la Millière. Paris, Miromesnil told Millière, seemed to believe that he would be the next lieutenant of police. Millière—apparently less inclined to indirection than the keeper of the seals—replied bluntly that he did not want the post; nor, he added, was there a chance it would be offered. The distaste the Parlement felt for him was too strong and too well-known; besides, Millière confessed, the repugnance was mutual. He could not, he indicated, tolerate subordination to two masters, especially if one of them was this body of judges he loathed. Millière, at least, took the power of the Parlement over the lieutenant of police seriously.[49] Indeed, there was reason to do so; for in the hands of this sovereign court lay the right to overturn many of the judicial decisions upon which the lieutenants of police relied to enforce their regulation of urban affairs. Using this leverage, the Parlement could and did assert itself against the lieutenant of police and those policies of which it disapproved.

In 1735 the Parlement set aside a decision handed down by René Hérault against two hay merchants and forbade the lieutenant of police from making any further efforts to interfere with their commerce. For fifteen years, from 1743 to 1758, it obstructed efforts on the part of the police to regulate the price grocers charged for butter, eggs, and cheese.[50] Three lieutenants of police found themselves unable to impose effective sanctions against grocers whose prices exceeded prescribed limits. Again and again the Parlement, hearing cases on appeal,

48. "The superiority of the Court [the Parlement] was purely formal, its orders of no significance, its anger a feeble display." Marc Chassaigne, *La Lieutenance-générale de police* (Paris, 1906), 122.

49. AN, K 1021, no. 3.

50. BN, MS JF 1316, fols. 140–41; BN, MSS JF 1322 and 1323 contain documents relating to this effort. The poor of the city relied heavily on these three commodities, making their availability at a reasonable price critical to the maintenance of order.

refused to uphold the fines imposed in police court. Only a number of concessions to the higher court in 1759 brought an end to its resistance and permitted Henri Bertin, then lieutenant of police, to control somewhat more effectively the price of three critically important commodities. As a subordinate magistrate functioning within the jurisdiction of the Parisian Parlement, the lieutenant of police found himself genuinely constrained by its will.

If both the sovereign court and the crown had a claim on the loyalty of the lieutenant of police and both means of exacting this loyalty, whose claim prevailed? Who ultimately controlled the police of Paris? Ordinarily, of course, the problem of ultimate control was not a serious one. Under most circumstances the lieutenant of police managed to conciliate the demands made upon him by his superiors and to satisfy sufficiently both magistrates and ministers. But in a century punctuated by discord between Parlement and crown, the issue of ultimate control remains both of interest and of importance.

In the face of conflict between those to whom he was responsible, with whom did the lieutenant of police side? That, ultimately and unhesitatingly, he stood beside the crown reflects in its own way the relative weight he gave his roles of intendant and of magistrate. Above all, the lieutenant of police was, in his own eyes, a royal administrator loyal to the crown. In February, 1747, when the Parlement and the royal council clashed once again over the papal bull *Unigenitus*, the lieutenant of police labored to keep his superiors in the government apprised of the Parlement's intentions. When the council invalidated an earlier act of the Parlement on February 21, Marville sent several agents into the area around the Palais to gather intelligence for the crown. Led by Inspector Perrault, they reported that a number of magistrates were advocating resistance but that considerable division and distrust existed in the ranks of the court. It would, they suggested, be several days before the Parlement could heal its wounds and respond. Clearly, in 1747 the police were taking their orders from the ministry, helping it to anticipate the moment and nature of any resistance the Parlement might offer.[51]

René de Maupeou's assault on the Parlement, an assault that temporarily destroyed it, underscored the government's control of the police. In January, 1771, police agents participated in delivering orders of exile

51. Inspector Perrault to Claude Feydeau de Marville, February 25, 1747, in BA, MS 10015.

to the magistrates; and in February, the lieutenant of police, Sartine, took up the task of stifling any propaganda on behalf of the Parlement. On February 7, one of Sartine's agents cautioned copyists and bookdealers sympathetic to the banished judges that any among them who displayed or distributed works treating the recent affair would suffer severe punishment.[52]

Neither the advent of a weaker king nor the boldness of a resurrected Parlement affected this established pattern of loyalty. In those situations which precluded allegiance to both crown and Parlement, the police continued to serve the crown. This fundamental commitment was apparent in the conduct of Thiroux de Crosne, the last lieutenant of police, who played an important part in royalty's final attack on the Parlement of Paris.

Needing money and badgered by the Parlement in its effort to raise the sums it required, Loménie de Brienne's government had decided to end this obstruction. On the night of May 5, 1788, police agents attempted to arrest two magistrates deemed particularly responsible for recalcitrance. Unsuccessful in this effort, the lieutenant of police and Marshal Biron, both acting under royal orders, supervised an armed occupation of the Palais where the two judges had taken refuge among their hastily assembled colleagues. For more than ten hours, from midnight until noon the next day, royal troops held the Parlement prisoner in its own chambers until, at last, the men they sought surrendered themselves. As soldiers conducted them to Crosne's office that day, neither of these magistrates can have doubted whose will weighed more heavily with the lieutenant of police. In the end, the crown, not Parlement, controlled the police.[53]

But the crown itself was no monolith. Rent with flaws, its authority lay, for the most part, in the hands of six men who sometimes cooperated in the task of governance, but who—no less frequently—invested considerable labor in intrigue aimed at one another. Around the chancellor or keeper of the seals, around each of the four secretaries of state, and around the controller general, factions formed and struggled for ascendancy. Unfortunately for the lieutenant of police, his extensive responsibilities made him, in one way or another, the subordinate of each of these men. One may, then, well ask whether each of these six officials had an equivalent claim on the loyalty of the

52. Inspector Dehemery to Antoine de Sartine, February 7, 1771, in BN, MS fr. 22114.
53. AN, 0-1 354, nos. 53–92.

police or whether the will of one among them was consistently preponderant.

On a formal level the question is not a difficult one. Theoretically, the lieutenant of police owed a preeminent allegiance to the secretary of state for the king's household. The claim of this officer rested on the manner in which authority was distributed among the four secretaries of state, who, in addition to functionally defined responsibilities, possessed an administrative jurisdiction that was delimited geographically. Under the authority of the secretary of state for the king's household fell much of the interior of France, including the city of Paris, and the principal royal agent there, the lieutenant of police.[54] This secretary's paramount authority over the police was, however, frequently no more than form. In fact, political circumstance and personal animosities or affections commonly placed such authority in other hands.

Consider, for example, those periods when France possessed a prime minister in title or fact—periods which, taken together, amount to more than a third of the reigns of Louis XV and Louis XVI. At such times, real control over the lieutenant of police lay not with the secretary of state for the king's household but with the first minister. Under Cardinal Fleury, the Count of Maurepas, and Loménie de Brienne, the lieutenants of police continued their weekly journeys to Versailles; they went, however, to meet with one man rather than with six. Lenoir reported that during the seven years Maurepas presided over affairs of state, he—the lieutenant of police—took his orders directly from the first minister; and the ascendancy of Fleury earlier in the century created a similar situation. Hérault, whose term as lieutenant of police (1725–1740) coincided roughly with Fleury's tenure of power, owed preemptive allegiance not to the minister of Paris but to Fleury himself.[55]

In the presence of a prime minister, Lenoir, Hérault, and—to some extent—Crosne under Brienne, found their own relative position enhanced and elevated. At such times, Lenoir recalled, the lieutenant of police found himself in circumstances much the same as those of an ordinary minister who—obliged to obey orders that came from some-

---

54. During a period of eight years following the disgrace of the Count of Maurepas in 1749, the Count d'Argenson managed to transfer authority over the city to his own department, that of war.

55. BO, MS 1422, p. 721; Duke d'Antin to René Hérault, August 5, 1730, in BA, MS 10006.

one other than the king—suffered a kind of demotion. The existence of a prime minister conferred greater independence on the lieutenant of police, freeing him from the need to conciliate six powerful superiors, liberating him from conflicting loyalty and contradictory command. It was in the presence of such a preeminent figure that the lieutenancy of police most closely approximated Roland Mousnier's description of it, becoming "a veritable Ministry."[56]

Though in theory the minister of Paris might claim ultimate authority over the lieutenant of police, the existence of a first minister undid this claim, creating a familiar discrepancy between theory and fact. Other circumstances produced a similar variance. Although the crown might, for extended periods, withhold the title of first minister, it did not bestow equivalent favor on all its principal servants. From the perpetual intrigue that surrounded the throne, from the struggle among ministers for favor, one or two among them often emerged with a disproportionate influence—with a preponderance that, while informal and ephemeral, was in the moment no less real. No lieutenant of police could permit such discrepancies in power to escape him; nor, under most circumstances, could he allow formal ties to one minister—the minister of Paris—to take precedence over the exigencies of political circumstance. Hence, after the death of Maurepas in 1781, it was not to Amelot, minister of Paris, that real control over Lenoir and the Parisian police passed; instead the head of the police conducted most of his weekly business at Versailles with the two ministers who had, in 1781, the surest hold on royal esteem—the Count of Vergennes, secretary of state for foreign affairs, and Hue de Miromesnil, keeper of the seals.[57]

Continual shifts in favor required that a lieutenant of police keep his finger in the air and be willing to move with the prevailing winds. Inflexibility could bring dismissal, as Lenoir twice discovered. In 1775, he had failed to adapt to Turgot's waxing influence and had, thanks to the controller general's unmollified hostility, lost his post. Having been reappointed a year later and having allied himself to Vergennes and Miromesnil, Lenoir once again ignored the growing influence of others. This time it was the Baron of Breteuil, secretary of state for the king's household and minister of Paris after 1783, whom he failed to

56. BO, MS 1422, p. 721; Mousnier, *Paris au XVIIe siècle*, 98.
57. BO, MS 1422, pp. 724–27. Of Vergennes, Lenoir reports that "this Minister enjoyed great esteem in the eyes of M. de Maurepas, after whose death, he had, more than the other Ministers, the confidence of the King."

cultivate and who compelled him to resign a second and final time in 1785.[58]

Personal bonds rather than political expediency might determine to which member of the government the lieutenant of police gave his loyalty. During his tenure, Joseph d'Albert took orders primarily from the controller general—his friend and benefactor, Turgot—while the Count d'Argenson, who headed the police briefly in 1720, looked to his father—the keeper of the seals—for direction. Neither d'Albert nor d'Argenson remained in office more than a year. The personal ties that had procured their posts and determined their allegiance also proved their undoing. D'Albert held office little more than a year before the fall of Turgot undermined his position and forced him to resign. D'Argenson followed his father into disgrace six months after having taken up the duties of his office. To be sure, a lieutenant of police could not do without still more powerful friends; even less, however, could he afford a single bond that was too close. Amid the shifting winds that blew at Versailles, most vessels of any size required more than one anchor.

There were, however, periods when the wind was constant and a man could dispense with elaborate precautions. At such times close association with the right individual might bring more than security against an ill-disposed minister; it could make the lieutenant of police as powerful and dangerous an adversary as any who stood in the first rank of royal servants. It was Nicolas René Berryer, linked as he was to Madame de Pompadour, who, in 1757, engineered the disgrace of the Count d'Argenson, then secretary of state for war; and, eight years earlier, the same lieutenant of police who had humbled the secretary of state for the king's household and forced his resignation.[59]

As Maurepas later noted, both of those compelled to resign had been ministers of Paris, and one finds it difficult to believe that the two blows that felled them, aimed as they were rapidly in the same direction, were random. They appear, under the circumstances, less the re-

58. Jacques Peuchet, *Mémoires tirés des archives de la police de Paris* (6 vols.; Paris, 1838), II, 412–13.
59. BO, MS 1422, p. 724. Lenoir reports that shortly before he died, Maurepas confided a piece of information to the lieutenant of police, paused, and then added: "If I had reason to think that you were against me, I would not tell you this. I have not forgotten that Marville brought about my disgrace by Louis XV, when I was Minister of Paris; and that Berryer accomplished the disgrace of M. d'Argenson when he held the same position." Since Marville was no longer lieutenant of police in 1749 when Maurepas fell from power, I have assumed that the memory of either Maurepas or Lenoir proved inaccurate

sult of purely personal intrigue than the revolt of one royal servant against the pretensions of another. They seem, indeed, an insistence by the lieutenant of police on a limited administrative autonomy and a stunning warning to one minister against pressing too far his claim of authority over the Parisian police.

Even lacking an ally as powerful as Madame de Pompadour, the lieutenant of police remained a figure no minister could sensibly ignore. Many of those who headed the police carried on a direct and private correspondence with the king, as well as with members of his family; and though much of what passed between Louis XV or Louis XVI and their lieutenants of police may have been of little political consequence, the correspondence itself was enough to promote caution and concern among the king's closest advisors; for with it went an independent leverage on the royal will, a means of manipulating the mechanism that made and unmade political fortunes.[60]

Ironic, but nonetheless indicative of this concern over the king's private correspondence, was the ministry's use of police informers to uncover any such correspondence. Royal ministers apparently did everything in their power to insulate the king and to insure that they controlled the information he received.[61] One wonders whether the government—the ministry—had better luck censoring royal mail and reading material than it did keeping undesirable books out of the hands and homes of the French people.

Louis XV and Louis XVI both seem to have maintained private correspondence with their lieutenants of police in part as a remedy against these efforts. From the lieutenants of police they sought, and believed they could obtain, accurate information—information that had not been filtered by the layers of personal and political ambition surround-

---

in recalling this incident and that one or the other was actually referring to Berryer who replaced Marville in 1747. Nonetheless, Maurepas had had a hand in forcing Marville's resignation; and it is possible that it was, indeed, the former lieutenant of police, who, by using sources of information still open to him, supplied the evidence of Maurepas's indiscretions regarding Madame de Pompadour that brought about his fall. Berryer's association with Madame de Pompadour, attested to by Peuchet (*Mémoires*, II, 123–24), who calls him her "confidential agent, her 'creature' in all respects," helps explain his successful assault on a minister of war and a secretary of state for the king's household.

60. See BO, MS 1422, pp. 719–21 on the nature of Lenoir's correspondence with Louis XVI and the royal family. MS 1799 in the *nouvelles acquisitions* of the *fonds français* at the Bibliothèque Nationale (hereinafter cited as BN, MS fr. n.a. 1799) contains several letters signed Louis and addressed to Berryer. They are brief and may well be in the king's own hand. BA, MS 10025, piece 195, is a letter from the queen to Marville dated July 31, 1749.

61. BO, MS 1422, p. 723.

ing the throne. The lieutenant of police constituted in their eyes, if not
in fact, one of the few mediums through which unrefracted light pene-
trated Versailles. He was a rare window in a wall of mirrors. Perceived
as such, as a relatively objective and honest source of information
about the great city the crown could not ignore, the lieutenant of police
became on his own, without the intervention or assistance of allies, a
powerful and potentially dangerous political opponent.

The choice of a new archbishop for Paris in 1781 suggests the occasionally decisive influence of a lieutenant of police and underscores
the bases of this power. In seeking a successor to Christophe de Beau-
mont, Louis XVI found himself faced with conflicting advice from two
determined parties. On one side stood the two most influential ministers in his government, Vergennes and Miromesnil, as well as the
king's aunts; on the other, the queen and most of the court. Vergennes
and those aligned with him supported the nomination of Leclerc de
Juigné, bishop of Châlons; the queen and her allies urged the appointment of Loménie de Brienne, the archbishop of Toulouse. Confronted
with dissension among those closest to him, Louis wrote his lieutenant of police, Lenoir, asking him for a prompt, careful, and secret
report on opinion in Paris regarding the character of Brienne. In his
recollection of the incident, Lenoir said simply, "I obeyed and M. de
Juigné was appointed."[62]

Given his ties to Miromesnil and Vergennes, it is not surprising that
Lenoir's report confirmed their advice to the king; but it is important
to note Louis's solicitude of opinion in his capital and the fact that, in
seeking a representation of this opinion, he turned to the lieutenant
of police. To speak on behalf of Paris was to speak with a voice that
neither a minister nor the king himself could treat lightly; and though
many claimed this right, it was the lieutenant of police more than any
other who exercised it. From such exercise and from his role as a source
of relatively objective information, the lieutenant of police derived
an influence sufficient to make him an independently powerful figure
—powerful enough at times to give pause even to an overbearing
minister.

Who controlled the Parisian police? To this question no single satisfactory response can be given unless one chooses to speak simply in
formal terms. One can say that, despite the ambiguous position of the
lieutenant of police, he obeyed the orders of the crown rather than

62. BO, MS 1421, p. 245.

those of the Parlement and that obedience to the crown was obedience
to the prime minister when such a position existed. At other times,
control over the police might rest with any of the six principal royal
officials. Which of them actually exercised this authority depended on
political and personal circumstance. Yet, in a sense, control of the
police often lay in a very direct way with the king himself. The un-
mediated correspondence Louis XV and Louis XVI conducted with a
number of their lieutenants of police gave these agents of the king
a certain independence from ministerial authority, making them at
times almost the peers of those who proudly obeyed the orders of no
man but the king of France.

THE CHARACTER OF THE POST

Subordinate to both Parlement and crown, simultaneously responsible
to six royal ministers and a king, the lieutenancy of police was inevitably drawn into political intrigue. It is not difficult under these
circumstances to understand why Lenoir called the post a "dangerous
honor" or to appreciate why flexibility and prudence were qualities
considered absolutely essential in one who would occupy it.[63] Without them a man found it exceedingly difficult to pick his way through
the maze of apparent loyalty and obligation in which he found himself. In their absence, it was unlikely he could circumvent the potential
for dangerous enmity and damaging embarrassment that lay scattered
along his path.

   The world in which a lieutenant of police moved required more of
him than the ability to mollify six ministers and several hundred magistrates. His was a world rent by an extended and complex set of social distinctions as well as by political struggle; and unlike many administrators, a lieutenant of police could not barricade himself against
this larger world. He had daily to confront persons drawn from the
far reaches of the social spectrum; and the success of these encounters,
the lieutenant of police believed, depended on his own sensitivity to
the exigencies of social circumstance and his capacity for appropriate
adaptation. Lenoir thought it vital that he not only make himself accessible to all, but that he be capable of conversing in whatever style
most suited his interlocutor. In the presence of laborers, a lieutenant of

---

63. BO, MS 1422, p. 43. For contemporary assessments of the attributes believed vital
in a lieutenant of police, see AN, K 1021, nos. 1–3; BA, MS 1001, piece 163; BO, MS
1422, pp. 893–95.

police had to appear "affable and without arrogance." Among those of
high social standing, undisciplined good nature must give way to elaborate form and careful regard for the sensitivities of rank. Encounter
with members of the upper class was, Lenoir reported, invariably
"difficult and delicate."[64]

Antoine Gabriel de Sartine, Lenoir's predecessor, is supposed to have
owned more wigs than any man in Paris and to have believed that
none of them was an unnecessary indulgence. Each permitted him to
effect some modification in his appearance that, however slight, augmented alterations in manner and, hence, rendered him a more artful
and adequate player of the roles each day imposed upon him. Whether
or not they existed, Sartine's wigs stand as an appropriate symbol for
the frequent social adjustments demanded of a lieutenant of police.
Writing after revolution had momentarily suspended the need for such
careful social discrimination, another lieutenant of police could not
help envying the relatively consistent posture permitted his postrevolutionary successors.[65]

While Lenoir described his post as dangerous, he would not have
quarrelled with those who qualified it as "painful."[66] The adjective
seems appropriate on several counts. Certainly considerable emotional
stress went with the stewardship of Paris. Responsible on the one hand
to a city of more than half a million persons for policy he did not
always have a hand in making, accountable on the other to an absolute
monarch for the conduct of hundreds of thousands of persons over
whom his control was obviously limited, the lieutenant of police could
hardly have failed to experience more than occasional anxiety.

But in calling his position painful or difficult, commentators referred
less to the psychological burdens accompanying it than to the time,
labor, and energy it demanded. All informed observers concurred that,
together with adaptability and prudence, a taste for hard work was
critically important in a lieutenant of police. "This post," said the
keeper of the seals in 1785, "requires unremitting work in one's office.
It permits but few distractions. It demands almost continuous residence [in Paris]."[67]

64. BO, MS 1422, pp. 891–92.
65. Peuchet, Mémoires, II, 362–63; BO, MS 1422, pp. 891–92.
66. BA, MS 10001, piece 165.
67. AN, K 1021, no. 1.

REWARDS

Despite the long hours, despite the psychological and physical strain that went with being lieutenant of police, men continued to vie for the post. Having acknowledged its dangers and difficulties, Lenoir spoke of its inescapable attraction.[68] Why? Given the labor it exacted and the risks it imposed, wherein lay its appeal? What rewards did the post offer as remuneration for the pain and danger it entailed?

Its compensations assumed a variety of familiar forms: upon those interested in status it bestowed considerable prestige; to those tempted by power, it promised extensive authority over a great city; before those whose taste inclined toward the tangible, it laid uncommon recompense; and to all, it held out the possibility that beyond the immediate rewards lay others still greater.

The lieutenancy of police was—all qualification aside—an honor. Dangerous it might have been, and painful, too; but only a handful of the administrative posts in France conferred more status. Intendant of the city of Paris in fact, if not in title, the lieutenant of police shared in the prestige that attached to the small elite which, throughout France, governed in the king's name. Indeed, among this group of approximately thirty-five men who bore the appellation of intendant the lieutenant of police was something more than a peer. While it is difficult to rank the intendancies with great confidence or precision, it is clear that among them a rough hierarchy existed. Near its top, perhaps beneath only the intendancy of Paris (the *généralité* which was an entity distinct from the city), stood the lieutenancy of police. When Hérault, who had held the important intendancy of Tours (ranking fourth in size, third in the amount of revenue it produced), was made lieutenant of police in August, 1725, he received a great many letters congratulating him on his promotion; and some of the correspondents viewed the new assignment not only as an elevation, but as the last step one might take before attaining one of the great offices of state. The attitude embodied in these letters suggests that, with one or two possible exceptions, no intendancy carried the prestige bestowed by the lieutenancy of police.[69]

As one of the crown's more important administrators, the lieutenant

68. BO, MS 1422, p. 43.
69. BA, MS 10001, pieces 159, 161.

of police received numerous marks of status and favor. Like a bishop or a member of the royal family he was appropriately addressed as "Monseigneur." His was the right of accompanying the king and queen on their trips away from Versailles to the more intimate and exclusive chateau of Marly.[70]

A lieutenant of police might expect promotion to the nobility or elevation within it. Sartine, a Spaniard by birth and without noble title, became the Count of Alby. The Count d'Argenson, lieutenant of police under Louis XIV, became the Marquis d'Argenson and the Marquis of Paulmy. Marville received the titles of Count of Gien and Marquis of Dampierre.

More meaningful than titles, perhaps, was the proximity of the lieutenant of police to the king. Henri Sée once suggested that it was possible to distinguish the upper level of the French nobility by locating those who had been presented to the king. Among a noble population of approximately four hundred thousand persons, we know that some twenty thousand had experienced this honor. One begins to appreciate the status of a lieutenant of police when one realizes that he had not merely been presented to the king a single time but that he saw him or corresponded with him on many occasions. He was not one of twenty thousand whose name had been uttered before the throne, but one of perhaps twenty who had the right of working alone with the king in his office.[71]

From this proximity to the crown sprang not only status but a portion of the power that lay in the hands of a lieutenant of police. No intendant, except once again perhaps the intendant of Paris, stood as close to the sources of power in France. Weekly trips to Versailles, Compiègne, or Fontainebleau kept him in regular, personal contact with each of the chief figures in the government and afforded him an uncommon chance to promote or dispute policy. There was more limited access to the king himself.

A network of agents within Paris permitted the lieutenant of police to perform a variety of services for the queen, members of the royal family, and other highly placed persons, thereby establishing a credit in favors upon which he could draw as needed. A role in determining the occupant of several thousand positions in the Parisian administra-

70. BA, MS 10015, piece 247.
71. Michel Antoine, *Le Fonds du conseil d'état du roi aux Archives Nationales* (Paris, 1955), 10.

tion meant that he was a patron of considerable importance, and his capacity to influence the crown's appointments did not end with the boundaries of the capital. In many of the letters the lieutenant of police received regularly from the secretary of state for the king's household, there are requests for an opinion regarding some individual who had petitioned the king or the secretary of state for a post outside Paris.[72] No doubt many of those who drafted these petitions were aware that the lieutenant of police would have a hand in deciding their futures and were consequently ready to render service for service, if asked.

To the part he played in bestowing offices, the lieutenant of police added another significant role—that of deciding what funds would be available to Parisian institutions in need of them. When, in 1765, the abbess of the Convent of Saint-Antoine wanted to repair her establishment and needed 300,000 livres to build new, safe dormitories for her nuns, she had to get the permission of the Conseil d'État to borrow this sum in Paris. And in making its decision, the council turned to the lieutenant of police for help. It commissioned him to inspect the convent, determine what repairs were really necessary, and recommend an appropriate ceiling for the loan the abbess sought. In the end the lieutenant of police suggested that 150,000 livres would be sufficient to meet the convent's needs, and it was this sum the council authorized the nuns to borrow.[73] Clearly, part of the power of the lieutenant of police derived from his control over the extent to which many institutions in Paris could tap public credit (and thereby compete with the crown). He was a man who had favors of a very concrete kind to dispense and who could, in consequence, count on extensive gratitude and reciprocation.

He could count, too, on fear; for, regardless of how much he actually knew about the daily affairs of individuals, men believed him to know a great deal. Rumors circulated that every third member of a gathering was an agent of the police. Not a house in Paris, it seemed, was without its informer. Believing or half believing such stories, few men were willing to risk offending one who held information that could do them considerable harm.

Regular contact with the ultimate sources of authority, the capacity

72. See, for example, any of the letters from the Count of Pontchartrain to Marc Réne d'Argenson, in AN, 0-1 362, or those from the Count of Saint Florentin to Sartine, in AN, 0-1 407.
73. Count of Saint Florentin to Sartine, August 13, 1765, in AN, 0-1 407.

to serve and to obligate the most influential persons in the realm, the means by which to bestow reward and the presumed means of punishing injury—these were abundant sources of strength and could not fail to tempt those who saw in power an irresistible luminosity.

While its material benefits may have been a less significant attraction than the power and prestige it offered, the lieutenancy of police provided financial rewards that one could not easily ignore. An annual income of 50,000 livres was not the modest sum Lenoir pretended it to be.[74] True, these earnings did not put a lieutenant of police in the same rank as a royal prince like Condé, whose yearly revenues were many times as great; but they surpassed the income of all but 250 noble families in France, exceeded the official earnings of all members of the Parisian Parlement, excepting only the first president, and were half again as large a sum as the average intendant received.[75]

To this initial income of approximately 50,000 livres the lieutenant of police added pay he received for his work on various commissions of the Conseil d'État. Thiroux de Crosne, lieutenant of police during the last four years of the Old Regime, obtained an additional 21,000 livres in 1787 from this source, giving him a total official income of 70,000 livres.[76]

Rumors circulated that a lieutenant of police had access to still larger sums. Those gaming houses the police permitted to operate were obliged to purchase the toleration they enjoyed. Amounting to some 300,000 livres a year during the latter half of the century, these fees, many Parisians believed, went in part to making the lieutenant of police a wealthy man.[77]

74. See BO, MS 1422, p. 969 for Lenoir's views on the adequacy of his salary; p. 469 of the same source and BHVP, c.p. 4725 contain information on the magnitude of this income and the expenditures it was supposed to cover.

75. Daniel Roche, "Aperçus sur la fortune et les revenus des princes de Condé à l'aube du XVIIIe siècle," Revue d'histoire moderne et contemporaine, XIV (1967), 217–43; Guy Chaussinand-Nogaret, La Noblesse au XVIIIe siècle (Paris, 1976), 77; François Bluche, Les Magistrats du parlement de Paris au XVIIIe siècle (Besancon, 1960), 169–72; Vivian Gruder, The Royal Provincial Intendants (Ithaca, N.Y., 1968), 237–38.

76. "Appointements de divers fonctionnaires de l'administration, fin du XVIIIe siècle," in subseries 4 of Series F at the Archives Nationales (hereinafter cited as "Appointements des fonctionnaires," in AN, F-4 1032). This additional income is listed as follows: appointements et gages (emoluments and pay) of the council, 10,000 livres; expenses, 6,000 livres; bureau du commerce, 3,600 livres; bureau des arts et métiers, 1,800 livres.

77. BO, MS 1422, pp. 895–96, 969. Lenoir denies that he or his predecessor, Sartine, appropriated any of this money, but the careful wording of his statement leaves one wondering about those who came before Sartine.

There were rewards still more tangible than money, small gratuities from those who courted the favor of men more powerful than themselves. In November, 1730, Hérault received a letter from an agent at Tonnerre, a small town on the Armançon River, near Auxerre. The correspondent, after discussing the wines of the region—those of Chablis—and quarrels among the residents of the town, went on to report having had the good fortune to come upon six pounds of fresh truffles. Without hesitation, he said, he had bought all 124 of them, packed them in moss, and turned them over to Hérault's messenger with instructions to deliver them to the lieutenant of police as quickly as possible.[78] While it is difficult to say how many such gifts a lieutenant of police received during the course of a year, it is clear that his material compensation was various and that figures like 50,000 or 70,000 livres give only an incomplete account.

In the end, immediate rewards—whatever their nature—were probably less significant in drawing men to the lieutenancy of police than the future the post seemed to promise. Important as was the position itself, many regarded it as merely the final corridor one traversed on one's way to the important chambers of Versailles.[79]

Five of the fourteen lieutenants of police reached the pinnacle of the administrative hierarchy in France: Marc-René d'Argenson became simultaneously keeper of the seals and president of the Conseil des Finances in 1718; his second son, Marc-Pierre, was secretary of state for war between 1743 and 1757; Nicolas Berryer had charge of the Department of the Navy for three years and then held the seals until his death in 1762; Henri Baptiste Bertin de Bellisle became controller general in 1759 and four years later, with the rank of minister, was made a kind of fifth secretary of state; finally, Antoine Gabriel de Sartine left the lieutenancy of police in 1774 to become, like Berryer before him, secretary of state for the navy. During the eighteenth century, 36 percent of those who became lieutenant of police ascended to one of the highest positions in the state, while no more than 12 percent of the provincial intendants reached these posts.[80] If it is true that the crown drafted its most powerful servants from the ranks of the

78. Déon to Hérault, November 7, 1730, in BA, MS 10006.
79. This was Lenoir's view toward the end of the Old Regime (BO, MS 1422, p. 892) and that of Hérault's correspondents in 1725 (BA, MS 10001, pieces 159, 161).
80. Gruder, *Intendants*, 54–55. The figure is eleven of ninety-four in Gruder's study of those who occupied intendancies between 1710 and 1776.

intendants, it is also true that it found these servants more frequently among its lieutenants of police in Paris. As an occupant of this position a man's chances of becoming a secretary of state or controller general were three times those of an ordinary intendant.

Those lieutenants of police who failed to reach the very top could nonetheless count after they resigned on becoming a conseiller d'état. This position, held by no more than forty men at a time, was of considerable prominence. As a group, the conseillers d'état yielded precedence only to the peers of France; and it was they, who, together with the maîtres des requêtes, staffed the committees and commissions of the Conseil d'État.

Having entered this select corps of administrators, a man who had been lieutenant of police enjoyed substantially more generous remuneration than his fellows. Below is a table summarizing the distribution of official income in 1787 among thirty-five conseillers d'état.[81]

Income in livres	Number of Councillors of State
0–10,000	11
10,000–20,000	7
20,000–30,000	10
30,000–40,000	3
40,000–50,000	3
50,000–60,000	1

Only two councillors drew more than 60,000 livres from the treasury, and both were former lieutenants of police: to Lenoir the crown payed almost 70,000 livres, while upon Sartine it bestowed a yearly income that approached 90,000 livres. A third former lieutenant of police, Feydeau de Marville, was one of only four who, according to the table above, received between 40,000 and 60,000 livres.[82]

Viewed as a group the lieutenants of police seem to have had remarkably good fortune upon quitting their post in Paris. Whether they became ministers or conseillers d'état, their success within the royal administration was uncommon, and those to whom the lieutenancy of

81. These figures and those that follow are from "Appointements des fonctionnaires," in AN, F-4 1032.

82. Only one other former lieutenant of police was alive in 1787. This was Bertin, whose name does not appear on the list.

police was offered undoubtedly regarded the proposal as something more than the promise of immediate prestige and power. Given prior experience, the offer would have appeared not merely of immediate value but also as an implicit pledge of relatively durable favor and reward. Those who became lieutenant of police made a pact that reached beyond today and tomorrow and, in accepting the offered post, marked for others the extent of their ambition.

BECOMING LIEUTENANT OF POLICE

One question remains. Admitting that a man might reasonably desire to be lieutenant of police, how did he manage to realize the aspiration? The answer is unsurprising. It is essentially the same as that others have given to a similar question regarding the provincial intendants, and so may be quickly summarized here. Like all who sought high administrative positions, those who became lieutenant of police began by acquiring training in the law. All fourteen lieutenants of police embarked on their careers as attorneys. From private practice, they quickly passed to some public post within the courts, becoming either judges or prosecutors. Four of the fourteen served early in their careers as one of the public prosecutors at the Châtelet; another filled a similar post before the tribunal known as the Requêtes de l'Hôtel. The remaining nine occupied some judicial position in a *parlement*, usually that of Paris, or on a presidial court, usually the Châtelet, again in Paris.

The next step, the most critical, involved obtaining a place among the eighty maîtres des requêtes. From this corps came all important servants of the crown, and no one could hope for a successful administrative career without having gained access to it. The requisites of admission were three: family or friends with influence; personal ability; and access to the approximately 100,000 livres which the charge cost. Marc-René d'Argenson, the second lieutenant of police, performed his judicial functions on the presidial court of Angoulême with rare ability for thirteen years and at any point during this time could have raised 100,000 livres. But it was not until he married a relative of the controller general, Pontchartrain, in 1693 that he obtained the connections without which neither ability nor money nor both together was sufficient to secure a place as maître des requêtes.

Having entered this elite corps—usually in his late twenties or early thirties—a man might, under special circumstances, pass almost directly on to the lieutenancy of police. Being the son of the keeper of the seals brought Marc-Pierre d'Argenson the post less than a year after he became a maître des requêtes. Others, without similar connections, might wait a very long time. Both Thiroux de Crosne and Louis Charles de Machault had been maîtres des requêtes for twenty-four years before being named lieutenant of police. A more frequent experience, however, was one involving about eight years of prior judicial and administrative experience on commissions of the Conseil d'État, as a provincial intendant, or as a president of the Grand Conseil.[83]

Elevation beyond one of these posts depended again largely on ability and connections. Of these two prerequisites, connections were far the more important. Especially useful to those interested in becoming lieutenant of police were ties to a man who held or had held the post. It was Sartine, who—upon becoming secretary of state for the navy in 1774—secured the position he had just vacated for his friend, Lenoir; and one supposes that Hérault had more than a minor role in seeing that his son-in-law, Marville, succeeded him as lieutenant of police. Of obvious utility was the protection of a minister, but one apparently did as well cultivating a royal mistress: d'Albert may have owed his appointment in 1775 to friendship with Turgot, but Ravot d'Ombreval came to office in 1724 because he had the support of his cousin, the Marquise de Prie; and both Berryer and Bertin, it was said, gained the position because Madame de Pompadour urged their name upon the king.[84]

A man did not, in general, quickly complete the road that led toward the lieutenancy of police. Most were in their early forties before reaching its end. Along the way lay a number of obligatory halts that impeded progress. Legal training and law courts, the wait for a place as maître des requêtes, judicial and administrative work on the Conseil

83. Before 1725, one finds men becoming lieutenant of police before being made provincial intendants or intendants of commerce or finance; after 1725, the sequence changes completely, and it is one or more of the intendancies that comes first in a man's career. This reversal may mark a change in the crown's attitude regarding the relative importance of the lieutenancy of police and those posts most resembling it.

84. BO, MS 1422, pp. 719, 730, 736; dossier no. 1 in MS no. 16 of subseries A in Series E of the Archives de la Préfecture de Police (hereinafter cited as APP, EA 16, no. 1); Henri Carré, Le Règne de Louis XV, 1715–1774 (Paris, 1909), 79, Vol. VIII, Pt. 2 of Ernest Lavisse (ed.), Histoire de France depuis les origines jusqu'à la révolution (9 vols.; Paris, 1900–1911); Biographie universelle, IV, 343–44, and LVIII, 138–41.

d'État, service in the provinces—all were stations at which a man had to pause on his way to high administrative position.

Ledgers recording these delays remain, and we rightly regard them as essential to the continuation of the journey. Other stops, though less well-recorded, were, if anything, more important. Long hours in court or council chamber availed a man little unless he also passed the requisite evenings in the homes of those well enough placed to publicize his talent before the king and his closest counsellors. Traveling the road he did, one who aspired to be lieutenant of police could ignore neither public edifice nor private dwelling along his way.

3

Subordinates and Organization

Royal edict and commission had invested the lieutenant of police with the authority to do Paris either considerable good or, through negligence and ineptitude, great harm. Yet this authority to shape life in the city and the power to do so were by no means identical. Authority the king of France could bestow with a brief gesture of the hand; but the capacity to exercise this authority was not so easily given. Its establishment required not a single royal act but rather sustained and durable support against others who claimed the newly granted authority for themselves; above all, it required a commitment of resources on the part of the crown, an allocation of funds with which to purchase tools for implementing one's will. We have seen that by edict in March of 1667 and by subsequent commission the crown granted the lieutenant of police remarkably extensive authority. We have yet to ask whether the means it placed at his disposal were commensurate with the responsibility it had imposed.

How many men was the lieutenant of police able to draw into his service, and in what ways did he secure their loyalty and obedience? Until these questions are posed and ways found of answering them, we cannot distinguish the formal right to act from the genuine capacity to do so; nor, it follows, can we really gauge the impact of the police on prerevolutionary Paris and those who inhabited it.

Still, to put such questions is not always to be able to answer them definitively. Between query and conclusion significant obstacles arise. There is the ambiguity surrounding usage of the word police and the difficulty of deciding what extent the term is to be given. There are the problems posed by fragmentary sources whose testimony often fails to interlock—random pieces from more than a single puzzle; there is, as well, an occasional superabundance of data and the dilemma of con-

tradiction. But such obstacles are not novel and hardly justify the sub-
stitution of anecdote for data or haphazard description for the attempt
to provide a clear and comprehensive account of structure. The problems I have cited ought rather to serve simply as a warning against
regarding what follows as irreversibly established, without need of
further scrutiny and consequent elaboration or correction.

NUMBER

Fashioning pieces of data into a single summatory figure is but a first
step in portraying adequately the size of the prerevolutionary police.
While it is essential to determine that over three thousand men and
women served the lieutenant of police in 1788, this number does not
assume full significance for us until it is set against the size of Paris
itself at that time and compared with other, contemporary figures
whose concrete ramifications are familiar to us.

If we take the population of Paris in 1788 to have been 600,000 and
number the police at 3,114, we may conclude that there was in Paris
on the eve of revolution one police employee to every 193 residents of
the city.[1] To gain some sense of the presence these figures represent,
we may juxtapose them to others whose meaning is clearer to us.
Below is a list of cities in the United States whose current population
(1970 census) most closely approximates that of Paris in 1788. The list

City	Population	Number of Police	Ratio, Police to Population
San Antonio	654,153	1234	1/530
Boston	641,071	3002	1/214
Memphis	623,530	1462	1/426
Saint Louis	622,236	2871	1/217
New Orleans	593,471	1801	1/330
Phoenix	581,562	1572	1/370
Columbus, Ohio	540,025	1326	1/407
Seattle	530,831	1394	1/381
Jacksonville, Fla.	528,865	1167	1/453
Pittsburgh	520,117	1581	1/329

1. The figure for the city's population is Marcel Reinhard's, *Paris pendant la Révolution*, I, 25–34. It permits one to give credence to the data contained in Jean de Lacaille's
unpaginated *Description de la ville et des fauxbourgs de Paris* (rprt. 1967; Paris, 1714)—
data which leads one to estimate a population of 550,425 for that date—and to the asser-
tions that one encounters in many documents that Paris continued to grow during the
eighteenth century. The figure for the police will be justified in what follows.

includes figures on the size of the police forces in each of these cities and, in each case, an indication of the ratio of police to inhabitants.[2]

It would seem today in the United States a resident of Boston or Saint Louis is best situated to translate numerical data on the pre-revolutionary police into a concrete sense of magnitude similar to that experienced by an eighteenth-century Parisian—into subjectively cor-respondent notions regarding the availability of service and the prox-imity of intimidation. Lacking the peculiarly favorable perspective of a Bostonian, we can yet offer a satisfactory answer to our initial ques-tion.

How large was the police force of Paris under the Old Regime? It was, it would seem, larger in relative terms than any police depart-ment existing today in a major American city, and larger in absolute terms than the present forces of either Saint Louis or Boston, both of which contain populations larger than that of Paris in 1789.

But gross figures like those used thus far can mislead. As suggested earlier, the activities performed by an American police force today and those performed by the Parisian police before the Revolution are by no means wholly coincident. Police was, during the eighteenth century, a more encompassing appellation than it is today, and among the 3,114 persons employed in one way or another by the lieutenant of police were a considerable number we would not today include on the rolls of a police department. Attempting to take this discrepancy between definitions into account, we arrive at a somewhat different estimate for the size of the prerevolutionary police. Of the 3,114 persons who constituted the Parisian police in 1788, 1,931 performed functions similar to those undertaken by a modern American force.[3]

If we use this new figure in place of the earlier one to obtain a ratio of police to residents, we find that eighteenth-century Paris resembled in this respect not so much Boston or Saint Louis as New Orleans. In having one individual whom we would consider a police agent to every 313 residents, prerevolutionary Paris remains even by modern stan-

2. Most of the data cited here is from *The World Almanac and Book of Facts, 1976* (New York, 1976), 210, 976. That for Boston was contained in a letter Police Commis-sioner Robert J. DiGrazia sent me on September 26, 1973. He and the Boston police were kind enough to supply me with more detailed information than that in the *Al-manac*.

3. See table 2. I have included in this number all those involved in administration and communications and in deterrent patrol; I have also included those employed under the heading investigation and intelligence as well as the forty-eight commissioners of the Châtelet.

Table 1 Allocations of Personnel:
Paris 1788 & Boston 1973

Function	Parisian Police 1788		Police of Boston 1973	
	Number	Percentage of Total	Number	Percentage of Total
1. Deterrent Patrol	1,483	47.62	2,050	68.29
2. Services	699	22.45	149	4.96
3. Inspection[1]	376	12.08	0	0.00
4. Investigation and Intelligence	360	11.56	255	8.49
5. Justice[1]	156	5.01	0	0.00
6. Administration and Communication	40	1.28	548[2]	18.26
7. Totals	3,114	100.00	3,002	100.00

SOURCE: Boston Police Department
1. This function in all its various forms is, in Boston, in the hands of various other agencies of the state and city.
2. In calculating this figure, I have assumed that all 425 civilian employees working with the Boston police are engaged in administrative tasks. No doubt this assumption has produced an inflated estimate of administrative personnel.

dards a well-policed city. While its police force may no longer appear in relative terms as larger than that of any contemporary American city, it nonetheless remains of considerable size, larger in fact than more than half the police departments in this country's thirty largest cities.

Comparing the eighteenth-century police force with its offspring in the French capital today may serve as a final indication of its size. Paris is at present patrolled and protected by a police force that is in absolute terms more than ten times the size of its eighteenth-century ancestor; but the current population for which this department is responsible is also slightly more than ten times what it was in 1789.[4] It

4. In comparing the Parisian police force of today with the police of the eighteenth century, neither of the figures I have already given for the latter is adequate. Once again the historian must allow for conceptual and administrative differences. The police in Paris still perform a number of functions performed by the prerevolutionary police in the capital, functions that do not fall within the province of police forces in the United States. They continue, for example, to provide protection against fire and to inspect food and drugs. They do not, however, any longer bear responsibility for lighting the city or removing waste. Taking these similarities and differences into account, it seems fair, for purposes of comparison, to number the prerevolutionary police at 2,485. The

does not seem unfair, then, to say that those who have a concrete sense of the size of the police force in Paris today have also a rough notion of how considerable it appeared in August and September of 1788 when ominous crowds began to appear in the streets of the capital.

DELEGATING AUTHORITY

If it is important to obtain an overview of the prerevolutionary police force, it is also essential to know something of its components and of the structure imposed upon them. What entities did it comprise and how was responsibility that had been invested in the lieutenant of police apportioned among them?

Delegation of authority had proceeded gradually since 1667 when the lieutenancy of police was created. In 1789 it was based partly on a division of the city into twenty quarters largely accomplished in 1702 by the second lieutenant of police, Marc-René d'Argenson, and partly on a somewhat elaborate functional specialization in whose progressive articulation several lieutenants of police had an important part.

Function

While the quarters were in many ways the older basis for distributing responsibility, function became during the eighteenth century a device at least as important. The authority conferred by the lieutenants of police ceased gradually to be an undifferentiated control over sectors of the city. As the number of police agents grew after 1708, they came increasingly to exercise responsibilities that were functionally distinct; and attention to this evolving differentiation permits division of the prerevolutionary police into six major sections, each containing elements engaged in roughly similar activities: five of these divisions (deterrent patrol, investigation and intelligence, public services, inspection, and justice) worked directly in the community, while the sixth—administration and communications—attended to internal problems of coordination, supervision, and direction. Within these six sections fall the units and individuals who actually constituted the Parisian police.

---

ratio of police to population for 1788 thus becomes 1/241. As of January 1, 1968, the Parisian police force numbered 36,052, while the population falling within its jurisdiction totalled 6,730,000. On this date, then, the ratio of police to population would have been 1/187. See Patricia Lemoyne de Forges, "La Police dans la region parisienne" in Patricia and Jean Michel Lemoyne de Forges, *Aspects actuels de l'administration parisienne* (Paris, 1972), 47–49.

Since Commissioner Lemaire drafted his "Mémoire sur l'administration de la police" in 1770, no one with the possible exception of Marc Chassaigne has seriously attempted to make sense of the structure of the prerevolutionary police. Some have been content with facile remarks regarding a few of its more prominent elements—commissioners, inspectors, and guard; others like Funck-Brentano have confused the traditional conceptual categories describing police responsibility and activity—religion, morals, health, supplies, roads, public order, sciences and liberal arts, commerce, domestics and day laborers, manufacture, and the poor—with actual structural divisions of the police.[5] The scheme proposed here attempts to avoid these mistakes. While it does not approach the problem of structure as Lemaire did, and might hence be viewed as conceptually anachronistic, its principal difference with the scheme of Lemaire is its attempt to employ more encompassing categories of analysis. Rather than list in order of prestige twenty varieties of police employee, I have tried to group agents of the police into six major categories. Defined in terms of function, these categories or sections have the advantage of both clarity and ready comparison with the elements of more modern police departments. As Table 1 suggests, such an approach facilitates an overview—a historical perspective on the police and changes in their role in an urban community.

DETERRENT PATROL

The Watch.—In 1789 more men were engaged in deterrent patrol than in any of the other major functions performed by the police. The oldest of the companies patrolling the city, if not the largest, was the Parisian watch (*guet*). While its origins may have extended back to the thirteenth century, it was not until about 1550 that it acquired the form in which a historian of the police encounters it. Commanded in the early part of the eighteenth century by an officer known as the *chevalier du guet*, the watch comprised a total of 150 men, a third of whom were cavalry.

Those who constituted the watch held their positions not as salaried employees but—like most magistrates and members of the financial administration—as officers and owners of their places. The price of a

5. BO, MS 1424 is a copy of Lemaire's manuscript; Chaissaigne, *Lieutenance générale de police;* Frantz Funck-Brentano, *Archives de la Bastille* (Paris, 1892–95), Vol. IX of Henry Martin (ed.), *Catalogue des manuscrits de la Bibliothèque de l'Arsenal* (9 vols.; Paris, 1885–99).

Table 2 The Functional Distribution
of Personnel

Function	Number 1788	% of Total 1788	% of Section	Earlier Figures
I. DETERRENT PATROL	1,483	47.62	100.00	
1. The Watch (*guet*)	74	2.38	4.99	150 (171
2. The Guard (*garde*)	1,040	33.40	70.13	725 (176
3. *Robe courte*	78	2.50	5.26	
4. *Maréchaussée*	179	5.75	12.07	
5. Archers, Hôpital Gén.	100	3.21	6.74	
6. Guardians of commerce	12	.38	.81	10 (177
II. INVESTIGATION AND INTELLIGENCE	360	11.56	100.00	
1. Inspectors of police	20	.64	5.56	40 (171
2. Subinspectors & spies	340[1]	10.92	94.44	
III. SERVICES	699	22.45	100.00	
1. Lighting	150	4.82	21.46	370 (171
2. Garbage collection	260[2]	8.35	37.19	170 (17
3. Fire Department	221	7.10	31.62	32 (17
4. Child care	42	1.35	6.01	
5. Mont-de-Piété	25	.80	3.58	0 (17
6. Dépôt de Filature	1	.03	.14	0 (17
IV. INSPECTION	376	12.08	100.00	
1. Public works & bldgs.	18	.58	4.79	0 (17
2. Censors	178	5.72	47.34	82 (17
3. Expert farriers	3	.10	.80	0 (17
4. Corporate officers	176	5.65	46.80	496 (17
5. Police architect	1	.03	.27	
V. JUSTICE	156	5.01	100.00	
1. Commissioners	48	1.54	30.77	43 (17
2. Clerks to the commrs.	48	1.54	30.77	
3. Bailiffs	48	1.54	30.77	
4. Prosecutor	1	.03	.64	1 (17
5. Clerks, police court	8	.26	5.13	
6. Criers	2	.07	1.28	
7. Collector of fines	1	.03	.64	

Function	Number 1788	% of Total 1788	% of Section	Earlier Figures
. ADMINISTRATION AND COMMUNICATION	40	1.28	100.00	
1. Lieutenant of Police	1	.03	2.50	1 (1718)
2. Administrative staff	35	1.13	87.50	8 (1730)
3. Police treasurer	1	.03	2.50	4 (1718)
4. Bursar	1	.03	2.50	
5. Printer	1	.03	2.50	1 (1714)
6. Notary	1	.03	2.50	
TOTALS	3,114	100.00		

This figure is for 1780 when secret funds amounted to 20,000 livres and may have stood as high as 460 in 789, if the request Crosne made in 1785 for an increase in these funds to 80,000 livres was granted. For etails on this request, see Crosne to controller general, in APP, DB 355.
One piece of evidence (BN, MS JF 1321, fols. 65–66, 74–75) suggests the number may have been closer to 00; but I have preferred Lenoir's testimony (BO, MS 1421, pp. 605–606), since Mildmay reports (The olice of France, 118) that each cart cost the police 2000 livres a year and we know that the funds allocated r garbage collection in 1780 amounted to 260,307 livres (BO, MS 1422, p. 971).

post in this company varied, of course, with rank. A vacant lieutenancy cost about 11,000 livres, while for his place an ordinary archer in the foot patrol would have paid only 1,400 livres.[6]

Since charges in the watch were venal, what a man earned depended on what he had paid. Income took the form of *gages*, or interest, paid at the rate of 5 percent on the price of the office. Hence, an archer could count on receiving no more than seventy livres a year for work that involved nightly patrol in the streets of the city and the inconvenience of life in the early morning cold. It would seem that an ordinary man with capital to invest and no masochistic tendencies could have found some less afflictive and no less profitable way of using his money. Why, one wonders, did anyone bother to purchase a place in the watch?

The answer is clear enough. With a position in the watch went not only the officer's ordinary 5 percent annual return on his investment but a number of privileges that were both financially and socially advantageous: exemption from the obligation to quarter soldiers and

6. For figures on both the unit's size and the price of a place in it, see the four unnumbered pieces comprising MS 356 in subseries B of Series D at the Archives de la Préfecture de Police (hereinafter cited as APP, DB 356), and AN, 0-1 360, nos. 169, 172, 175.

from the potential burdens known as *tutelle* and *curatelle*; exemption
from payment of the *taille* on rural property within a specified distance
from Paris and freedom from all taxes raised within the city itself; and
finally the right of *committimus* with its guarantee of a relatively convenient and inexpensive legal recourse against injury.[7] Perhaps equally
important was the fact that becoming an archer of the watch did not,
in fact, mean spending one's nights far from a warm bed.

During the seventeenth century the watch had ceased to be an effective and reliable unit. In a decree dated February 19, 1691, the Parisian
Parlement had to remind members of the company that with the benefits of their positions went the duty of regular patrol; but the enjoinder
seems to have had little lasting effect.[8] During the first half of the eighteenth century, the watch, with the tacit consent of authorities in
Paris, ceased altogether its desultory and half-hearted efforts at patrol.
Its sole responsibility became the maintenance of a guardpost in the
courtyard of the Châtelet, where night and day it was to receive and
guard prisoners others had apprehended and dispatched to the cells of
the old fortress.

But even this reduced labor proved too much for the watch; and in
September, 1771, the government, lamenting the inconveniences of a
venality it had so recently assaulted elsewhere, abolished all offices in
the ancient company. At the same time, it created a new unit to replace the old watch. Known officially by the name of its predecessor,
the new watch was in fact no longer anything more than a part of the
guard (as such it was sometimes referred to as "la compagnie d'étoile"
—the company of the star—to distinguish it from the three other companies constituting the guard). Reduced to half its former size and composed not of venal office-holders but of men who received a salary from
the crown, the reformed watch served at the Châtelet until 1783 when
it returned as a unit of the guard to its ancient task of patrol.[9]

7. *Tutelle* ("tutelage") and *curatelle* ("guardianship") were forms of financial and
legal responsibility that an adult might by law be obliged to assume for a minor who had
no one competent to care for him or his interests. The *taille* was the principal tax under
the Old Regime, literally the government's "cut" of one's income; and letters of *committimus* (from the initial Latin word in such letters, which began "We commit") conferred the privilege of having one's legal disputes, provided they were not criminal in
character, heard before a high court such as a *parlement* or the Grand Conseil. Immediate access to one of these tribunals spared an individual the time and expense of several
appeals.
8. Box 26, file 120, piece no. 3, in subseries I of Series AD at the Archives Nationales
(hereinafter cited as AN, AD-I 26, 120, 3); AN, 0-1 360, no. 175.
9. AN, 0-1 360, nos. 175, 368–88; APP, DB 356.

The Guard.—Long before its reform in 1771, the evident inadequacy of the watch had led the crown to create three additional armed companies in Paris. Though established at different moments, the three units became known collectively as the guard (*garde*). The first of these new entities, created in 1667 as part of the general reform that produced the lieutenancy of police in the same year, was a mounted company of forty-three horsemen. Known as the *compagnie d'ordonnance de cavalerie* or *compagnie d'ordonnance à cheval*, this unit had an existence independent of the watch, owing its allegiance not primarily to the *chevalier du guet* but to its own leader, Blondeau, whom Colbert had appointed and who took his orders directly from the lieutenant of police. Half a century later, in 1719, one of Blondeau's successors, a man named Louis Duval, received command of a second company, this one a unit of infantry (often called the *garde des ports*), newly created to patrol the city's ports and stockpiles at night, as well as the broad boulevards that had taken the place of the old walls. Finally, the following year, in 1720, the crown created the third and last component of the eighteenth-century Parisian guard, another new company of infantry (the *compagnie d'ordonnance d'infanterie* or *compagnie d'ordonnance à pied*) whose assignment, like that of the original cavalry, was patrol of the entire city.[10]

Together these units of the guard proved a more effective force than the watch had ever been, in part simply because the entity they constituted was larger. Already in 1725, only five years after its third company had been added, the guard would have been approximately three times the size of the old watch. By 1760 the guard counted 725 men in its ranks, and by 1788 it had become a force of over 1000. More than seven times the size of the watch, the guard might reasonably have been expected to do a better job.[11]

Size, however, was not all that made it a more adequate instrument in the hands of authority. As important as their number was the prior military training and experience of many guardsmen, for to the former soldiers in the guard's ranks discipline and basic skills like marksman-

10. BA, MS 10282 contains several short histories of the watch and guard. See also AN, AD-I 26, 120, 8; AN, 0-1 360, nos. 172, 180; APP, DB 356; and Jean Chagniot, "Le Guet et la garde de Paris à la fin de l'ancien régime," *Revue d'histoire moderne et contemporaine*, XX (1973), 58–71.

11. AN, 0-1 360, nos. 272, 280, 388 *bis*; *Almanach parisien*, 1771 (Paris, 1771), 13; Chagniot, "Le Guet et la garde," 59–60. In 1725 the company of cavalry and the *garde des ports* together numbered about 350. I do not have figures for the second company of infantry but assume it to have contained at least 100 men, even at this early date.

Table 3 Commanders of the Watch and Guard

Watch	Guard
Chopin, *chevalier du guet*, 1683–1733	Blondeau, inspector of the guard, 1667–?
	Jean Duval, inspector of the guard, ?–?
	Louis Duval (Jean's son), inspector of the guard, ?–1733

Watch and Guard

Louis Duval, captain-commander of the guard and inspector of the watch, 1733–1745

Louis Le Roy de Rocquemont (Duval's son-in-law), captain-commander of the guard and inspector of the watch, 1745–1765; *chevalier du guet* and commander of the guard, 1765–1770

Le Laboureur de Blérenval, *chevalier du guet* and commander of the guard, 1770–1775

Jean Baptiste Dubois, *chevalier du guet* and commander of the guard, 1775–1788

Rulhière, *chevalier du guet* and commander of the guard, 1788–1789

SOURCES: BA, MS 10282; Jean Chagniot, "Le Guet et la garde de Paris à la fin de l'ancien régime," *Revue d'histoire moderne et contemporaine*, XX (1973), 59–62.

ship were not as foreign as they had been to the small investors constituting the watch. Of 981 men who were enrolled in the guard between 1766 and 1770, 314 admitted to having served previously in the army. Others may well have been deserters unwilling to reveal their prior association with the military. But more important than either the experience or the number of its members was the fact that the guard harbored no man who owned his place. All who served with one of its companies drew not yearly interest on an investment but a salary paid every other month from the royal treasury, a salary upon which most of these men depended for their survival. Of this same group of 981 men who entered the guard between 1766 and 1770, 834 can be classified on the basis of their father's profession. Only 4 of these 834 guardsmen came from families whose lands or investments permitted them to live without working. Sons of small farmers (30 percent of the total) and artisans (29 percent) greatly outnumber those from other social categories enrolling in the guard. Sons of professionals, for example, account for only 3 percent of this enrollment and the offspring of domestics for only 2.5 percent.[12] Thus, against guardsmen who failed to perform their duty, there was available a prompt administrative sanction, whereas serious action against a member of the watch—a man who owned his office—involved protracted legal action in the courts.

Loyalty and ready obedience could be expensive. In 1771 the three companies of the guard cost the crown almost 466,000 livres. How much of this sum an individual guardsman received depended less on his rank than on the company to which he belonged. Two of the three units composing the guard, the two largest, served on foot, and pay in these at all levels was at best only a third of what members of the mounted company earned. While an ordinary cavalier received three livres a day, a *fusilier*, or rifleman, in the foot patrol got at most only one livre; and though leadership of a mounted brigade brought four livres a day, command over a detachment of foot patrol meant only twenty-five sous or one and a quarter livres.[13]

Despite these differences in wage, all three companies performed essentially the same function—that of patrol. While one unit moved on foot among the ports and along the boulevards of Paris, the horse guard and the other company of infantry circulated throughout the remainder of the city. Drunkards and prostitutes, persons gambling in public—these and others whose conduct they deemed disorderly the guard took in tow, conducting them to the home of the nearest commissioner, whose duty it was—regardless of the hour—to admit the guardsmen and to determine provisionally whether the individual brought before him was to be confined until trial or released.

During its rounds at night the guard rattled doors as it passed, noting those left unlocked in violation of police regulations forbidding this. When night settled on the city, there were to be no retreats for the unwanted, no shelters and no hiding places from the police. Hunting the homeless and the unemployed—those for whom the city had no place and who became in consequence its enemies—the guard poked about in shadowed spaces and saw to it that refuges like the wine shops and cabarets closed their doors at the prescribed hour.

With the routine of patrol went other duties. Detachments of the

12. Chagniot, "Le Guet et la garde," 65–66.
13. An, 0-1 360, nos. 387, 388 *bis*.

guard were obliged to respond to all calls for assistance and, in the event of fire, to cordon off the area immediately affected in order to prevent accident, interference, or looting. At public celebrations and processions it had a similar task, serving once again to restrain the curiosity and emotion of crowds.

But patrol remained the primary function, and to perform it each of the three companies constituting the guard was divided into smaller units. These, in the case of the two units of foot patrol, were known as squads, and their size altered with changes in the size of the companies themselves. Take, for example, the larger of the two companies serving on foot, whose responsibilities were not confined to the ports of the city. In 1754 this company numbered 400 men distributed among fifty-seven squads. Each squad of seven contained a sergeant, one corporal, an *appointé* or under-corporal, and four riflemen. By 1771 when the same company had grown to just over 500 men, the squads, too, were larger, containing not seven men but twelve.[14]

These changes in size were closely linked to changes in the way the company operated. Initially without base of any kind, its squads had moved continuously day and night through the streets, each following the route it had been assigned only hours earlier; but in 1720 began a partial modification of this procedure based on the erection of stations which guardsmen were to man regularly. In July of that year, the crown established a guardpost in the Place Louis le Grand (now the Place Vendôme) and ordered that it be staffed each day by a squad of the foot patrol. To this initial post the crown added others: four in April, 1721, two more in October, 1723, two in July, 1728, and another in February, 1732. By 1754, there were fifteen of these stations or guardhouses, and by 1789, at least fifty.[15]

Their locations derived not primarily from an effort to distribute detachments of the guard evenly about the city, but rather from authority's sense of its own vulnerability and from its experience of disorder. The supply and distribution of items essential to life must always be of concern to those in power, for the fate of a government is directly linked to its ability to guarantee the availability of food, fuel, and other vital commodities. Let disorder or shortage appear in the markets of a

14. William Mildmay, *The Police of France* (London, 1763), 56. Mildmay's figures appear to be approximate, for they do not always fit neatly together. AN, 0-1 360, no. 388; BO, MS 1424, p. 61.
15. AN, AD-I 26, 120, 8, 19; Mildmay, *Police of France*, 56–57.

capital and the survival of a regime can immediately become problematic. It is understandable, then, that a number of the new guardposts in Paris were to be found proximate to the city's markets and to the ports and stockpiles that supplied them.

But what of those guardposts that were not so situated? How are we to account for their placement? At least a partial answer lies in the ordinances by which the crown created several of the new establishments. Explaining its decision of July, 1720, to place a squad of the guard on permanent duty in the Place Louis le Grand, the government argued that such a step was necessary to prevent the disorder that was resulting from exchange of stock in John Law's year-old Compagnie des Indes; and when it added a ninth guardpost to those that already existed in February, 1732, locating it next to the cemetery of Saint-Médard, it clearly intended that the new post should intimidate and silence the fanatical convulsionists who, for almost five years, had provoked tumultuous gatherings in the district.[16] A number of the guardposts were, in other words, authority's response to specific incidents of disorder in the city. Throughout the eighteenth century they stood as extraordinary and costly monuments, as government's ironic commemoration of those who had once harassed or threatened it. In affixing these tiny structures to a map of the city, one is also inevitably sketching a partial geography of discontent under the Old Regime.

The details of this geography may be found on Map 3 and in Tables 4 and 10, which confirm, for example, the Faubourg Saint-Marcel's reputation for tumultuousness. There were in 1770 more guardsmen stationed in the quarter containing this section than in any other quarter in the city. One also finds a relatively large contingent of guardsmen in the quarter of Saint-Germain-des-Prés, where much of the nobility chose to reside during the eighteenth century. If prior experience suggested surveillance or intimidation of the city's poor, it also apparently prompted disproportionate protection of the rich.

Until the 1760s, squads of guardsmen assigned to the new guardposts manned them only during the day, from 6:00 A.M. to 9:00 P.M. during the warmer, lighter half of the year, and from 7:00 A.M. to 5:00 P.M. during late fall, winter, and early spring. At night the foot patrol abandoned its fixed posts and circulated throughout the city. In 1754, for example, while fifteen of one company's fifty-seven squads were on

16. AN, AD-I 26, 120, 8, 19.

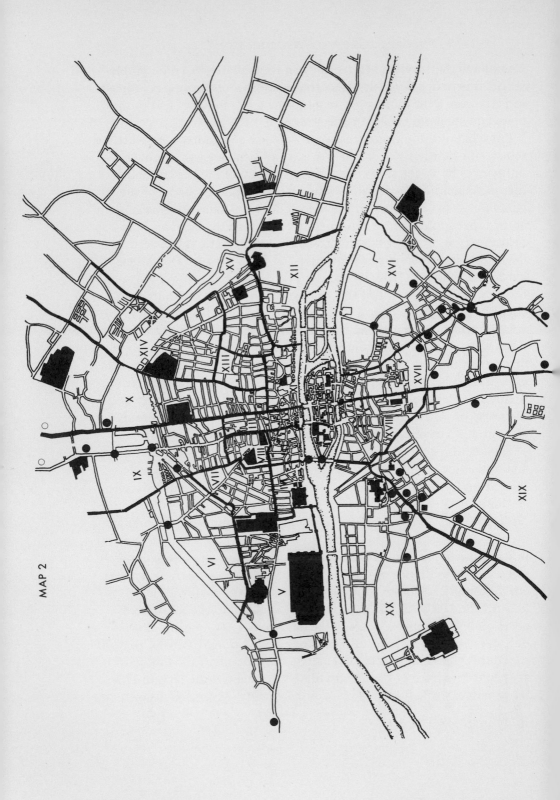

MAP 2

Map 2
GUARDPOSTS, 1714

Symbols

● Gardes Françaises, 11 men to a post.
○ Gardes Françaises, 6 men to a post.
■ The Parisian Guard, 10 men to a post.

Number of Men in Each Quarter

1. Luxembourg (XIX)—86 men.
2. Place Maubert (XVI)—66 men.
   Saint-Benoît (XVII)—66 men.
3. Saint-Denis (IX)—50 men.
4. Saint-Germain-des-Prés (XX)—33 men.
5. Cité (I)—22 men.
   Palais-Royal (V)—22 men.

6. Saint-Martin (X)—17 men.
7. Montmartre (VI)—11 men.
   Eleven quarters contained no guardposts.

The Major Sections

Left Bank—23 posts, 251 men.
Right Bank—10 posts, 100 men.
Cité—2 posts, 22 men.
West (west of the rues Saint-Martin and Saint-Jacques)
   —22 posts, 224 men.
East—13 posts, 149 men.

SOURCE: Jean de Lacaille, *Description de la ville et des fauxbourgs de Paris* (1714; reprint ed., Paris: Éditions Les Yeux Ouverts, 1967).

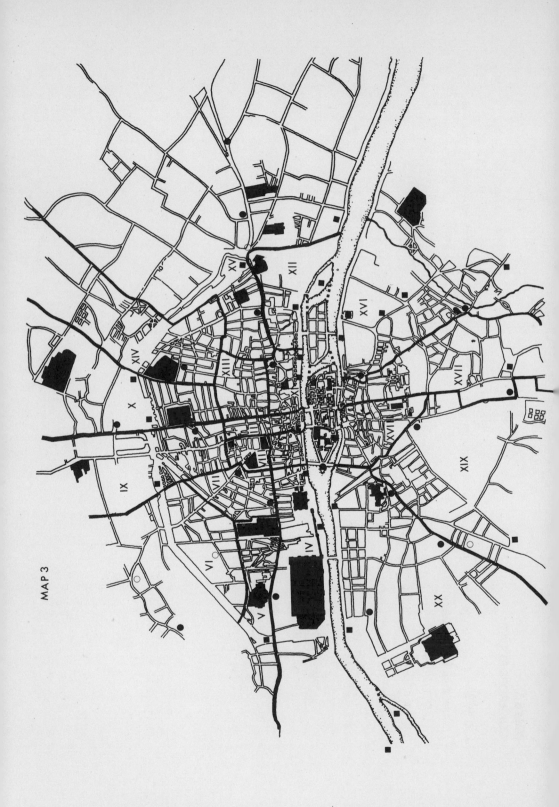

MAP 3

Map 3
GUARDPOSTS, 1770

○ Mounted patrol, the *compagnie d'ordonnance à cheval*, 5 men to a post

● Foot patrol, the *compagnie d'ordonnance à pied*, 12 men to a post

■ Guard of the ports and boulevards, 10 men to a post

SOURCES: AN, AD-I 26, 120, 8, 9, 19, 28; royal order, October 26, 1723, AN, H-2 1880(6); AN, Y 11810; royal order, May 5, 1722, BA, MS 10282; BHVP, MS n.a. 477, fol. 22; BN, MS JF 450, fol. 162; BN, MS JF 1103, fols. 71–133; Deharme, "Plan de Paris, 1763" in Alphand [ed.], *Atlas des anciens plans*; Alletz, *Géographe parisien*, I, 57–59.

Table 4 The Distribution of the Guard, 1770[1]

Quarters & Sections	Cavalry		Infantry		Ports & Boulevards		Totals		% of Total	
	Posts	Men	Posts	Men	Posts	Men	Posts	Men	Posts	Men
Cité (I)	0	0	2	24	2	20	4	44	8	8.5
Saint-Jacques-de-la Boucherie (II)	0	0	0	0	0	0	0	0	0	0
Sainte-Opportune (III)	0	0	0	0	0	0	0	0	0	0
Louvre (IV)	0	0	1	12	3	30	4	42	8	8
Palais-Royal (V)	0	0	0	0	1	10	1	10	2	2
Montmarte (VI)	2	10	1	12	0	0	3	22	6	4
Saint-Eustache (VII)	0	0	2	24	0	0	2	24	4	5
Les Halles (VIII)	0	0	1	12	0	0	1	12	2	2.5
Saint-Denis (IX)	0	0	1	12	1	10	2	22	4	4
Saint-Martin (X)	0	0	1	12	2	20	3	32	6	6
La Grève (XI)	0	0	1	12	2	20	3	32	6	6
Saint-Paul (XII)	0	0	0	0	1	10	1	10	2	2
Sainte-Avoie (XIII)	0	0	0	0	0	0	0	0	0	0
Temple (XIV)	0	0	1	12	0	0	1	12	2	2.5
Saint-Antoine (XV)	1	5	3	36	2	20	6	61	12	12
Place Maubert (XVI)	0	0	2	24	5	50	7	74	14	14.5
Saint-Benoît (XVII)	0	0	1	12	1	10	2	22	4	4
Saint-André-des-Arts (XVIII)	1	5	0	0	0	0	1	5	2	1
Luxembourg (XIX)	1	5	1	12	1	10	3	27	6	5

Cité	0	0	2	24	2	20	4	44	8	8.5
Right Bank	3	15	12	144	12	120	27	279	54	54
Left Bank	2	10	7	84	10	100	19	194	38	37.5
East	1	5	9	108	15	150	25	263	50	51
West	4	20	12	144	9	90	25	254	50	49

SOURCES: AN, AD 1, 26, 120, 8, 9, 19, 28; royal order, October 26, 1723, AN, H-2 1880(6); AN, Y 11810; royal order, May 5, 1722, BA, MS 10282; BHVP, MS n.a. 477, fol. 22; BN, MS JF 450, fol. 162; BN, MS JF 1103, fols. 71–133; Deharme, "Plan de Paris, 1763" in Alphand (ed.), Atlas des anciens plans; Alletz, Géographe parisien, I, 57–59.

1. Does not include sixteen brigades (eighty men) of the mounted guard which were not assigned to any fixed post but which circulated throughout the city.

duty each day of the week in the guardhouses, the remaining forty-two served at night and never set foot in the new stations. Their assignments were not single posts but carefully prescribed routes, the details of which were entrusted only to the sergeants commanding each squad, and even to them only at dusk each day when the squads had assembled for duty in the square named after the *chevalier du guet*. [17] Lieutenants of police throughout the eighteenth century insisted on this secrecy and on the absence of any permanent tie between a detachment of the guard and a section of the city as a means of reducing the harm done by corrupt or garrulous guardsmen.

Sometime during the 1760s, Sartine altered this hybrid mode of operation in which procedures dating from the seventeenth century governed the guard's operations at night, while the innovations of the eighteenth century controlled its conduct during the day. Fixed in a single place, detachments of the guard were easier for those in need of help to locate than they had been before 1720; but there were many parts of the city in which the presence of stationary units was not felt. At night the difficulty was exactly the opposite: squads of guardsmen appeared in every corner of the capital but were not always easy to find at precisely those moments when someone needed them.

Considering these two systems, Sartine apparently decided that by integrating them the disadvantages of both could be eliminated. Essential to this reform was an increase in the size of squads from seven men to twelve. Almost twice as large as they had been, these units were subsequently able to patrol the streets and simultaneously to provide a fixed, immediately accessible presence to those in need. Sartine's reform divided the enlarged squads into two equal sections of six men. While one section manned the guardhouse to which the squad had been assigned, the other went off on patrol in the surrounding area. Every two hours the units exchanged places. Under the new system squads no longer served each day or every other night; instead they worked twenty-four hours at a time with equivalent periods of liberty. In 1771, for example, the larger company of foot patrol, comprising forty-two squads, had only twenty-one of them on duty at any one time. [18]

While the other company serving on foot—that responsible for the

17. Mildmay, *Police of France*, 56–57; AN, AD-I 26, 120, 9. Of the forty-two squads assigned to patrol after dark, half worked one night, half the next.
18. BO, MS 1424, pp. 60–63; AN, O-1 360, no. 388 *bis*.

boulevards of the city and the ports—also established its own guard-posts and began using them as bases,[19] the mounted company of the guard continued, for the most part, to operate without them. Yet its procedures did not wholly escape the impact of the new station houses. Their gradual establishment—frequently provoked rather than planned —affected all three companies of the guard, generating among them a cooperation and coordination that had not previously existed.

Composed of forty brigades in 1754, each containing five men, the mounted patrol appeared larger than it was in fact. The mobility of its detachments, the fact that they sat elevated above most men and objects passing in the street gave them a prominence their numbers alone would not have accorded.

Though the size of a brigade remained constant throughout the century, the actual strength of the company as a whole fluctuated. William Mildmay, an Englishman who was in Paris in 1754, appears to have seen it at its peak; for by 1771, of the 200 cavaliers Mildmay had counted, only 105 remained. Nonetheless, during the 1770s this decline in strength ended, and by 1780 the company again numbered 160.[20] Its sudden resurgence may be linked to Saint-Germain's reform of the army and particularly to his suppression in December, 1775, of the king's musketeers. With their disappearance, the mounted guard became the only unit of cavalry left in the capital, and this situation may well have appreciated its value in the eyes of the government, recommending not only its conservation but its reconstruction.

Elements of the mounted guard were on duty at all times, four of its brigades serving during the day and fifteen at night.[21] Only as each brigade went on duty did its commander receive orders prescribing the route he was to follow. His orders, as in the case of the foot patrol,

19. *Almanach parisien, 1771,* 13; Alletz, *Géographe parisien,* I, 57–59. Data on this company is not easy to reconcile. Mildmay gives its size in 1754 as 300 (*Police of France,* 88); Lemaire estimates its size in 1770 as 268 (BO, MS 1424, p. 61), while a payroll dated 1771 records it as 152 (AN, 0-1 360, no. 380); the *Almanach parisien* puts its strength at 225 in 1771, while Alletz numbers it at 240 in the late 1760s. Given estimates of the guard's size as a whole in the 1780s and what we know of the size of the other companies, the latter figure appears most plausible as an estimate of this unit's strength in 1789. Changes in the number of its squads and in their size are unclear. Given estimates of the company's total strength and Alletz's testimony regarding the number of posts it was supposed to man, I have assumed that in 1770 there were twenty-four squads in this unit of the guard, each containing ten men.

20. Mildmay, *Police of France,* 54–55; BO, MS 1424, p. 51; AN, 0-1 360, no. 388 *bis; Almanach parisien, 1771,* 13.

21. Mildmay, *Police of France,* 55. Mildmay does not explain what has become of the two brigades for which these figures do not account.

were a closely kept secret until the last minute. Mildmay reports that even greater care was taken at night than during the day to render the course of the brigades unpredictable: halfway through an evening, he says, the initial orders were frequently countermanded and new routes assigned the men on duty.

With the creation of guardposts for the foot patrol, these routes acquired at least an element of constancy. As the number of posts grew, brigades of the mounted guard began, with whatever permutations, following courses that took them past the new guardhouses. By their passage the mounted brigades permitted scattered units on foot to communicate with one another; and their recurring circuit of the guardposts meant that a squad of foot patrol in need of assistance would not have long to wait. Even for the still largely itinerant mounted company, then, the new guardhouses had, by 1750, become, if not bases of operation, at least essential parts of its routine, points of collaboration between it and other units of the guard.

Assuming that the capabilities of individual guardsmen did not decline dramatically during the eighteenth century, it is likely that the guard as a whole was a much more effective unit in 1788 than it had been at the end of Louis XIV's reign. Aside from quadrupling in size, it had become a more integrated and flexible force. The institution of fixed stations, begun in 1720, facilitated communication and gave mounted brigades a means that had not before existed of locating and supporting units of the foot patrol, which themselves had become doubly useful. Sartine's reforms, implemented during the 1760s, permitted the squads serving on foot to provide a given sector with both constant patrol and a stationary, accessible presence. Despite the disdain evident in some of Lenoir's references to the guard,[22] the force which served him in 1780 was undoubtedly superior to that which had patrolled Paris seventy years earlier under d'Argenson.

The Company of the Lieutenant de la Robe Courte.—In 1526 the crown added to the growing number of magistrates at the Châtelet yet another, the *lieutenant criminel de la robe courte* (lieutenant criminal of the short robe).[23] Established primarily as a weapon against those the government labeled vagabonds, the new magistrate possessed

22. BO, MS 1422, p. 64, for example.
23. Antoine, *et al., Fonds judiciaires*, 168. The short robe indicated the partly military nature of his functions and distinguished him from his colleagues of the long robe (lieutenant civil, lieutenant criminal) whose work was primarily judicial.

powers of summary justice and commanded his own troop of twenty men. While this lieutenant's company grew slowly in the decades that followed, his own importance as a judge diminished. The culmination of this latter process was an edict of July, 1783, that stripped him of all judicial function. Though the office itself did not disappear, its occupant suffered a considerable blow to his prestige. So, in its own way, did the company as a whole, which, under the terms of the edict, largely surrendered its function of patrol and assumed instead the lesser task of manning a station in the courtyard of the Châtelet from which post it guarded the prisons of the old fortress. Amidst these changes the company continued its older happy chore of conducting those condemned to death to their places of execution.[24]

Numbering seventy-eight men in 1783, the company comprised, in addition to its commander and five lieutenants, twelve brigades of six men, each commanded by an officer known as an exempt. The procedures and reliability of these brigades are matters that remain unclear. Until 1783 all who served in them held their places as commissions from the *lieutenant de la robe courte.* The edict of that year, however, revoked the commander's right to issue such commissions and converted all positions of command in the company to venal charges.[25] Following these changes, lieutenants received 1,500 livres a year, interest (*gages*) and exempts 1,200; ordinary archers in the company earned one livre a day, the same sum paid riflemen of the guard.

While the entire company was at the disposal of the lieutenant of police, he seems to have called regularly on several of the same officers and their brigades to perform special services. For those involved, the additional work meant added income. A brigade commanded by Baudin, for example, divided an extra 1,572 livres among themselves in 1763, while in the same year another under the command of an officer named Morelle received more than 5,000 livres in additional pay. All told, perhaps half the company participated to some extent in these special assignments.[26]

The work they undertook seems to have been largely the location and arrest of particular persons whom the government wished incarcerated. In a letter to the controller general of finances, Nicolas Desma-

24. AN, K 716, no. 4; BN, MS JF 1419, fols. 252–57; Mildmay, *Police of France,* 59.
25. The edict (BN, MS JF 1419, fols. 252–55) orders that all positions in the company become venal, but a later payroll (*ibid.,* fols. 256–57) suggests that in the end the order affected only exempts and lieutenants.
26. AN, 0-1 361, nos. 324–44. These are police payrolls from the years 1763–1768.

retz, dated February 23, 1715, the lieutenant of police, d'Argenson, reports a number of such operations carried out under his orders by an officer of the *robe courte* named Bazin. In the summer of 1712, d'Argenson had commanded Bazin to find a Breton noble, named Noel, whose petitions to the king concerning affairs of state had produced something other than the desired effect. Having spent fifteen days searching the capital, Bazin and his men at last located their quarry. On July 13, they seized Noel and escorted him to a waiting carriage that carried him off to the prison of For l'Évêque. In the months that followed, the same little band with Bazin at its head tracked a widow who had fled from the archbishop's prison in Lyon to Paris, arrested a number of persons trafficking in base coinage or involved in sending money out of the country, and journeyed to Rouen to locate a receiver of the Farms whom they conveyed to Paris and accommodations in the Bastille.[27]

The Maréchaussée.—While the lieutenant of police might, on occasion, send agents from Paris into the provinces to make an arrest, he more frequently relied in such cases on the detachments of *maréchaussée* scattered throughout France. After 1720, more than thirty companies of *maréchaussée*—one in each *généralité*—patrolled the roads and villages of the French countryside. The size of each of these companies depended to some degree on the extent and importance of the *généralité* in which it served, but most numbered approximately a hundred men. At the head of each company was a *prévôt-général* who, like the *lieutenant criminel de la robe courte*, combined the functions of judge with those of a cavalry commander. Responsible for affairs and operations throughout the entire *généralité*, each *prévôt-général* had the assistance of a varying number of lieutenants (rarely more than four) who supervised subdivisions of the *généralité* known as *arrondissements.* They in turn relied on exempts, or brigadiers, beneath them, who were the actual commanders of the eighteen to twenty-four brigades that formed a company.[28]

Mildmay reports that the brigades of a company were stationed in major towns, towns that were, as nearly as possible, at equal distances from one another and, in any case, no more than half a day's ride apart. Whatever the precise distance separating them, brigades of *maréchaus-*

27. BN, MS fr. 6791, fols. 21, 23–27.
28. Mildmay, *Police of France*, 28, 35–41; royal ordinance, February 11, 1774, in APP, DB 355.

sée met regularly at the perimeters of their districts to exchange descriptions of offenders and to coordinate efforts at apprehension. The descriptions of important fugitives went beyond adjacent units to the headquarters of the *maréchaussée* in Paris where copies were printed and distributed by mail to the approximately six hundred brigades dispersed throughout France.[29]

Obviously this network was available to the lieutenant of police, who derived valuable information from it and who, like others, used it to pursue those he sought into every corner of the realm. Police payrolls from the years 1762–1768 suggest the extent of this use. On each of these lists appear sums disbursed to several detachments of *maréchaussée* for work they have done at Sartine's bidding. During these years brigades at Caen and Macon, at Quimperlé and Lyons, at Nantes and Senlis undertook assignments in their districts for the lieutenant of police.[30]

Nonetheless, this use of the provincial *maréchaussée* was irregular, dictated it seems by special circumstances. Only rarely does the name of the same provincial brigade appear more than once on the police payrolls. With the *maréchaussée* of Paris, however, the contact was frequent and routine, sufficiently so to consider these detachments, at least, an element of the police.

Unlike other *généralités*, Paris had not one company of *maréchaussée* but several. Among these was the unit known as the company of the *Connétablie* (literally, "constabulary"). Both the unit itself and its commander, the *prévôt-général* of the *Connétablie*, took precedence over all other elements of the *maréchaussée*. To the commander of the *Connétablie* fell the right of inspecting companies other than his own and the power of overturning on appeal the judicial decisions of their commanders, the other *prévôts*. The privileged company itself was relatively small, consisting of four brigades each numbering fourteen men. These, though formally subject to the marshals of France (whence the name *maréchaussée*), regularly performed duties assigned them by the lieutenant of police. Most common among these assignments was the guarantee of order outside the three "spectacles" of the capital—the Opera, the Comédie-Française, and the Comédie-Italienne.[31]

29. Mildmay, *Police of France*, 29–30.
30. AN, 0-1 361, nos. 324–44.
31. Regulation issued by the marshals of France, January 16, 1786, in APP, DB 355; Mildmay, *Police of France*, 25–26.

A second company of *maréchaussée* based in Paris was that commanded by the *prévôt-général* of the Hotel des Monnaies (currency). Established during the seventeenth century to cope with counterfeiters, this unit performed a more specialized function than other sections of the *maréchaussée* and cooperated closely with the Cour des Monnaies. Nonetheless, its members took orders from the lieutenant of police as well as from the sovereign court. In 1744, for example, a lieutenant in this company, together with those he commanded, received in the relatively brief span of two months eighteen assignments from Marville, all involving orders for arrest. While the size of this company during the eighteenth century is unclear, it probably numbered no fewer than fifty men.[32]

The third and last of the units of *maréchaussée* based in Paris was the company of the *prévôté* of the Île-de-France.[33] Through it the lieutenant of police extended his hand into the villages and towns immediately surrounding the capital, for it was this unit that patrolled the small settlements and rural areas of the *généralité* in which Paris lay. Learning from one of his inspectors in September, 1773, that a number of persons selling counterfeit lottery tickets had taken refuge outside Paris, Sartine turned, as had his predecessors in similar situations, to the *prévôt* of the Île-de-France, sending him descriptions and ordering him to see that a search was undertaken.[34]

The company of the Île-de-France contained eight brigades in 1751 and comprised ten little more than a decade later. Nine of the brigades had a normal complement of five men, while the tenth, based at company headquarters in Paris, was made up of eight. With assignment to the brigade stationed in Paris went salaries exceeding those paid members of other units. Brigade commanders outside the city received between 900 and 1,100 livres a year, a sum no greater than that a simple cavalier earned in Paris. Cavaliers who served in the countryside sur-

32. BA, MS 10029, piece 32; Mousnier, *Paris au XVIIe siècle*, 93. Mousnier puts its strength during the seventeenth century at about fifty and I have no more recent data.
33. Marcel Marion in his *Dictionnaire des institutions de la France aux XVIIe et XVIIIe siècles* (New York, 1968), 362–63, argues that there were in 1789 four companies of *maréchaussée* in Paris. To those I have listed, he adds one serving under the *prévôt général* of the *généralité* of Paris. Because I have found no mention of this fourth unit and because one of the documents I consulted speaks of "le prévôt général au gouvernement-généralité de Paris et Isle-de-France," I have included only three, believing that Marion's company of the *généralité* may have been only another appellation for the company of the Île-de-France.
34. BN, MS fr. 22116, fol. 327.

rounding the capital earned 792 livres a year. Mildmay reports that, in addition to their salaries, members of the *maréchaussée* received a bounty of 100 livres on every offender they captured, provided that the man was later convicted. In turn, an equivalent bounty, paid from the salaries of those cavaliers presumed negligent, went to any private person who captured a wanted man. In this way, by inducement and sanction, the government sought to enhance the vigilance and efficacy of the *maréchaussée.*[35]

Brigades of the company of the Île-de-France had their headquarters astride most, if not all, the important roads leaving Paris: at Saint-Denis to the north on the road to England; at Bondy and Charenton to the east along the highways to Germany, Switzerland, and Savoy; at Villejuif on the road to Lyon and Italy; at Bourg-la-Reine as one journeyed south to Orléans and points beyond; and on the west at Saint-Germain-en-Laye. Three of the nine brigades operating outside Paris occupied stations along the heavily traveled road to Versailles. To this single route leading southwest from Paris the company consigned almost a third of its strength, with brigades positioned at Passy, Sèvres, and Montreuil-près-Versailles. None of the nine brigades was more than fifteen miles from the center of Paris.

Exempts of the Police.—The only definite testimony regarding this unit is that provided by Mildmay who clearly distinguishes it from the company of the *lieutenant de la robe courte* and from the bands of men employed by the inspectors of police. He reports that in 1754 there were fifty "exempts de police" who patrolled the streets and public places of Paris and who, on occasion, delivered *lettres de cachet.* Lemaire, however, does not mention these men; and references to them in correspondence and reports are ambiguous, leaving one unsure whether the word "exempt" is meant to designate officers in the *robe courte*, the guard, or the *maréchaussée* who bore this rank, or whether it refers to the members of yet another distinct unit. In Lenoir's papers, the term appears to serve as a general designation for employees of the police who had no official title.[36] Given this ambiguity and because I have not found the exempts on any police payroll, I omit them from calculations regarding the size of the police force and assume that Mildmay was referring to men I have included under another title.

35. BN, MS JF 1310, fols. 9–10; AN, 0-1 360, nos. 271, 368; Mildmay, *Police of France*, 34–36.
36. Mildmay, *Police of France*, 51–53; BO, MS 1422, pp. 965–67.

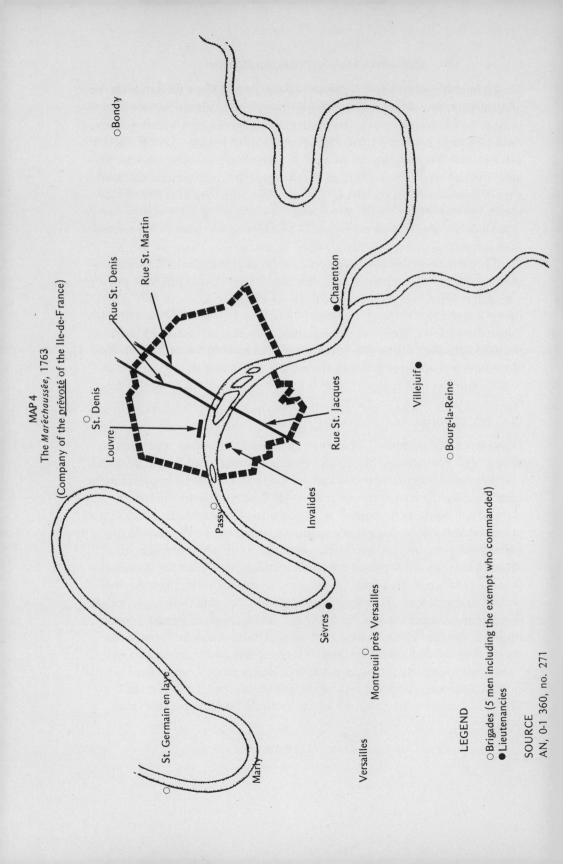

MAP 4
The *Maréchaussée*, 1763
(Company of the <u>prévôté</u> of the Ile-de-France)

Bondy

Rue St. Martin

Rue St. Denis

Charenton

St. Denis

Louvre

Rue St. Jacques

Villejuif

Invalides

Bourg-la-Reine

Passy

Sèvres

Montreuil près Versailles

Versailles

St. Germain en laye

Marly

LEGEND

○ Brigades (5 men including the exempt who commanded)
● Lieutenancies

SOURCE
AN, 0-1 360, no. 271

Archers of the Hôpital Général.—Attached to the vast complex—
half prison, half agency of relief—known as the Hôpital Général were
100 armed but apparently unimposing men whose task it was to patrol
the streets of Paris, clearing them of idlers and beggars. Divided evenly into ten brigades, the archers of the Hôpital began their patrol each
morning at eight; with two hours for lunch they resumed their rounds
at two in the afternoon and continued until six. Their service ended
with the coming of night, and squads of guardsmen were left to carry
on without the support—such as it was—that this unit provided during the day.

While an archer of the Hôpital wore no uniform, his wage equalled
that of the guardsmen who did. Ordinarily members of brigades got one
livre a day and their commanders a livre and a half. As one of the seven
governors of the Hôpital Général, the lieutenant of police had unques-
tioned authority over the archers; and, if Mildmay's description is accurate, it was an authority he exercised almost to the exclusion of
those who shared his title of governor.[37]

Guardians of Commerce.—In a letter dated May 12, 1770, Sartine
expressed his displeasure at seeing the guard used to seek out and arrest debtors. Such employment he seems to have considered a waste of
its time, and this dissatisfaction may have found its culmination in
edicts of November, 1772, and July, 1778, that created first ten, then
twelve guardians of commerce (*officiers-gardes du commerce*). Despite
the title attached to them, the new positions were not venal offices but
commissions exercised under the great seal. Appointment to them was
in the hands of the lieutenant of police, whom the edicts enjoined—
whenever possible—to select the new guardians of commerce from
among officers already serving in the company of the *robe courte.*

Any creditor with a court order for the arrest of a negligent client
could make his way to an office located in the heart of the city where,
six hours a day (9:00 A.M. to noon and 3:00 P.M. to 6:00), he could
submit the paper he carried to an official trained in law. If the document was valid, the official passed it on to one of the guardians of
commerce who became solely responsible for its execution. Each arrest
a guardian made brought him sixty livres and each report on an individual he had been unable to capture earned him twenty. Circum-

37. Mildmay, *Police of France*, 53–54; BO, MS 1422, p. 688.

stances obliged the guardians to earn their money, for few of those they sought were anxious to step forward and follow obediently to prison.[38]

The Army.—Between the police and the army there was during the eighteenth century an unquestionable distinction that I do not propose to challenge here; nonetheless, a discussion of forces patrolling Paris and maintaining security there would be incomplete without mention of the Gardes Françaises and Gardes Suisses. Both of these units, elements of the king's military household, had long been quartered in and about Paris; both were disciplined regiments of infantry that served together in time of war as a military brigade. While estimates of their combined strength vary, we can, perhaps, accept Lenoir's assertion that together they numbered between seven thousand and eight thousand men.[39]

Throughout the eighteenth century the Gardes Françaises maintained fixed posts scattered about the city, each staffed by eleven men. If the number of these posts declined as the Parisian guard began establishing stations of its own (from thirty-three in 1714 to perhaps seventeen in 1789), the two regiments continued to play an important role in preserving order in the capital. Lenoir suggests that the troops came to be considered only an auxiliary force as the century progressed and the police forces themselves grew. Gardes Suisses and Françaises were called upon to assist the police only when the guard and the *robe courte* were unable to maintain order.[40]

But with the city's sudden expansion in 1782 to perimeters traced by the new wall of the Farmers-General, the situation changed. Detachments of both regiments began patrolling the streets each evening in support of the guard. Lenoir, who was lieutenant of police at the time, asked in addition that the Gardes Françaises station troops permanently in two of the poorer sections of the city, the Faubourgs Saint-Antoine and Saint-Marcel—both enlarged by the recent change in the city's boundaries. The commander of the regiment acceded to this request, and new army posts went up on the eastern edges of the capital. Gardes Suisses and Gardes Françaises, which for a number of years had

38. Sartine to the syndics of the commissioners, May 12, 1770, in AN, Y 13728; BN, MS JF 1416, fols. 195–201 (edicts creating these positions), 212–14 (reports of resistance to the guardians of commerce).

39. Before 1775 one might also mention the two companies of musketeers, one garrisoned opposite the Louvre, the other in the Faubourg Saint-Antoine; but these disappeared in 1775. BHVP, MS n.a. 477, fol. 20 (Cf. BO, MS 1423, pp. 369–81).

40. BHVP, MS n.a. 477, fols. 20–21.

gradually reduced their contribution to ordinary efforts at maintaining order, began after 1782 to recommit themselves.[41]

For some time there seems to have been pressure on the government to abandon the guard and other police forces in Paris and to rely exclusively on the army to keep order. Such a move, it was argued, would spare the crown expense while at the same time providing it with a more formidable and steadfast troop in the city.[42] The renewed use of the Gardes Françaises and Suisses after 1782 may represent a partial concession to these arguments as well as a response to the extension of the city's perimeters.

Certainly, too, the attitude of the lieutenant of police himself contributed to the reengagement of the army. Considering the city's own units a very mediocre force, he, more than anyone else, had urged construction of the new stations in the Faubourgs Saint-Marcel and Saint-Antoine and had contended that these should be staffed not by detachments of the Parisian guard but by disciplined troops of the line.

Lenoir's enthusiasm for the two military units undoubtedly derived not only from a respect for their discipline and strength but from a chain of events that had given him, unlike his predecessors, direct authority over the Gardes Françaises and Gardes Suisses. Lenoir had been lieutenant of police only a few months when, on the morning of May 3, 1775, serious disorder erupted in the capital. Crowds of men and women, angered at the rising cost of bread and fearful of imminent scarcity, began looting the markets and bakeries of the city. Learning of the tumult and its extent, the new lieutenant of police called on the commander of the Gardes Françaises, Marshal Biron, for immediate assistance; but, according to Lenoir, "Marshal Biron, despite the entreaties and earnest petitions of the Lieutenant of Police, refused to commit detachments of his regiment on the pretext that he had received no order from the King to do so."[43] This intransigence and the inability to issue superseding orders directly to elements of the regiment cost Lenoir his job; for, without assistance from the military, he had been unable to suppress the disorder promptly.

The experience was one Lenoir did not forget; and when recalled to the lieutenancy of police in June, 1776, he made his acceptance of the

41. BO, MS 1422, p. 65.

42. AN, 0-1 360, no. 180. This is an interesting memoir, probably written in 1767 or 1768, which disputed such arguments.

43. BHVP, MS n.a. 477, fol. 22. Lenoir managed to get such an order issued, but it arrived two days after the rioting had subsided.

post conditional on the king's granting him the direct authority he had lacked a year earlier. The crown consented, and thereafter neither Lenoir nor his successor, Crosne, had any difficulty requisitioning troops. Those manning the new stations in the Faubourgs Saint-Marcel and Saint-Antoine even received a portion of their wages from the police and obeyed incidental orders from Lenoir as readily as those issued by Marshal Biron himself.[44]

INVESTIGATION AND INTELLIGENCE

Inspectors of police.—Though the initial power to judge and punish crime in the city lay with the lieutenant criminal of the Châtelet, the administrative tasks of preventing it and of pursuing its perpetrators were in the hands of the lieutenant of police, who, of course, delegated them to others. As the burden of patrolling Paris rested most heavily on the Parisian guard, so the inspectors of police bore the greatest share of responsibility for investigating crime in the city.

A king in need of money had created the first police inspectors in February, 1708. Under the circumstances, it is not surprising that the forty new venal positions contributed less to the establishment of an able and effective police force than they did to the royal coffers. For some time the new police agents served largely as adjuncts to the commissioners in their sectors of the city, as additional presences to be called on in case of need, as ready hands to perform whatever random service a superior might require. A number of the posts—perhaps those the crown was unable to sell—went to servants in the households of the lieutenants of police.[45] Without status, without requisite experience or qualifications, the new inspectors occupied neither a prominent nor an important place in the Parisian police force.

In 1740 this situation began to change. Feydeau de Marville, having succeeded his father-in-law as lieutenant of police in 1739, seems to have taken the first step; for it was probably he who persuaded the crown to suppress the office of inspector as it then existed. In place of the forty positions extant since 1708—often competing for the limited number of tasks assigned inspectors—the government, in an edict of March, 1740, created twenty new ones bearing the same title but costing considerably more. The move was more than another effort to raise money. It appears rather as an attempt to eliminate incompetent per-

44. *Ibid.* The squads at these posts probably numbered eleven men.
45. BO, MS 1422, p. 10.

sonnel and to construct a respected and effective corps of investigators, a branch of the police whose daily concern would be the assembly of intelligence.

Domestic servants were no longer to serve as inspectors of police. In an effort to invest the office with a new dignity, the crown barred anyone from holding it who had not attained the rank of officer in the king's armies. To assure itself that new inspectors were at least minimally qualified, it insisted that five years of experience accompany the military title. And, as further guarantee that only men of proper standing should hold the post, the government attached to it a price beyond the means of most.[46]

Surveillance and investigation became the province and duty of the new officers. Each of them examined daily registers of hotels and boardinghouses in a given district; each regularly visited the shops and stalls of secondhand merchants in the same area to peruse records and search out stolen articles; and each frequently spent hours collecting information about individuals whose conduct had attracted the attention of the lieutenant of police or one of his superiors.

Beyond these common tasks, the inspectors began to acquire particular responsibilities. Marville's successor as lieutenant of police, Nicolas Berryer, continued the effort to establish an effective body of investigators by instituting a limited specialization among the inspectors of police. According to Berryer, "nothing is more important than to classify and delegate the various details that together constitute the business of the police. The officer who has to concern himself with but one set of affairs gets the hang of them, imposes an order on them, and acquires knowledge about them which permits him to do a much better job, with greater ease and speed."[47]

The single set of affairs to which Berryer assigned an inspector was known as a "département." How many departments Berryer himself created is not clear; but together with those established by Sartine,

---

46. Mildmay states that the office cost 11,500 livres in 1754 (*Police of France*, 50). Thirty years later it sold for between 20,000 and 24,000 livres (receipt from receiver of the *parties casuels* to Inspector Joseph Martignier, [?], 1782, in APP, DB 355, and BO, MS 1422, p. 966). This increase in price suggests the new prominence and importance reform had given the position by the 1780s. Inspectors became men of some social standing. In a report made to his successor on those who had worked for him, Sartine reports that Inspector Marais was a good officer but that he loved too much the parties that took place at the home of Count Dubarie and the homes of other "seigneurs," where he was often invited (Sartine to Lenoir, June 5, 1775, in BA, MS 12436).

47. BO, MS 1424, pp. 57–58.

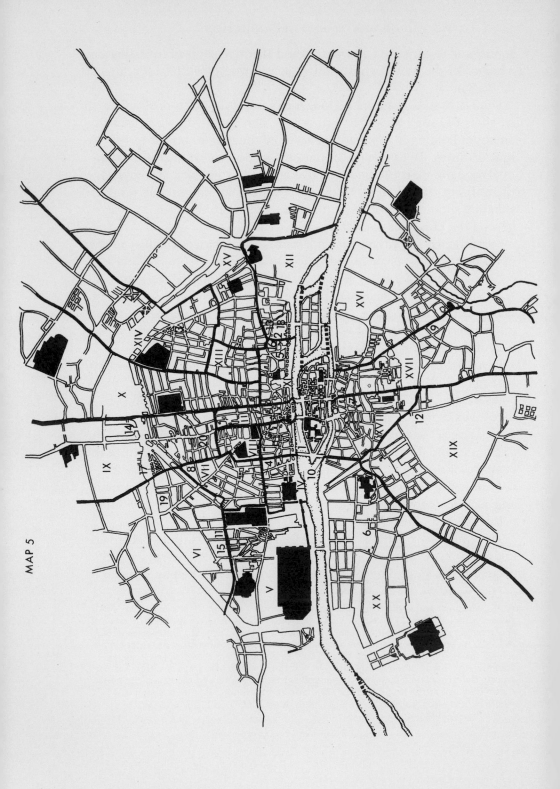

MAP 5

Map 5
THE INSPECTORS OF POLICE, 1742

1 Framboisier
2 Brébant
3 Pommereuil
4 Pillerault
5 Presle
6 Bardet
7 Roussell
8 Préolle
9 Ferrat
10 Joinville

11 Arborat
12 Adam
13 Machy
14 Le Grand
15 Doucet
16 Poussot
17 Bonamy
18 Saghat
19 Beaubigny
20 Lefèvre

SOURCE: *Almanach royal, 1742*, 284–85.

MAP 6

Map 6
THE INSPECTORS OF POLICE, 1789
The Inspectors with Dates They Entered Office

1 Paillet (1782)
2 Le Houx (1771)
3 Sommelier (1767)
4 Quidor (1778)
5 Willemein (1778)
6 Le Chenetier de Longpré (1777)
7 La Ture Morelle (1774)
8 Santerre de Tersé (1774)
9 Vaugien (1773)
10 Noël (1778)
11 Bossenet (1786)

12 Royer de Surbois (1782)
13 Patté (1774)
14 Pere (1780)
15 Poisson (1782)
15a Poisson's office, which differed from his residence
16 Henry (1771)
17 Boisset du Tronchet (1766)
18 De Saint-Paul (1785)
18a De Saint-Paul's office
19 Lescaze (1776)
20 Carpentier (1788)

SOURCE: *Almanach royal, 1789,* 426–27.

who enlarged upon Berryer's work and gave it a form that remained
little changed until 1789, they numbered at least twenty-five. In
Table 5 are listed the twenty-five departments along with the number
of persons staffing each. Though inspectors and commissioners shared
responsibility for seven departments, all but one of the remainder were
in the hands of a single individual, eight the charges of inspectors and
nine entrusted to commissioners.

The remaining department, that concerned with criminal affairs,
was the largest of them all and, in the eyes of the lieutenant of police,
probably the most important. Staffed first by three and then, after
1776, by four inspectors of police, this department, more than any
other, devoted itself to investigation. To it, by way of the commissioners scattered about the city, came reports from individuals who
had been attacked or robbed, and to it fell the task of hunting down the
assailant and the thief. The inspectors responsible for criminal investigations seem to have pursued them eagerly and with some success,
arresting regularly each year more men and women than the entire
Parisian guard.

Work they divided by region, each of the four being responsible for
all investigations in his section of the city. Every day they assembled
at the Office of Criminal Investigation (the *bureau de sûreté* or, in
1789, the offices of Mr. Garon) to discuss reports they had received,
to pass along information they believed important to a colleague, and
to coordinate work on particularly important cases. Unlike other inspectors and presumably to encourage cooperation rather than competition, their bonuses, fees, and expenses went into a common fund
which they divided evenly among themselves.[48]

Departments other than that of criminal affairs were as much concerned with the steady surveillance and intelligence that prevented
abuse as the investigation that uncovered and punished it. Some occupied themselves with a particular form of activity (commerce in a
given commodity, gambling, dramatic presentation, or printing), while
others kept watch over specific sorts of people (pawnbrokers, wetnurses, members of a club, prisoners, soldiers, or foreigners).

One group honored by special attention from the police were the
city's prostitutes. Though law had long forbade their existence, a succession of police administrators, finding the position of these women
inveterately strong, had at last struck a compromise that tacitly con-

48. BO, MS 1424, pp. 64–81, 118.

Table 5 Structural Divisions of the Police
The Departments, 1750–1789
(*les départements*)

Department	Number of Commissioners	Number of Inspectors
1. Calf market	1	1
2. *Spectacles* (Opera, Comédie-Française, Comédie-Italienne)	3	1
3. Bourse (stock exchange)	1	1
4. Pawnbrokers and usurers	1	1
5. Charlatans (medicine and drugs)	1	1
6. Gambling	2	1
7. Wetnurses	1	1
8. Criminal investigation and mendicancy		3 (1750–76) 4 (1776–89)
9. Military affairs		1
10. Librairie (booktrade)		1
11. Foreigners		1
12. Circles and clubs		1
13. Horse market		1
14. Prostitutes and kept women		1
15. Confidence men (*escrocs*)		1
16. Pederasty		1
17. Les Halles (provisionment, especially grains)	1	
18. Poultry market	1	
19. Hay and fodder	1	
20. Prisoners of state (often political prisoners)	1	
21. Police prisoners (prostitutes, beggars, vagabonds)	1	
22. *Maisons de force* (prisons)[1]	1	
23. Native Protestants (registry of deaths)	1	
24. Foreign Protestants	1	
25. Livestock market (cattle, pigs, sheep)	1	
TOTALS	19	18 & 19

SOURCES: BO, MS 1423, pp. 55–62; BO, MS 1424, pp. 53–55, 57, 139, and 143; AN, Y 13728, *passim*; BO, MS 1422, p. 688.
1. The department known as *maisons de force* carried responsibility for overseeing those prisoners detained by royal order, not for acts against the state, but at the request of some individual (often a relative), or upon presumption of guilt that went unproven in court.

doned their presence.[49] In return the police expected certain forms of cooperation. To avoid the generation of public outrage and consequent charges of laxity or corruption on the part of the police themselves, they insisted that these women stay off the street and out of windows. Appearances were critical, and those who offended them by whatever indiscretion could expect no immunity.

By making it illegal to rent to prostitutes, the police sought to confine such women to a few tolerated houses and thereby simplify the tasks of surveillance and control. A single inspector of police had charge of the department concerned with prostitutes. In addition to investigating the complaints of angry wives or puritanical neighbors, this inspector saw to it that the locations and owners of all tolerated brothels were a matter of record. As a matter of course those who ran such houses were obliged to file regular reports on the men who frequented them.[50] It was also understood that no proprietor was to admit an unknown girl to her household without first presenting her to the inspector who, according to Lemaire, "was to ask her all questions necessary to determine whether or not she had ever had intercourse with a man." If the girl maintained that she had, the inspector, before recording her name in the register he maintained, sent her to a surgeon or midwife whom he asked to confirm the girl's testimony. A madam bold or careless enough to neglect this obligation could expect not only imprisonment, but several days and several forms of humiliating public exposure.[51] In this way the police sought to leave the "corruption" of young women in nature's hands and to prevent financially interested parties from tampering with the process.

The pay an inspector received depended largely on which department he was assigned by the lieutenant of police. Because all twenty inspectors had invested approximately twenty thousand livres in their offices, all received an annual interest on this sum of about one thousand livres. Apart from this, however, incomes varied with the kind and quantity of work demanded of a man. In all, fees paid the inspectors amounted to more than two hundred thousand livres a year from

49. Berryer seems to have been the initiator of this compromise and of the policy of toleration it embodied; but his innovation remained a novelty in 1753 and, at that, an unpopular one. A report filed by one inspector in March of that year quotes the Marquis of Paulmy as predicting that Berryer's successor will certainly close the brothels and imprison the women operating them (BA, MS 10252, fol. 31).

50. For examples of such reports, see BA, MS 10252, fols. 43–53 or 74–97.

51. BO, MS 1424, pp. 86–87.

at least 1763 until the end of the regime. Though this would have meant an additional ten thousand livres a year to each inspector, the money was not distributed evenly.

Variations in income could be considerable, as in 1763 when Inspector Legrand received less than fifteen hundred livres in fees while his colleague, Inspector Durocher, got over twenty-one thousand livres. Nor was this particular discrepancy unique: in the same year the crown paid Inspector Framboisier almost twenty-two thousand livres and gave Inspector Lahaye only a little more than one thousand livres.[52]

To these sums paid by the government an inspector might add additional fees collected from private persons. Inspector Dehemery, for example, apparently received one hundred livres from an individual who, presumably with the inspector's assistance, had obtained a *lettre de cachet* against a member of his family.[53] Hotels and roominghouses were obliged to pay a monthly fee to the inspectors who examined their guest registers; and though varying with the size of the establishment and generally quite small, these fees—collected with sufficient energy—were of some importance.

Whatever the annual total, much that an inspector earned he did not keep; for out of his gross income, he had to pay not only the salaries of assistants, but the cost of both equipment and privately rendered services required in the course of his work. Having acquitted himself of these obligations, no inspector would have been left with as much as ten thousand livres, and most probably retained between two thousand and five thousand livres a year.[54] While such a sum did not constitute wealth, it did place the inspector in comfortable circumstance. Outside Paris, businessmen gladly retired when they had assured themselves of a similar income.

Somewhat surprisingly the highest sums paid to inspectors did not

52. AN, 0-1 361, nos. 324–41; BO, MS 1422, p. 97.

53. Ernest Coyecque, *Inventaire de la Collection Anisson sur l'histoire de l'imprimerie et la librairie principalement à Paris* (2 vols.; Paris, 1900), I, vii–ix.

54. Lenoir reports that the most lucrative department, that of Les Halles, was worth at most 10,000 livres, and this was in the hands not of an inspector but of a commissioner (BO, MS 1424, p. 115). Mildmay reports that commissioners who paid 30,000 livres for their offices in 1754 had a net income of 6,000 livres (*Police of France*, 49). If the ratio between cost of office and annual profit was approximately the same in the case of an inspector, we can calculate his net earnings in 1754 as 2,300 livres, for we know that the price of an inspector's office in that year was 11,500. By the 1780s, though the same office cost 20,000 livres, it is unlikely its returns had shown similar growth; nonetheless, assuming they had, an inspector would have earned 4,000 livres.

go to those who had served longest, but to men who, while experienced, were still young enough to work diligently. The average length of service among inspectors in 1768 was eleven years, and it was upon men whose service approached this duration that the lieutenant of police relied. Inspectors Framboisier and Durocher, who each received more than 21,000 livres in 1763, had had six and ten years of experience. In contrast Inspector Joinville with thirty-three years of service in 1763 got only 651 livres and Legrand who had served twenty-six years in 1763 received less than 1,500 livres. Novice inspectors fared, if anything, a bit worse than their senior colleagues.[55]

Subinspectors and spies.—Whatever his particular responsibility, an inspector of police did not work alone. The number of his assignments and the covert procedures often employed in their undertaking obliged him to seek the help of others. Some assistants he employed openly, and upon these he imposed a variety of tasks; others worked for him clandestinely at a single chore—the provision of intelligence. While the public was content to call all who served the inspectors of police in whatever way *mouches* or *mouchards*, the police themselves had a slightly more discriminating set of appellations permitting them to distinguish between covert and ordinary agents. Those who worked for them under cover they most often designated *observateurs* (observers), while those employed openly they spoke of in the popular idiom as *mouches* or as *sous-inspecteurs* (subinspectors), *commis* (agents), or *préposés* (employees).[56]

Men in the latter group an inspector generally employed to locate and arrest persons he sought or to follow individuals whose conduct had aroused his suspicion. To those of his subinspectors who proved themselves most able he might commit more delicate tasks. Struggling in 1751 to discover the author of an illegal newsletter printed in Paris and distributed in the provinces, Inspector Dehemery used one of his assistants to impersonate a curious provincial. Dehemery already knew who distributed the newsletter and where in Paris it could be read. Equipped with this information, his assistant found a furnished room nearby and began going regularly to read the gazette. Sometime

55. *Almanach royal, 1768*, 364–65; AN, 0-1 361, nos. 324–41.
56. Though *mouche* is the French word for fly and seems, in this sense, apposite, Peuchet claims that both *mouche* and *mouchard* in their application to police agents derive from a famous spy of the sixteenth century named Mouchy (*Mémoires*, I, 11). BO, MS 1424, pp. 59–60.

later, having ingratiated himself with the man and woman who made it available, he explained that he had to return home to his province and told them he would very much like to continue reading their news-sheet. He asked that it be sent to him regularly; and, after several days of hesitation, the couple agreed. No doubt pleased with his success, the subinspector left an address belonging to a contact of Dehemery's in Soissons, paid three livres for the first eight issues, and feigned a departure. Eventually, of course, Dehemery received each of the eight issues for which he had indirectly paid. One of these contained a hand-written note giving the address to which payment for subsequent is-sues was to be sent; and the inspector, after comparing the handwriting on this note with samples in the police files, concluded that the author of the gazette was a man named Sarrazin, who had been arrested on a number of previous occasions for the same offense. With some difficul-ty Dehemery and several subinspectors managed to locate Sarrazin and, on entering his lodgings, to grab him before he slipped through a trapdoor in the ceiling onto the rooftop and away into the night.[57]

Most subinspectors—those serving someone other than Dehemery who was responsible for the booktrade and censorship—could not have carried off the impersonation that led to Sarrazin's capture, for most were probably not literate. Subinspectors came, on the whole, from the lowest levels of Parisian society. Some the police recruited among men and women actually in prison, but many more came from the ranks of those who stood at the jailer's gate. Given the reputation of prisons like Bicêtre and Salpêtrière, it was not difficult to persuade even those who hated authority to trade their services for a wage and liberty. Bar-gains of this kind were clearly useful to the police; for, in gaining the assistance of men and women who had lived by theft or at the expense of public credulity and superstition, they gained access to the people and parts of Paris that most interested them.

Most subinspectors, or *commis*, began their careers as what the po-lice called *observateurs*—informers and undercover agents. For a time a newly recruited police agent continued to frequent old associates, passing what he learned along to the inspector who had engaged him. Invariably, however, his ties with the police became known and former contacts whom he had not already betrayed remained silent and sullen in his presence or disappeared altogether from their regular haunts.

57. Inspector Dehemery to Nicolas Berryer, undated, in BN, MS fr. 1214, fol. 23.

With his previous connections severed, the undercover agent became by a kind of natural progression a subinspector—a man with keen eyes and a trained ear, who, in a crowd, could spot those faces meriting attention, and who, conversant in the argot of the underworld, made a man's own diction his enemy, a mark threatening always to betray him.

Agents drawn from the city's prisons or courtrooms and blackmailed into services were of unquestionable value to the police; but their employment brought concomitant difficulties, as the case of Marie Dion suggests. Abandoned by a husband who found life with her intolerable, Marie—known since her marriage as la Maréchal—became mistress to a Parisian banker. During the course of their liaison, she managed in one way or another to steal fourteen thousand livres from her new companion, who, upon discovering the theft, had her arrested. Confined in the Châtelet, la Maréchal quickly extended the duration of her sentence by offering one of the jailers six louis to murder her former lover. It was a bit much to ask, even of an eighteenth-century prison guard; and Marie was transferred to Salpêtrière to serve out her new sentence. There, somehow in 1747, she met an employee of the police named Durot who offered her release on the condition that she become an informer. Marie accepted the proposition and for three years served Inspectors Poussot and Dadvenel, passing gradually from the position of undercover agent to that of subinspector.

During the early summer of 1750, the lieutenant of police received a number of complaints charging that la Maréchal was using her place with the police to extort money and services. Berryer ordered an investigation and placed its conduct in the hands of Commissioner Chastelus. Inquiry revealed that on numerous occasions (at least twelve), la Maréchal had sold prisoners their freedom and had gone so far as to have innocent individuals arrested in order, later, to barter with them for their liberty. One poor woman had been sent to prison three times on Marie's recommendation and three times had paid the price of her release. Ordinarily la Maréchal demanded five or more louis, a sum lovers were often willing to pay when the imprisoned women could not. To the genuinely destitute she offered other terms, accepting stolen silverware from some and permitting one woman to serve her as maid.

There were other needs Marie's position permitted her to fill. A woman of strong and indiscriminate sexual appetite, she sat one day in a carriage conveying a woman she had arrested to prison. Obviously interested in her captive, Marie made her an offer: "if she would promise to love her and come live with her, she [Marie] would have her out of prison in less than fifteen days." Not realizing what was in store for her, the young woman, Geneviève Pounnier, gratefully accepted the proposition, agreeing as well to appear and testify against the authors of the newsletter whose sale had led to her arrest.

Twelve days later la Maréchal gained the woman's release, loaned her the money she needed to pay her prison expenses, and conducted her home. There she immediately began making the sexual demands on her that continued for more than a year. Surprised that after two weeks in the female prison of Salpêtrière Geneviève should feel any reluctance, la Maréchal confided that "if she knew the pleasure two women could give one another, she would give up Durot [Geneviève's lover] and men would cease to mean anything at all to her." After somewhat more than a year of this servitude, Geneviève went to Inspector Poussot and asked for his help.

This act and the complaints of others ended la Maréchal's extortion and brought about her confinement; [58] but the corruption she represented within the Parisian police was never contained. It could not be, for it came unavoidably with those the inspectors believed themselves obliged to employ.[59] If hiring rogues gave the police a power and perception they would otherwise have lacked, the practice also made malfeasance an endemic disease and generated public attitudes that hindered the work of the police. Distaste, fear, and a desire for distance were common responses to an agency that, while imprisoning some who offended the community, paid a regular salary to others.

Unlike the subinspectors, not all undercover agents, or *observateurs*, came from the same low level of Parisian society. The kind of individuals the police chose for domestic espionage depended naturally enough on the milieu they wished to penetrate. For public places

58. On the case of Marie Dion see the series of affidavits contained in the dossier bearing her husband's name of Maréchal, in BA, MS 11732.

59. While other dossiers in the BA (see, for example, that of Hubert Maillot in MS 11232) suggest the entrenched presence of corruption, not all subinspectors were, in Lemaire's words, "extremely bad subjects," recruited in jail. One *commis* working for Inspector Troussey in 1773 had worked as a soapmaker and still had his own shop; another was a fourteen-year-old boy who worked in Troussey's house as a domestic.

where men gathered to discuss the affairs of the day, it was necessary
to find individuals who were "above all presentable, that is to say,
well-dressed, and who ran absolutely no risk of being suspected as
agents." To keep àbreast of illegal gambling, the police employed men
like the chevalier Montblanc—men who, while making a pretense of
nobility, lived by their wits and by the adroitness with which they
insinuated themselves into the company of those with a taste for
chance.[60]

Not all undercover agents were in the pay of an inspector. Each lieutenant of police engaged agents of his own who reported to no one else.
Sartine and Lenoir, for example, both benefited from the services of a
woman in her sixties who, Lenoir tells us, "was received into the best
homes in Paris," and who, in turn, "entertained at her own home,
several times a week, courtiers, men of letters, socialites, and these
idle persons one sees everywhere and who meddle in everything. She
served, on days she entertained, a tea the cost of which the police paid.
Her house, where gathered persons of all conditions and of good and
bad company, was not regarded as completely open; only a few women
attended; there were no games; people spoke there with complete freedom." Through this agent and by means of the weekly teas at which
she presided on his behalf, Lenoir contends he often learned more of
importance than he did through his inspectors and their contacts.[61]

In selecting their undercover agents the police showed themselves
men of broad view, employers free from any taint of social discrimination. To complement the work of their prominent hostess who could
not, after all, entertain the whole of Paris, Sartine and Lenoir employed
retired domestic servants to visit the homes and *hôtels* of those unable
or unwilling to attend the police teas. Garrulous old comrades, still at
work in such places and happy to see a friend, gladly shared tales about
their employers. Lenoir states that, toward the end of his term in office,
he also began employing persons in the Parlement and the clergy, as
well as lawyers and doctors who had access to the Masons and other
secret organizations that were forming. These measures became necessary, he reports, as social fashion changed, as men and women lost
interest in the salons and began attaching themselves to clubs and
secretive societies. The inspectors of police were, as we have seen, no

60. BO, 1424, p. 59; dossier of La Bate (Montblanc's real name), in BA, MS 11751.
61. BO, MS 1422, p. 98.

more narrow in choosing their subordinates than was their superior. Having selected the most respectably attired individuals they could find for work in the city's coffee houses, they sought out prostitutes and secondhand dealers (*revendeuses*) to help them keep watch over the streets. In their pursuit of intelligence, there were none whom the police, out of distaste or esteem, hesitated to approach and, if possible, hire.[62]

Police agents or spies, eighteenth-century Parisians believed, were everywhere—ubiquitous ears that caught each small hint of discontent. Historians have, on the whole, done little more than repeat the popular rumors, suggesting, for example, that the crown spent the extraordinary sum of one million livres a year to maintain a force of three thousand spies in Paris.[63]

It suited the police that stories like this should circulate. According to Lenoir, the common belief that nothing which happened in Paris went unnoticed by the police was far more helpful to him than a host of paid undercover agents could have been. To nurture this useful popular conviction, he says, the lieutenant of police made a practice of feigning "to know what many persons acting without calculation or commission came to tell him."

The actual number of those paid to provide intelligence to the police was far smaller than rumor supposed. Had it not been, Lenoir added, "neither those funds assigned to secret and unforeseen expenses of the police in which were comprised those for intelligence, nor the sums from other funds to which the Lieutenant of Police was thought to have access, would have sufficed for even the initial cost of such an inquisition."[64] While he does not tell us precisely how many undercover agents the police employed, we can make a rough estimate of their number.

As Lenoir indicated in the passage just cited, a portion of the money

62. *Ibid.*, 29, 98; for data on one of the secondhand dealers, Marie Anne Forget, see her dossier in BA, MS 11746; on the use of prostitutes, see BO, MS 1424, p. 88 and BA, MS 10252, fols. 43–97.

63. Arthur Michel de Boislisle (ed.), *Lettres de M. de Marville, lieutenant de police au ministre Maurepas* (3 vols.; Paris, 1896–1905), I, x, and repeated in Robert Forster's *European Society in the Eighteenth Century* (New York, 1969), 397. The claim is remarkable. Were it accurate, it would mean that the government had as many men collecting intelligence in Paris as it had, in the form of the *maréchaussée*, policing all of rural France.

64. BO, MS 1422, pp. 97–98.

spent on intelligence came from a fund that was designated secret. We
know that in 1780 this fund totaled 20,000 livres.[65] In the same year
the crown paid about 210,000 livres to the inspectors of police over
and above what they received as interest on the cost of their offices.[66]
If, given our previous discussion of their earnings, we estimate at 3,000
livres the annual net income of each inspector, we may (subtracting
the 60,000 livres that went to the twenty inspectors from the original
210,000) conclude that together the inspectors had 150,000 livres with
which to purchase the services of subordinates. Joined to the secret
fund administered by the lieutenant of police, this would have amounted to a total of 170,000 livres for use in the hire of subinspectors and
spies.

Fortunately, we know not only how much money was available to
pay such personnel, but how much it cost to obtain their services.
Lemaire tells us that subinspectors received three livres a day plus
occasional bonuses for work well done. If we assume most of them
worked with some regularity, that is, about fourteen days a month,
each would have made 42 livres a month or 504 livres a year.[67]

In contrast to the uniform sum paid subinspectors, the *observateurs*
or undercover agents were paid according to their social standing and
the value of their work, some getting as little as 30 livres a month and
others as much as 150 livres.[68] The yearly income of an undercover
agent might, then, have fallen anywhere between 360 livres and 1,800
livres, though one doubts that very many approached the upper end of
the scale. Most, in the end, would probably have received no more than
what was paid the subinspector, that is to say, roughly 500 livres a

65. *Ibid.*, 970–71. This sum varied throughout the century. It seems to have reached
its peak during the 1730s, when concern over the *convulsionnaires* prompted the government and the police to augment the number of undercover agents. Between 1732 and
1737 the government allocated 8,000 livres a month to police intelligence (BN, MS fr.
6791, fols. 51–112). The same fund for all of 1784 amounted to only 12,000 livres
(office of the lieutenant of police to the controller general, February 12, 1785, in AN,
F-4 1017).

66. BO, MS 1422, p. 971. Lenoir's figures, which are based on a copy of a treasury
document he possessed for the year 1780, find confirmation in the payrolls submitted by
the crown to the treasury in 1768 (AN, 0-1 361, nos. 341–44).

67. BO, MS 1424, p. 60. The assumption about regularity of work seems reasonable
given data on three subinspectors in a letter from a man named Bergeot to Sartine,
August 26, 1773, in BA, MS 12436; and the total annual income it suggests (540 livres)
corresponds roughly with the 480 livres we know a subinspector named Duplessix was
making each year during the 1740s (from an unnumbered piece listing eight foreign
ambassadors under surveillance, in BA, MS 10293).

68. BO, MS 1424, pp. 59–60.

year. Taking this figure as the cost of employing either an undercover agent or a subinspector and dividing it into the 170,000 livres available for this purpose, we may calculate that the total number of *mouches*, as the Parisian public called them, could not have exceeded 340 men and women.

It is important to stress that this figure applies only to the number of agents who were, in some sense, regularly employed and whom we may legitimately consider a part of the Parisian police. It does not take account of those who sometimes accepted a ticket to the Opera in exchange for information—or those who became increasingly congenial and talkative with each round of drinks an inspector bought, or those who went to the police out of fear, vengeance, the desire to eliminate a rival, or even, on occasion, a sense of duty. How many such people there were is obviously difficult to say. Surely their number depended in part on the state of popular attitudes toward the mores and values enforced by the police; but this is a variable whose effects it is difficult to measure in concrete terms.

More helpful, perhaps, is the correlation that exists today between the length of time a detective has served on a police force and the number of persons to whom he can turn for information. Even a novice in an American police department has, after six months, developed a few contacts, while an experienced detective may have twenty-five or thirty. The head of an investigative branch with twenty-five years of service may have as many as a hundred.[69] Knowing, as we do, that after 1750 inspectors of police had been in their posts an average of about eleven years, we might assume that their contacts in the community resembled those of a veteran detective today. Proceeding on the basis of this assumption, it does not seem unreasonable to suggest that together the Parisian inspectors drew on the services of five hundred to six hundred occasional informers, men and women who, without formal ties to the police, were, nonetheless, essential to its successful operation.

SERVICES

Police departments today find themselves performing a number of services for the community which have little to do with the patrol and investigation that are thought of as their primary tasks. Control of

69. For these figures I am indebted to Biagio Dilieto, chief of the New Haven Police Department, who was kind enough to talk with me at some length on August 9, 1973.

traffic and parking, charge of an animal shelter or a lost-and-found—
these and other tasks have often devolved upon the police because
there has been no other agency available to undertake them. During
the eighteenth century the responsibilities of this kind conferred on
the Parisian police were of considerable magnitude. Upon them fell the
great burdens of seeing that the city was lit at night and cleaned during
the day. They were responsible for protecting the community against
fire and oversaw the program by which thousands of Parisian mothers
surrendered newly born infants to wetnurses from the surrounding
provinces. Of these services themselves and their significance I shall
speak later; here I mean only to establish, insofar as possible, the
numbers and, in some cases, the identity of those who performed
them.

   Lighting.—Conceived by La Reynie, the first lieutenant of police, as
a means of making Paris safe at night, the lighting of the city had, by
1714, become a major enterprise, requiring the work of at least 370
men. As new lamps were added, this number continued to grow until
1769, when a technological innovation permitted the police to reduce
the force of lamplighters to 150 men. (For justification of these figures
and a more complete discussion of the role the police played in lighting Paris, see the section on deterrence in Chapter Five.)

   Cleaning and garbage collection.—Beginning in 1704 the cost of removing rubbish from the city was paid out of funds allocated to the
police. Following this date, two-wheeled carts rolled regularly through
Parisian streets collecting the refuse residents had amassed in front of
their homes. One-half hour before the carts arrived (between 8:00 and
9:00 A.M. in summer), twenty employees of the police passed throughout each quarter sounding a small bell which warned residents that
they were to begin assembling waste and dirt in neat piles for garbage
collectors. These piles were then loaded by the two men who attended
each cart—one working with shovel, the other with broom—and
transported to refuse dumps outside the city. In 1714, 85 carts and 170
men were at work cleaning the capital; by 1754 there were 130 carts
and 260 attendants. Those engaged in this work, Lemaire tells us, were
farmers (*laboureurs*) who worked land near Paris and who had decided
that horses capable of drawing plows could also pull garbage carts. Each
of them was really a small entrepreneur, employing and receiving ap-

proximately two thousand livres a year for the labor he performed with his horse and cart on behalf of the city.[70]

Protection against fire.—Responsible during the eighteenth century for keeping Paris clean, the police were also charged, as they still are today, with protecting the city against fire; and to perform this duty they employed a steadily increasing number of men as the century progressed. The initial company of firefighters numbered 32 men when it was definitively established in 1716. Six years later the unit had doubled in size, and by 1789 it contained 221 men.[71] Later we will trace this growth in greater detail and examine its ramifications for the city (see "A Limit to Hazard" in Chapter Six). Suffice it here to say that the dramatic expansion of this company of firemen represents one of the significant and admirable achievements of those who administered the eighteenth-century Parisian police.

Child care.—Another such achievement was the apparatus the police created to secure, insofar as one could, the lives of thousands of newly born infants whose parents could not or would not care for them. As we shall see in Chapter Six, two administrative centers established by the police worked during the eighteenth century to find surrogate mothers for these children. Employing something like fifty men and women, these two agencies had the task of drawing into the capital the many peasant women the city required each year to feed its offspring;[72] and upon their success in this endeavor, upon their ability to attract and satisfy a sufficient number of wetnurses, hinged thousands of new lives.

Mont de Piété.—Not until December, 1777, did letters patent obtained by Lenoir create the last of the major institutions in Paris operated by the police. Judged from almost any perspective the Mont de Piété was a remarkably successful innovation. In conception, and in fact, it was at the outset essentially a state-run pawnbrokerage; it became, within a brief period, a major financial institution as well.

In creating the new institution, Lenoir aspired to do two things: to

70. Mildmay, *Police of France*, 117–19; BO, MS 1424, p. 99; Lacaille, *Description de Paris*, unpaginated; BO, MS 1421, pp. 605–606.

71. BN, MS JF 1325, fols. 103–106, 113–16; letters patent, December 11, 1785, in AN, F-4 1017.

72. *Almanach royal, 1789*, 425–26; BO, MS 1421, p. 365.

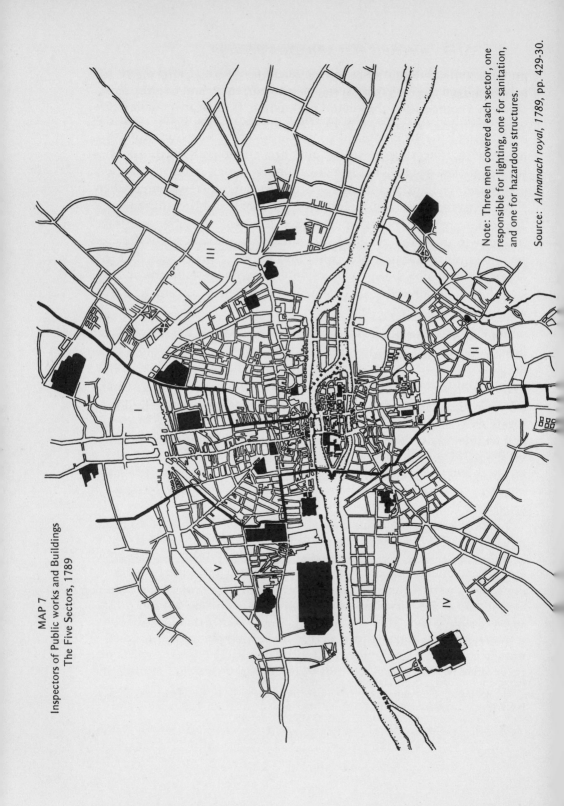

MAP 7
Inspectors of Public works and Buildings
The Five Sectors, 1789

Note: Three men covered each sector, one
responsible for lighting, one for sanitation,
and one for hazardous structures.

Source: *Almanach royal, 1789*, pp. 429-30.

protect from exorbitant rates of repayment those who found themselves obliged to convert possessions into currency; and to eliminate, through a competition they could not sustain, the private pawnbrokers who constituted a principal market for stolen goods in Paris.

Located in the Marais, a block from the Hôtel de Soubise, the Mont de Piété succeeded in fulfilling both these aspirations. Its first director, Framboisier de Beaunay, Lenoir transferred from his previous post as head of the *bureaux des nourrices*. Beaunay, drawing initially on funds provided by the police for the money it became his business to advance to others, quickly made the institution self-sufficient. Men and women, offered far better terms than those granted by private lenders, flocked to the new establishment. Given their numbers, the Mont de Piété passed from self-sufficiency to the making of considerable profit. Investors, admiring both its work and its stability, hurried to Beaunay to make funds available and contented themselves with interest that, while paid at a rate beneath that offered elsewhere, was received regularly and in the amount promised. By 1781 or 1782—four or five years after its creation—the Mont de Piété was handling 33 million livres a year (a sum equivalent to about 15 percent of all revenues received by the state in 1781) and drawing envious, covetous glances from those responsible for royal finances. Beyond the profits it returned to investors as interest, Lenoir's new institution turned its annual earnings over to charitable purposes, particularly to obtaining the release of mothers and fathers imprisoned for failing to pay wetnurses they had engaged, and to sustaining the cost of returning many unredeemed articles to the destitute clients who had pawned them.

To assist him in managing this enterprise Lenoir had furnished Beaunay with a staff of roughly twenty-five persons, individuals to keep accounts, to receive and appraise the items brought in by the public, and to manage the store in which unredeemed articles were sold.[73]

Dépôt de Filature.—In the same year he created the Mont de Piété, Lenoir established on the rue de Bourbon, near the Gate of Saint-Denis, a workhouse in which women who were out of work and in need of money could find employment spinning thread. Though the fruits of their work were sold and the money obtained went to maintaining the workhouse, additional funds for its support were required. These Lenoir drew from sums the police collected as licensing fees from the

73. BO, MS 1424, pp. 151–52; BO, MS 1423, pp. 357–67; *Almanach royal, 1778*, 496.

operators of billiard halls. Operating this institution for the lieutenant of police in 1789 was a man named Nau. Whether or not he had assistance in the task is unclear.[74]

INSPECTION

The enforcement of police regulations in Paris required constant surveillance. There was, in addition, a need to see that those services for which the police paid and bore responsibility were honestly performed. Many sections of the police played a part in performing these tasks: elements of the guard on patrol; the commissioners and inspectors in each quarter; informers employed by the lieutenant of police. But in addition to these individuals, whose primary responsibilities lay elsewhere, there were others associated with the police or employed by them for whom inspection of various objects and activities constituted their entire function.

Inspectors of public works and buildings.—During the early part of the century, the inspectors of police in each quarter kept watch to see that those who lit and cleaned the city did their jobs properly. With the reform of 1740 that halved the number of inspectors, and with the increasing delegation of specialized responsibilities to this diminished company, the need arose for men who had time to inspect the streets of the city, making sure that the money spent to light and clean them was not being wasted. There was, as well, a need to note structures in dangerous disrepair and to see that those on the verge of collapse were condemned.

Though no one specifically assigned to these tasks appears in the *Almanach Royal* until 1772, it is clear that at least twenty years earlier Berryer had begun the creation of a separate section of the police to undertake them. By 1772 this section included seven men: one supervisor—Vannier—who had worked under Berryer, and six others—two serving on the Left Bank and four on the Right. Seventeen years later there were eighteen inspectors and subinspectors of public works (*inspecteurs d'illumination et nettoiement*). Where there had been one supervisor in 1772, there were now three, one bearing particular responsibility for illumination, another for hazardous structures, and the third for proper disposal of waste. The fifteen men who remained divided the city into five sections, three men to a section, each again

74. BO, MS 1422, p. 691; *Almanach royal, 1789*, 431.

specifically responsible for one of the company's major concerns and each reporting to the appropriate supervisor.

Salaries for both inspectors and subinspectors were reasonably decent in 1789, the one drawing 2,100 livres a year and the other 1,800.[75]

Censors.—Throughout the eighteenth century the relationship between the police and the office responsible for regulating the booktrade (known as the *direction générale de la Librairie*) was both intimate and complex. It attained maximum simplicity in 1763 when, following Lamoignon de Malesherbes's resignation as director of the Librairie, the post passed into the hands of the lieutenant of police, Antoine Gabriel de Sartine. For thirteen years, until Lenoir asked to be relieved of the additional burden it imposed, the Office of the Booktrade became a branch of the police.

Having always been obliged to judge the religious, moral, and political propriety of printed sheets and brochures, the lieutenant of police now acquired responsibility for books. With his new charge came a staff of 127 censors, divided into seven groups, each with responsibility for works falling into one of seven classes: theology, jurisprudence, medicine and natural history, *belles lettres* and history, geography and travel, mathematics, and prints. There was, in addition, an individual known as the police censor (*censeur de la police*) who examined dramatic works intended for the theater.

Between 1763 and 1776, exercising their powers to increase or diminish the size of this company, the lieutenants of police added something like 40 new censors, bringing to about 160 the number of men at work in this section.[76]

Expert farriers.—So important was the horse to labor and transport during the eighteenth century, and so frequent the deception and dishonesty afflicting the exchange of these animals that, in 1782, the police added three farriers to their ranks—experts, men long familiar with horses, trained to recognize disease or defect. Any buyer who had purchased his animal at the horse market in the Faubourg Saint-Marcel and who believed himself cheated or deceived might, within a week's

---

75. Inspector Pasquier to Hérault, November 23, 1727, in BA, MS 10321; AN, 0-1 361, no. 273; memoir, Louis Thiroux de Crosne to controller general, undated, in APP, DB 355; *Almanach royal, 1772,* cxcv; *Almanach royal, 1789,* 429–30.

76. Peuchet, *Mémoires,* II, 383; BO, MS 1422, p. 574; Marion, *Dictionnaire des institutions,* 76; APP, EA 16, nos. 15–20.

time, demand that a police expert inspect the animal. If the farrier's
report sustained the buyer's claim, an inspector of police responsible
for affairs at the market compelled a refund. For each such inspection
the farrier (*maréchal expert*) received three livres and fifteen sous.

In addition to assessing claims of fraud, the three police farriers
spent their days visiting stables throughout the city, intent on detect-
ing and containing any communicable malady. They looked, in particular, for the symptoms of glanders, a deadly and highly contagious disease that could, if not discovered promptly, cripple the city's capacity
to supply itself by land. Any horse showing signs of this infection they
seized, destroyed, and burned.[77]

Officers of the industrial and mercantile corporations.—Among the
duties of the lieutenant of police fell the task of supervising and regulating most manufacture and commerce conducted in Paris. Those
who headed the police realized the enormity of the ambition and believed it reasonable only within an economic context that preserved
the medieval commercial and industrial guilds. Each of the societies
possessed organizational hierarchies that permitted government to
exact obedience from many by commanding a few. In this fact lay the
crux of their importance to the police and the reason that every Parisian lieutenant of police but d'Albert, the friend and protégé of Turgot,
sought to preserve them. Officers of the guilds had long subjected each
member artisan or merchant to similar standards and procedures; by
controlling the content of these standards, the police managed to convert each set of corporate officers into auxiliary agents, into a means by
which vast aspiration escaped ludicrous incapacity.

Prior to Turgot's famous edict of February, 1776, there had been approximately 140 commercial and industrial corporations in Paris. The
men in charge of each were known variously as *jurés*, *gardes*, and
syndics. Numbering sometimes two, sometimes as many as six, new
officers were selected at the Châtelet in the presence of a public official
who obliged those chosen to swear publicly to uphold and enforce the
regulations governing their corporation. In the oath they took the new
officers promised to inspect regularly work done within the guild by its
members and to report, in less than twenty-four hours, any violation
they detected to the public prosecutor.

77. BO, MS 1424, pp. 143, 156.

To encourage diligence on the part of a corporation's officers (and compliance by its members), the head of the police occasionally sent a police commissioner and several guardsmen to accompany them on their rounds. On June 16, 1779, Lenoir wrote Commissioner Dupuy to tell him that a detachment of the guard would be available to him the next morning when he began his tour with the syndics of the barber's guild. He was to meet them at the guardpost on the Pont Neuf at 5:00 A.M.[78]

By oath, then, the roughly 560 officers of the Parisian corporations became, during the period of their tenure, semipublic officials, deputized and expert police inspectors who, with occasional prompting, kept watch over the economic life of the great city.[79]

JUSTICE

The commissioners.—Since the fourteenth century a company of men known as *commissaires-enquêteurs-examinateurs* (commissioners-investigators-examiners) had assisted the provost of the Châtelet and his lieutenants in the performance of their duty. Initially numbering twelve, the company had, by the late seventeenth century, quadrupled in size. Its forty-eight members, dispersed throughout the city, bore extensive responsibilities within each of the major jurisdictions of the Châtelet. Simultaneously subordinate to the lieutenant civil, the lieutenant criminal, and the lieutenant of police, the commissioners were, in a sense, judicial handymen, whose particular tasks no one has yet fully and carefully described. Inventorying the property of those who had died or declared themselves insolvent, validating the accounts of certain corporations and the statements trustees made to their wards, hearing criminal complaints, authorizing the burial of the dead, conducting searches and inquiries on behalf of the crown—the commissioners had obligations that appear at times without limit.[80]

Within this enormous province of responsibility they apparently de-

78. BO, MS 1422, p. 444; BN, MS JF 1330, fols. 12–14, 41–42; MS JF 1333, fols. 38–40; Mildmay, *Police of France*, 102; Marion, *Dictionnaire des institutions*, 144–51; Lenoir to Commissioner Dupuy, June 16, 1779, in AN, Y 12830.

79. As the number of officers varied between two and six, I have chosen four. This multiplied by 140, the number of corporations until 1776, gives 560. After 1776 and the reduction in the number of guilds to forty-four, there would have been 176 officers.

80. BO, MS 1424, pp. 37–55; Antoine, *Fonds judiciaires*, 170; unnumbered memoir dated 1805, in AN, F-7 3006.

voted the bulk of their energy and time to police affairs; [81] but these affairs themselves took a considerable variety of forms. As the first subordinates available to the lieutenant of police, the commissioners of the Châtelet had been delegated tasks as extensive as his own and powers to accomplish them that were both judicial and administrative. If it was their duty to judge preliminarily matters that would later receive final disposition in police court, they were also expected—particularly at the outset—to act as investigators and inspectors, to search homes and offices, to walk the streets and see that butchers cleaned their slaughterhouses regularly, that water carriers filled their buckets only at specified places along the river. By the end of the eighteenth century, at least twenty commissioners had been assigned particular administrative responsibilities (departments) ranging from the interrogation of state prisoners at the Bastille to inspection of the city's poultry market.

Given the range of functions these men performed even within the realm of police affairs, no single classification of their activity can be wholly adequate. A case might be made, as I have suggested, for designating them inspectors; but it is important to remember that, unlike any other employee of the police, the commissioners wore the robes of magistrates and that it was primarily upon these men that the lieutenant of police relied in exercising the judicial powers with which he had been invested.

When there was crisis and turmoil in the city, it was not the role of investigator or inspector that the commissioners were asked to play. Their part clearly became that of judge. In a letter to Commissioner Dupuy (one of the two commissioners in the quarter of Saint-Benoît), dated May 21, 1789, the lieutenant of police, Thiroux de Crosne, reports that on the following day, Friday, a sentence will be executed against the demonstrators (*séditieux*) recently arrested during a riot in the Faubourg Saint-Antoine. As there may be trouble and disorder, Crosne continues, Dupuy is to remain at home all day "to hear those

81. AN, Y 12224 contains two "Répertoire des minutes" of Commissioner Tourton, 1697–1731. These record his attention to civil matters under three categories: "procès verbaux de scellés," "comptes," and "partages." Criminal and police affairs are subsumed under the heading "plaintes, enquêtes, et informations." In the year 1712, all forms of civil cases handled by Commissioner Tourton numbered 11, while police and criminal actions together totaled 321. Of this latter total, the vast majority appear to have been within the province of police jurisdiction. See also AN, Y 13728, which contains letters addressed by the three lieutenants of the Châtelet to two commissioners. The great majority are from the lieutenant of police.

individuals who are brought before him and to decide on their fate."[82]

In fact, if not in form, the lieutenant of police delegated much of his judicial authority to the commissioners, even under ordinary circumstances. Indeed, most judgments pronounced in police court were probably no more than formal validations of decisions already made elsewhere by the commissioners. Sentences handed down by the lieutenant of police usually embodied the recommendations he received from the public prosecutor at the Châtelet, and these recommendations depended, in turn, on the outcome of preliminary inquiries conducted by the commissioners. An incomplete register records sixty-two such inquiries in 1773: twenty-two of them concerned the transport or sale of contraband, most of it tobacco; eleven dealt with "insolent beggars"; seven with the theft or falsification of lottery tickets; another five treated the cases of guild members who had refused to obey the officers of their corporations; there were two reports on resistance to the employees of the General Farms (tax collectors) at the barriers of the city, and two more on persons alleged to have sold printed matter without licenses; finally three reports concerned wetnurses against whom complaints had been brought, two of them charged simply with inadequate care, and the third, a woman named Mary, with having returned a small but healthy girl to a soldier of the guard, who definitely recalled having entrusted her with his son.[83]

That these reports on a case were sometimes more than recommendations is suggested by a letter Lenoir wrote Commissioner Gillet on March 7, 1781. The lieutenant of police reported that he had ordered a coachman accused of having seriously injured a pedestrian brought before Gillet. He wanted the commissioner to decide the case and to send the man to prison if he was guilty. The report Lenoir concluded by requesting was clearly meant to embody, not merely a recommendation, but a delegated judicial decision, which the lieutenant of police would proceed to sanction with a formal sentence.[84]

The records of the commissioners themselves testify to their role as judges—judges who, by resolving immediately the many minor disputes that arose each day on the city's streets, spared the lieutenant of police considerable time in his court. In a notebook begun the twenty-

---

82. Crosne to Commissioner Dupuy, May 21, 1789, in AN, Y 12830.
83. Register of reports (procès verbaux) from the commissioners to the clerk of the Chambre de Police, 1773, in AN, Y 9646.
84. Lenoir to Commissioner Gillet, March 7, 1781, in AN, Y 13728.

eighth of October, 1785, Commissioner Danzel recorded matters brought before him each day by the guard. Some days contain a single entry, some as many as four. Take June 3, 1786, for example:

9:30 a.m. Mr. Pia, corporal of the post at the market St. Martin, at the request of Thérèse Bourgot, wife of Mr. Dangé, arrested and brought before us a water carrier named Simon Dillan, residing on the rue de Vertu in the home of the Widow David, for having thrown water at Mrs. Dangé when she had her back turned. Enjoined the said individual to be more circumspect and released him.

7:00 p.m. (Heard, warned, and released two men arrested for fighting.)

10:00 p.m. (Heard a musician arrested for causing a disturbance at the "académie" of the comte d'Artois. Released him after he signed promise never to return there.)

12:30 a.m. Mr. Pelletier, sergeant commanding the post on the rue Meslée, arrested and brought before us at the request of Gaspard Louis Baeot, paper merchant . . . , a sculptor named Pierre Vigoureux . . . , for an altercation involving a dog that the said Gaspard had found and the said Vigoureux claimed belonged to him. (Danzel, weary perhaps, does not tell us who got the dog.)[85]

A quarrel, an accident, a crime—it was to the nearest commissioner that men generally turned with news of anything extraordinary or threatening in their lives, and with demands for action or support. To this officer fell the duty of initial response; and by the quality and the decency of his action, those concerned judged not only him, but the police force itself. In the quarters of a commissioner, government regularly and directly confronted those whom it governed and, by its conduct, either enhanced or subverted its own authority.

We need to know more than we presently do about the men who, throughout the eighteenth century, filled these prominent posts. Lenoir assures us that the commissioners of 1780 were vastly more capable and dedicated individuals than those who had served fifty years earlier. He says that there were few companies of magistrates, even those that were much larger, which counted so many learned and able men among them; "forty-eight individuals of equal worth," he continues, "will not be found again."[86]

85. Commissioner Danzel's notebook of arrests (agenda de la garde), 1785–1786, in AN, Y 11810.
86. BO, MS 1422, p. 890; MS 1424, p. 115 (this is one of Lenoir's notes to Lemaire's manuscript).

These estimations are, however, retrospective; and it is important to contrast them with the complaints Lenoir frequently registered with the commissioners while he was still serving as lieutenant of police. Consider but one example, a letter he addressed to two commissioners shortly after he assumed office: "I fear," he begins, "that they [i.e., the other commissioners] seek to avoid all operations to which no special honorarium is attached." He adds that these commissioners are not making the searches he has ordered them to conduct nor are they reporting promptly to the criminal investigators cases of theft brought before them. He is angry, he says, and will take further steps to remedy the situation if reprimand does not suffice.[87]

What point we are to assume between these two perspectives will remain unclear until further work is done on the commissioners. The demands on a commissioner's time were, like those on the lieutenant of police himself, considerable; and it is no demonstration of personal inadequacy that some of them went unmet. That one commissioner—Tilloy Desnoyettes—was accused of misconduct and arrested is of less significance in judging the worth of others than the pressure his colleagues exerted on him to resign.[88]

Whatever else one may say about them, it appears that those who became commissioners were trained for the legal work that was such a large part of their job. Born in 1729 in Paris, Tilloy Desnoyettes attended the Collège des Quatre Nations and, at the age of twelve, began his study of law in the office of a Parisian notary. After eleven years in this office and others like it, Desnoyettes ended his legal apprenticeship and gained admission to the company of attorneys authorized to practice before the Parlement of Paris. Two years later, at the age of twenty-five, connections permitted him to buy the office of commissioner. By the time he became a magistrate, Desnoyettes had spent thirteen years—more than half his life—studying and practicing law.

To become a commissioner cost a man about 50,000 livres in 1760. By 1784 the price had climbed beyond 100,000 livres; and the increase, Lenoir suggests, demonstrated a growing esteem for the office. One hopes that he is right, for a commissioner could hope to earn little else. Beyond the 5 percent interest he collected on money invested in

87. Lenoir to commissioners, undated, in AN, Y 13728.
88. On this incident and for the biographical material that follows, see the dossier of Desnoyettes, in BA, MS 12399.

his office, there were often only debts. The largest supplementary income to which a commissioner might aspire was that attached to the department responsible for Les Halles—the city's central market. While this position was said to be worth almost 10,000 livres a year in revenue, it imposed, according to Lenoir, even greater expense. Few other commissioners had incomes approaching this figure or, one assumes, comparable expenses. In 1763, thirty of the forty-eight commissioners charged by the lieutenant of police with either a department or with incidental additional duties received a total of 45,000 livres as remuneration for their labor and costs. While the average share of this sum would obviously have been 1,500 livres a man, actual income ranged from the 146 livres paid Commissioner Thiot to the 6,390 livres his colleague Chenon received. By 1780 this group of commissioners, those most active within the police administration, was getting 83,000 livres, or almost twice what they had received in 1763. One presumes that this sum was divided as unequally as had been the earlier one, in recognition of both unequal work and unequal favor.[89]

Other judicial personnel.—If the lieutenant of police would have found it impossible to perform his judicial duty without the aid of the commissioners, there were others as well who assisted him with this task. It is important here at least to mention them. There were the clerks employed by the commissioners, one at least and perhaps several, to each magistrate. There were, in addition, a variety of individuals associated with the police court itself and with the Châtelet: the crown's prosecutor at the Châtelet who cooperated closely with the lieutenant of police in the formulation of sentences and the control of the guilds; the clerks (there were eight) who served alternately in the civil and police chambers; a host of bailiffs (*huissiers*) upon whom the courts of the Châtelet and the commissioners relied for the delivery of their orders; a collector of fines (*receveur des amendes*) imposed in police court; and, finally, the two criers whose job it was to read and post at prominent intersections in the city those sentences which the lieutenant of police intended should serve as deterrents.[90]

89. *Ibid.*; BO, MS 1422, pp. 949, 970–71; MS 1424, p. 115; AN, 0-1 361, nos. 324–27.
90. For a description of these posts and their work, consult the appropriate articles in the *Encyclopédie méthodique: Jurisprudence* (10 vols.; Paris, 1782–1791); for justification of my decision to count forty-eight bailiffs as part of the police, see Lenoir to commissioners, December 15, 1781, in AN, Y 12830.

ADMINISTRATION AND COMMUNICATION

Administrative staff (commis des bureaux). — The lieutenants of police had always required the services of secretaries to receive, draft, and
dispatch their extensive correspondence. While the number of men
employed at this task may have grown during the latter part of the
seventeenth century and the early years of the eighteenth, such growth
could not have been dramatic; for, by 1730 there were still only eight
secretaries working for the head of the police. Undoubtedly the four of
them who were most active had already developed among themselves
lines demarcating separate responsibilities; but they continued nonetheless to constitute a single administrative division or "bureau,"
working under the supervision of one man, a first secretary (*premier
commis*) whose relationship with the lieutenant of police was particularly close. During much of the thirty years that separated René Hérault's administration from Sartine's, this first secretary seems to have
been a man named Chaban, who—during the course of his service—
built a considerable reputation for ability among those who knew
him.[91]

But toward the end of his career Chaban became an obstacle to the
reform of an overgrown and increasingly awkward secretariat. Only
after Chaban's retirement late in the 1760s did Sartine begin a major
reorganization of the administrative staff, adding new employees and
dividing the ungainly single secretariat into six physically separate
and independent divisions, each with a chief who reported directly to
the lieutenant of police.[92] Table 6 summarizes the responsibilities he
conferred on each of the new administrative sections, indicates its
initial size, and records subsequent growth for which Lenoir or Crosne
was responsible. The first six of the divisions listed on the chart are
essentially those created by Sartine. Division seven, the *bureau des
contentieux* (office of conflicting claims), had initially been a part of
division four; Lenoir made it a separate entity. Division eight was
Crosne's creation, the result of withdrawing from the secretariat two
responsibilities Sartine and Lenoir had left in its hands. As Map 9
shows, all of these administrative divisions except the Mont-de-Piété
had their offices in the northwestern sector of Paris, along with many

91. BA, MS 10006, fols. 846–89; BO, MS 1422, p. 961.
92. BO, MS 1422, p. 961.

Table 6 Structural Divisions of the Police Administrative Offices, 1789
(*les bureaux de police*)

| Office | Number of Employees | | | Responsibilities |
	1770	1785	1789	
1. Secretariat	3	4	4	State prisons. Book trade. Personnel. Asylums, nursing homes. Correspondence with other bureaux. Miscellaneous affairs.
2. Offices of Mr. Puissan	6	6	6	Provisonment. Lighting. Disposal of waste. Licensing. Fire department. Hospitals. Inspection of bldgs. Police prisoners. Reports from the guard. Fairs.
3. Offices of Mr. Chauve	3	5	5	*Maisons de force.* Royal orders of confinement (*lettres de cachet*).
4. Offices of Mr. Mascrey	8	8	7	The industrial and commercial corporations. Examination of their accounts, all matters concerning their regulations and revenues. The *capitation* levied against them.
5. Offices of Mr. Spire	3	4	5	Commerce and manufacture as activities. Prohibited textiles. Royal lottery. Banking. Religious affairs. Police payrolls—receipt of claims for reimbursement.
6. Offices of Mr. Garon	4	3	3	Criminal affairs (*sûreté*). Jews.
7. *Bureau des contenieux*	—	2	3	Civil affairs decided during *police contentieux* at Châtelet.
8. Offices of Mr. Barbaud	—	—	2	Funds for charity. Military affairs and the Parisian militia.
Totals	27	32	35	

SOURCES: *Almanach royal, 1770*, 556–57; *Almanach royal, 1785*, 424–26; *Almanach royal, 1789*, 423–25.

other agencies of government. It was this part of the city that power had chosen as its abode, leaving to wealth and style the southwest, to learning and youth the southeast, and to labor and poverty what was left, particularly the growing faubourgs on the eastern edge of the city.

There remained, despite the reconstruction, a first secretary, a *premier commis*; but Duval, the man who occupied this post, was without the overriding authority and power Chaban had possessed: [93] section heads like Puissan and Collot now had independent access to the lieutenant of police; and one member of the staff, a man named Marolles, shared more intimately in Sartine's affairs than the first secretary. Inspector Troussey tells us in a statement he drafted that Marolles was to Sartine what another individual named Royer was to Joly de Fleury, the *procureur général* of the Parlement, "that is to say, his most confidential agent."[94]

In forty years, the eight secretaries working for the police in 1730 had become an administrative staff of twenty-seven. By 1789 their number had grown to thirty-five; and if one adds those in administrative tasks at the *bureau des nourrices*, the total climbs to forty-nine. To appreciate these figures it is useful to note that in 1789 the intendant of Paris employed a staff of only six; and that following reform of the Department of Finance by both Necker and Loménie de Brienne, the newly consolidated royal treasury (the intendancy of the treasury), which J. F. Bosher has called "the largest and most expensive section of the Department of Finance," comprised in 1789 seven administrative divisions and forty-eight employees.[95] Whether one counts the administrative staff of the police as thirty-five or forty-nine, it is clear that, by eighteenth-century standards, it had become uncommonly large.

In hiring men to serve on this staff, Lenoir reports, the lieutenants of police searched for persons who had already had legal and financial training in the offices of a notary or a public prosecutor. Once employed by the police, administrative personnel tended to stay on and, as Lenoir put it, to grow old in their jobs. A number of them could

93. Under Marville and Berryer, Duval—while not perhaps Chaban's equal—had occupied a very prominent role in the police administration. (See BA, MS 10025, piece 11; MS 10026, pieces 9, 102; dossier of Louis Girard, in MS 11747.) After Sartine's reform, the term *premier commis* was applied not only to the first secretary, but to the heads of each administrative division as well.

94. Dossier of Inspector Troussey, in BA, MS 12436.

95. *Almanach royal*, 1789, 347; J. F. Bosher, *French Finances 1770–1795: From Business to Bureaucracy* (Cambridge [England], 1970), 218.

MAP 8

Map 8

HÔTELS OF THE LIEUTENANTS OF POLICE:
THE ADMINISTRATIVE HEADQUARTERS

1   Vieille Rue du Temple, 1724.

2   Rue de Clery, near the Rue Montorgueil, 1725.

3   Rue Neuve des Petits Champs in the Hôtel Mazarin, 1728–1731, 1740–1741.

4   Rue du Bouloir (Bouloy?)ₕ 1731–1737.

5   Rue Sainte-Avoie in the Hôtel de Beauvilliers, 1737–1740.

6   Rue de Jouy in the Hôtel d'Aumont, 1741–1744.

7   Rue Saint-Honoré in the Hôtel Noaille, 1744–1751.

8   Rue de l'Université, 1751–1757.

9   Rue Neuve Saint-Augustin in the Hôtel de Gramont, 1757–1780.

10 Rue Neuve des Capucins in the Hôtel de Police, 1780–1789.

SOURCES: *Almanach royal, 1718–Almanach royal, 1789.*

MAP 9

Map 9
THE ADMINISTRATIVE OFFICES OF THE POLICE
1771 AND 1789

1771

A *Bureau du cabinet*
B Offices of Mr. Puissan
C Offices of Mr. Rossignol
D Offices of Mr. Collot
E Offices of Mr. Collart de Tilleul
F *Bureau de sûreté*
G *Bureau des nourrices* [1]
H *Bureau des recommandaresses* [1]

1789

1   Secretariat
2   Offices of Mr. Puissan
3   Offices of Mr. Le Chauve
4   Offices of Mr. Mascrey
5   Offices of Mr. Spire
6   Offices of Mr. Garon
7   *Bureau des nourrices* [1]
8   *Bureau des recommandaresses* [1]
9   *Bureau des contentieux*
10 Offices of Mr. Barbaud
11 Mont de Piété
12 Dépôt de Filature

1. First appear in *Almanach royal* of 1777. In the text they are treated under services rather than under administration. (On the functions of the administrative offices of 1789 and their counterparts of 1771, see Table 6.)
SOURCES: *Almanach royal, 1771, 339; Almanach royal, 1789, 423–25.*

count thirty years of service: Rossignol, chief of one of Sartine's administrative sections in 1770, had worked for five lieutenants of police, beginning with Hérault in 1730; and Garon, an employee in the division of criminal investigation in 1770, was still there almost twenty years later, having become the division's chief. These terms of service are significant, for they suggest a source of continuity in policy and an evolution toward bureaucracy. New lieutenants of police, at least after 1730, did not often tamper with the administrative personnel they found already at work, men for whom service with the police had become a career. Instead, they relied on these individuals to teach them their job. The heads of the administrative divisions, Lenoir says, were the conservators and the guardians of the policies, the forms, and the usages of the police. Lengthy experience rendered them indispensable to a new lieutenant of police and made them far more than file clerks, copyists, or research assistants. No doubt they did such work, but they were also counsellors whose recommendations only a lieutenant of police with experience of his own would have readily contradicted or set aside.[96]

The relationship of this staff to those inspectors and commissioners who had charge of departments falling within their purview is unclear. We know that the three or four inspectors responsible for criminal investigation spent two hours every day in the administrative office charged with these matters, perhaps dictating letters, requesting research, and going over reports prepared for them.

That not all was cooperation is suggested by a letter Inspector Dehemery sent the lieutenant of police in 1764 and marked on the outside "for M. de Sartine only." Dehemery contends that, since the days when Berryer was head of the police, he had been asked to investigate and approve those applying for licenses as colporteurs and bill-posters (afficheurs). Now, he complains, one of the administrative staff, a man named Laurent (employed, following Sartine's reform, in division two —the section responsible for issuing licenses), has begun recommending individuals for licenses without consulting him. The results, the inspector claims, have been tragic. Laurent has done nothing but propose his friends, without giving the slightest regard to their pasts or their characters. One of those recently receiving a license had, accord-

96. BO, MS 1422, pp. 5, 892, 962, 985; BA, MS 10006, fols. 843–89; Almanach royal, 1770, 556–57; Almanach royal, 1789, 425, 429.

ing to Dehemery, previously been arrested six times by the police. The inspector concludes petulantly that he is not going to hide these facts from Sartine because he knows Laurent has not spared him in conversations with the lieutenant of police.[97]

Despite their unfortunate tone, Dehemery's accusations help explain why men who obtained administrative posts with the police held on to them. Their positions gave them the capacity to dispense favors and made them, in consequence, persons of some power, individuals to be taken seriously and cultivated by whatever means one had at one's disposal. While the salaries attached to administrative posts averaged about 4,100 livres a year, an early police archivist claims that actual income was on occasion ten times as much.[98] Despite stories of fine carriages and splendid homes, it is very hard to believe that any employee of the police, excepting the lieutenant himself, made 40,000 livres a year. Nonetheless, given the utility of their good will, it is possible—perhaps probable—that members of the administrative staff received, as supplement to their regular wages, significant gratuities and gifts.

Treasurers and bursars.—Between 1704 and 1729, eight men were responsible for the handling of police funds. War and its exigencies had (as happened in the case of the inspectors of police four years later) led Louis XIV to fill what may have been genuine administrative need with a superfluity of personnel. Instead of a single treasurer of police funds and a single controller, the king, in an edict of 1704, created four of each.

While this arrangement served the immediate needs of the royal purse, it was of little use to the police; and in happier times, the crown began to remedy its mistake by eliminating four of the eight financial offices it had sold. Further reductions followed, leaving but a single treasurer of police by the 1770s. In October, 1779, as part of an attempt to consolidate and simplify its cumbersome financial apparatus, the crown joined to this remaining office responsibility for a number of other funds that had previously been managed separately,

97. BN, MS fr. 22116, fol. 40.
98. BO, MS 1422, pp. 970–71. The first secretary in 1780 received 12,000 livres. The remaining thirty or thirty-one employees earned a total of 127,035 livres or approximately 4,100 livres apiece, though doubtless the sum was not divided evenly. Peuchet, *Mémoires*, I, 12–13.

Table 7 The Treasurer and the Bursar, 1780

DISBURSEMENTS BY TREASURER

Expense	Monthly	Quarterly	Yearly
1. Salary of lieutenant of police		x	
2. Salary of first secretary		x	
3. Pay (*gages*) of inspectors of police			x
4. Rent for Hôtel de Police		x	
5. Garbage collection and rental of dumps	x		
6. Lighting for the city and the road to Versailles	x		
7. Fire department		x	
8. Secret expenses (espionage)	x		

DISBURSEMENTS BY BURSAR

Expense	Monthly	Quarterly	Yearly
1. Salaries for administrative staff (*commis des bureaux*)	x		
2. Lighting for offices		x	
3. Salary (*traitements fixes*) of the commissioners		x	
4. Fees (*vacations*) of the inspectors of police		x	
5. Salaries for various supernumeraries		x	
6. Expenses for the militia of Paris	x		
7. Pensions to former employees	x		
8. Alms to individuals and relief to poor religious communities	x		
9. Miscellaneous expenses		x	
10. Unforeseen expenses (wood to provide heat for offices during part of June and September; removal of snow; additional vegetables for Lent; cleaning bridges)			x

SOURCE: BO, MS 1422, p. 971.

like that for operating the royal stud farms. With this augmentation of responsibility the treasurer of police became *trésorier général des dépenses diverses* (general treasurer for miscellaneous expenses). Nonetheless, amid his extended obligations, the treasurer of miscellaneous expenses continued to draw funds for operating the police from the royal treasury and continued, as well, to make disbursements of these sums only on written order from the lieutenant of police.[99]

It is perhaps appropriate that the title treasurer of police should have disappeared in 1779, for it masked the diminishing role its bearer played in handling and managing the funds of the police. During most of the eighteenth century, the lieutenants of police had employed and kept close at hand a bursar (*préposé*) to make the many small payments daily operation of the police required. Unlike the treasurer, installed in his own *hôtel* and secure in an office he owned, the bursar worked in whatever building served the lieutenant of police as headquarters and stood subject to immediate dismissal should his work prove unsatisfactory. This dependence and proximity made him, as the century progressed, the manager of increasingly large sums. By 1780 the bursar handled and disbursed almost half the funds appropriated for police use (615,212 livres out of a total of 1,400,486); what is more, as a result of a reform promoted by Lenoir and accepted by Necker, the sums he managed no longer had to pass first through the hands of the treasurer. After 1780 the portion of police funds for which he was responsible came to him directly from the royal treasury.[100]

PROFESSIONAL CONSULTANTS

Among those upon whose professional services the lieutenants of police drew from time to time, three seem to have worked closely and regularly enough with the police to be counted among them, the first of a growing number of such persons police departments would find themselves obliged not simply to consult but to hire. From the inception of his office the lieutenant of police had required the services of a printer: initially to prepare sentences he had handed down and intended to post; later, and increasingly as internal procedures became standard, to print the time-saving forms required by any bureaucracy.

99. Edict of May, 1729, in AN, AD-I 26, 117; letters patent, October 31, 1784, in AN, AD-IX 389. Rouillé de l'Estang bought this office in 1779 for the handsome sum of 400,000 livres.

100. BO, MS 1422, pp. 897, 970–71.

In addition to a printer, there were a police notary and a police architect. In 1775, the latter was a man named Egresset, who, among other duties, inspected and vouched for the safety of all structures raised to accommodate spectators at processions or celebrations; it was he, as well, who bore responsibility for examining structures reported hazardous by police inspectors and for indicating to the lieutenant of police repairs he found necessary.[101]

While not engaged with sufficient regularity to consider them employees or subordinates, it is important to mention the doctors (other than those associated with the *bureau des recommanderesses*) and druggists upon whom the police called from time to time for assistance. There were also interpreters and handwriting experts. In an undated letter to Malesherbes, Sartine provides information requested by the director of the booktrade: "Enclosed is the last letter you were kind enough to send me. I made suitable use of it. The experts I have consulted about the 'Mémoires de Bordeaux' are in agreement that Descourti wrote as much as a third of the manuscript of these mémoires. Give me the pleasure, Monsieur, of letting me know whether the opinion of these experts can be of use to you."[102]

Scientists, of course, were also useful, as a letter from Lenoir to Condorcet suggests. The lieutenant of police asks that the Academy of Sciences name someone to assess a claim by the Baron de Bormes to have discovered a process by which a deceptive imitation of gold can be produced.[103]

Finally, there was the use made of parish priests. Later we shall see how priests cooperated with police efforts to control the quality of wetnurses brought into the city and to guarantee the care of deported infants. Here we may note simply that a number of letters addressed to the lieutenant of police from Parisian parish clergy and dated May, 1739, suggest that priests were also enlisted to assist in periodic crackdowns on beggars. The priests were apparently replying to a recent letter from Hérault in which he had asked them to report any indigent provincials they had noticed in their parishes.[104]

101. Printed forms appear in police papers after 1760 (see AN, Y 12830 for examples); BO, MS 1422, p. 985; Joseph d'Albert to Egresset, June 10, 1775, in AN, Y 13728.

102. A document headed "taxe des témoins," and dated 1764, in AN, Y 13728; BN, MS fr. n.a. 3348, fol. 280.

103. BHVP, MS n.a. 481, fol. 188.

104. BA, MS 10321, *passim*.

Space: The Quarters of Paris

While functional distinctions were increasingly important to the organization of the police during the eighteenth century, structure and the delegation of authority also depended inevitably on delimiting responsibility in spatial terms. Elements of the foot patrol walked specified districts surrounding their posts, and garbage collectors traversed each day only those streets of which they had charge. The perimeters bounding such areas were often temporary and subject to change; far from competing with or obstructing the demarcation of authority in functional terms, they served the process and made it practicable in a city the size of Paris. But of the most important divisions of the city, the quarters, or police sectors, the same could not always be said.

These quarters, as they existed during the eighteenth century, were essentially the work of Marc-René d'Argenson, the second lieutenant of police. Finding, in 1702, that the recent growth of Paris had made older circumscriptions of responsibility unreasonable, d'Argenson divided the city into twenty sectors and assigned responsibility for each to several of those who were at the time his principal agents, the commissioners of the Châtelet.[105] Each of the two or three commissioners in a quarter had particular charge of a smaller district known as a department. His authority in this district and his duties were extensive, covering almost the entire range of police activity. The commissioner was at once judge, inspector, fire chief, patrolman, and investigator. In 1702 it was necessary that he fill each of these roles, for there was, as yet, no one else to do so. But as subsequent lieutenants of police augmented their force, adding elements whose work was defined largely in functional terms (investigators in 1708, a fire department in 1716, inspectors of public works and buildings about 1750), the once universal authority of the commissioners within their bailiwicks was increasingly infringed and diminished. This process pushed the commissioners into specialization of their own, into the role of judges and into accepting the particular administrative responsibilities delegated some of them by the lieutenant of police.

But many commissioners did not welcome these changes and sought

---

105. Decree of the Conseil d'État, February 14, 1702, in Delamare, *Traité de la police*, I, 110–12.

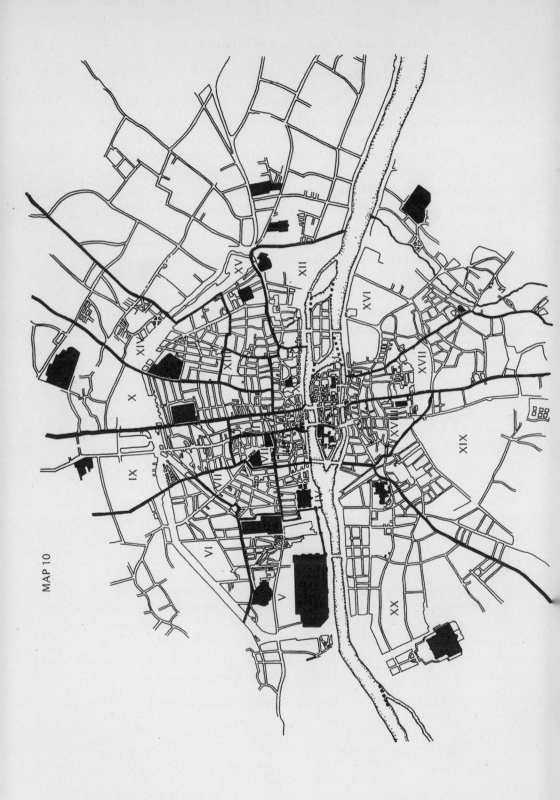

MAP 10

Map 10
THE QUARTERS OF PARIS, 1702–1763

I	Cité	XI	La Grève
II	Saint-Jacques-de-la-Boucherie	XII	Saint-Paul
III	Sainte-Opportune	XIII	Sainte-Avoie
IV	Louvre	XIV	Temple
V	Palais-Royal	XV	Saint-Antoine
VI	Montmartre	XVI	Place Maubert
VII	Saint-Eustache	XVII	Saint-Benoît
VIII	Les Halles	XVIII	Saint-André-des-Arts
IX	Saint-Denis	XIX	Luxembourg
X	Saint-Martin	XX	Saint-Germain-des-Prés

SOURCES: Lacaille, *Description de la ville.*

MAP 11

Map 11
THE CHARACTER OF THE QUARTERS, 1763

MARKETS

A Market d'Aguesseau
B Market de Bussi
C Marché aux Chevaux
D Market of the Cemetery of Saint-Jean
E Les Halles
F Marché-Neuf
G Market of the Patriarchs
H Marché au Pain, courtyard of the Saint-Germain fairgrounds
I Market of the Place Maubert
J Market of the Place Saint-Michel
K Market of Saint-Nicolas-des-Champs or of Saint-Martin
L Market of the Quinze-Vingts
M Petit Marché du Temple
N Market of the Temple
O Market of Saint-Paul
P Market of the Porte de Paris

PRIVILEGED ENCLAVES AND DISTINCT JURISDICTIONS

1 Abbey of Saint-Germain-des-Prés
2 Bailliage of the Palais
3 Jurisdiction of the chapter of Notre Dame and the Grand Chantre
4 Jurisdiction (temporalité) of the Archbishop
5 Fief of the Archbishop, known as La Grand Bastelier
6 Bailliage of Saint-Martin-des-Champs
7 Bailliage of the Temple
8 Bailliage of the Arsenal
9 Bailliage of the Sainte-Geneviève
10 Bailliage of Saint-Jean-de-Latran
11 Louvre and Tuileries (Prévôt de l'Hôtel)
12 Luxembourg (Count of Provence)
13 Palais-Royal (Duke d'Orléans)

GARDENS

I of the Arsenal
II of the Infante
III of the Luxembourg Palace
IV of the Palais-Royal
V of the King
VI of the Hôtel Soubise
VII of the Temple
VIII of the Terrain
IX of the Tuileries

THEATERS

□ Opera
■ Comédie-Française
● Comédie-Italienne
➤ Toll gates of the Farms

SOURCES: Lacaille, *Description de la ville;* Deharme, "Plan de Paris."

to preserve a definition of their authority that left them unencumbered in their districts. From their perspective, the quarters and their subdivisions were not an integral and necessary concomitant to functional specialization, but an alternative to it. The persistence of this basically spatial sense of authority is suggested by a letter Lenoir wrote the commissioners on January 19, 1780.[106] He sees with regret, he says, that a number of the commissioners are neglecting the particular duties he has assigned them in previous correspondence, while others presume in their districts to treat matters over which they have no authority. Nine years before the Revolution, the lieutenants of police were still trying to impose a new conception of authority on the oldest element of their force.

Despite the claims to which they led on the part of the commissioners, d'Argenson's quarters remained, throughout the century, essential to the structure of the police. When investigators were added to the force, they were assigned to a quarter and expected to handle all matters of whatever kind arising in that district. Even after 1740 when they had begun to specialize—a few, for example, handling cases of theft while another kept watch over foreigners in the city—they remained attached to their quarters and continued to perform common tasks within them. Every inspector of police, regardless of special assignment, examined the registers of hotels and guest houses in his district; and every inspector was responsible for looking into the ordinary private complaints one neighbor in his district might make against another.

The division of the city into quarters also provided one of the bases on which inspectors of public works divided their duties, there being one team of inspectors responsible for each of five clusters of quarters. The guard, too, after capturing an individual in the midst of an offense, sought first to carry him before the commissioner in whose department the arrest had been made. Finally, it was through the quarters that the police sought to consult the community or recruit its aid. The lieutenants of police kept lists of the eminent persons in each sector of the city and, when occasion required, ordered the senior commissioner in each quarter to assemble them for consultation or help.[107]

The character of a quarter affected considerably the tasks performed

106. Lenoir to commissioners, January 19, 1780, in AN, Y 12830.
107. For three such lists compiled for Feydeau de Marville in 1744, see BA, MS 10322. On these lists, the names of notaries, attorneys, and merchants figure most prominently.

by both the commissioners and the inspector assigned to it. Major
investments of time depended invariably on the number of bakers'
and butchers' shops, since these had to be closely watched; on the
presence of public gardens—gathering places for prostitutes and pimps;
on whether a quarter contained privileged enclosures like the Temple,
the abbey of Saint-Germain-des-Prés, the *hôtel* of an important noble,
or the Palais—sanctuaries from which habitual offenders of one kind
or another might harass a district; on the number of streets in an area,
and on the size and character of its population.

Linked to the quarters as well were a number of the particular responsibilities the lieutenant of police delegated to both inspectors and
commissioners. Lemaire tells us that, insofar as possible, special assignments were coordinated with territorial responsibilities, so that,
for example, charge of the Opera would, throughout much of the eighteenth century, have gone to a commissioner in the quarter of the
Palais-Royal and responsibility for the Mont de Piété to one of the two
commissioners in the quarter of Sainte-Avoie.

Assigned to a particular quarter, a commissioner at times had difficulty residing there; six of the forty-five commissioners holding office
in 1718 lived outside their districts; and in 1789, there were still five
among forty-eight unable to find housing in their quarters. During the
last years of the Old Regime, Lenoir and Crosne recognized the need to
eliminate this difficulty and guarantee both appropriate residence and
office space to their agents; but by the time the Bastille fell, they had
managed to establish permanent headquarters for only two commissioners, one in the quarter of Les Halles, the other in Sainte-Avoie.[108]

While some commissioners were finding the quarters with which
they were charged too far from them, others were discovering that their
districts were too large. Paris had not ceased to grow and to change
after 1702; and by the middle of the century, d'Argenson's police sectors required alteration. The need was particularly apparent in the
quarters of Saint-Martin, Montmartre, and the Palais Royal, where
appended faubourgs had grown considerably. In 1762 or 1763, Sartine
ordered that the boundaries of these districts be redrawn in order to
reduce their extent.[109]

108. BO, MS 1424, pp. 55, 115.
109. Cf. Lacaille, *Description de Paris*, unpaginated, with Deharme's map (1763) in
Alphand (ed.), *Atlas des anciens plans*; and see BN, MS fr. 22153, fols. 75–82, a draft
decree which complains about the imbalance in the size of the quarters d'Argenson had
established.

MAP 12

Map 12
THE COMMISSIONERS, 1718

ASSIGNED SECTORS AND RESIDENCE

1 Socquart (II)	10 De Soucy (III)	19 Thomin (XVI)	28 Nicolet (XIX)	37 Thienot (V)
2 Mazure (XII)	11 Bizotton (XX)	20 Tourton (IV)	29 Hubert (X)	38 Regnard le jeune (VII)
3 Le Maistre (VIII)	12 Du Bois (XVIII)	21 Camuset (XI)	30 Le Comte (XIX)	39 Petit (XIV)
4 Delamare (I)	13 Menyer (XIX)	22 Langlois (II)	31 Aubert (IV)	40 Laurent (VIII)
5 Gallyot (XIV)	14 Duplessis (VIII)	23 Borthon (XVII)	32 Regnard (XVII)	41 Parisot (XIII)
6 Labbé (XV)	15 Duchesne (I)	24 Cailly (XIII)	33 Desacq (IX)	42 Blanchard (?)
7 Marrier (VII)	16 Daminois (V)	25 Poget (III)	34 Fremin (XVI)	43 Regnard de Lessain (?)
8 De la Jarrie (XV)	17 De la Vergée (V)	26 Demoncrif (X)	35 Ysabeau (I)	44 De Launay (XX)
9 Duchesne (XI)	18 Chaud (XVIII)	27 Deslandes (VI)	36 Guerin (IX)	45 Croizet (XVIII)

UNDERSTAFFED QUARTERS

QUARTER	COMMISSIONERS ASSIGNED	COMMISSIONERS IN RESIDENCE
II	2	0
IV	2	1
VII	2	1
XIV	2	1
XX	2	1

SOURCE: *Almanach royal, 1718*, 192–95.

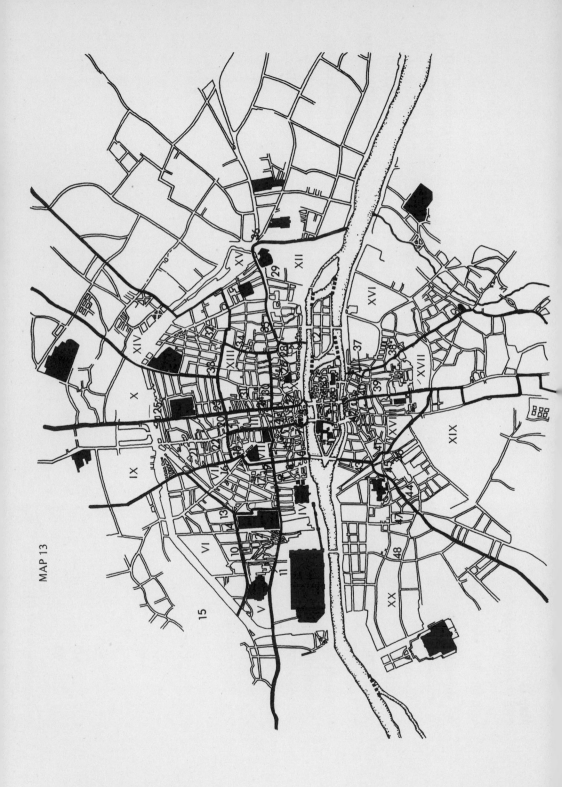

MAP 13

Map 13
THE COMMISSIONERS, 1789

ASSIGNED SECTORS AND RESIDENCE

1 Mouricault (I)
2 Chénon (I)
3 Chenu (I)
4 Sirebeau (II)
5 Thiot (II)
6 Dorival (III)
7 Guyot (III)
8 Fontaine (IV)
9 Leger (IV)
10 Serreau (V)
11 Convers-Desormeaux (V)

12 Ferrand (V)
13 De la Porte (VI)
14 Joron (VI)
15 Michel (VI)
16 Le Rat (VII)
17 Simonneau (VII)
18 Vanglenne (VIII)
19 Landelle (VIII)
20 Chénon, fils (IX)
21 Thibert (IX)
22 Le Seigneur (IX)
23 Dupuy (X)

24 Carre (X)
25 Odent (X)
26 Fourcart (XI)
27 Le Blond (XI)
28 Pierre (XII)
29 Baudet du Larry (XII)
30 Duchauffour (XIII)
31 Alix (XIII)
32 Prestat (XIV)
33 Berton (XIV)

34 Grandin (XV)
35 Gueulette (XV)
36 Boin (XV)
37 Lucote du Champe-mont (XVI)
38 Grutter des Rosiers (XVI)
39 Dubois (XVII)
40 Dassonvillez (XVII)
41 Danzel (XVIII)
42 Le Roux (XVIII)
43 Defresne (XIX)

44 Duchesne (XIX)
45 Le Bas (XIX)
46 Hiltebrandt de Villiers (XX)
47 Picard-Desmarets (XX)
48 Beauvallet (XX)

UNDERSTAFFED QUARTERS

QUARTER	COMMISSIONERS ASSIGNED	COMMISSIONERS IN RESIDENCE
VIII	2	1
X	3	2
XII	2	1
XIX	3	2
XX	3	2

SOURCE: *Almanach royal, 1789*, 394–96.

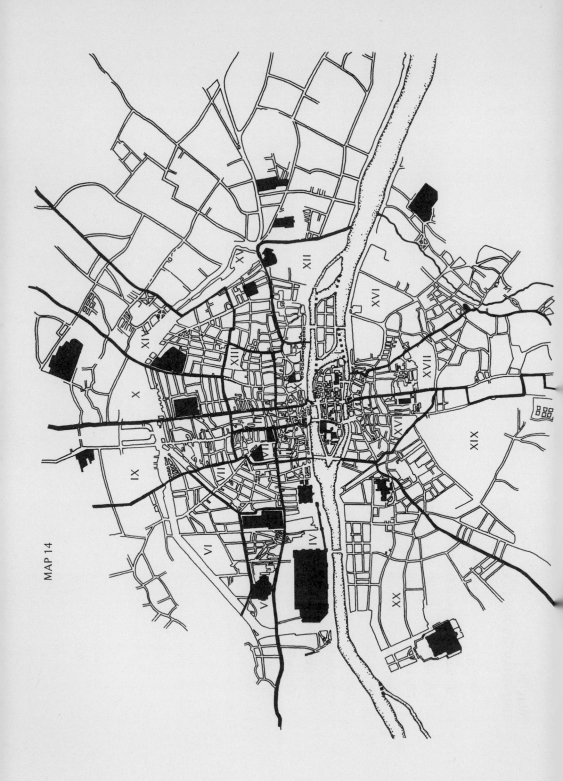

MAP 14

Map 14
THE QUARTERS OF PARIS, 1763–1789

I	Cité	XI	La Grève
II	Saint-Jacques-de-la-Boucherie	XII	Saint-Paul
III	Sainte-Opportune	XIII	Sainte-Avoie
IV	Louvre	XIV	Temple
V	Palais-Royal	XV	Saint-Antoine
VI	Montmartre	XVI	Place Maubert
VII	Saint-Eustache	XVII	Saint-Benoît
VIII	Les Halles	XVIII	Saint-André-des-Arts
IX	Saint-Denis	XIX	Luxembourg
X	Saint-Martin	XX	Saint-Germain-des-Prés

SOURCE: Deharme, "Plan de Paris."

Other lieutenants of police sought to adapt their force to changes in population without altering the perimeters of the quarters. Instead they chose to reassign commissioners, moving them to the areas in which they were most needed. In this way the quarter of Montmartre, which had but one commissioner in 1719, acquired two more by 1789, and the districts of Saint-Antoine and Saint-Germain-des-Prés, which each began the century with two commissioners, finished it with three. The new officers in these sectors came from Les Halles and Saint-André-des-Arts, which, during the same period, both lost one of the commissioners originally assigned to them.

Whatever the difficulties associated with them, whatever the need to modify and adapt them, the quarters remained essential to the delegation of authority within the police. In 1778, Lenoir acted to enhance their utility by encouraging coordination rather than isolation and rivalry among the agents working in each of them. A letter to the senior commissioner in each quarter dated March 20 ordered him to see that the inspector and the other commissioners in his district begin meeting regularly once a month. No problem was to fall beyond the scope of these gatherings, but Lenoir urged those present to concentrate particularly on devising ways in which they might concert their labor. The "good of the force" (le bien du service) demanded such an effort; and, to be sure it was undertaken, the lieutenant of police wanted careful monthly reports. The initial results of the newly instituted gatherings seem to have pleased Lenoir, for two months later we find him congratulating all those involved on the utility and wisdom of the suggestions that had emerged from their meetings.[110]

During the seventy-four years that separate the death of Louis XIV from the collapse of the Old Regime, one notes two principal changes in the Parisian police: growth and an increasing internal specialization. For these developments, which must have made the police a more effective instrument, no single lieutenant of police was wholly responsible: Marc-Pierre d'Argenson dramatically expanded a fire department his father had helped found; Charles de Machault and Taschereau de Baudry oversaw the addition of two new companies to the guard; René Hérault established crude facilities for regulating the deportation of infants; Marville purged the force of incompetent investigators, while Berryer, his successor, encouraged those who remained to concentrate

110. Lenoir to commissioners, March 20, 1778, in AN, Y 13728; Lenoir to commissioners, May 26, 1778, in AN, Y 12830.

their attention and talents on a single concern; Lenoir enlarged both
the size of the police force and the scope of its activity by establishing
a major institution of credit, a workhouse for women, and a small corps
of men to keep watch over the hundreds of horses that, like those they
served, lived and worked in Paris.

But of the eleven men who occupied the lieutenancy of police between 1718 and 1789, Antoine de Sartine, more than any other, refash-
ioned the force Louis XIV, La Reynie, and d'Argenson had bequeathed
to the eighteenth century. He alone dared redraw the police sectors
d'Argenson had traced in 1702, and it was he who expanded the administrative staff and gave specialization within it a definite and durable form. Sartine continued Berryer's effort to provide investigators
with particular responsibilities and enlarged the small staff his predecessors had established to inspect public works and buildings; during
his tenure the direction of the booktrade and of censorship came under
the authority of the police, the fire department doubled in size, and
Hérault's facilities for wetnurses acquired both new locations and
larger, more specialized staffs. Though his work has not attracted as
much attention as that of the seventeenth-century lieutenants of police La Reynie and Marc-René d'Argenson, Sartine must certainly be
counted as one of the principal architects of a police force which served
as model to much of modern Europe.

EXACTING OBEDIENCE

Not all three thousand men who served the lieutenant of police wore
chains of the same cast or weight. Like France itself under the Old
Regime, the Parisian police was a collection of still distinct entities,
whose ties to a common superior were far from uniform in kind or
strength. Appreciating this variety in the form of subordination is as
essential to understanding the power of the lieutenant of police as the
effort to number his agents.

Kinds of Control

The police force of the eighteenth century was partly a new creation
and partly a rearrangement, a coalescence, of older institutions. Individuals and groups constituting it fell into two groups: those who,
while formally subordinate to the lieutenant of police, were largely free
from the threat of direct sanction; and those whose formal subjection
was reinforced by their vulnerability to punishment and their depen-

dence on discretionary reward. Comprised within the first group were primarily those elements of the police whose existence predated that of the lieutenancy itself, groups which retained ancient privileges and which stubbornly resisted their infringement. The watch (until 1771), the clerks, criers, and bailiffs at the Châtelet, the syndics of the corporations, the men who served in the company of the *robe courte*, and, to some extent, the commissioners themselves—all belong in this category. In the second group, one finds those whose posts were created subsequent to 1667 as intentional additions to a nascent police force: the investigators, the inspectors of buildings and public works, the administrative staff, members of the fire department and the guard, those managing the Mont de Piété, and some of those who worked in the *bureau des recommendaresses* and the *direction des nourrices*. If we assume that the authority of the lieutenant of police was greater in those cases where it was accompanied by the power to sanction, we have still to ask what forms sanction took and what effect it had.

Control of other men invariably involves, in one form or another, the power to punish or the capacity to reward. Both means lay at the disposal of the lieutenant of police, but not always to the same extent. His ability to punish or intimidate was more limited in some cases than in others. While he could exercise the severe sanction of dismissal against elements of the guard and fire department, against members of his administrative staff, guardians of commerce, and inspectors of public works, the commissioners and inspectors of police were immune to such action. As owners of their offices, they could be removed only by judicial action. In gaining compliance from these important elements of his force, a lieutenant of police had to rely less on intimidation than inducement and his capacity to reward. Because he determined the sectors in which commissioners and inspectors worked, the nature of any assignment they might be given, and the wage they earned, tools to encourage their obedience were at his disposal. In the case of the commissioners there was added leverage, for all forty-eight of these men hoped eventually to become chief commissioner in their quarter; and it was again the lieutenant of police who controlled access to these posts and to the precedence, prestige, and honorarium they conferred.[111]

111. BO, MS 1424, p. 115; Commissioner Aubert or Hubert to Hérault, February 6, 1730, in BA, MS 10006. In 1777, the honorarium senior commissioners received amounted to about 250 livres apiece (Lenoir to the commissioners, January 22, 1777, in AN, Y 13728).

As a judge and as a powerful administrator with almost discretionary access to royal orders of confinement, the lieutenant of police was equipped to do more than fire those whose work greatly displeased him. Lenoir assures us that he did not hesitate to obtain the administrative confinement of subinspectors and spies guilty of serious disobedience or abuse; and, as judge in his own court, the head of the police could order the fining or imprisonment of garbage collectors and lamplighters who were grossly negligent. In 1750 we find an inspector of police urging one of Lenoir's predecessors to use his power to punish sparingly. Inspector Poussot asks Berryer to be lenient with two subinspectors whose credulity had led them to make an unauthorized arrest. To be sure the two men had "captured" not a woman who had been whipped and banned from the city but the wife of a now rather angry municipal employee; still, the mistake was a mark of the men's enthusiasm and was, after all, less their fault than that of the informer who had misled them. Poussot knows his subordinates must pay for their indiscretion, but he expresses the hope that Berryer will order no more than three or four days of confinement.[112]

If the lieutenant of police had the power to punish some of those who served him poorly, it was less this capacity than his ability to reward that proved the most versatile tool for fashioning loyal subordinates. Its utility reached beyond commissioners and inspectors to the fringes of the force. Based in part on control of the sums allocated for police activity, it brought the lieutenant of police not only the service of his own spies but more ready compliance from detachments of the *maréchaussée*, the watch, and the guard. Officers and agents in these units who did their work well might count on receiving special assignments from the head of the police, tasks like patrolling a fair that brought both a break in routine and additional income. And there were other favors the lieutenant of police could grant those who obeyed his orders or heeded his requests. When, for example, two soldiers in the Gardes Françaises agreed to furnish him with information he sought, Berryer reciprocated by giving one of the friends an order for the release of his imprisoned mistress. Limited though it may have been, this power to shape the course and content of lives no doubt on occasion permitted the lieutenant of police to purchase forms of loyalty and service that currency could not buy.[113]

112. BO, MS 1424, p. 118; BA, MS 10134, fols. 303–304.
113. AN, 0-1 361, nos. 324–44; BA, MS 10134, fol. 494.

Supervision

The powers of sanction and reward depend for their efficacy on proper application. Firing the inept and commending the able both require accurate information about the work of subordinates, and this information depends in turn on the quality and extent of an employer's supervision. What means did the lieutenant of police possess for overseeing and judging the labor of three thousand men?

Obviously, he relied on the heads of branches to inform him. After 1750 in any case, and probably before, the lieutenant of police met weekly with the lieutenant criminal, the head of the guard, and the commander of the *maréchaussée* to hear their reports and to discuss matters affecting public order. We have seen that, beginning in 1778, Lenoir demanded monthly reports from the senior commissioners in each quarter. No doubt these reports, treating district meetings attended by commissioners and inspectors, helped him gauge the worth of the men involved, as did his own weekly meetings with all commissioners and inspectors who had charge of a department. With those in the criminal division he conferred daily; and the work of his administrative staff was still more familiar to him; for, though it seems almost incredible, almost every official act of this staff, down to the granting of a passport or the issuance of a cab license, required his signature.[114]

Lieutenants of police did not depend simply on heads of sections or their own observations to keep them informed about subordinates. They tried also, where it was possible, to encourage the different elements of the force to keep watch over one another. In a letter to the commissioners dated January 8, 1766, Sartine writes, "I enclose a copy of the instructions I have sent the inspectors concerning the procedure they are to follow in investigating complaints I turn over to them. I have reason to believe they are not always respecting this procedure and ask you to be sure the reports they submit to you conform with it." Another letter to the commissioners enjoins them to see that any member of the guard reporting to them upon summons or with a prisoner be given a form indicating the time of his appearance and the

114. BO, MS 1422, pp. 392, 966–67. Most officials of the Old Regime labored against an extraordinary incapacity and unwillingness to delegate authority. The police were not unique in this regard. Lenoir tells us that it was not until the 1760s, under Choiseul, that the minister of war began permitting principal subordinates to sign his name. Other ministers regarded the innovation as a dangerous threat to their authority and refused to experiment with it.

moment he was dismissed. Without such forms, Sartine says, the officers of the guard have considerable difficulty keeping their men from taking extensive unauthorized breaks. After 1772, inspectors of public works kept watch over the labor of garbage collectors and lamplighters, while throughout the century secretaries and office staff had helped the lieutenant of police keep track of the commissioners, and the commissioners themselves had supervised the syndics of the corporations.[115]

Finally, as part of their attempt to oversee the labor of three thousand men, the lieutenants of police employed a number of clandestine "observers," most of whom were assigned to watch brigades of the guard. In 1762, for instance, observers received one livre a day to see that patrols kept to the routes and schedules they had been assigned. Lenoir reports that the lieutenants of police made every effort to persuade other employees that they, too, were being watched. One commissioner named Holland may have been inclined to give credence to these rumors when he received the following letter from Sartine: "It has come to my attention, Monsieur, that you have received the sum of 15 livres from several of the hat salesmen who display under the arch of the Petit Châtelet. You undoubtedly believe yourself authorized to collect this fee, but I would like to know by what right you thought you were due such a sum. I ask you to send me the money." There are similar letters to other agents, all of which taken together suggest that the lieutenants of police did more than give orders and forget them, that, in one way or another, they were monitoring the work of their subordinates and, hence, were generally able to reward and punish appropriately.[116]

Obstacles to Control

MULTIPLE SUBORDINATION

A number of those who served the lieutenant of police had other superiors as well. The commissioners, for example, took orders from all three lieutenants at the Châtelet, and one is led to ask how much their multiple subordination curtailed the power of the lieutenant of police. In this case, the response seems clear. Though they might complain

115. Sartine to commissioners, November 21, 1772, in AN, Y 13728.
116. AN, 0-1 360, no. 272; Mildmay, *Police of France,* 58; BO, MS 1422, pp. 97–98; Sartine to Rolland, November 30, 1765, in AN, Y 12830; Hérault to Inspector Roussel, February 26, 1735, in BA, MS 10031; Lenoir to the corps of inspectors, dated simply 1782, in AN, Y 12830.

from time to time about the attention commissioners were giving civil affairs, the lieutenants of police both demanded and got the vast majority of the time and energy these men had to give.[117]

In general the formal right of others to command men subordinate to the lieutenant of police seems to have gone unused and, except in moments of political crisis, largely unnoticed. No one had seriously questioned the lieutenant of police's authority over the watch and guard of Paris until 1770, when the Parlement, in the midst of conflict with the crown, began to reassert old claims on these units. The immediate cause of renewed interest on the part of the Parlement was a tragedy the guard had failed to prevent in the Place Louis XV. Here, on the night of May 30, 1770, as Paris celebrated the marriage of the dauphin to the Austrian princess Marie-Antoinette, two enormous crowds met—one entering and one leaving the Place by way of the Rue Royale. The press that ensued produced panic among those who were being forced together from two sides. With no place to go but into a pit opened by construction workers, more than a hundred people were either crushed or fell to their deaths; more than a thousand were injured.

Eager to prevent any recurrence of such a disaster, the Parlement initiated an investigation wherein it examined the conduct of a number of individuals and agencies, including the guard. But as its enquiry proceeded, the concern of the Parlement, its memoranda make clear, moved beyond the work of the guard on a single evening to a more basic issue, the issue of who controlled this body of uniformed men. Together watch and guard constituted a force of nearly one thousand men, armed and already ensconced in Paris. Command of this force became a matter of increasing importance as the chasm between crown and Parlement deepened.

Dispute between the two sides took the form of an apparently innocent disagreement over the words "watch" (guet) and "guard" (garde), both of which were loosely applied to the units patrolling Paris. The Parlement claimed that the term guard ought really to be forgotten. Paris, it contended, possessed only a watch despite the crown's lamentable effort to create a distinct force "known since only recently by the special name, guard of Paris." The new company, it pointed out, had no flag of its own; and how, it asked rhetorically, could any company

117. See the papers of Commissioner Tourton (AN, Y 12224) or those of Commissioners Gillet and Coquelin (AN, Y 13728).

without a flag be bold enough to claim independent existence. Clearly, the so-called guard was nothing more than an appendage to the properly accoutered watch.[118]

The significance of the argument was, of course, that officers of the watch were proprietors of their positions and, as officials of the Châtelet, constituted part of a judicial establishment that was both willing and obliged to obey orders issued by the sovereign court.

Unfortunately for the Parlement, previous royal policy had by 1770 robbed its argument of whatever force it might once have had. Beginning in the seventeenth century, as has been noted, the crown had gradually created three companies of men who, far from being owners of their positions or officials of a court, depended solely on it for their wage. By 1770 these units, which the crown chose to call the guard, were together ten times the size of the watch. If one appellation—with all its connotations of appropriate subordination—had to suffice for both groups, "watch" no longer appeared the sensible alternative.

While constructing a far more numerous force, whose allegiance was not problematic, the crown had proceeded simultaneously to emasculate the watch, depriving it of both leadership and significant function. When the *chevalier du guet*, Chopin, died in 1733, the crown did not name a new man to fill the post but instead returned the 120,000 livres paid for the office to Chopin's family and appointed—on revocable commission—a commander of the guard whom it made simultaneously inspector of the watch. Without a leader the watch degenerated. Partly as a result of its decay and partly perhaps to encourage it, the crown barred the company from its ancient duty of patrol, ordering it instead to occupy itself permanently with guard duty in the courtyard of the Châtelet. In 1765, a humiliated and weakened watch offered no resistance when the government ordered the commandant of the guard, Louis Le Roy de Rocquemont, to assume the title *chevalier du guet* and to take command—still as a removable commissioner, not an office owner—of the leaderless company.[119]

Five years later, by which time it was too late, the Parlement grasped the impact of these changes. "Not being able to attack this sovereign court directly . . . , all possible methods have been successfully employed to give to this company [the watch] only a shadow of existence

118. BN, MS JF 450, fols. 142–43.
119. Decree of the Conseil d'État, March 31, 1733, in APP, DB 356; royal declaration, July 12, 1765, in APP, DB 356.

and to mutilate it to the point that it can never again completely re-establish itself." [120] The reforms of the government, aimed at strengthening the guard and weakening the watch, had been nothing but a clever way of removing from the control of Parlement "that which forms the most essential part of the Parisian police."

In an effort to undo this situation and to refashion its authority over armed force in the city, the Parlement seized upon the accident in the Place Louis XV to discredit the guard and resurrect the useful fiction of a single entity, subordinate to the city's sovereign court. Summoning Rocquemont before it, the court asked the *chevalier du guet* "whether, given the title he bears and that of so-called commandant of the so-called Guard of Paris, which is nothing more than the Watch, he recognizes himself as subordinate to the court." Rocquemont found it expedient to reply affirmatively, but within weeks Sartine had found a way of blunting the Parlement's assault on his control over the guard. Rather than permit this body to determine the nature and terms of the reform for which it clamored, he drafted his own edict for proclamation by the crown. While it granted some changes and catered to the Parlement's distaste for the word "guard," Sartine's edict maintained the semantic distinction which the judges, if they were to reassert themselves, felt they had to obliterate. "[W]ithout mentioning the Guard of Paris, it [the edict] refers to and recognizes the Watch so as not to confound it [with the Guard] and confirms the declaration of 1765 in which the Guard of Paris is recognized." [121]

If the case of the guard is representative, the formal right of others to appropriate their subordinates did not seriously infringe on the power of the lieutenants of police. Fitfully exercised, these competing claims —even when advanced by a body as significant as the Parlement of Paris—proved difficult to realize. Those who challenged the lieutenant of police for the loyalty of his agents seem generally to have lacked not only his practice in command but equivalent support from the king and a similar arsenal of sanctions.

PROTECTION

The principal obstacle a lieutenant of police encountered in the exercise of his authority was not the legal obligation some subordinates had toward other officials, but rather the informal ties linking them to

120. BN, MS JF 450, fol. 142.
121. AN, 0-1 360, no. 194.

patrons or "protectors." Though the head of the police possessed a number of means by which to exact obedience, his actual use of these tools was at times circumscribed by the powerful protection some police agents enjoyed. The case of Inspector Dehemery provides us with a glimpse of the limitations on the power of a lieutenant of police and with a sense for the indirection that he found necessary in proceeding against the protégés of others.

Though Sartine had apparently grown disillusioned with Dehemery's work by 1764 and wished to dispense with him, he could not proceed straightforwardly as might a superior today. Instead, he had first to undermine the support Dehemery could expect from his protectors, a maneuver that naturally provoked indignation and protest from the inspector:

> M. de Sartine has been complaining to several persons who do me the honor of protecting me that I have given him no information regarding the printing and display of the Archbishop's pastoral . . . . In the end, it seems that this magistrate seeks not only to humiliate and hurt me, but to defame me before my protectors, for I am certain that he has already convinced some of the most respected among them—whose kindnesses are especially dear to me—that I am a man not to be trusted . . . . It is very sad and very disagreeable for me, a man who has served 24 years with, I dare to say it, an honor and distinction that is not common among the police and who has enjoyed during 21 years the complete confidence of his superiors, to see myself persecuted and exposed every day to such disagreeable rumors.[122]

The extent to which the lieutenants of police were able to control their agents depended not merely on the formal right to issue orders, nor on their capacity for supervision and their powers of sanction, but also on the informal connections of the subordinate, on whether he was part of one of the Old Regime's numerous systems of protection and hence shielded by powerful figures.

At many points during the eighteenth century the lines of authority emanating from heads of administrative organization met lines joining a protégé to his protector. The same man might be simultaneously protégé to a duke or president of the Parlement and an administrative subordinate of the lieutenant of police. The last two men to head the police, Lenoir and Crosne, seem to have struggled against this situation, seeking to establish the primacy of administrative ties. They appealed often to abstractions like "public well-being," "the good of the

122. BN, MS fr. 22097, fol. 515–16.

force," and even a "humanitarian sentiment" in their attempts to build a sense of duty that had no single individual as its object.[123]

Earlier lieutenants of police had contented themselves, when they were able, with purging those whom they could not control. If Hérault unwittingly retained an agent named Beauchamps whom he had hired in 1737 at the behest of Count d'Argenson "without perceiving that Beauchamps was an agent meant to spy on him, a man who had taken this position only in order to have a title and be well-placed to serve Monsieur d'Argenson,"[124] other lieutenants of police proved considerably more suspicious. In 1773 Sartine managed to rid himself of an inspector of police named Troussey whom he believed to be a protégé of his political foe, Joly de Fleury.

At 2:00 A.M. on the morning of August 5, one of Sartine's agents, bearing royal orders of confinement, had arrested Troussey and conducted him to the Bastille. From his quarters in this prison of state, the inspector wrote Sartine often, trying in each letter to name and confute the real motive behind his incarceration, a motive he did not initially decipher. At last, he believed himself to have hit upon the difficulty. The lieutenant of police had, he learned, ordered agents to arrest and interrogate his assistants; and the questioning of these men, he also discovered, had centered on their role in conveying messages from Troussey to the procureur general, Joly de Fleury. Sartine knew such messages had been sent and apparently suspected he was being betrayed.

In several lengthy attempts at justifying himself, Troussey reminded Sartine that the lieutenant of police himself had encouraged the inspector's initial involvement with Joly de Fleury. When Troussey had hesitated to pursue this engagement beyond its beginnings, Sartine had urged him to continue and to report regularly on the procureur general's remarks and requests. Troussey had agreed, expressing his conviction that he could "easily penetrate and know all that Monsieur de Fleury thought about Monsieur de Sartine." (Knowing Joly de

123. For examples, see Lenoir's letters to the commissioners in AN, Y 13728. The frequency with which Lenoir had to repeat these sermons suggests that, at least in the case of the commissioners, they did not have the desired effect. Symbolic of Lenoir's attempt to create a sense of impersonal authority was his move in 1780 or 1781 to new quarters which he designated not the Hôtel de Lenoir as his predecessors would have done, but the Hôtel de Police. The police as an institution was to have an existence of its own and space independent of that housing the man who happened temporarily to run it.

124. BN, MS fr. 22080, no. 18.

Fleury's distaste for him, Sartine had apparently smiled and replied that the assignment, as Troussey conceived it, ought not to be too difficult.)

The inspector also pointed out that he had carried information to the lieutenant of police regarding Joly de Fleury's personal life, recording on paper for police files the procureur general's own comments concerning his wife's regular infidelity. In addition, Troussey had warned Sartine that the procureur general intended to try to replace the concierge of the Châtelet—Sartine's protégé—with one of his own men, permitting the lieutenant of police to frustrate this attempt. Nonetheless, at some point, for reasons that are unclear, Sartine began to suspect that Troussey's ultimate allegiance had shifted; the culmination of this suspicion was Troussey's arrest and, eventually, his exile to Nancy. Circumstance assisted Sartine in disposing of Inspector Troussey. The man had fallen into debt and his financial obligations provided a convenient pretext for disgrace; but we do not know how many other men, only ostensibly in the service of the lieutenant of police, gave him no sufficient excuse for replacing them.[125]

Anyone who has read extensively in police papers of the eighteenth century cannot but be struck by the frequency with which the word "protector" and its concomitant "protégé" appear. The phenomenon of protection was sufficiently common and so important that police reports and interrogations invariably seek to establish its existence. Indicating a man's protector was essential to articulating his identity, to judging him enemy or friend, and to predicting his conduct and preparing for it.

Appreciating the extent and importance of these systems of protection is, I believe, vital to writing the history of eighteenth-century France, whether that history be political, administrative, or social. Protection or patronage was not simply a pension accorded an artist in return for dedications or performance. Protection was, under the Old Regime, a form of franchise bestowed on men and women who had never touched pen or brush. It was the means by which persons escaped impotence and the position of outsiders in their own society. In the end, it was less one's standing vis-à-vis the law than one's relationship to other men that brought rights, reasonable security, and a modicum of power in eighteenth-century France. Indeed, law and the

125. Dossier of Inspector Troussey, in BA, MS 12436.

courts themselves were frequently no more than a form and an arena
for contests decided, not according to statute or precedence, but by the
influence of protectors. In the papers of Lieutenant of Police Hérault,
we find a letter dated August 26, 1730, thanking him for writing the
avocat général of the Parlement. The gratitude came from an individual who was conducting a suit against the community of surgeons and
who told Hérault that "despite the strength of my cause, I needed protection as strong as yours not only to bring [this affair] to an end but
to resist that [the protection] of Monsieur Maréchal who is responsible
for this case." [126]

Because protection was valuable, because it was a form of franchise
that not all might come by and an essential requisite of any successful
career, no protégé was anxious to relinquish his status once he had
obtained it; and it is this fact—the value of protection, the reluctance
to surrender it—that makes the phenomenon important to a study of
the police or any other administrative entity during the eighteenth
century. One cannot understand the limitations on the authority of a
lieutenant of police, or any other executive agent, until one realizes
that among those he employed were a number whose primary loyalty
was not to him—to their administrative chief—but rather to the protectors, who had secured them employment and who were the source
of what legal and financial security an ordinary man might enjoy under
the Old Regime.

---

126. [?] to Hérault, August 26, 1730, BA, MS 10006. The signature on the letter is
illegible.

4

A Context:
The Administration of Paris

To many retrospective observers, eighteenth-century Paris has appeared to lie awkwardly extended along the banks of the Seine, resting like a grand serpent, swollen and rounded from recent feeding. In its belly lay the considerable remnants of other creatures, victims of an appetite that had outstripped the beast's own powers of digestion. Consumed but frequently alive and conscious, the victims—whole villages, monasteries, collegiate churches and their environs—jostled one another in the darkness and quarreled over allocations of space. Periodically recollecting the serpent, one and then another of them protested that their ingestion and inconvenient confinement changed nothing, that legal status was unaffected, that ancient privilege and power remained intact, notwithstanding the vexatious circumstance in which they found themselves. This movement, these refractory rumblings from within, occasioned the French capital considerable discomfort; and, as if deliberately intending to accentuate its distress, a succession of kings and events had given the city more than a single master, indeed, a grand collection of governors, who, in acting without consultation, might demand of it a series of graceless contortions that ill suited its tumid and distended form.

Prior to the Revolution, Paris and its suburbs contained almost fifty seigneurial jurisdictions, each claiming inviolable authority over men and lands whose destinies had ceased to be distinct from that of the city itself. At the very heart of the capital were the temporal jurisdictions of the archbishop and the chapter of Notre-Dame; on the Right Bank, the privileged enclosure of the Palais-Royal and those of the Temple and of Saint-Martin-des-Champs; across the river, the Palais du Luxembourg and with it three more privileged jurisdictions—those of Saint-Jean-de-Latran, of Saint-Germain-des-Prés, and of Saint-

Geneviève; a step further, on the periphery of the city and just beyond, lay the seigneuries of Auteuil, Montmartre, Belleville, Charonne, Gentilly, Chatillon, and Vaugirard, to name but a few.

In addition to these feudal remnants scattered about in its midst and along its fringes, Paris contained a bevy of royal jurisdictions and privileged properties: the Louvre and the Tuileries, subject to the prévôt de l'hôtel; the Bastille and the Invalides, each subordinate to its own governor; a *parlement* and a *bureau des finances*, both claiming a voice in the administration of the city and both ensconced on what we know as the Île de la Cité, a third of which—the bailliage of the Palais—constituted yet another separate jurisdiction; a *chambre de la maçonnerie* (also known as *chambre des bâtiments*) and the *Connétablie*, each having its own quarters in the Palais and each concerned with certain aspects of life in the capital (the former primarily with enforcement of building codes and the latter with litigation involving soldiers); across the river, on the Right Bank, the Châtelet, a *grenier à sel* (to try violators of the salt tax), the bailliage of the Arsenal, and—housed in the Hôtel de Ville—what remained of the once independent municipal government.[1]

The proximity of so many distinct authorities claiming judicial and administrative powers only roughly defined over interwoven groups of individuals, over convolutions of activities and snarled sections of the city, produced—one hardly need say—considerable confusion and conflict among those with a voice in the affairs of Paris. Magistrates of the Parlement quarreled with agents of the king; officers of the Hôtel de Ville contested powers assumed by judges at the Châtelet; feudal seigneurs railed against the encroachments of royal authority—variations on the theme of conflict are numerous, and few historians who have worked on eighteenth-century Paris have been able to resist toying with the familiar notes.

But there is a second theme—that of consultation and cooperation—

1. BN, MS JF 1310, fol. 74 (a list Feydeau de Marville sent Joly de Fleury, the chief prosecutor of the Parlement of Paris, on May 29, 1746, naming ten seigneurial jurisdictions in the city and thirty-nine in the suburbs). BN, MS fr. 8058 contains an extended list of royal jurisdictions (fols. 113–482) still active in Paris in the eighteenth century. It also lists the seigneurial jurisdictions in and about the capital. For discussions of the jurisdictions in Paris, both royal and seigneurial, see Jean Lucien Gay, "L'Administration de la capitale entre 1770 et 1789," *Mémoires de la Fédération des sociétés historiques at archéologiques de Paris et de l'Île-de-France*, VIII, (1956), 314–37; Mousnier, *Paris au XVIIe siècle*, 62–135; and Antoine, *et al.*, *Fonds judiciaires*, passim.

which merits more attention than it has yet received. Quarrelsome though they could be, those most engaged in the governance of Paris commonly labored to avoid contention. Their efforts at cooperative administration—institutionalized some time before 1728 in the Assemblée de Police—were far more ordinary phenomena than the disputes so often stressed by historians. To neglect these efforts, to ignore the search for accommodation and concurrence they embody, is to leave an important part of Parisian history untold; for it was cooperation not conflict that kept the great city alive.

Figuring prominently in both the disputes among Parisian administrators and their labor at collaboration were the police of the city. The extensive responsibilities conferred on the lieutenant of police in the latter half of the seventeenth century gave him from the start an important place in the life of the capital and embroiled him inevitably with other municipal authorities—with seigneurial magistrates and royal officers, who saw in the activity of the police a threat to their own ancient prerogatives. Given the quarrels that arose, it is natural to ask how the police fared in them, to seek the results of their encounter with individuals and institutions that challenged their authority, to want to know whether the lieutenant of police managed prior to the Revolution to establish formal right to anything resembling the considerable place his successor, the prefect of police, today occupies in the affairs of Paris. But having posed these questions, it is essential to take a step further and ask how important, in fact, jurisdictional dispute and its results were in deciding where lay the actual power to govern Paris.

THE RIGHT TO GOVERN: COMPETING JURISDICTIONS

Feudal Remnants

In January, 1746, the lieutenant of police, Feydeau de Marville, routinely fined four tavern owners who had been guilty of serving food and drink after the hour prescribed for closing. The taverns involved, however, lay outside the city proper, in the seigneury Clichy-la-Garenne, and the four proprietors appealed this decision to their lord, Gaspard Grimond de la Rivière (a farmer-general), who carried the case before the Parlement of Paris, claiming that the right to police a seigneury belonged to its lord alone and that the conduct of the tavernkeepers violated no regulation he had ever issued. A royal magistrate like the lieutenant of police had no right, Rivière argued, to intervene in the affairs of a seigneury. Unfortunately for the farmer-general, members of the Parlement—themselves royal magistrates—found his contention unappealing. On April 4, they upheld the earlier judgment of the lieutenant of police.

Strangely animated by this case, the procureur general—the chief prosecutor—of the Parlement wrote Marville nine days later, requesting from him a list of all seigneuries in Paris itself and in the surrounding suburbs. It was his intention, he said, to obtain a parlementary decree that would underscore the significance of the recent decision against Gaspard de la Rivière and that would, in general terms, reaffirm the right of the lieutenant of police to act in all seigneurial jurisdictions, both those within the city and those surrounding it.[2]

Are we to interpret this intention and the decree in which it culminated as a major victory for the lieutenant of police, as a final subjection of at least one of the groups contesting his authority in Paris? Hardly. The Parlement's act in 1746 was but one of a long series of royal efforts to curtail the power of feudal jurisdictions in the capital. A year before establishing the lieutenancy of police, the Council of State had acted to subordinate them to the Châtelet and its officers. In a decree of November 5, 1666, the council declared that the right to police Paris and its suburbs belonged to the *prévôt* of the Châtelet and his lieutenants; all other authorities, royal and seigneurial, it barred from exercising this function.[3] There were to be no privileged sanctuaries from the officers of the Châtelet and no resistance to their efforts at guaranteeing public security and well-being.

Eight years later the crown dramatically reaffirmed its intention that there should be no immunity from the police powers of the Châtelet. By an edict issued in February, 1674, it suppressed nineteen of the most important seigneurial jurisdictions in the city; with a single gesture, uncommonly disdainful of the past, it swept aside the cumbersome remnants of another age—the jurisdiction of the Temple and that of Saint-Germain-des-Prés, the temporal authority of the archbishop of Paris and that exercised by the cathedral chapter of Notre-Dame.

2. BN, MS JF 1310, fols. 69–74.
3. AN, AD-I 22B, 1, 2. Parlement had issued decrees of similar content on August 3, 1536, and July 3, 1537; letters patent of September 25, 1372 had excluded all judges but the *prévôt* of Paris (the formal head of the jurisdiction known as the Châtelet) from the exercise of general police powers.

Had the government stood determinedly behind this edict, Parisian seigneuries would have ceased once and for all to contravene the authority of the Châtelet and its new lieutenant of police. But no sooner was the edict published than the crown began issuing exemptions. In April, yielding to protests from the archbishop, it found a device for restoring his temporal authority in the city; months later, in January, 1675, the abbey of Saint-Germain-des-Prés regained its judicial power; in August, 1676, came the turn of the chapter of Notre-Dame; and, in 1678, Saint-Jean-de-Latran, the Temple, and Saint-Martin-des-Champs obtained exemption. Within five years of its issuance, the edict of February, 1674, was a dead letter.[4]

Its demise was an early blow to the authority of the lieutenants of police, a blow only partially countered by subsequent acts like that proposed and sponsored by the procureur general in 1746. In parts of Paris, the power of the police remained, until 1789, conditional on the cooperation of seigneurial baillis or, in case of resistance, on the backing of the Parisian Parlement.

Royal Jurisdictions

Like the feudal institutions in Paris, several royal properties in the capital claimed exemption from the ordinary processes of justice and administration. Police powers at the Louvre, the Tuileries, and the Palais du Luxembourg (until it became part of the appanage created for the Count of Provence in 1771) lay in the hands, not of the lieutenant of police, but in those of the prévôt de l'hôtel and his lieutenants, charged, as they were, with maintaining order in all royal residences.

A letter Lenoir wrote the secretary of state for the king's household on March 23, 1782, indicates in concrete terms the kind of problem this arrangement could create for the lieutenant of police. Several days earlier, it seems, a woman, wishing to evade her husband, had taken refuge in the home of a friend named Madame Boisgelin. The husband, however, had had little difficulty discovering her hiding place and had impulsively made his way to the house his wife had chosen as a sanctuary. Pushing past the servant who greeted him at the door, the angry man mounted the stairs to Madame Boisgelin's bedroom, ensconced himself, and refused to leave until his wife consented to return home

4. BN, MS fr. 8058, fols. 29, 39–40, 43, 51, 60; Delamare, *Traité de la police*, I, 134–36.

with him. Little pleased at this intrusion, the mistress of the house dispatched a servant to demand immediate assistance from the lieutenant of police; but unfortunately for Madame Boisgelin, her residence stood sufficiently proximate to the Louvre or the Tuileries to be within the jurisdiction not of the police but of the prévôt de l'hôtel. Barred from responding to this request for aid, Lenoir sent a subordinate in search of some official attached to the prévôté de l'hôtel—a man competent to intervene. Only when a three-hour search failed to produce such an individual did the lieutenant of police take it upon himself to order one of his own agents to go to Madame Boisgelin's.

Led before Lenoir, the imprudent husband received a lecture on proper and improper means of recovering one's wife and was released. That, however, was not the end of the matter. When officers of the prévôté—wherever they were—learned what had happened, they immediately protested to the secretary of state for the king's household, arguing that Lenoir's conduct amounted to an infringement of their prerogatives. Seven years before the Revolution, as late as 1782, the lieutenant of police found it necessary to answer such a charge and to justify the exercise of his authority in the very heart of Paris.[5]

Rights of police jurisdiction belonging to the prévôt de l'hôtel and his officers extended beyond royal buildings and properties. They encompassed as well two groups of individuals dwelling in the city: merchants serving the court and persons bearing the title *commensal du roi* (literally "table companion of the king"—a title accorded, among others, many members of the king's household, officers of the sovereign courts, and a number of persons involved in financial administration). Like the prévôt's jurisdiction over certain properties, this authority over people also impinged on the power of the lieutenant of police and, on occasion, obstructed his efforts to administer the capital.

On August 21, 1722, Marc-Pierre d'Argenson fined a paper merchant named Blainvillain thirty livres for having refused to pay a tax collected in his district to underwrite the cost of lighting its streets. Blainvillain, who apparently furnished paper to the court, had, as a merchant serving the king, claimed exemption from both this financial exaction and the authority of the lieutenant of police. In a sentence issued on September 1, the prévôté de l'hôtel upheld these claims.

5. AN, 0-1 361, no. 271.

Voiding d'Argenson's decision against Blainvillain, it forbade any bailiff to serve the previous judgment and warned the receiver of fines at the Châtelet—a man named Dautel—that, should he insist on collecting the fine d'Argenson had assessed, he would be compelled to return from his own funds a sum four times as large. Six decades later, zealous as ever in defending its position, the prévôté de l'hôtel continued to stand between the lieutenant of police and small pieces of the city he was supposed to govern.[6]

A third of what is known as the Île de la Cité, the area bounded on the west by the rear of the Place Dauphine and on the east by the streets connecting the Pont Saint-Michel with the Pont au Change, was also partially shielded from the power of the police. This portion of the capital, known because it once had been a royal residence as the Palais (palace), not only housed the sovereign courts of the city but constituted as well a separate jurisdiction—the bailliage of the Palais. To the magistrates of the jurisdiction, to the bailli and his lieutenant, belonged most police functions performed within its perimeters and the right to decide civil and criminal affairs arising there. While an edict of October, 1712, had permitted the lieutenant of police to receive registers from hotel keepers in the area and had charged him with administrative responsibility for lighting and cleaning the Palais, the same edict had reserved to the bailli all powers of compulsion.[7] Hence, without cooperation from this official, the lieutenant of police could not readily sanction individuals within the Palais who chose to disregard the limited number of regulations he was authorized to issue there. Throughout the eighteenth century, the bailliage of the Palais, lying in the center of Paris, stood as yet another bastion against the power of the police.

While one must understand that there were barriers to the authority of the lieutenant of police in the capital, it is also important to note that during the eighteenth century the area these encompassed diminished and that two institutions in particular, the *bureau des finances* and the *bureau de ville*, lost ground before the police.

---

6. BN, MS fr. 22114, fols. 103–104; for the details of another quarrel between the prévôté de l'hôtel and the lieutenant of police, this one occurring in April, 1783, see AN, 0-1 361, nos. 10–12.

7. For the complete terms of this edict which sought to define the powers of the bailli of the Palais vis-à-vis those of the lieutenant of police, see BN, MS JF 1418, fols. 129–30.

In a room on the eastern perimeter of the Palais sat a group of men who sought to exercise and protect administrative prerogatives that reached throughout the city. Royal ordinances of October, 1489, and October, 1508, had granted this body—the treasurers of France—responsibility for the streets of the capital and for the highways of the surrounding *généralité*. Though this authority slipped into other hands late in the sixteenth century, the treasurers regained it in 1635 when the crown once again entrusted them with all matters relating to public roads. Henceforth, the treasurers of France, sitting as the *bureau des finances* for the *généralité* of Paris, were to oversee the construction and maintenance of streets in the capital. Three of their number served by royal commission as directors of paving in Paris, while all of the approximately twenty-five treasurers decided questions of "alignement," that is to say, questions concerning the proper breadth of roads and the right of incursion on public thoroughfares. Responsibility for settling matters of *alignement* was not the power to determine the course of a street (this was an affair for the Council of State, acting through letters patent) but rather the obligation to protect this course from infringement (in the form of a sign or temporary structure) once it had been decided upon.[8]

With authority over the streets of Paris came the right to inspect buildings that bordered them and to condemn any structure that, through lack of maintenance or inept construction, jeopardized passage through the city. But the police, too, had been granted this power over hazardous structures; and, needless to say, the efforts of two distinct jurisdictions to exercise concurrently the same authority led to occasional conflicts.[9]

More than occasional were the controversies arising from the bureau's claim to administer Parisian streets. Lieutenants of police—responsible for provisioning the city by land and, hence, themselves vitally interested in the condition of roads—did not always share the *bureau des finances'* generous interpretation of what constituted a passable street. For three years, Hérault and his successor, Marville, fought what they considered the bureau's unwillingness to protect

8. Isambert, Jourdan, and Decrusy, *Recueil des lois*, XVII, 270–71; Nicolas Toussaint Le Moyne [Des Essarts], *Dictionnaire universel de police* (7 vols.; Paris, 1786–89), I, 247–51.

9. See AN, AD-I 26, 120, 18. While I have found no concrete instance of conflict, this royal declaration of August 18, 1730, in providing for the resolution of such disputes, implies their occurrence.

the rights of passage and transport; but, failing to obtain needed support from the Parlement, they were forced in 1742 to abandon the struggle.[10]

There were to be few other victories for the *bureau des finances* during the eighteenth century. Ignored by the crown, which preferred delegating its authority elsewhere, the bureau watched as functions it believed rightly its own slipped into other hands. In a memorandum to the keeper of the seals dated June, 1787, it charged the lieutenant of police and the *bureau de ville* with arrogating to themselves essential elements of its authority. But protest did not restore power. By the closing years of the Old Regime—if one accepts the agency's representation of its own position—it had ceased to play a major part in the governance of Paris. Tangible evidence of its degraded and moribund condition were the unfilled gaps in its ranks. In 1789 more than a third of the offices in the Parisian *bureau des finances* lay vacant, unsold and unsought, spurned even by a community of investors renowned for the willingness with which it ordinarily exchanged cash for the most modest of public titles.[11]

The *bureau des finances* and the police might struggle for control of Parisian streets, but the city's broadest avenue, the river Seine itself, escaped the authority of both. Jurisdiction over it was the right of the *bureau de ville*, eighteenth-century heir of the once powerful guild of river merchants whose authority had earlier extended beyond the banks of the Seine to encompass the entire city. Once the organ through which commercial interests in Paris had sought to govern independently and to resist royal attempts at controlling the city, the *bureau de ville* had fought an unequal battle and retreated slowly back to the original source of its wealth and its power—the river. As it withdrew, it surrendered most of the city to the prévôt of Paris and his lieutenants at the Châtelet, chief agents of the crown.

To complete their victory, French monarchs chose not a complete destruction of the *bureau de ville*, but rather subversion of its initial character. Leaving its authority over the river intact, they saw to it that men of their own choosing were named under the title prévôt des marchands—provost of merchants—to head the remnants of municipal government in Paris. In choosing this course, in conserving a domesti-

---

10. See BN, MS JF 1318, fols. 1–42.
11. Gay, "Administration de la capitale," 332; Marion, *Dictionnaire des institutions*, 61.

cated *bureau de ville*, they preserved yet another claimant to authority in the capital—the oldest of them all.[12]

Despite their common subjection to the crown during the eighteenth century, the Châtelet and the *bureau de ville* continued to find new terrain for their ancient contest over jurisdiction. In 1700 the government had made a major attempt to end the recurrent feuds. An edict issued in June of that year traced in detail lines meant to distinguish definitively the authority of the two jurisdictions, but the labor proved fruitless. In a letter to Joly de Fleury dated May 9, 1728, we find a president of the Parisian Parlement complaining that once again his court has before it a dispute over jurisdiction between the *bureau de ville* and the officers of the Châtelet. Wearily, he expresses the hope that the procureur general can find a device that will end the repeated conflicts and give the Parlement a deserved and necessary peace.[13]

How well Joly de Fleury succeeded we may judge by a letter Lenoir sent the commissioners of police on August 18, 1780: "the bailiffs of the *bureau de ville*, who wish to make their functions commensurate with your own, Messieurs, daily undertake tasks that jeopardize rights belonging to you and to the jurisdiction of the Châtelet." Such excesses, Lenoir continues, must stop; and to see that they do, each commissioner is to report any municipal bailiff he finds performing duties that are rightly those of a police officer.[14]

If a device, indeed, did exist for differentiating once and for all the authority of the police from that of the *bureau de ville*, the high courts and councils of the Old Regime were unable to find it. To say, as these organs essentially had, that one jurisdiction should have charge of the river and of commerce associated with it, while the other was to administer all else, left much undecided. Who was to control the peripheral areas—the quays, for example, so necessary to commerce by water, but undeniably distinct from the river they defined? And what of bridges—of the homes and shops that lined them during the eighteenth century? Were these rightly a part of the river they spanned or

12. The *bureau de ville* comprised the prévôt des marchands, four assistants known as *échevins*, a royal prosecutor (*procureur du roi*—like most administrative bodies under the ancien régime, the *bureau de ville* was also a court), a clerk, and a keeper of accounts (*receveur du domaine*). Though the form of electing a prévôt des marchands was preserved throughout the eighteenth century, the king's will, not that of the small body of electors, determined the successful candidate.

13. Delamare, *Traité de la police*, I, 195; President Lambert to Joly de Fleury, May 9, 1728, in BN, MS JF 1327.

14. Lenoir to commissioners, August 18, 1780, in AN, Y 12830.

the banks they joined? The edict of June, 1700, had tried to resolve
these problems by giving authority over the quays to the lieutenant of
police, except insofar as matters affecting navigation were involved.
Tracing the precise limits of this exception occupied legal minds until the regime fell. Bridges the edict divided in half horizontally, the
underside falling within the purview of the *bureau de ville*, while the
upper half, with whatever buildings it sustained, was within the jurisdiction of the police.

There were other sources of controversy. In surrendering the bulk of
the city to the Châtelet, municipal officers had retained authority over
the capital's walls (many of which had become in the latter half of the
seventeenth century wide boulevards for whose maintenance, cleaning, and illumination the *bureau de ville* remained responsible), its
fountains, and its sewers. They continued to control, as well, the extensive Place de Grève, which extended westward and south from the
Hôtel de Ville and which served as an important place of assembly
under the Old Regime. These incursions into the territory of the police
created additional surfaces for contact between the two jurisdictions
and, naturally enough, further abrasion. The same could be said of the
particular power granted the lieutenant of police over commerce in
hay, a commodity which, together with wood and grain, constituted
one of the city's three essential fuels during the eighteenth century.
Much of the hay consumed in Paris arrived by boat; and, had the banks
of the Seine been a definite and genuine boundary between Châtelet
and *bureau de ville*, its exchange and management would have fallen
under the jurisdiction of the prévôt des marchands. Tradition, however, had conferred this responsibility on the officers of the Châtelet;
and a decree of the Parisian Parlement in July, 1673, had reinforced the
dictates of custom, specifying the lieutenant of police as the particular
officer who should exercise the ancient right. Officials at the *bureau de
ville* suffered over this breach in their authority, believing that police
agents frequently used the access it gave them to the river to meddle in
matters beyond their competence.[15]

Given these sources of difficulty and the numerous conflicts that in
fact ensued, one may ask how the two sides fared. Does one of them
appear to have made gains at the other's expense, or did the recurrent
contest between them during the eighteenth century leave their re-
spective powers largely intact and unaffected?

15. BN, MS JF 1316, fols. 91–92.

According to Sebastien Mercier, by 1780 there was little substantial to quarrel over, for the police had carried the struggle on all fronts. The authority of the *bureau de ville*, said Mercier, had vanished: "The Prévôt des Marchands, the King's prosecutor, [and] the *échevins* have lucrative, honorary positions; but from the standpoint of power, they are phantoms, everything being in the hands of the police, even the provisioning of the city."[16] While this judgment exaggerates the debasement of the *bureau de ville* (which, after all, retained its authority over the vital highway that was the river and which, during the last twenty-four years of the regime, was headed by men of considerable administrative stature),[17] it rightly indicates that in contests over jurisdiction the police had gained an upper hand.

The greatest losses of power and prestige suffered by the *bureau de ville* had come prior to the eighteenth century as a result of royal efforts to reduce its independence. Further erosion of its position after 1718 was reasonably minor and a consequence not of continued royal hostility (the prévôt des marchands was by this time as much an appointed agent and ally of the crown as the lieutenant of police) but of the bureau's own relative weakness. It is unlikely that the prévôt des marchands had a tenth the number of men working for him that served the lieutenant of police.[18]

Juxtaposed to the police the *bureau de ville* frequently came off appearing unprepared and incompetent. When fire broke out on the Petit Pont in 1718, pumps inspected and maintained by the police arrived promptly to help fight the blaze. Four other pumps, entrusted to the Hôtel de Ville and housed closer to the fire than any of those in the hands of the police, never appeared. Had they, their presence would have been of little use, for no one had bothered to keep them in working order. An investigation of the mishap cost the prévôt des marchands the authority he had, until then, exercised jointly with the lieutenant of police over the nascent Parisian fire department.[19]

16. Louis Sebastien Mercier, *Tableau de Paris* (rev. ed., 12 vols.; Amsterdam, 1782–88), II, 37–38.

17. Three of the four men who served as prévôt des marchands between 1764 and 1789 (Bignon, La Michodière, and Le Peletier) had attained the rank of conseiller d'état in the royal bureaucracy, a rank that suggests administrative experience and ability equivalent to that of Sartine and Lenoir, the lieutenants of police during the same period.

18. On the employees of the *bureau de ville*, see any *Almanach royal* of the eighteenth century, that of 1789, pp. 440–41, for example.

19. BN, MS JF 1325, fols. 9, 113–16.

The *bureau de ville* suffered a further loss of power once shared with the police following another accident, the accident that had injured more than a thousand persons in May, 1770, in the Place Louis XV. After investigating the events of that night, the Parlement attributed significant blame for the tragedy to the *bureau de ville* and concluded that henceforth, except in the City Hall itself and the adjacent Place de Grève, the direction and management of all public ceremonies and celebrations would belong to the lieutenant of police alone.[20] These diminutions of the bureau's authority, while not themselves of monumental significance, suggest a gradual disillusionment with municipal officers, a loss of confidence in their capacity to execute orders, and an inclination on the part of ministers and magistrates to rely instead on the police—an entity whose very size made it a more dependable and effective instrument.

In repeated contests with other jurisdictions, then, the Parisian police gained more ground than they lost during the eighteenth century. Despite an occasional local defeat, their formal authority in the city grew with the passage of time and at the expense of other institutions. Feudal seigneurs, once independent municipal officers, and diverse royal agents all suffered incursions on their prerogatives, with perhaps only the prévôt de l'hôtel escaping, what appeared to some, a long series of police depredations. But despite the cries they raised, the advances of the police were, for the most part, minor alterations of traditional boundaries; and, in the end, the jurisdictional lines in Paris, however drawn or redrawn, were by the eighteenth century less important to the concrete practice of administration than we have long supposed.

THE EXERCISE OF POWER: COOPERATION AND THE ASSEMBLÉE DE POLICE

Most major decisions affecting Paris were the work not of a single jurisdiction in the city, but of several authorities acting in concert. To provide the capital with a modicum of coherent and unified direction, a small group of magistrates met regularly in what was known as the Assemblée de Police; and it was a place in these gatherings, much more than success in jurisdictional disputes, that conferred on would-be administrators a major role in formulating policy for the capital.

20. On this incident whose ramifications were manifold, see BN, MS JF 45, fols. 137–92.

Places in the assemblée were few. Only four men (and through them three institutions) had a regular part in its gatherings: from the Parlement of Paris, which claimed a general supervisory role in the city, came the first president of that court and its procureur general; from the *bureau de ville* came its chief, the prévôt des marchands; and from the Châtelet, there was, as one might expect, the lieutenant of police. These four magistrates sufficed to constitute the Assemblée de Police, and ultimately it was they alone who had a voice in its decisions.[21]

Still, others ordinarily attended—experts with whom the members wished to confer, subordinates who had been charged with inquiry or supervision of some kind, magistrates from other jurisdictions whose cooperation in a given matter was deemed essential. During the decade of the 1730s one finds the administration of the Hôpital Général (a vast collection of ten separate hospitals, hospices, and prisons) making more frequent appearances in the assemblée than any of the other occasional participants. Three times early in 1731 these administrators presented themselves to discuss the quality of the provisions they were receiving and to ask the assemblée to warn their suppliers against fraud. They returned on many other occasions to report on an embryonic clothing industry the assemblée had ordered established within the hôpital.

Private persons of stature, men of some use to those who governed Paris, might also find themselves briefly a part of these gatherings. Samuel Bernard, the well-known financier, attended two sessions of the assemblée during the summer of 1731. He had been invited to join in deliberations regarding provisionment of the capital and was asked to cooperate in efforts at containing the price of bread in Paris. The assemblée wanted Bernard to begin immediately disposing of grain he controlled and to proceed with its sale in such a way as to assure a steady supply of flour and bread in the markets. Fearing other shortages, the members also asked their guest to use his considerable means and his extensive connections to bring oats, rice, peas, butter, and livestock into the city. Space in public structures, they promised, would

21. On occasion one finds three others present: the *avocat général* of the Parlement and the king's prosecutors from the Châtelet and the *bureau de ville*; but their presence was not essential. The name *assemblée de police* was also applied to weekly meetings convoked by the lieutenant of police and attended by the lieutenant criminal, the *prévôts* of the *maréchaussée*, and the commander of the guard. These gatherings, however, were far less concerned with charting policy than with considering the tactics of implementation.

be available to store whatever quantities of these items Bernard could furnish.

If financiers were of sufficient use to the assemblée to sometimes find a place in its meetings, so too were scientists and inventors. To a session in April, 1733, the Assemblée de Police invited several foreigners who claimed to have produced a fire pump superior to that then in use in Paris. As it was spring, the magistrates sensibly adjourned to the out-of-doors for a demonstration, which, it seems, left them unimpressed. Despite this failure, members of the assemblée no doubt preferred such visual diversions to some of the lengthy technical disquisitions they inflicted on themselves in the name of public good. Participating in subsequent meetings, at the request of the assemblée, were a number of learned men: one came to discuss industrial use of the Gobelins stream and consequent pollution of the Seine; another to report on the feasibility of brightening the face of Paris by requiring that all structures in the city receive periodic coats of whitewash; a third appeared to lecture on the scales used in Parisian commerce and to give his views on preventing fraud.[22]

Dukes and architects, too, found their way into the assemblée; but, like the scientists, the financiers, and the administrators of subordinate institutions, they came not as members who attended by right but rather as guests, present because they had been invited. Whatever the list of those in attendance, power within the Assemblée de Police lay in the hands of the four magistrates who were its core.

Essential to appreciating the place of the assemblée in the administration of Paris is the realization that it alone viewed the capital as whole and could, given the power of its members, treat it as such. One must understand as well that meetings of the assemblée were not simply a forum within which three separate institutions did one another the courtesy of reporting unilateral decisions; they were instead genuine efforts to ignore jurisdictional lines and to act collectively on behalf of the entire city. Though authority over the municipal water supply belonged in theory to the prévot des marchands, it was the assemblée as a whole that made decisions affecting this supply and its distribution within Paris; and while power to control most prices in the capital belonged formally to the lieutenant of police, this was a power he exercised only after obtaining the concurrence of his col-

22. Entries for January 25, April 5, 26, June 26, July 19, 1731, April 29, December 31, 1733, January 14, 28, February 11, July 29, August 5, 1734, in BN, MS fr. 11356.

leagues in the assemblée. In August, 1769, for example, we find Sartine urging the representatives from the Parlement and the Hôtel de Ville to approve an increase in the price of candles without which, he says, the supply of tallow to the city will remain inadequate. Nine years later, Lenoir went before the same group to ask that it check the rising cost of meat by imposing a ceiling of eight sous a pound on common cuts. Disorder would ensue, he feared, if the price were not contained. Important here are not the different policies advocated by Sartine and Lenoir but the fact that such advocacy before others was necessary, that four men participated in making a decision which, formally, was the prerogative of one.[23]

Even the sovereign court of the Parlement, which claimed a general and encompassing authority over Paris, did not generally act without first gaining, through its representatives in the Assemblée de Police, the counsel and support of this body. Having decided that it must issue regulations aimed at eliminating dangerous buildings in the capital, the Parlement asked its first president to draft, within the assemblée and with the concurrence of its other members, a set of such regulations.[24]

Most legislation affecting Paris, whether it eventually appeared as a decree of the Parlement, as an ordinance of the *bureau de ville*, or as a regulation from the hands of the lieutenant of police was, in fact, the work of men from each of these jurisdictions, acting together. Lines dividing the most important institutions in Paris were finally less significant in determining where authority and power lay than in deciding what legal form the exercise of both should take.[25]

Because the Assemblée de Police did not act in its own name, because its decisions invariably appear, masked and disguised, as the work of older, established institutions, it is no wonder that its place in the administration of Paris has gone so long unnoticed.[26] Yet to read the minutes of its meetings is to realize the magnitude of this over-

23. *Ibid.*, fols. 14–20; BN, MS JF 1333, fols. 129–30; Lenoir to commissioners, February 7, 1778, in AN, Y 13728.

24. BN, MS fr. 11356, fol. 82.

25. Power over these lines themselves, insofar as it was in the hands of living men and not in those of tradition, lay as well with the Assemblée de Police. The last minutes we have of meetings—those from 1739 and 1740—show the assemblée beginning work on royal declarations aimed at redefining the competences of Châtelet, Hôtel de Ville, and *bureau des finances* (BN, MS fr. 11356, fol. 405).

26. Chassaigne devotes a sentence to the assemblée in his *La Lieutenance générale de police* (see pp. 117–18) and Gay gives it equally brief attention in his article on the

sight, for the assemblée had a part—frequently a decisive one—in shaping most legislation concerned with the capital. Proposals touching Paris, whether they came initially from a private citizen or from a minister, passed inevitably into its hands for scrutiny and comment.

From the father of the philosophe Helvétius, a man who was himself physician to the queen, the assemblée received a plan aimed at providing decent medical treatment for Parisian prisoners. Unfortunately, funds for the program were to come from the establishment of a lottery of which, the assemblée decided, there were already too many in the capital. In 1737, the assemblée received from the controller general, Orry, drafts of two royal declarations that would have created in the capital a number of new financial offices. Since these were to be attached to the Hôtel de Ville, the prévôt des marchands had been assigned by his colleagues to report on the proposals; but it was the assemblée as a whole that decided unanimously against Orry's project, viewing it as nothing more than a ruse by which to raise money, devoid of value for the city.[27]

Twenty years later records show the secretary of state for the king's household asking the assemblée for its views on a proposal that would have moved part of the meat industry outside Paris; and while the secretary, Saint-Florentin, may have regarded the response he received as counsel, members of the assemblée apparently considered their letter a decision. In a brief note for himself on the action he and his colleagues had taken, Joly de Fleury confidently scrawled "rejected." Ministers who acted precipitously, without consulting the assemblée, apparently had occasion to regret their haste. Early in 1740, the controller general (Orry again) granted a Monsieur Puisneuf letters patent authorizing him to open and develop a new street on the eastern edge of Paris. Pressed, it seems, by the Duke of Villeroy, who had a considerable investment in Puisneuf's scheme, Orry had moved without the advice or concurrence of the assemblée. When this group met on April 7, 1740, it did not hesitate to review and condemn the controller general's conduct. The letters patent Orry had issued completely ignored established limits on urban development, and they carried with them the too blatant appearance of special favor, an appearance Puisneuf

administration of Paris (see p. 319). Neither goes beyond reciting what he has found in Commissioner Lemaire's work on the police, completed in 1770 (cf. the above citations with BO, MS 1424, p. 35).

27. BN, MS fr. 11356, fols. 325–27.

insisted on magnifying by vaunting loudly the powerful protection he enjoyed. Quickly and without dissent, all four members of the assemblée agreed that the enterprise must not proceed. As a group and individually, they began to press the controller general to revoke his rash authorization of Puisneuf's project.[28]

Letters patent and royal declarations, decrees of Parlement and municipal ordinances, police regulations and edicts of the crown—behind the manifold forms authority assumed in eighteenth-century Paris, there was often a single face, that of the Assemblée de Police; and the power of the lieutenant of police over urban policy was far more closely linked to his place in this body than to the outcome of petty feuds between the Châtelet and other jurisdictions in Paris. But if this is so, what was his position in the assemblée? Alone, or in alliance with others, can the lieutenant of police be said in any way to have dominated its proceedings and directed, more than others, its determinations? Surely, precedence among members was not his but belonged instead to the first president of the Parlement. It was this magistrate who hosted meetings at his spacious residence and who presided over them.[29] Nonetheless, as all who have studied the Old Regime know, precedence and power can never be presumed synonymous; and, in fact, there seems to be no compelling reason for judging the first president a preponderant figure in the Assemblée de Police. By citing appropriate passages from minutes of meetings, one might make any of the four members appear a prevailing force. Minutes from the gathering of March 28, 1737, for example, read simply, "nothing important occurred, the Lieutenant of Police having suddenly fallen ill this morning." This inscription, one might argue, clearly implies that the lieu-

28. Count of Saint Florentin to Joly de Fleury, June 22, 1759, in BN, MS JF 1333; BN, MS fr. 11356, fol. 411. Though the outcome of their efforts is unrecorded, the minutes suggest that the assemblée's members had no doubt they could alter the decision of the controller general.

29. Ordinarily, the assemblée convened every other Thursday afternoon, though not infrequently meetings had to be rescheduled because one member found it impossible to attend. The first meeting of which we have record was that held Thursday, December 2, 1728; and while a prefatory note scrawled upon the minutes from this session makes it clear that there had been previous gatherings, we have no way of knowing how many. Nor do we have minutes from any meeting after that of September 1, 1740, though we know without question that the Assemblée de Police was still functioning as late as 1778 (Lenoir to commissioners, February 7, 1778, in AN, Y 12830) and may, I think, presume that it endured for another eleven years. Indeed, it is just as our record breaks off in 1740 that the assemblée begins to take on one aspect of a distinct and durable institution, acquiring about this time its own permanent secretary to record and preserve its deliberations (see BN, MS fr. 11356, fol. 404).

tenant of police stood at the very heart of the assemblée, that he was its single indispensable figure, the one man without whom it could not function. But proceeding through the minutes, one finds under February 6, 1738, a similarly suggestive entry regarding the prévôt des marchands.

Viewed as a whole, the minutes we have—those spanning a decade of meetings—suggest that two men, the procureur general and the lieutenant of police, may have been particularly forceful in the assemblée. Theirs at least are the voices that appear most frequently in the hurried and often brief notes that remain. Both speak with authority and as men perhaps better informed than their colleagues. Still, one senses that potency within the assemblée depended greatly on individual personality, on the forensic skills members carried with them on any given day, and on the shifting configuration of moods amid which they happened to find themselves.

The power a single individual exercised over urban policy could be amplified by alliances contracted within the assemblée or without it. As chief royal commissioner in Paris, the lieutenant of police often carried into the assemblée an authority augmented by his close association with the government. One index of his proximity to the crown lies in the correspondence of the secretaries of state for the king's household. As the individual ultimately responsible for Paris, this secretary of state issued the crown's directives to those who represented it in the city, and one might expect the frequency of these directives to reflect, in part, the importance to Versailles of the various royal agents in Paris. Listed below are the number of letters the secretary of state for the king's household sent in three sample years to the four members of the Assemblée de Police. The figures suggest the government's relatively close collaboration with the lieutenant of police.[30]

	1702	1765	1788	Averages
First President	7	12	10	29
Procureur General	37	32	23	31
Prévôt des Marchands	0	16	83	33
Lieutenant of Police	114	98	216	143

Supplementing the ties of correspondence were weekly sessions with the crown's ministers, regular meetings and conversations with

30. An, 0-1 362, 407, 461, 432–33, 484, 499.

powerful figures who at times gave the lieutenant of police the support he needed to overcome opposition to a given project from his colleagues in the assemblée. Hérault, for example, managed in 1738 to bring about the reinstitution of a duty on butter, cheese, and eggs entering Paris, despite the determined resistance of both the procureur general and the first president. The lieutenant of police won his victory by drawing into the struggle not only the controller general, but the first minister himself, Cardinal Fleury.

Hérault pressed for the imposition as a means of furnishing needed funds to the Hôpital Général and as a device which, in creating royal officials to collect the tax, would supply men who could also be used by the police to control traffic in these articles. While agreeing that money was needed for the Hôpital Général, the procureur general and the first president of the Parlement argued that it should come from funds the crown was improperly spending on the military. The issue, debated for more than a year, apparently brought the lieutenant of police and the first president close to blows at one meeting of the assemblée; study of the incident provides a rare and excellent example of how policy affecting Paris was made. A royal declaration reestablishing the tax and embodying Hérault's triumph appeared on May 10, 1738.[31]

That lieutenants of police strengthened their hand in formulating urban policy by invoking support from the government is not surprising. More remarkable, having gone so long unmentioned, are the alliances these same men contracted with their colleagues in the assemblée as a means of obtaining from a preoccupied or reluctant minister action which they considered important to Paris. Such alliances, involving as they did lieutenants of police and leaders of Parlement, have perhaps been ignored because they violate accepted notions of political alignment under the Old Regime. Be this as it may, they existed and served on more than one occasion to enhance the power of the police in the capital.

Believing that one of the female prisons in the city badly needed reconstruction and having without success urged Cardinal Fleury to provide funds for the work, Hérault took his case before the Assemblée de Police on March 10, 1729. Here he found the concurrence and support he needed. Joly de Fleury, the procureur general, promised to seek out

31. BN, MS JF 1322, fols. 153–58, 160, 174–76.

the cardinal and to join in pressing him for the needed money. In the meantime, the assemblée decided, women presently confined in the prison would be given quarters elsewhere, quarters that did not constitute a threat to their lives.[32]

Members of the Assemblée de Police cooperated in a similar fashion on other matters. Several times during the decade of the 1730s they joined together not to refurbish buildings in the city but to repair a damaged legal structure. There were in Paris powerful individuals who openly flouted certain of the city's statutes and who, in so doing, encouraged a more extended disregard. Alone, the lieutenant of police did not have the stature to check this affront to the law. He could not by himself enforce a general ban on gambling against men like the Duke of Gesvres and the Prince of Carignan; nor could he impose Lenten abstinence on princes of the blood, or regulations regarding excessive luxury on the dukes of Saint Simon and d'Antin. Faced by the effronteries such persons offered urban authorities, he turned again to his colleagues in the assemblée, who took turns badgering the first minister, Cardinal Fleury, urging him to visit or summon the transgressors and to use whatever exhortations were necessary to gain their future compliance.

At a meeting of March 24, 1729, Joly de Fleury reported to members of the assemblée on his recent attempt at getting the cardinal to act against the seigneurs. The procureur general was clearly dissatisfied with Fleury's response. Indeed, though the conversation had occurred four days earlier, he still fumed at the first minister's desire to avoid confrontation, labeling the excuses he had heard "feeble" and "specious." He urged a willing assemblée to continue, in the strongest possible terms, to press the cardinal for action. While the results of this persistent collaboration were no doubt modest, they must certainly have exceeded those the lieutenant of police could have obtained acting alone.

The Assemblée de Police worked to extend police authority not only to those individuals who while dwelling within Paris believed themselves beyond its laws, but to a number of the archaic independent enclosures that dotted the city as well. Having heard the lieutenant of police report on a fire that broke out within the Arsenal on the night of

32. On this incident and those that follow, see BN, MS fr. 11356, fols. 80–86, 93, 350–54. This MS contains the surviving minutes of the Assemblée de Police.

April 24, 1729, members of the assemblée, aware of the powder stored in this compound, commended the good fortune that had spared Paris a major explosion. Hérault's tale moved the first president of the Parlement to deplore the existence of so many privileged places in the capital, places whose officials did not act with the same vigilance and care as the police. He found it, he said, incredible that almost no water had been stored in the Arsenal as a precaution against fire, and he moved that the assemblée present to the first minister a proposal that would henceforth subordinate the Arsenal to police authority.

Traditional representations of government in eighteenth-century Paris have ignored the Assemblée de Police and, in so doing, have come to exaggerate the fragmentation of administrative authority in the capital. They have portrayed the city as something approaching a battleground, the scene of unremitting conflict among jealous and petty jurisdictions; and amid these struggles, they have dwelt, above all, on one—that which engaged on one side the authority of the crown, embodied in the lieutenant of police and, on the other, the power of the great sovereign court in the city, the Parlement.

No one who has studied eighteenth-century Paris would want to deny that there is truth in these accounts; and yet they are, as they stand, caricatures that leave one wondering how a beast as unfortunate and as rent with internal disorder as the capital fed itself and survived until 1789. If there was, on occasion, disagreement among those who governed Paris—between Parlement and police, between police and *bureau de ville*—there was also frequent, indeed regular, collaboration. If the first president of the Parlement and the lieutenant of police spent part of one Thursday afternoon shouting at one another, they more often used these occasions to eliminate differences and to coordinate labor at Versailles on behalf of Paris.

Any portrayal of perpetual administrative conflict within the capital and of a static alliance between police and crown against Parlement is, to say the best one can, inadequate; for such a portrait ignores the fact that the lieutenant of police was an urban administrator as well as a commissioner of the crown and that, as such, he frequently shared not the perspective of ministers responsible for all of France but that of those—prévôt des marchands and leaders of Parlement—who were deeply immersed in the problems of a single city. While a controller general, worried in 1738 about raising revenue for the king, might believe it necessary to export grain and disregard the risk of shortage in

Paris, the lieutenant of police and the magistrates of Parlement both found such a course unacceptable and joined together to obtain a temporary ban on grain shipments out of the country.

For each occasion on which one finds the police at odds with the Parlement over urban policy, one might find a corresponding situation in which the two joined forces against Versailles in the name of Paris. The preeminent power lieutenants of police exercised over the capital during the eighteenth century derived not simply from competitive success against other jurisdictions, a success founded on close ties to secretaries of state and ministries of the crown, but from the pursuit of allies in Paris as well and from a readiness to cooperate with their fellow magistrates in the Assemblée de Police.

Part II

The Uses of Power: Operations

5

A New
Wall

About 1670, acting on orders from the crown, workmen began pulling
down the walls that since the fourteenth century had shielded Paris
from its enemies. Their work did not so much mark a new sense of
security as it did a conviction that mortar and stone had become ob-
solete, that the ancient walls—having already been breached—were
useless, and that new strategies of defense were required. It is more
than coincidence that, while men and animals struggled with the debris of fallen ramparts, the government was at work trying to create an
effective urban police force. The new entity was to stand during the
eighteenth century and subsequently as successor to the condemned
and outmoded fortifications that had once encircled the city. It was to
give the capital a more adequate barrier against danger, a security traditional ramparts had ceased to afford. Paris did not under Louis XIV
become an open city; instead, it acquired, as it had under Charles V and
Philippe Auguste, a new wall, one better suited to altered circumstance, one which in this case could be used against an enemy who
now appeared more often within the city than without it.

THE FACE OF THE ENEMY

Parisians had known danger in many forms: in the ninth century they
had seen it in the guise of Norman plunderers; three hundred years
later it had come dressed as an English soldier; and in 1590, it had
appeared in the uniform of the king of France. During the seventeenth
century and during the eighteenth, with France an ascendant interna-
tional power, danger ceased to be external but did not disappear. Instead, Parisian authorities began to discover that an enemy dwelt in
their midst, an enemy against whom walls had already proven ineffec-
tual and whose defeat would require new measures of defense.

189

Who was this enemy? Who was it that police and prominent Parisians feared as a threat to order and security in the capital? To these questions there is more than a single answer, but one group above all others attracted the attention of Nicolas de La Reynie and his successors. This was the motley collection of individuals known in official acts as *gens sans aveu*, those who lived at or beyond the fringes of society, beggars and vagabonds, "such," in the words of an old English statute, "as wake on the night and sleep on the day, and haunt customable taverns and alehouses, and rout about; and no man wot from whence they came, nor whither they go."

Together mendicant vagabonds in eighteenth-century Paris probably never numbered more than ten thousand persons; yet they were, in the eyes of the police, the most dangerous group in the capital. Almost 90 percent of the city's crime was crime against property, and it was clear to the police that the vagabond, poor and without income, played a very prominent role in the various forms of theft afflicting the city.[1]

Parisian authorities considered the act of mendicancy itself a reprehensible form of theft. In asking alms from the pious and the humane, able-bodied men and women were taking money that rightly belonged to the weak, the crippled, and the aged. A royal edict of July 18, 1724, charges that vagabonds merit severe punishment in that "they steal the bread of the truly poor in arrogating to themselves charity destined for others." Some of those who begged on the city's streets were, indeed, guilty of fraud. Inspector Poussot recorded his encounter with one such man in July, 1746.

> I performed yesterday a miracle to the satisfaction of all about. I arrested a beggar who had his head wrapped in several cloths, and that part of his face which was visible appeared to be so covered with leprosy that no one dared look at it. He had before him a kind of tub as if to collect the pus that ran from his sores, a large crucifix, a rosary, and the languid air of one who was going to die. The Commissioner [who was accompanying Poussot] took ahold of part of the man's cheek, saying "I am going to cure you this instant." He found that what lay beneath was quite healthy. I made the man wash his face, take off the cloths mentioned above, and then had him walk from the Châtelet to the Rue Saint-Germain. Everyone was well-satisfied and began crying "miracle."

1. The police counted only three thousand vagabonds in 1785, though the year before there had been twice that number (BO, MS 1422, pp. 691, 703). On criminality and the incidence of theft, see Porphyre Petrovitch, "Recherches sur la criminalité à Paris pendant la seconde moitié du XVIII° siècle," in André Abbiateci, *et al.*, *Crimes et criminalité en France 17ᵉ–18ᵉ siècle*, Cahiers des *Annales*, No. 33 (Paris, 1971), 208.

The substance used to alter his appearance in this way is egg white and flour which he then smears with beef blood.[2]

The idleness of the vagabond disturbed authorities. It, too, constituted a form of theft, for one man's inactivity deprived both agriculture and industry of the labor necessary for collective survival. Indirectly, but no less certainly, the vagabond was robbing his fellows of bread and the state of revenues it might have had in the form of additional taxes. Each summer, in a concrete expression of this viewpoint, the police intensified their campaign against mendicancy, their objective being to force beggars out of the city in time to make them of use as agricultural laborers in the approaching harvest.[3]

Vagabonds were, authorities believed, an immediate danger not only to the property of Parisians but to their persons as well. A police report submitted to the government in 1780 claimed to prove that during the preceding thirty years the majority of assaults committed both in Paris and in the realm as a whole had been the work of homeless beggars, acting sometimes alone and sometimes in small bands.[4] But it was not simply the vagabond who waited in some shadowed doorway that Parisians had reason to fear; even those who sought alms in the light of day could be dangerous, as Etienne Alvarez discovered one May afternoon in 1773.

Alvarez was walking along the Rue des Cordelliers about one o'clock, trying to make his way through a crowd that had gathered to watch Marshal Biron's arrival in the city. A beggar appeared, stood in his path, and refused to step aside, insisting on some kind of offering. Having asked the man once or twice to let him pass, Alvarez asked again; and this time something in the tone of his voice, or perhaps some movement of the cane he carried, provoked the beggar, who— angered or frightened—leapt at Alvarez, snatched away the cane he held, and began threatening him with it. After an undignified scuffle, Alvarez recovered his cane, straightened his clothes, and continued on his way; but the beggar, a man named Ambroise Langlois, did not view the affair as finished. Gathering a group of confederates, he set off after his ungenerous adversary, and, had a number of men in the crowd not intervened, the beggars would have taken what Alvarez had been unwilling to give. As it was, the pursuers were routed, and Langlois found

2. Royal edict, July 18, 1724, in AN, Y 17112; BA, MS 10136, fol. 72.
3. BN, MS fr. 11356, fol. 421.
4. BO, MS 1422, pp. 689, 692, 694.

himself carried first before Commissioner Roland and then on to the prison of the Châtelet.[5]

Perhaps less dangerous as individuals than the vagabonds but far more numerous were the capital's domestic servants. Estimates suggest that there were between fifty thousand and one hundred thousand domestics in Paris during the eighteenth century. Whether serving in the home of a commercial family or a family of noble standing, each servant in the city roused the suspicion of the police. As early as 1666, domestics had attracted the attention of the special Conseil de Police established in part to discover and to eliminate the sources of insecurity in Paris; and one hundred years later, a lieutenant of police was still convinced that most of the thefts committed in the capital were the work of servants.[6]

Police distrust of the city's domestics was mixed with both repugnance and disdain. Le Moyne's *Dictionnaire de la police* describes household servants as the "scum of the countryside," as men and women devoid of virtue, bringing with them nothing but danger. More than one lieutenant of police shared this view. Lenoir, for example, contended that while other groups of poorly paid workers might occasionally cause the city difficulty, they also provided it with invaluable service. Domestics, however, contributed nothing, in his view, but disorder and the example of their sloth. On many occasions, he contrasts the merit of workers in commercial and industrial enterprise with the inutility and menace of the city's servants. "Labor in stores and shops," he says, "was for the workers the basis of their discipline, while the obligation to serve in the homes and in the retinues of their masters was, for most domestics, nothing more than a device for supporting idleness."[7]

5. AN, Y 9515, pieces 369–71.
6. Reinhard, *Paris pendant la révolution*, I, 102; BN, MS fr. 16847, fols. 75–80; BO, MS 1422, p. 645. Petrovitch's study of criminality, based on the records of prosecuted cases at the Châtelet, calls into question the judgment of the police: he and his colleagues estimate that, while domestics constituted 17 percent of the population, they made up only 8 percent of those appearing at the bar of the Châtelet. The authors of this excellent study are aware that there are particular problems with their figures for domestics, suggesting that many thefts committed by servants went unreported. Lenoir confirms this judgment, arguing that it was not simply many, but most, such thefts that never found their way to the prosecutor. The penal code of the *ancien régime* prescribed death as the sole penalty for a servant convicted of stealing from his master, regardless of the value of the article involved. Under the circumstances, most Parisians, to their credit, were unwilling to report thefts committed by a domestic, preferring simply to dismiss the individual they suspected.
7. BO, MS 1422, p. 645.

In the eyes of the Parisian police, it was not the worker and the laborer who constituted the most dangerous segment of the city's population. To be sure, the thousands of artisans and store clerks inhabiting the faubourgs of Saint-Antoine and Saint-Marcel had to be watched, but they were on the whole far less threatening than other elements in the community. Lenoir recalls that the workers of these faubourgs played "no important part in either the insurrection of May 3, 1775 caused by the shortage of flour or in earlier disorders, known as 'révolutions parlementaires.'" And, if criminal activity is used in place of rebellion to measure the relative menace of worker and servant, Lenoir reminds us that "crime was more common among domestics than among workers (*ouvriers*) and laborers (*manouvriers*)."[8]

Prior to 1789, the face of the enemy in Paris had wholly different features than the visage men subsequently learned to fear. It was not a revolutionary urban proletariat that menaced the city, but a thieving servant population that depended on the aristocracy and was of necessity, at least in Marxist terms, a socially conservative force. During the eighteenth century, those who most threatened Paris—the vagabond and the domestic—belonged, in the eyes of the police, not to a class that labored but to a *classe fainéante* (lazy, do-nothing class).

To this idle and dangerous class the police would have added the city's prostitutes who were, in a sense, more to be feared than either the domestic or the vagabond. A dishonest servant could deprive a man of property, and a desperate vagabond might do a man physical harm as well in the course of robbing him; but only encounter with a prostitute could injure a man spiritually as well as physically and financially. There were, according to the police, three kinds of prostitutes: those who walked the streets, those who received their clients in a house, and those—the most attractive and extravagant—who had managed to find one man willing to maintain them. All three sorts menaced a man's soul; but it was the street walker (frequently afflicted with syphilis) who most endangered his person, and the elegant mistress who posed the greatest threat to his property.[9]

As one of the city's enemies, as part of the *classe fainéante*, prostitutes had, like the vagabond, to endure the permanent attention of a

8. *Ibid.*, 598,.645; Petrovitch, "Criminalité à Paris," 245. Lenoir contends that there were invariably more unemployed domestics than jobless commercial and industrial workers; and this circumstance (which again the work of Petrovitch tends to confirm) offers a ready explanation for the higher incidence of crime among servants.

9. BO, MS 1424, pp. 83–89.

police inspector specially assigned to keep track of them. They had, too, to put up with intermittent harassment from the entire force. On November 16, 1778, Lenoir announced in a letter to his commissioners a new campaign against those who practiced this unproductive and degenerate profession: "With the Chevalier Dubois [commander of the guard] I have just taken measures to effect in every section of the city the arrest of the prostitutes who, at the end of each day and during the night, undertake their infamous commerce in the streets, in public places, and along the boulevards. I am writing the governors and concierges of the public gardens ordering that they expel and arrest them. Thus attacked from all sides, there is reason to hope that the number of these girls and women will diminish and that they will occasion less scandal."[10]

Recent work on criminality in Paris suggests that women as a whole were a greater menace to urban life during the eighteenth century than they are currently, accounting then for two to three times the percentage of offenses they do today. During the disorders that erupted in Paris in August and September of 1788, it is not surprising to find women playing a more important role than they might presently. The night of August 29, for example, it was a crowd of women, apparently led by a prostitute named Saint-Amand, that sacked and destroyed a guardpost at the Halle Neuve. There is also the suggestion that women played an inordinately large part in the Jansenist movement that so plagued the monarchy. One police informer speaks of the Jansenists during 1730 as "being almost entirely composed of women" and grows indignant at the crowds of females who each day fill to overflowing the church of Saint-Germain-le-Vieux, one of the two Parisian parishes still in the hands of the Jansenists. As Jansenists, as beggars, as domestic servants and prostitutes, women formed a considerable contingent among the city's foes—one worthy of more attention from the police than their counterparts today receive.[11]

In a society half of whose population was under twenty, it is not surprising to learn that the face of the enemy was often young. Adolescents apparently figured prominently in the crowd that invested the Palais after the exile of the Parlement in August, 1787. For an entire

10. Lenoir to commissioners, November 16, 1778, in AN, Y 12830.
11. Petrovitch, "Criminalité à Paris," 234; BN, MS JF 1103, fols. 109–10. Joubert to Hérault, March 12, 1730, in BA, MS 10006.

week following this event, disorder reigned in Paris. Mobs gathered
daily in the streets and the gardens of the Palais-Royal. Composed, according to police reports, largely of *jeunes gens* (young people), these
gangs roamed the city, looting shops, forcing entry into the court
chambers of the Châtelet, and beating anyone bold enough to express
sympathy for the government.[12]

Children stole from parents, from teachers, and, with the help of an
adult, from strangers. They might also on occasion threaten more than
property, being, it would seem, among the more ardent anticlericals in
Paris. In July, 1735, the monks of the Abbey Sainte-Geneviève wrote
Hérault, the lieutenant of police, seeking his protection against what
the monks described as a band of children of all ages. The youngsters,
who came, according to the monks, from the Faubourg Saint-Marcel
and principally from the Place de l'Estrapade, gathered every day outside the walls of their monastery and began hurling "not only all kinds
of garbage, but even stones weighing two and three pounds" into the
garden of the enclosure. This bombardment began at sunrise, the
monks claimed, and went on until dark. It had buried the garden's
shrubs and grass under debris and had made walking out-of-doors a risk
few clergymen were willing to take. When the monks ventured outside the monastery to stop the barrage, they inevitably attracted a
crowd of parents who sided with their offspring and drove the clerics
back behind their walls. The monks had no recourse, they said, but to
ask the police for help.

Hérault summoned before him a number of the parents and warned
them that they would be held responsible should the attacks on the
monastery continue. Threatening them with exemplary corporal punishment, he said he could not overlook the fact that others besides the
monks of Sainte-Geneviève—"persons of the highest distinction and
of the highest rank in the realm"—had often found themselves targets
for undisciplined bands of children.

Six years later Hérault's successor was still trying to protect congre-
gations of clergymen from gangs of small Parisians. This time the
children involved came from the northern edge of the city, from the
quarter of Saint-Denis. Again it was the parents who appeared before
the lieutenant of police, but on this occasion they learned that the

---

12. AN, 0-1 361, nos. 13–14.

youngsters themselves would be punished should the stoning continue. Marville told them he would have those who persisted whipped and confined.[13]

There were others still younger than children whom the city came to regard as enemies and to treat as such. Every year the police took into custody approximately four thousand small vagrants, infants newly born and quickly abandoned. Like the prostitute, these tiny beings began appearing on the streets as night settled over the city. Often they came with a small note attached on which appeared their name, their sex, and the date of their baptism. Night after night detachments of the guard carried five or six or ten of the little creatures to the foundling hospital, but there were always more.[14]

Many of these infants had traveled no more than a few blocks to reach the places where they lay; but a large number of others had come farther, surviving long journeys by carriage or boat from distant villages. Because Paris had a foundling hospital that afforded unwanted children a chance to survive, reluctant mothers all over France paid boatmen and wagoners what they could to smuggle into the capital hundreds of small, wet, and sometimes noisy bundles. The strain on the city became overwhelming, and in 1772 orders went out to every intendant in France and to the commanders of each detachment of *maréchaussée* that they were to prohibit and prevent transport of infants into Paris. Boats, carts, and carriages bound for the capital were to be searched and any unattended infant removed to the nearest hospital. Meanwhile, in Paris itself and along its perimeters, the police labored to repulse this strange and damaging assault on the city's resources.[15]

If it is ironic to find infants viewed as enemies of a great city, there are others whom one is surprised to find were also regarded as such. In the course of work to guarantee Paris adequate supplies, most lieutenants of police appear to have acquired a considerable distrust of the

13. On theft by children, see Peuchet, *Mémoires*, II, 108; regarding their assaults on clergy, see AN, AD-I 26, 120, 20.

14. Mildmay, *Police of France*, 81. The figure 4,000 is for mid-century. In 1751, 3,783 babies were admitted to the foundling hospital in Paris. The figure at the beginning of the century had been closer to 2,000, while in the last decade of the Old Regime it generally approached, and sometimes surpassed, 6,000. See Ernest Labrousse, *et al.*, *Des derniers temps de l'âge seigneurial aux préludes de l'âge industrial (1660–1789)* (Paris, 1970), 73–74, Vol. II of Ferdinand Braudel and Ernest Labrousse (eds.), *Histoire economique et sociale de France* (Paris, 1970–); AN, Y 13018 (this is a log of the guard's activity in which the discoveries of abandoned infants are recorded).

15. BN, MS JF 1236, fols. 88–98; deliberations of the officers of the Hôpital Général, in AN, Y 13728.

merchant, viewing him, in Lemaire's words, as inclined to fraud and as among those "avid to profit from public misfortune." While recognizing that the periodic shortages experienced in Paris had many causes, the police were generally inclined to believe that selfish commercial interests had a hand in generating many of these deficiencies. Hérault spoke for others who held his office when, in 1735, he drafted a report for the Parlement in which he charged that hay was unavailable in the capital largely because merchants were hoarding it, waiting for a rise in price that would enhance their profit. Human greed and individual disregard of public good had emptied the ports and markets of the city. As men whose cupidity occasionally led them to choke off the supplies of food and fuel upon which life and civil order in Paris depended, the city's merchants had a place among those whom the police regarded with undisguised suspicion.[16]

So, too, did moneylenders, particularly those known as *preteurs sur gages*, or pawnbrokers, who, the police were sure, consciously fenced much of the property stolen in the capital.

The king's soldiers were yet another group that aroused abnormal distrust on the part of the police. Both troops stationed in Paris and those there only briefly to recruit or visit contributed more than their share to urban disorder. As men inordinately sensitive about their honor and as dedicated patrons of the city's cabarets, the Gardes Suisses and Gardes Françaises—supposedly in Paris to maintain order—probably created more disturbances in the capital than they managed to quell. The registers of police patrols record frequent encounters with disorderly and belligerent soldiers from these two regiments. On a Monday night, for instance, in October, 1747, a police patrol was called to a cabaret where eight inebriated and boisterous Gardes Suisses were making a nuisance of themselves. When ordered by the patrol to leave, the offended soldiers declined and declared that it was rather the police who would be obliged to go. It does not, perhaps, speak well for the French army to report that the king's troops were eventually led as prisoners from the cabaret.[17]

Visiting soldiers shared the intemperate thirst of their comrades stationed in Paris and were driven, in their efforts to quench it, to similar

16. BO, MS 1424, p. 124; BN, MS JF 1316, fols. 105–106, 152–55.
17. AN, AD-I 22B, 6, 8; entry dated October 9, 1747, in AN, Y 13018. According to Lenoir, discipline among the Gardes Françaises and Suisses improved during the eighteenth century. By 1780, he contends, these troops had ceased to commit the same number of "excesses" in Paris they had fifty years earlier (BHVP, MS n.a. 477, fol. 23).

excesses. At one o'clock in the morning on November 12, 1747, a police patrol summoned to one of the many cafés in Paris found a royal dragoon, armed with a sword and clothed only in a nightgown, chasing the proprietress of the establishment. Despite appearances, the guard determined that it was only a drink that interested this particular soldier. Questioning revealed that he had found a law forbidding the sale of alcohol after eleven o'clock unconscionable and had decided to compel at least a momentary revision of the cruel regulation.[18]

More dangerous than drunken dragoons were the calculatingly sober recruiters who came to Paris hunting men to fill out the depleted ranks of their units. Again and again boys and young men followed a recruiting officer into some cabaret, drank to excess, and disappeared. Some were lucky and managed to escape, but rarely without the help of a courageous stranger and the police. In January, 1747, a woman noticed a boy struggling with soldiers and called out for help on his behalf. Several men who tried to intervene were beaten, but their efforts delayed the abductors long enough to cost them their captive, for the woman who had initially given the alarm had gone in search of the police. When she returned with a detachment of the guard, roles were suddenly reversed: the recruiting sergeant found himself a prisoner and the boy went free.[19] If life in the capital had its annoyances, it also brought the ordinary resident a protection against military arrogance and brutality that was unknown elsewhere in France.

Some among the enemy in Paris threatened property and person; others menaced inhabitants in less tangible ways, corrupting souls and robbing men of what the crown, the high clergy, and the police deemed proper loyalties. A number of the philosophes belonged in this group, as did the many less celebrated individuals who turned out illegal newsletters known as *nouvelles à la main* in which members of the royal family, the court, and the government were ridiculed and defamed, but those whom the police pursued with special fervor were the Jansenists who, in their eyes, threatened the attachment of the Parisians to both monarch and church. It had been a Jansenist, the police believed, a man named Gaspard de Vise, who had been the principal force behind the fanaticism and disorder that erupted during the 1720s and early 1730s in the cemetery of Saint-Médard. A standing order

18. Entry dated November 12, 1747, in AN, Y 13018.
19. BA, MS 10015, fol. 7.

for this man's arrest went unexecuted because agents were unable to corner him.

Throughout the century the police worked to uncover the clandestine gatherings of other Jansenists and to record the names and addresses of all who participated in these assemblies. Lenoir was convinced that the Jansenists had allied with Protestants both in France and elsewhere "to destroy the clergy of France and to overturn royal authority."

Their power in the restored Parlement of Paris was particularly dangerous; and Lenoir deemed it necessary to begin paying "several magistrates and lawyers" who were members of this court to report on the conduct and speeches of Jansenist colleagues. Of special interest to him were two men whom he judged to be the most "fanatical" leaders of the Jansenist party in the Parlement, men named Fréteau and Camus.[20]

Also of interest, of course, were the publicists who served such men, the printers willing or eager to publish their speeches and the colporteurs who accepted the risks of distributing them. Both of these groups, too, were carefully watched by the police. Like food merchants, they were an essential part of life in the capital. Yet, like these merchants, they were also a great potential menace, one that had to be kept under surveillance and carefully controlled; if it was not always possible to prevent an individual from speaking his mind, one could at least limit the public exposure given hostile comment by keeping close watch over presses and peddlers. So, for example, in June, 1760, Sartine informed his inspector of the booktrade that a recent remonstrance made by the *parlement* of Rouen was a genuine threat to the monarchy and ordered him to be vigilant, seeing that any colporteur who dared distribute this statement was immediately arrested.[21]

Obviously suspect of subverting loyalty to the French crown were the foreigners who visited Paris, both those who came as representatives of their governments and those who were ostensibly no more than tourists. The police kept ambassadors from a number of states under surveillance, while their attention to travelers and tourists centered on three groups in particular. Dutchmen and Germans they sus-

20. BA, MS 10026, fol. 135; MS 10029, fols. 75, 77; BO, MS 1423, p. 35.
21. Unnumbered list of those the police considered dangerous, in BA, MS 10249; BN, MS fr. 22115, fol. 286.

pected of clandestine assistance to the Jansenist party in France, and this distrust led a police agent in 1763 to suggest to Sartine that a way be found of eavesdropping on the confessionals of two German priests then in Paris in order to determine whether they were using the privacy of this sacrament to plant sedition. Two years later, Sartine noted in a letter to Inspector Buchot the arrival in Paris of two young Prussian artists. "I think it necessary," he says, "to keep track of their activity and of their encounters for fear that their voyage has a purpose other than that they have claimed."

That the police took special notice of English tourists is hardly surprising, given the prolonged enmity between France and her island neighbor, and given, too, the unwelcome political doctrines that unavoidably accompanied the visiting Englishman.

Italians brought with them neither pernicious religious views nor subversive political opinion. They were, nonetheless, among those whom the police treated with particular distrust. Lenoir explains why in a letter he wrote Commissioner Gillet on October 11, 1779. In going over guest lists from hotels, the lieutenant of police says, it is important to take special note of foreigners and, among these, especially of Italians and Piedmonters, whose reasons for being in Paris are usually dubious. It is the Italians, Lenoir continues, who supply most of the thieves and pickpockets at work in Parisian crowds and in the capital's theaters and its opera.[22]

There is a sense in which most of those who threatened Paris were foreigners. Of the domestics whom the police regarded with so much distrust, 87 percent came not from the capital but from the provinces of France. Most of the city's prostitutes, too, were immigrants to Paris, as were the majority of the able-bodied mendicants whom the police called vagabonds and pursued with such great energy.[23]

It was immigrants who accounted for most of the crimes committed in Paris and who played a preeminent role in the civil disorders that erupted during the last years of the Old Regime. One historian has found that two-thirds of those tried in the criminal court of the Châ-

22. BN, MS fr. 16847, fols. 75–80; unnumbered list in BA, MS 10249 which begins "foreigners in Paris" and ends "women living in high style"; unnumbered list from the 1740s naming envoys under surveillance, [?] to Sartine, December 7, 1765, and Inspector Buchot to Sartine, September 8, 1767, all in BA, MS 10293; BA, MS 10026, fol. 135; AN, K 1021, nos. 1–2; Lenoir to Commissioner Gillet, October 11, 1779, in AN, 13728.

23. Reinhard, *Paris pendant la révolution*, I, 103; BO, MS 1424, p. 84; A majority of the so-called vagabonds were probably unemployed domestics (BO, MS 1422, p. 645) who were, as we have seen, mostly immigrants.

telet after 1755 were not native Parisians but came instead from provinces to the north and east of the city; and if one examines the lists of those who appeared in the Chambre de Police charged with something more than a routine offense, one finds an even higher proportion of immigrants: of sixty-one persons sentenced to exile or prison on May 25, 1759, for example, only fifteen were Parisians by birth. Provincials figure prominently, too, in every major civil disturbance occurring in Paris between 1775 and 1789. According to George Rudé, 80 percent of those arrested during the bread riots of 1775 had been born outside the city, as had 66 percent of the men and women involved in the Reveillon riots of April, 1789, and 63 percent of those who joined in storming the Bastille three months later. Of thirty-two men and women arrested for their part in the riots of August and September, 1788, only nine (28 percent) were native Parisians.[24]

On the basis of this data, one might argue that it was not Parisian crowds that saved a revolution or imposed one on the rest of France, but rather that these deeds were the work of provincials, of immigrants frustrated and desperate at the tenuousness of their place in the capital, of men and women who quickly realized that the city to which they had come was anything but "open." It is perhaps symbolic that the first target of the revolutionaries in July, 1789, was not the Bastille, but the newly completed wall of the Farmers General that encircled the city. Rudé argues that the principal objective of those who attacked this barrier was not to permit free entry of consumer goods but to control the access of persons and arms to the city. It is as if the rebels believed large numbers of comrades waited outside the city to aid them—more provincials to secure the revolt in Paris; and, indeed, thousands of persons appear to have entered the capital during the summer of 1789. Lafayette estimated the number of "strangers or *gens sans aveu*" in Paris during the week following the fall of the Bastille at thirty thousand.[25]

24. Petrovitch, "Criminalité à Paris," 238, 240; an unnumbered document headed "rolle des prisonniers . . ." (roll of prisoners), in AN, Y 9539; George Rudé, *The Crowd in the French Revolution* (Oxford, 1959), 249; BN, MS JF 1103, fols. 71–133. Rudé, using other sources (series Y at the AN) and treating 1788 together with 1787, counts a total of fifty-five arrests for the disorders of both years. Among this total, he finds only seventeen provincials (31 percent), a number inferior to that provided by the list at the BN for 1788 alone. In each of the instances cited in this paragraph, the percentage of immigrants involved exceeds—insofar as we can tell—the percentage of immigrants among the population as a whole (see Reinhard, *Paris pendant la révolution*, I, 37–39).
25. Rudé, *The Crowd in the French Revolution*, 19.

Doors that bolted shut at 10:00 P.M., commercial and industrial communities locked against the intrusion of any newcomer, carriage terminals and hotels under constant surveillance by the police—what provincial could have failed to notice that the capital remained during the eighteenth century what it had ever been—a fortress with its walls intact, a bastion from which men looked down with disdain on those who came seeking a new beginning or simply a way to live. To the stranger Paris offered little hope of a decent livelihood. Immigrant men might wait in a public square or at the ports for a chance to transport some heavy load; some of the women might be allowed to serve in the city's homes; but for many newcomers there were no options but prostitution, mendicancy, and theft. Parisians ridiculed the provincial immigrant, exploited him, denied him both dignity and a genuine place among them. It is no wonder, then, that, in the end, he became the foremost of the city's enemies.

STRATEGIES OF DEFENSE

Whether one measures the preoccupations of the police by reference to the distribution of personnel or by an examination of expenditures, it is clear that the provision of security and the maintenance of order were overriding concerns. In 1780 the police were dedicating 70 percent of their personnel and two-thirds of their financial resources to these objectives.[26] But how, in concrete terms, did they go about pursuing these goals? By what means did they seek to provide Paris with the safety and civil peace walls had once given the city?

Provisions and Order

Understandably the police preferred preventing crime and riot to suppressing them, and this preference led them to give considerable attention to the problems of provisioning Paris; for, like many historians of France, municipal authorities had long perceived a striking correlation between internal disorder and augmentations in the price of food and essential commodities. Before a special session of the Parisian Parlement convoked on November 28, 1768, to consider ways of obtaining badly needed supplies of grain for the capital, the lieutenant criminal of the Châtelet, Testart Dubys, rose to join in deploring the scarcity of

26. See tables 2 and 8. In calculating 70 percent of personnel I include all those involved in deterrent patrol (47 percent), investigation and intelligence (12 percent), lighting (5 percent), and censorship (6 percent).

this vital provision. His position, he said, gave him more cause than most to lament the shortage, for each day he witnessed its consequences: "Crimes grow more numerous not because the human heart is more corrupt, but because the resources of this society have become limited. Among the criminals who fill our prisons, the majority are more wronged than guilty. At the first opportunity they explain that misery prompted their crime, and investigation confirms what most have said. Consumed by their need, misled by it, many of those I have seen finish shamefully because they and their families were dying of hunger." There was no doubt, he concluded, that the present dearth of grain was the immediate cause of an increase in the number of crimes perpetrated in Paris.[27]

To these views more than one lieutenant of police would have subscribed, adding only that such shortage could provoke massive disorder as well as individual crime. One only need read the dispatches Thiroux de Crosne sent the procureur general of the Parlement during the Reveillon riots of April, 1789, to realize that he regarded adequate supplies of food a barrier against disorder every bit as important as armed force. Within the same hour on April 28, 1789, Joly de Fleury received two messages from the lieutenant of police. In the first, Crosne reported that at 6:00 P.M. the crowd on the eastern edge of the city was still growing. It had become so thick in the large avenue Faubourg Saint-Antoine that police informers were having trouble getting in and out to supply information. Troops sent to contain the assembly had been driven back and were waiting for reinforcements. In the second dispatch, written one hour later, after fresh troops had arrived and opened fire on the crowd, Crosne told the procureur general that he had given orders that the markets of the city be extraordinarily well stocked with bread on the following day. Bakers in the Faubourg Saint-Antoine who were unable to bake would, Crosne said, be furnished with bread to sell. The following morning, the lieutenant of police found it possible to report that abundant displays of food had completed the task of pacification. The markets, he wrote, were impressively full and there had, that morning, been no sign of further trouble.[28]

Crosne was not the first lieutenant of police to appreciate the link between provisions and order in the capital. His predecessors had long understood the connection and had, in an effort to minimize crime and

27. AN, K 1022, no. 14.
28. BN, MS JF 1103, fols. 158–60, 168.

Table 8 Police Expenditures
(All figures are in livres)

	(1) 1780	% of Total 1	% of Total 2	(2) 1718	(3) 1753	(4) 1764	(5) 1789
SECURITY[1]	1,488,537	45.24	66.00				
Guard and watch	660,000		29.26		420,000		768,244
Maréchaussée (Ile-de-France)	195,000		8.65		120,000	21,038	261,588
Supernumeraries (Robe Courte)	41,160	2.94	1.82				
Inspectors	216,690	15.47	9.61			177,804	
Secret funds (espionage)	20,000	1.43	.89				
Lights	355,687	25.40	15.77	300,000 (1704–22)	300,000		
PUBLIC SERVICES	408,621	29.18	18.12				
Garbage removal	260,307	18.59	11.54		206,000		116,000
Fire protection	81,790	5.84	3.63		20,000		
Relief	66,524	4.75	2.95				
ADMINISTRATION & COMMUNICATION	190,474	13.59	8.44				
Lt. of police[2]	28,000	2.05	1.28				
First secretary	12,000	.85	.53				
Staff	127,035	9.07	5.63				
Rent, light, heat	22,639	1.61	1.00				

JUSTICE	82,800	5.91	3.67	
Commissioners	82,800	5.91	3.67	58,350
MISCELLANEOUS (Pensions, Paris militia)	85,058	6.08	3.77	
TOTAL 1[3]	1,400,490	100.00		1,070,615 (1759–80)
TOTAL 2[4]	2,255,490	100.00		1,554,000 (1787–89)

SOURCES: (1) BO, MS 1422, p. 971; AN, AD-IX 389; (2) AN, F-4 1017; (3) BN, MS JF 1321, fols. 65–66, 74–78, 130–31; BN, MS JF 1325, fols. 113–16; Mildmay, *The Police of France*, 93–95, 117–22; BHVP, c.p. 4725; AN, O-1 361, pieces 329–32; BO, MS 1422, p. 968; (5) AN, AD-IX 389; AN, F-4 1017.

1. This total does not include the very considerable cost of maintaining the various prisons in the city. Mildmay says he was told that operating the largest of these, the Hôpital Général, cost 2,700,648 livres in 1753, when its various element contained 12,868 persons. The figures for the guard and watch are from 1781.
2. This is the sum given on Lenoir's table of expenses (B, MS 1422, p. 971), even though on p. 969 he had indicated that the income of the lieutenant of police amounted to 55,000 livres a year. Presumably, the additional 26,200 livres was paid out of a fund other than that assigned to the police.
3. Lists of police expenses did not ordinarily include money spent to maintain the guard and the *maréchaussée* of the Ile-de-France. This total excludes these expenses.
4. Includes expenditures for guard and *maréchaussée*.

civil disturbance, sought to control both the supply and the price of essential commodities entering the city. The task was enormous, involving labor both in Paris and outside the city in the provinces of France and in neighboring countries.

Under ordinary circumstances, when harvests and production were normal in regions supplying the capital, the police spent their time monitoring exchange in the city's markets, attempting to see that merchants did not demand more for a product than they had been authorized to charge. As part of their effort to enforce limits on prices, the police regulated the days and hours during which basic items could be sold and prescribed the locations where such sale could take place. Hence, most articles were available in the markets only on Wednesday and Saturday and all basic foods could be sold initially only at the central market. In July, 1724, we find Ravot d'Ombreval, then lieutenant of police, fining a grocer named Roger 200 livres for not carrying all the butter he had brought into Paris straight to Les Halles. A commissioner of police, up prowling about at 4:00 A.M., had spotted Roger as he had stopped clandestinely to unload a portion of his cargo.[29]

While prescribing the place at which initial exchange could occur made the task of surveillance somewhat easier, the police had, as already noted, another motive in requiring that foods be transported first to the central market. According to Commissioner Lemaire, authorities believed that by creating abundant displays of grain and produce they were "consoling" the more indigent members of the community, encouraging them to believe that they would not go hungry. Display, he said, "sustains the poor, encourages them; it removes and banishes from their minds the fears and uncertainties most capable of causing them to contemplate the ruin and misery which pursue them and which, in excess, drive them to despair."[30] One hardly need add that beyond despair lay acts of crime and rebellion, and that, in the end, it was to prevent these that the police obliged merchants to exhibit large quantities of food in a public setting.

Efforts to control prices were likewise an attempt on the part of the police to avoid dangerous levels of despair and anger. All lieutenants of police had the power of specifying the prices at which important commodities could be sold, a power they were inclined to use. To enforce

29. BN, MS JF 1323, fols. 231–32; MS JF 1333, fol. 103; BO, MS 1424, p. 53.
30. BO, MS 1424, p. 127.

their determinations they relied not only on commissioners and inspectors of police but on the officers of the mercantile communities.
Even Joseph d'Albert, whom Turgot had made lieutenant of police to
preside over the destruction of the Parisian guilds, was obliged to create substitutes for these officers who had run the guilds and aided the
police. D'Albert's plan was to divide each of the city's twenty quarters
into a number of *arrondissements* (the quarter of Saint-Benoît, for example, was to have four) containing no more than three hundred merchants and artisans. Inhabitants of each *arrondissement* would then
participate once a year in choosing three officers (one syndic and two
assistants) responsible in that area for enforcing the economic regulations of the police.[31] Seen in this light, d'Albert's administration of
Paris under Turgot represents less an effort to end police regulation
of the economy than an attempt to alter the manner in which such
regulation was enforced. The new syndics created by d'Albert were to
be responsible not for overseeing a single craft or profession, as had
their predecessors under Lenoir, but for a particular section—an *arrondissement*—of the city.

Given its preeminent place in the lives of most Parisians, bread was
a commodity whose price was of particular concern to the police. Its
cost, while carefully controlled, fluctuated with changes in the price of
grain. On May 29, 1769, Sartine noted in a letter to the commissioners
that the price of both grain and flour had dropped and ordered them to
inform bakers in their districts that bread was to sell for no more than
thirteen sous the four-pound loaf. The previous autumn Sartine had
told the bakers they were not to raise their prices for the time being,
but that at the end of the month he intended to permit a slight increase. He was, he said, constantly torn between the bakers and the
public, wishing to be just and helpful to the one, but being unable to
ignore the complaints of the other, especially those of the poor among
them, which touched him deeply.

The police sought to control the price of more than grain and bread.
On September 21, 1777, Lenoir wrote his commissioners saying that
attempts by the city's butchers to raise the price of meat from eight
sous a pound to nine were to be resisted. Livestock, he pointed out,

---

31. Albert to Commissioner Gillet, March 18, April 6, and May 20, 1776, in AN, Y
12830.

were selling for exactly what they had the year before, leaving the butchers nothing to justify their demands but an avarice that could not be tolerated.

While keeping watch over the price of meat, the police also interested themselves in the cost of other essential food, in the price of candles, and in the charges made for important services. In January, 1771, for example, Sartine expressed dissatisfaction with the city's cabdrivers and the unreasonable fees they were asking of those they transported to a park near the École Militaire. Henceforth, he told his agents, the drivers were to demand no more than forty sous for this trip.[32]

Those who failed to comply with prescribed limits on prices could expect a warning and, if this did not suffice, a summons to appear before the Chambre de Police where they ordinarily received a fine ranging from one hundred to three hundred livres. To this fine the lieutenant of police sometimes added the burden of unwelcome publicity in the form of an order that the sentence should be published and posted. The value of these sanctions, however, depended on support from the procureur general and the Parlement to whom a defendant in the Chambre de Police might appeal his case. Five lieutenants of police, beginning with d'Ombreval in 1724 and ending with Bertin de Bellisle in 1758, found it very difficult to control the price of butter in Paris because the Parlement continued throughout this period to overturn their sentences against violators.[33]

If, under ordinary circumstances, the police confined their attention to Paris itself and devoted themselves to discovering and punishing merchants who asked more for an item than regulations permitted, periods of shortage broadened the scope of their work. It was during times of scarcity, particularly in the worst years of shortage—1726, 1752, 1768, and 1774—that the police acted not only to control prices but to augment supplies and to see that the hungry actually had means of purchasing food.

Each day the lieutenant of police received reports on the quantities of supplies entering Paris and could compare these with records from previous years to determine the adequacy of what the city was receiv-

32. Sartine to commissioners, September 6, 1768, May 29, 1769, January 12, 1771; Lenoir to commissioners, September 21, 1777, in AN, Y 13728.

33. BN, MSS JF 1322–23 contain documents relating to this struggle with the city's grocers (*fruitiers-orangiers*). The story is a long and complex one, closely tied to the crown's efforts to reestablish a tax on butter.

ing. In May, 1768, when the police began to note a decline in supplies of livestock reaching the capital, Sartine dispatched an agent into the provinces of the Bourbonnais and the Lyonnais with orders to report on the number of sheep and cattle he observed and on what he perceived as the real reasons for scarcity in the Parisian markets of Sceaux and Poissy. (As late as March, provincial correspondents had written that there was no diminishment in the number of available livestock, and the lieutenant of police could not help suspecting a conspiracy among suppliers.) Sartine gave the man 30,000 livres before he left— 10,000 in currency and 20,000 in letters of exchange—and ordered him to buy what animals he could for Paris. It appears likely that the lieutenant of police sent another man westward into Normandy on a similar mission. Both were warned to proceed with great discretion in order to avoid what Sartine described as the "usual inconveniences" that arose when merchants learned of an impending scarcity. The reduced supply of livestock in the spring of 1768 was linked to the poor harvest the previous autumn and the high price of grain. When grain was scarce, farmers gave up the work of fattening livestock since they could make more money selling the grain directly than by converting it into fattened animals. Sartine was no doubt aware of this fundamental difficulty but was also concerned that it not be exacerbated by those who, upon learning of an approaching shortage, would have hidden what livestock they had until the price climbed high enough to suit them.

The shortage of livestock continued through 1769 and into 1770. In January, 1770, Sartine wrote the intendants of ten provinces (including Turgot at Limoges and Crosne at Rouen) asking them to indicate the quality and quantities of livestock in their areas, the prices at which animals were selling, and the reasons which, in their judgment, accounted for reduced supplies to Paris. At the same time he again sent his own agents into the provinces, ordering them to try to answer the same questions and to buy wherever they could for the markets in the capital. Calculating the city's needs at 2,200 cattle per week and foreseeing shortages despite the work of his commissioners in the provinces, Sartine sent men across the borders of France—north into the Low Countries and east into the states of Germany.

These agents were to persuade foreign merchants to bring livestock into Paris at their own expense by offering them a bonus of ten livres on every head of cattle and five sous for every sheep. Failing in this, they were to buy the animals outright on behalf of the crown, taking care to purchase enough to keep the price reasonable in Paris but not so many as to drive it to levels that would discourage French farmers from raising livestock. Sartine's agent in Germany, obliged to buy the animals there, could not initially understand his failure to get the foreign merchants themselves to venture into France.

On his return to Paris, however, the reluctance of the Germans became comprehensible. Seven years earlier, in a decree issued April 17, 1763, the Conseil d'État had sought to increase the numbers of livestock reaching market by reducing duties imposed on animals entering France and by eliminating internal tariffs altogether. Sartine's commissioner was appalled to discover that no office of the General Farms along the road from Germany was observing this edict. At the frontier with Breisgau he had been obliged to pay twelve sous a cow; he was asked for another ten passing through Colmar; for ten more at the frontier of Lorraine; for ten again to traverse the province of Bar; and for still ten more at Saint Dizier on the Marne. The commissioner reports that at each office of the Farms he invoked the edict of 1763, which he knew by heart since he had often helped execute it, but all to no avail. The ignorant employees of the Farms had never heard of the edict and for seven years had been zealously collecting duties to which they had no right. One can only too well imagine, he says, the difficulties, the losses, and the fears foreign merchants suffered in their dealings with these men.[34]

Agents sent to buy in the provinces and abroad, investigators dispatched to uncover hoarding, reduced internal and external tariffs, bonuses paid on scarce commodities—these were some of the means employed by police and crown to increase supplies reaching Paris during periods of shortages. The police tried as well to take measures within the city to see that essential foods reached not only the markets but the people as well. In 1768 Sartine sought and obtained additional funds from the government to subsidize 500 bakers who, without such help, would have been forced out of business by the high price of grain. The lieutenant of police also obtained money that permitted him to offer work to many men in the construction industry who had lost their jobs as a result of the winter's severe cold. During difficult moments in 1771 and again in the spring of 1778, the head of the police ordered bakers throughout the city to accept as payment from the poor

34. Auguste Molinier, *Inventaire sommaire de la collection Joly de Fleury* (Paris, 1881), xxvi; BN, MS fr. n.a. 6765, fols. 4–6, 20–49, 109–85, 193–95, 203–20, 241–46.

coins they would not ordinarily have taken. Police agents then went about collecting the questionable pieces and reimbursing the bakers with a more acceptable currency.[35]

Generally, the police worried about shortages and the disorder they might cause. In the case of alcohol, however, it was abundance, particularly in certain hands, that worried them. From time to time the lieutenant of police issued a reiteration of regulations whose observance he deemed most important to public order. These ordinances "concerning public safety and tranquillity" reflect a keen sense for the correlation between excessive consumption of alcohol and antisocial behavior. To preserve the dignity of religious observance the sale of alcohol was forbidden Sunday mornings and during religious festivals; and those who chose to disregard this provision were often not difficult to locate and punish. There was, for example, Mr. Caron, proprietor of a cabaret at the corner of the Rue Bourbon and the Rue Petit-Carreau. Having decided to do business on the day of Corpus Christi, Caron opened his doors early in the morning to three regular customers—a butcher named Vinot, a glassmaker called Tardu, and one of the butcher's helpers, Barre. Quickly, these three had raised their spirits enormously and climbed to the second floor of the cabaret where they could watch a religious procession pass beneath them. Carried away by enthusiasm for the holiday, Tardu and Barre began firing pistols they had brought with them. The two celebrants kept at it for some time, dispersing the procession, and sending neighbors for the nearest commissioner of police.

To eliminate noise and hazard at night, all establishments serving alcohol were obliged to close at 10:00 P.M. during the winter and at 11:00 P.M. between April 1 and November 1. Significantly, no cabaret was to admit or sell liquor to vagabonds or prostitutes; nor were soldiers to be served after a specified hour, earlier than that for ordinary customers. In addition, no cabaret was to sell wine and spirits except in a room that opened onto the street where police patrols could, without difficulty, observe what was going on.[36]

35. AN, K 1022, no. 14; Lenoir to commissioners, April 4, 1778, in AN, Y 13728.
36. For two examples of police ordinances concerning public safety, see AN, AD-I 26, 120, 5 (issued by Marc-René d'Argenson in 1716) and APP, DB 355 (Lenoir's ordinance of May 21, 1784). The Conseil de Police convoked in 1666 showed itself suspicious not only of alcohol but of tobacco as well, suggesting that "users and sellers of tobacco" were among those who ought to be carefully watched (BN, MS fr. 16847, fols. 75–80). AN, AD-I 22B, 6, 22.

Censorship and the Control of Rumor

Crown and police sought to preserve order in Paris by controlling the supply and exchange not only of food but of ideas. Whether cast in the form of drama for the theater or in that of a book, a pamphlet, a poster, a song, or a simple verbal declaration, ideas had to be examined and regulated. Those that offended church or state or accepted notions of proper conduct the police sought to suppress. In their efforts to control the circulation of ideas under the Old Regime, the police hunted down books and men condemned by the censor, pursued educators whose religious views were unacceptable, and worked, now and then, as an agency of propaganda, concerned not simply with uprooting undesirable opinions but with planting in their place others judged more useful.

While attacks on the church and government both provoked action by the police throughout the eighteenth century, there seems to have been a change in either the relative frequency of these two offenses or in governmental sensitivity to them. Prior to the administration of René Berryer, which began in 1747, religious publications and pronouncements—particularly, of course, those of the Jansenists—appear to have drawn more attention from the police than works concerned simply with affairs of state. Peuchet reports that d'Ombreval passed much of his term as lieutenant of police enforcing the religious orthodoxy prescribed by a royal declaration of May 14, 1724, and René Hérault—d'Ombreval's successor—gained a reputation during his fifteen years in office as the "great buttress of the Molinist, Jesuit, [and] bishops' party." In March, 1730, Hérault received a letter from a priest named Joubert expressing regret that the lieutenant of police was receiving so many letters threatening him for the zeal with which he had been executing royal orders against the Jansenists. The priest urged Hérault to remain firm and harsh with these "disguised Calvinists."[37]

Following the succession of Madame de Pompadour's protégé, Berryer, to the lieutenancy of police in 1747, the attention of the police appears to have shifted progressively from religious works to those treating government and current affairs. In a largely useless, anecdotal work on the lieutenants of police, Théodore Edme Bourg does reproduce a short list of pamphlets confiscated by the police under Lenoir.

37. Peuchet, *Mémoires*, I, 275; Mathieu Marais, cited in Chassaigne, *Lieutenance générale de police*, 61; Joubert to Hérault, March 12, 1730, in BA, MS 10006.

Notes in the margin of this list indicate the reasons each work was seized, and one remarks immediately that not one of them is judged an offense to religious doctrine. All are attacks on the administration, on the court, or on the queen.[38]

If, in the span of thirty years, the police learned to hunt political pamphlets with more energy than the Jansenist *Nouvelles ecclési-astiques*, their interest in pornography appears to have remained reasonably constant during the same period. Berryer's term in office did not alter the enthusiasm with which they confiscated prints depicting "the art of reproduction" or pieces of sculptures which, it was felt, could only further the steady corruption of morals.[39]

Until October, 1763, when Sartine became director of the book-trade, the lieutenant of police was less concerned with determining what books deserved proscription than with locating and punishing the authors, printers, and the distributors of works others had judged offensive. In pursuing books brought to his attention by a minister, by the director of the Librairie, or by the archbishop of Paris, he relied primarily on the investigative ability of a single inspector of police, responsible for surveillance of both the booktrade and of traffic in periodicals and pamphlets. To this individual the lieutenants of police turned not only for the solution of specific cases but whenever they found themselves faced with broad demands for a more rigid or a more careful enforcement of the censorship. In a letter written to Inspector Dehemery in February, 1767, Sartine asked not for the capture of a particular offender but for general counsel on strategy: "I am under great pressure to propose ways of stopping illegal books from entering France and of ending the abuses currently practiced by printers. . . . You have information concerning this part of my administration from which I wish to profit. You know how much this problem disturbs the king; you love the good and are loyal to your duty; you are fond of me and know my feelings for you—there you have the sum of the reasons for pressing ahead with this matter. Don't lose an instant."[40]

Trapping individuals who produced and circulated proscribed books ordinarily required great patience and long hours of surveillance. Dehemery reports spending two weeks watching a building he suspected

38. Théodore Edme Bourg, *Biographie des lieutenants-généraux, ministres . . . , [et] préfets de police en France, et de ses principaux agens* (Paris, 1829), 93–94.

39. For a few examples of police attention to pornography, see BN, MS fr. n.a. 1214, fol. 357 and Sartine to commissioners, April 27, 1765, in AN, Y 13728.

40. Sartine to Inspector Dehemery, February 2, 1767, in BN. MS fr. 22123.

housed a Jansenist press. Though this persistent attention eventually led to the arrest of eleven persons and to the seizure of a clandestine press, no one had apparently enjoyed the long hours spent hidden in doorways and alleys. In 1755 Dehemery or some other members of the force proposed that the police save themselves the ordeal of hunting underground presses by operating one of their own. Given the immunity it would enjoy and a willingness to do work at modest fees, such a press could monopolize all illegal printing done in Paris. Care would have to be taken in selecting a director for the new press. He ought to be a Parisian printer with extensive contacts among men of letters, someone widely respected whose reputation would attract manuscripts from literary figures. Presumably, the more harmless works would appear and be distributed without hindrance, though the identity of the authors would be known and noted; works deemed genuinely dangerous the police would follow to points of storage and seize in a manner that would not compromise those who had printed them. Though Berryer was favorably impressed by this scheme, we do not know whether he eventually implemented it.[41]

Police efforts to control circulation of undesirable books reached beyond Paris itself. In addition to using customs officials on the edges of the city to see that no proscribed works entered Paris, the lieutenant of police sent agents both into the provinces and, occasionally, on secret missions abroad. In 1766 Sartine designated Commissioner Mutel and Inspector Dehemery to act as his agents at the fair of Beaucaire and in the city of Toulouse. They were to seize any book they judged contrary to religion, state, or public morality. On April 30, 1771, Dehemery and another police agent named Gautier received orders from Sartine to proceed to Caen where, in the company of a subdelegate from that intendancy, they were to search the shops of all printers and bookdealers. Finding anything relating to the Brittany affair, they were, without being seen, to apprehend, detain, and interrogate the individual in whose possession this material was discovered. The two police agents bore a letter to the commander of the *maréchaussée* in Caen ordering him to furnish whatever assistance was required.

Ten years later, to stop the circulation of what were considered libelous attacks on the crown, Lenoir sent an inspector of police, Receveur, into Holland and the Austrian Netherlands to discover "the several

41. BN, MS fr. 22096, fols. 70–76; MS fr 22122, fol. 138.

shops in which these abominable works had been printed." Receveur's mission was successful, and shortly after his return to Paris, he was sent north again, this time accompanied by a second inspector named Brugières, to arrest secretly and smuggle back into France the printers involved. The mission, highly sensitive because it violated the sovereignty of other states, proceeded smoothly. In Brussels the two French agents took into custody a handful of printers and seized a number of incriminating manuscripts. By making liberal use of money and imagination, they managed to get their captives out of the Netherlands and back to Paris. Greatly pleased, Lenoir and Vergennes, minister of foreign affairs, began planning a similar mission into England to seize a Frenchman named Bossière, the last of those believed responsible for the defamatory attacks on crown and government that had been entering Paris.[42]

These missions abroad reflect a certain impotence at home; for despite the best efforts of the police in Paris, proscribed books continued to circulate. The principal reason for the ineffectiveness of the police is well-known. Numerous influential persons simply refused to cooperate, displaying books sought by the police in their homes, protecting the authors of these works, and, at times, even joining in the production of material the government regarded as seditious. The archbishop of Paris was driven to write Lenoir, complaining that heretical books by Diderot, Helvétius, d'Alembert, and Raynal were being kept openly in the *hôtels* de la Rochefoucault, d'Aubusson, and de Mirabeau; that they were defiantly displayed by members of the Parlement, the learned academies, and the royal court. Lamoignon de Malesherbes, after learning that the police had at last discovered and arrested the author of a work that had offended the crown, confessed to Sartine that he had for some time known the identity of the author but that affection for the man had bound him to silence, despite his position as director of the booktrade. To his astonishment—perhaps—Lenoir learned from the abbé Jabineau in 1779 that the same Malesherbes, Armand de Miromesnil (keeper of the seals, 1774–1787), Antoine Séguier (magistrate in the Parlement, member of the Académie Française), and the current first minister himself, the Count of Maurepas, had all had a

42. Duke of Daumont to Hérault (requesting a "passport" for books he wishes to enter the city), December 2, 1730, in BA, MS 10006; BN, MS fr. 22101, fols. 103–104; [?] to Joly de Fleury, April 28, 1782, in AN, F-4 1017. There is evidence in the same file that a preliminary mission to London had been undertaken during the summer of 1781. On this same affair see also BO, MS 1422, pp. 104–105.

hand in writing the proscribed pamphlets that earlier in the decade had attacked Chancellor Maupeou and his administration.[43]

If books and longish pamphlets had to be controlled, so too did shorter publications—those amounting to no more than a few pages. Over these, whether they assumed the form of a newsletter, a brochure, or a poster, the police had complete authority throughout the century. They not only pursued and seized items in this category that had given offense, but also acted as censor for all works under eight pages in length, determining what might be legally printed and in what form it was to appear. Responsibility for keeping proscribed posters and newsletters off the streets belonged, as previously noted, to the same inspector who had charge of the booktrade.

Essential to this portion of his assignment was careful selection and surveillance of the 120 colporteurs permitted to sell brief printed works and of the 30 to 40 *afficheurs*, or billposters. No one became either a colporteur or a billposter without police scrutiny of his past and a final act of approval by the lieutenant of police. Upon obtaining one of these positions men were obliged to wear a sign bearing the word "colporteur" or "afficheur" when they worked and a number by which they could be identified.

In 1776 Sartine named two former sergeants of the guard to work as Inspector Dehemery's assistants, giving them particular responsibility for surveillance of the colporteurs and billposters. Five years later, he added a third man to this team of agents, which devoted most of its energy to stifling comment on current affairs and to silencing quarrelsome Jansenists and Jesuits. It was a difficult task. During the years Dehemery and his associates undertook it, they invariably placed several informers among the colporteurs and knew the identities of those who sympathized with each of the vocal parties in Paris. They knew, too, which among the 120 were inclined to sell proscribed works simply for profit. And yet Dehemery reported that it remained very difficult to prevent the distribution of illegal materials, for all the colporteurs were extremely cautious, refusing to sell proscribed works on the street or to anyone they did not know. Trapping them, he argued, would require frequent searches of their homes; but even this expedient, he believed, might prove insufficient against their care.[44]

If the police did not visit the homes of colporteurs as often as they

43. BO, MS 1421, p. 110; MS 1423, p. 268; BN, MS fr. n.a. 3348, fols. 70–71.
44. BN, MS fr. 22116, fols. 2–7, 40, 67, 145, 218–24; MS fr. n.a. 1214, fols. 81–85.

might have liked, they did find their way into many other private dwellings and into the Palais itself while hunting Jansenist literature or the remonstrance of a sovereign court. The search for Jesuit propaganda took them in 1764 into a number of the convents in Paris, including the Convent of the Visitation on the Rue Saint-Jacques, which had as its mother superior the sister of the chancellor.[45]

Neither graffiti nor hand-drafted posters escaped the attention of the police. In January, 1771, Sartine ordered all commissioners to see that any writing found on the walls was removed and advised them that notices they found posted were to be sent on to his office. Sartine's successor cannot have been pleased as he read a placard tacked to a tree in the gardens of the Tuileries Palace on July 22, 1782: "How long Frenchmen will we refrain from being men? How long will we close our eyes to our sad situation? Will our spirits be forever sufficiently vile, sufficiently base to remain the slaves and victims of a tyrannical, imbecile government? To arms, for God's sake, to arms, and down with those who do not range themselves under the standard of liberty. All is ready; let us break our chains and build a glorious destiny at the expense of our tyrants." The author of this call to revolt had printed his message in large capital letters which did not correspond to anything experts on handwriting could find in the police files; and though a second poster bearing similar sentiments and cast in the same form appeared several days later, their source remained a mystery.[46]

It was not the written word alone that concerned the police. As is well-known, they also made considerable efforts to compel circumspection in speech and song. One of their principal instruments in this enterprise was the informer, stationed in cafés and other public places or, in the guise of a domestic, in private homes. No lieutenant of police hid the fact that he employed spies. Indeed, Sartine and Lenoir did what they could to publicize the existence of these agents and to exaggerate their number, believing that a myth of ubiquitous surveillance was the best of all deterrents to angry or careless comment on the regime.

That there would be those who, nonetheless, chose to speak against government and church, the police did not doubt. They hoped, however, to minimize the impact and fertility of such acts by greatly lim-

45. BN, MS fr. n.a. 1214, fol. 242; MS fr. 22101, fol. 5; MS fr. 22097, fols. 518–19.
46. Sartine to commissioners, January 21, 1771, in AN, Y 13728; AN, 0-1 361, nos. 285–87.

iting the right of assembly. If gatherings of day laborers and those
without regular employment were feared as conducive to popular disturbances, the suspicion of private meetings extended to all
groups in the community. Marc-Pierre d'Argenson expressed this distrust in an order he sent the masters of a guild in 1723. He forbade
them "ever again to gather on a holiday or a Sunday in the church of
Saint-Médard, or in any other place, under pretext of religious devotion
or brotherhood," and he promised prison "and even more severe penalties" to any who should violate his order.[47]

Lenoir reports that no club or organization but the Freemasons was
tolerated under Louis XV and that all twenty of this society's lodges in
Paris were kept under some form of surveillance. The lieutenants of
police judged the Masons harmless, and Lenoir notes that lists of mem-
bership kept in police files included not only a number of his subordinates, but the names of some of the king's foremost councillors—
names like Amelot, Maurepas, and Vrillière.

In 1775 the first minister, acting against the advice of his lieutenant
of police, authorized the formation of an association known as the
Société Libre d'Émulation and, during the ten years that followed,
tolerated the establishment of other groups committed to meeting regularly and in private. This, Lenoir contends, was a foolish deviation
from accepted policy. The police found it difficult to penetrate all the
new clubs and found in many of those to which they did gain access a
distressing dissemination of sedition. By the time the government took
alarm in 1786 and ordered the lieutenant of police to close all clubs and
societies, the damage, Lenoir says, had been done.[48]

Their role in the regulation of ideas led the police inevitably to involvement in education. The colleges and other educational institutions in Paris had many ordinary contacts with the lieutenant of police,
calling on him for help in maintaining discipline among their pupils,
for assistance in obtaining financial aid from the government, and for
judicial interpretations of their statutes. It was also well understood
that any man who wished to head a college had to pay court not only
to the archbishop of Paris, who approved royal choices, but to the
lieutenant of police, who often determined whom the king would
propose.[49]

47. AN, AD-I 22B, 10, 2; sentence against merchant-producers of gold, silver, and silk
cloth, March 15, 1723, in AN, Y 9500.
48. BO, MS 1423, p. 241.
49. For instances substantiating these generalizations, see BA, MS 10294, passim.

Throughout the century it was the duty of the lieutenant of police to watch over educational institutions in Paris on behalf of the crown and to see that instruction given in them encouraged loyalty to king and church. Police reports from the 1730s and the early 1740s evince great concern over the hold Jansenists had obtained on many schools in the city. One of these documents notes that "most of the primary schools [*petites écoles*] in Paris are in very bad hands" and recommends that the vicar general of the archbishop and the lieutenant of police visit each of these institutions, interrogate those in charge, and purge any who show undesirable sympathies.[50]

Of equal concern, the report continues, is the fact that the Jansenists (frequently described by this document as "the Party") control three-fourths of the convents in the capital. The implications of this domination are enormous, for most young women of any means spend time in these institutions as boarders and learn in them false doctrine that they will certainly pass on to their children. To halt this infection of the young, the police and the church must visit each convent in the city to determine which require reform. Each deviant house must be given a strong, inflexibly orthodox superior and a confessor upon whose loyalty the government may count. Finally, any convent in which more than half the sisters remain insubordinate ought to be barred from receiving any boarders whatsoever.

The situation, according to this police report, is little better in the Hôpital Général, particularly in the Salpêtrière, where thousands of poorer girls and young women in the city are contaminated by heresy and then released to communicate their malady to others. Here, too, a purge of the ecclesiastical personnel is essential.

The report's conclusion is grim: "public instruction in Paris is almost entirely corrupt and is leading toward a general revolution in religion." The government must, in its own interest, arrest and then reverse this movement, for "alterations in matters of religion shake the foundations of the strongest states and only too often end in overturning them."

Given the recommendations and warnings of this report, it is not surprising to find Hérault and the vicar general of the archbishop visiting the College of Sainte-Barbe on a Saturday morning in October, 1730, where, after assembling students and instructors in the chapel, the lieutenant of police read royal orders exiling six of the institution's

50. BO, MS 1422, p. 572; unnumbered, undated report, in BA, MS 10294.

directors and installing in their places others newly chosen by the crown and church. Nor is it unexpected that the police should have guided election of a new rector at the university or managed (with a finesse and attention to detail worthy of today's political strategists) the campaign of 1738–1739 to get the faculty of arts to revoke its appeal against *Unigenitus.*[51]

Regulating opinion required that the police silence those whose views they judged deviant or dangerous, but it also required that they work from time to time in a more positive fashion to disseminate views or attitudes useful to the government. While it was the church that served as the monarchy's chief propagandist, the police also had a part in this labor, though one that was both less significant and intentionally less prominent.[52]

Their role was not that of an open advocate who appeared regularly to reiterate and defend the principles of monarchy and Catholicism; rather, their chief task as propagandists was the clandestine management of rumor in the interest of the government. The police kept close track of the talk circulating in Parisian cafés and, on occasion, sought to spread stories of their own. Hence, in 1766 we find one lieutenant of police ordering a subordinate to circulate assurances at the Bourse that there would be no *lit de justice* and another, under orders from the foreign minister, commanding undercover agents in January, 1747, to begin praising the Spanish king loudly in public places for the benefit of this monarch's spies. It has long been recognized that the lieutenant of police used the tolerated gazettes as well as his network of informers to plant stories useful to the regime.[53]

51. Cardinal de Fleury to Hérault, October 14, 1730, and unnumbered, undated reports to Feydeau de Marville, in BA, MS 10294.

52. On the church's role, see, for example, the crown's order to all bishops in France during the disturbance in the spring of 1775 caused by a rise in the price of bread. These ecclesiastics were to see that every curé in every diocese read a statement giving the government's view of the current crisis, which did not, the statement argued, result from a real shortage of grain or from an "excess of misery" but rather from the presence of lying and financially interested provocateurs in the parishes of the realm. AN, K 1022, nos. 24, 24 *bis.*

53. Despite their concentration on manipulating rumor, the police did, nonetheless, employ literary figures to attack some of the doctrines deemed most pernicious. Lenoir reports that during the reign of Louis XVI he was paying only one man, the poet Laurent Gilbert (1751–1780), to controvert the philosophes (BA, MS 1421, p. 223). The implication is that his predecessors had engaged a larger number of individuals to perform this task. BA, MS 10029, *passim;* Marquis d'Argenson to Feydeau de Marville, January 3, 1747, in BA, MS 10293; BN, MS fr. 22123, fol. 8; Henri Quentin [Paul d'Estrée], "Journal du lieutenant de police Feydeau de Marville," *Nouvelle Revue retrospective,* VI, (1897), 97–120, 169–216, 265–88.

Nonetheless, Lenoir tells us, the public credited the police with more influence over opinion and conduct than they actually possessed. The lieutenant of police, he says, was not always able to control a crowd's attitude toward figures of the government and the court who visited the capital. Modestly, Lenoir confesses that there were limits to what his agents and his money could do. Some public demonstrations of affection or distate, he insists, were genuine, the results of circumstance rather than manipulation. For example, he says, neither considerable expense nor the best efforts of his men were able to produce anything more than isolated cries of "long live the Queen" among the crowds that watched Marie-Antoinette enter Paris in the last years of his administration. Lenoir implies that it was often difficult for the lieutenant of police to persuade those who received this kind of indifferent or hostile reception that he had had no part in provoking it.[54]

Deterrence

While the police understood that the prevention of disorder involved controlling both supplies of food and the circulation of ideas, they did not, it must be said, invest the bulk of their resources in either of these activities. Instead, they devoted themselves primarily to the task of intimidation. While one inspector of police and a few assistants were employed to control traffic in illegal books and a relatively small collection of special commissioners worked at keeping the city supplied with food, almost fifteen hundred police agents (not to mention the detachments of Gardes Françaises and Suisses) patrolled the streets and environs of the city. This number constituted almost half the entire force, and maintaining it in the last decade of the Old Regime consumed approximately 40 percent of the funds available to the police. In the face of such figures, one cannot doubt that it was upon fear, rather than bread or a carefully tended morality, that the police counted in preventing crime and civil disturbance.

Dressed in blue uniforms and clearly visible to all, the Parisian guard walked city streets less to detect crime than, by its very evident presence, to deter it. The patrols of guardsmen were undoubtedly a credible threat, even to crowds, for police ordinances and activity had given these patrols a monopoly on firearms. Since at least 1716, it had been illegal for anyone else in the city to bear this most intimidating of weapons. Domestics and laborers were to have nothing in their posses-

54. BO, MS 1423, pp. 337–38.

Table 9 Sections of Paris: Population and Services

Section of the City	Estimated Population (1714)	% of Total Population	No. of Commissioners		% of Commissioners		No. of Guardsmen (Guard e Garde Française)		% of Guardsmen	
			1715	1789	1715	1789	1714	1770	1714	1770
West	284,800	51.7	26	29	58	60	224	254	60	49
East	265,625	48.3	19	19	42	40	149	263	40	51
Right Bank	337,100	61.2	31	33	69	69	100	279	26.8	54
Left Bank	168,125	30.6	12	12	27	25	251	194	67.3	37.5
Cité	45,200	8.2	2	3	4	6	22	44	5.9	8.5
Northwest¹	175,150	31.8	17	19	37.8	39.6	83	132	22.3	25.5
Northeast	161,950	29.4	14	14	31.1	29.2	17	147	4.6	28.4
Southwest	90,900	16.5	8	8	17.8	16.7	119	98	31.9	19
Southeast	77,225	14.0	4	4	8.9	8.3	132	96	35.4	18.6
TOTALS	550,425		45	48			373	517		

SOURCES: *Almanach royal, 1715,* 192–95; *Almanach royal, 1789,* 394–96; BN, MS JF 1325, fol. 218; Lacaille, *Description de la ville;* Deharme, "Plan de Paris"; for sources on the guard in 1789, see Map 3.
NOTE: Estimates of population are based on multiplying the number of houses in each quarter (Lacaille, in his *Description de la ville,* supplies this data) by twenty-five (for a discussion of this figure, see Reinhard, *Paris*

sion that might be used as an instrument of violence; more respectable citizens might wear swords or carry walking-sticks; but guns were the prerogative of public authority alone.[55]

It is worth noting that at the beginning of the century, in 1714, the police appear to have devoted almost 70 percent of their strength to patrolling the Left Bank of the city, an area that contained but 30 percent of the capital's population; and that during the seventy-five years that followed, they slowly shifted their personnel northward across the river until, by 1789, the percentage of men and patrols on the Right Bank corresponded roughly to the population located there (see Table 9). While this change may suggest a diminished apprehension of the

55. The prohibition against carrying firearms found in d'Argenson's regulation of 1716 (AN, AD-I 26, 120, 5) is extended to their manufacture, display, and sale in an ordinance issued by Lenoir in 1784 (in APP, DB 355).

No. of garbage carts, 1714	% of Carts	No. of Lanterns, 1714	% of Lanterns	No. of fire pumps, 1716	% of pumps	No. of fire stations, 1789	% of stations	No. of fountains, 1763	% of fountains
47	55.3	3026	54.7	8	50	15	60	29	53.7
38	44.7	2506	45.3	8	50	10	40	25	46.3
55	64.7	3488	63	8	50	14	56	35	64.8
24	28.2	1637	29.6	8	50	9	36	17	31.5
6	7.1	407	7.4	0		2	8	2	3.7
29	34.1	1837	33.2	4	25	9	36	20	37
26	30.6	1651	29.8	4	25	5	20	15	27.8
16	18.8	1033	18.7	4	25	5	20	8	15.8
8	9.4	604	10.9	4	25	4	16	9	16.7
85		5532		16		25		53	

pendant la révolution, I, 32). Calculating twenty-five persons per house probably exaggerates the population of peripheral quarters and, in compensation, underestimates that of central districts.
The division of the city into four sections excludes the quarter of the Cité.

young gathered together in colleges and pensions in the Latin Quarter and of the residents of the Faubourg Saint-Marcel, it does not indicate any extraordinary suspicion of the Right Bank or the vast Faubourg Saint-Antoine, which seem only to have acquired their proper share of police patrols and guardposts.

The lights which the first lieutenant of police had begun installing above city streets and those which his successors added were a substantial part of the endeavor to deter crime. Darkness was a mask, a disguise that everyone could afford, and its recurrent availability had always encouraged some to believe they might steal or murder without having to answer for these acts. To push the darkness back, to put anonymity and the boldness it engendered out of reach, the police had for a time to enlist the services of more than four hundred men and devote annually a considerable portion of their budget to buying tallow, oil, and glass.

Lanterns in considerable numbers had begun to appear above the streets of Paris in 1666, and each year that passed brought new lights to make the city brighter. By 1714, 5,500 lanterns burned at night in Paris; and forty years later, there were another 1,000. In order that the city might be wholly illuminated within half an hour, no lamp-lighter had charge of more than fifteen lanterns; and, given this limitation on the work of a single individual, it took at least 370 men to light Paris in 1714. By 1754 the task engaged another 65.

Undoubtedly, this corps of part-time lamplighters continued to expand until 1769, when Sartine introduced a new, more effective lamp that burned oil rather than candles and employed two, three, and sometimes four reflectors to intensify the light it cast. This innovation permitted a remarkable reduction in the number of lanterns required to light the city. Their number was more than halved, amounting after the introduction of the new device to about three thousand; and as each lamplighter now had charge of twenty lanterns, 150 men did the work it had previously taken 435 to do.[56]

The identity of these men was, until 1769, in the hands of those with some standing in the city. Every year in August the residents of each quarter gathered at the home of a commissioner of police to select those who would have charge of the district's lanterns. Since 1704, the cost of materials—candles, glass, iron—for lighting the streets had been a part of the police budget, but requisite labor the crown exacted without remuneration. All who inhabited the city were subject to the obligation, though, of course, when his turn came, any person of even modest prominence delegated the chore to a household servant.

In 1727 a part of the responsibility for lighting the quarter of Saint-Benoît devolved on a dealer in horses named Gornin. Like many others, Gornin and his wife decided to convert the undesired burden into a boon by cutting away and keeping a half-inch of every candle furnished them. Though considerably more adept than others who insisted on taking two or three inches at a time, they did not escape detection and went, along with the less clever, to jail.

Sartine's reform of 1769, by dramatically reducing the number of

56. The preceding figures and the discussion of lighting which follows derive from Alletz, *Géographe parisien*, I, 65; Lacaille, *Description de la ville*, unpaginated; Mildmay, *Police of France*, 122; *Almanach parisien, 1771*, 13; BN, MS JF 1321, fols. 130–31; Inspector Pasquier to Hérault, November 23, 1727, in BA, MS 10321; BO, MS 1421, pp. 599–600; MS 1424, pp. 103–105.

persons required to light the city, seems to have made it possible to
remunerate service and, hence, to eliminate both the elections that
had occurred in each quarter and, perhaps, much of the petty theft that
Gornin and others had practiced. After 1769, day laborers were regularly employed as lamplighters.

The cost of paying these men and maintaining the lanterns they ser-
viced was considerable. In 1780 it
accounted for 15 percent of the police budget and was, after the guard
itself, the greatest single expense
undertaken by the police. The type
of lantern first employed by the
police in 1667 remained in use for
just over a century. It consisted of
a small metal box with numerous
panes of glass on each of its four

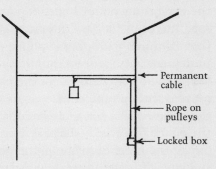

Permanent
cable

Rope on
pulleys

Locked box

sides and space for a candle at its center. Suspended fifteen feet above
the middle of the street, the lantern gave only meager light, and metal
fittings for the several panes of glass on each side caused shadows large
enough to hide a man. Until well into the eighteenth century, the
police tried to improve this system simply by adding more lanterns, so
that by 1750 lights hung only fifteen yards apart on many streets. Still,
the results were not satisfactory; and in 1769, acting through the
Academy of Sciences, Sartine called upon the city's inventors to recommend a more efficient means of lighting the city. The plan he eventually found most suitable was one suggested by Argant and Quinquet,
two men known until then for their skill in lighting interiors. It
involved replacing the old lanterns with new ones that would burn oil
rather than candles. The new lanterns had but a single pane of glass on
a side and used reflectors to intensify the light they cast. The number
of reflectors and oil-burning nozzles in each lantern depended on where
the light was to be hung: those at intersections had four nozzles and
four reflectors, while those hung along a single street had but two.

At the beginning of each year, both before and after Sartine's reform,
the commissioners of police received a long, carefully calculated table
prescribing the hours at which the lanterns should be lit and the length
of time they should burn. Using this data, compiled and supplied in
order to take all possible advantage of the full moon and the light it

furnished, the commissioner sent an assistant through his district ring-
ing a small bell to notify lamplighters that it was time to begin their
work. Lenoir reports that prior to 1769 the lights of the city never
burned beyond 2:00 A.M., but following the changes made by Sartine,
they remained lit on nights they were used until dawn.

By illuminating the night and circulating armed patrols throughout
the capital the police hoped to encourage the potential criminal or
rebel to reconsider and set aside his antisocial inclinations. As a further stimulus to do so, the police occasionally joined other authorities
in demonstrating for the public the many disagreeable consequences
that issued from defiance of the law. Public punishment, marked by
parades through the streets, signs affixed to the criminal explaining
the nature of his act, and carefully graded forms of shame and death,
the police believed essential to maintaining order. Though apparently
one of the more humane lieutenants of police, Lenoir invested considerable effort in trying to persuade Louis XVI not to abolish the salu-
tary act of breaking men on the wheel. An occasional exhibition of
slow and agonizing death, he argued, had in itself almost completely
eliminated the crime of murder so common in Paris at the start of the
century.[57]

A less evident part of the effort to deter crime than public execu-
tions, light, and patrols by the guard was the attention the police
gave Parisian families and their domestic problems. In the structure of
the family and the strength of its bonds, lieutenants of police saw a
major deterrent to antisocial behavior, and it is astonishing to discover
how much time they spent trying to buttress this social entity. Much
of their correspondence with the secretary of state for the king's household, one finds, is devoted not to important matters of state or urban
policy but instead to the many petitions both received from families
with a problem. To read this correspondence is to realize the sad extent of domestic unhappiness under the Old Regime and the remarkable readiness of individuals to turn to public authority for assistance
and relief: husbands who could no longer tolerate their wives and who,
in asking for their incarceration, offered to pay the costs of their food;
wives with long stories of abuse, who made similar requests and similar offers; mothers, sick of a lazy son and willing falsely to portray him

57. BO, MS 1423, pp. 422–23.

as a thief simply to be rid of him; fathers who believed that only speedy confinement could save their daughters' chastity.[58]

In the face of these appeals, the lieutenants of police did what they could to hold the family together. In a letter to the commissioners dated December 15, 1774, Lenoir chastises them for granting the requests of parents who ask to have a child imprisoned. Forbidding them henceforth to grant any such request on their own authority, he reminds them that, far from correcting conduct, prisons only serve to corrupt children and that a young person who remains with his parents and under their supervision is far less likely to become a menace to others than one who does not.[59]

On more than one occasion, Lenoir found himself approached by a wife who had become involved in an affair that she could not discreetly end or a liaison that had led to an awkward pregnancy during the husband's absence. On such occasions, acting as he believed his predecessors had, Lenoir did everything he could to help the woman hide her secret, believing that it was essential to help her preserve her marriage. We find Berryer acting in similar fashion in June, 1755, when he learned from the curé of Saint-Benoît that one of his parishioners, the wife of a president of the Cour des Monnaies, had complained during confessional of an affair with a man who threatened to inform her husband if she stopped seeing him. Berryer, anxious to encourage this inclination toward reform, promptly arranged a pretext for having the lover arrested and exiled from Paris.[60]

These acts were more than whimsical or gallant efforts at charity. They stemmed from a clear sense of the social utility of the family and of the contribution it made to deterring disorder. Life in a family taught men loyalty to an entity larger than themselves and gave them an extended sense of identity, which led them to restrain relatives from immoral or illegal acts that they believed would necessarily discredit them as well. One's own pride and reputation were inevitably impli-

58. See AN, 0-1 361, *passim* for a sample of this correspondence and the familial problems with which it tried to cope. Its abundance, suggested by the registers of correspondence leaving this secretary's office (see, for example, 0-1, 369, 0-1 395, 0-1 405, 0-1 417, 0-1 432), is significant and finds too little place in A. M. Boislisle's *Letters de M. de Marville, lieutenant général de police au ministre Maurepas 1742–1747* (3 vols.; Paris, 1896–1905). Lenoir reports that most of the 200 petitions he received each week concerned domestic affairs (BO, MS 1422, p. 989).

59. Lenoir to commissioners, December 15, 1774, in AN, Y 13728.

60. BO, MS 1422, pp. 913–25; BA, MS 10252, no. 15.

cated in the conduct of those who shared one's name, and this extension of identity, Lenoir recognized, "stimulated every individual in a family to watch his relatives with care—an important aid to maintaining public order—since a single misstep that might have dishonored one was felt to compromise the honor of all."[61]

Detection and Identification

Not all enemies of order in Paris could be deterred or intimidated. Adequately defending the capital and its residents required that the police undertake not only the prevention of crime but its detection as well, and the identification of its perpetrators. Both of these operations were primarily the work of the inspectors of police, created by the crown in 1704 as a ploy by which to raise money, but reorganized under Berryer and Sartine into a reasonably effective force of investigators.

Increasingly after 1740 these agents had begun to specialize, to limit their attention and efforts to particular kinds of offenses or to specific groups of individuals. Thus, among the twenty inspectors of police, one came to have special responsibility for the detection and arrest of charlatans, another for surveillance of foreigners, and a third for keeping an eye on soldiers (see Table 5). Of particular importance were the three men (four after 1776) who formed the department known as the *sûreté* and who were charged with investigating theft, armed assault, and murder.[62] It is indicative of police attitudes regarding the city's enemies that these men, responsible for identifying thieves and murderers, were also given—as a matter of course—the task of coping with vagabonds and beggars.

This specialization among inspectors undoubtedly increased their effectiveness, permitting them to learn the habits and techniques of a particular adversary and, working within a single milieu, to build a more adequate network of contacts. An investigator who was able to specialize could master information relevant to his work and begin to perceive patterns amidst the detail. Acts of theft ceased to appear distinct and unconnected; seditious or irreligious pamphlets were seen to

61. BO, MS 1423, p. 181. This sense of identity and honor extended to all classes, Lenoir contended; to prove his point, he could have cited petitions like that dated January 27, 1778 in which a day-laborer named Étienne Guinot expressed fear that his son would soon bring shame on the entire family (in AN, Y 13163).

62. On the activities of one of these inspectors between 1767 and 1769, see the register of Inspector Sarraire, BA, MS 10145.

have a common source; and, as styles in word and deed became familiar, the city's enemies began, for the first time, to appear finite in number.

Assigning inspectors specific responsibilities permitted a more productive cooperation within the police force. Information gathered by chance was less readily lost or misplaced, since men knew to whom it might profitably be directed. Lenoir could command commissioners to take advantage of each incidental arrest made by the guard for petty theft, ordering them to see that a member of the *sûreté* had a chance to inspect and interrogate the individuals brought before them.[63]

In their pursuit of criminals, police inspectors did not work alone. By law and under the threat of losing their right to practice, all doctors and surgeons had immediately to report to the police any individual they treated for a wound. Midwives were under a similar obligation, being required to furnish the names of those they assisted in delivery and to note any whose behavior or whose circumstances suggested an inclination to infanticide or desertion. Dealers in secondhand merchandise and pawnbrokers had to maintain ledgers recording all purchases or loans, the dates of these transactions, and the names and addresses of each of those who had pawned or sold some article. These ledgers inspectors examined regularly in their search for stolen property and those responsible. The police also made daily checks of the registries all hotels and roominghouses in the city were obliged to keep, hunting culprits whose names they knew and noting the names of all outsiders —those "who do not ordinarily reside in Paris"—whose motives they invariably suspected. As a further means of discovering newcomers to the city, the police required all who operated boats or vehicles that entered the city to furnish them with a list of any passengers they carried; and despite inadequate ways of storing and retrieving information, the practice of branding thieves and vagabonds with appropriate letters permitted the police, if they wished, to pick out in any group of new arrivals those whose pasts made them undesirable visitors or immigrants.[64]

In addition to those obliged by law to furnish the police with information useful in tracking wrongdoers, there were others who performed this service for financial recompense. The number of these

63. Lenoir to commissioners, October 6, 1777, in AN, Y 13728.
64. AN, AD-I 26, 120, 5; BO, MS 1423, p. 919; MS 1424, p. 56; Lenoir to inspectors, November 16, 1778, in AN, Y 12830; Peuchet, *Mémoires*, I, 283.

individuals—of undercover agents and informers—increased and diminished as one lieutenant of police replaced another. On the basis of the financial data available, it appears that there may have been more police spies at work in Paris during the 1730s under Hérault than at any other time during the century. Secret funds allocated for espionage during this period amounted to almost 100,000 livres a year and this sum coupled with money assigned to the inspectors may have sufficed to employ almost 500 agents and informers. Under Sartine and Lenoir, the number of spies diminished, falling to something like 350. Crosne, when he entered office in 1785, asked for funds that would have permitted him to increase the force to about 450 men, but we do not know whether he obtained the money his plans required.[65]

Among those employed by the police as informers were persons from many social settings: domestics engaged to report on both their fellows and their masters; mountebanks to furnish information on illicit gambling in the city; prosperous-looking residents to sit with open ears in coffee houses; a socialite or two to watch over the salons; judges and lawyers from the Parlement to report any colleague bold or rash enough to speak against the government. A number of men stood watch outside the *hôtels* of those ambassadors to France whose conduct happened at any moment to interest the crown; others spent days and nights following ordinary foreign visitors, intent on discovering their purposes in the city. Reports from 1749 and 1750 record descriptions, activities, purchases, and plans—when these could be discovered—of two English lesbians, a sixty-year-old Neapolitan troubadour, a "Dutch captain" (in fact, the son of an Alsatian merchant who had served in neither the Dutch army nor that of any other country), and the prince de Massau Sarbruck, who had once commanded a regiment of Germans serving the French.[66]

With the aid of these informers and undercover agents, the police sought to locate foreign agents, discontented Parisians who spoke carelessly of the government, domestics who stole from their masters, and professional gamblers who exploited the wealth, the rashness, and the pride of young noblemen.

In hunting murderers and thieves, the police believed prostitutes to

65. On secret funds during the 1730s, see BN, MS fr. 6791, fols. 51–112; on calculating the number of spies, see Chapter Three. The difficulty for the 1730s is that we do not yet know how much money was going to the inspectors and through them to the employment of informers. Memoir, Crosne to controller general, undated, in APP, DB 355.
66. BO, MS 1423, p. 35; BA, MSS 10249, 10284, 10293, *passim*.

be of great use; for they managed to tempt many of these men, outsiders in Paris without ordinary companionship from women, into
leaving whatever refuge they found, into momentarily giving up their
discretion and anonymity. Drunk and anxious to impress, such men
sometimes revealed more than was wise about themselves and the
money they spent. From the time of Berryer, the lieutenants of police
tolerated those houses of prostitution whose matrons agreed to file
weekly reports on their customers. During the early 1750s the police
were receiving regular information from at least seven such houses in
the city; and it is probable that efforts to eliminate the ordinary street-
walker stemmed as much from a desire to force lonely men into these
monitored establishments as from a sense that women who worked
the streets were an offense to standards of decency.

The brothels of eighteenth-century Paris may have given many men
nothing but the pleasure they paid for, but for some they proved to be
a baited trap. Set to ensnare the unwary thief or deserter, these establishments occasionally caught a person of prominence, furnishing the
police with information that could be used to blackmail him. Berryer,
for example, must have learned with interest that the new papal
nuncio in France, Monseigneur Blancheforte, had become attached to a
girl at Madame Baudouin's and was having her brought to his home
regularly. Of even greater interest would have been the report that the
girl was pregnant and that "she had led the new papal nuncio, whom
she sees two times a week at his residence, to believe that the pregnancy is his doing."[67]

Though Lenoir does not mention by name the shadowy yet famous
cabinet noir ("black bureau"), or cabinet secret des postes ("secret
bureau of the posts"), he does indicate that the lieutenants of police
obtained data useful in locating men they sought not only through
their networks of informers, but by a clandestine examination of correspondence sent through the public mails. Undertaken in conjunction
with the intendant general of the posts, this opening of sealed letters
was not, he contends, as common a practice as many believed.[68]

Confinement and Exile

To surprise and capture those they sought, the police learned during
the eighteenth century to make use of the night rather than to fear it,

67. BA, MS 10252, fols. 43–53, 74–97; MS 10251, fol. 241.
68. BO, MS 1422, p. 117.

as public authority long had. Ordinances issued by the lieutenants of
police obliged Parisian proprietors and tenants to lock entrances to
their buildings at 10:00 P.M. After this hour, with the streets relatively
deserted and all doors barred against him, a vagabond's chances of elud-
ing the police were significantly reduced. Subinspectors, working in
teams but walking separately and dressed appropriately for the section
of the city they were patrolling, eyed carefully those they passed in the
street (particularly, it seems, those carrying packages). Anyone who
aroused their suspicion they quickly encircled and pulled into a waiting carriage to face interrogation by a commissioner of police. The
pedestrian, whoever he might be, was surprised, outnumbered, and
trapped on city streets from which there was no exit.[69]

Having learned the identity and address of a man he sought, an inspector of police generally waited for the late hours of the night to
make his arrest. These moments, Commissioner Lemaire tells us,
were invariably "the most convenient," since the suspect was likely to
be home, unprepared to escape, and since the arrest could generally be
made without creating any disturbance or drawing the attention of an
unfriendly crowd.

But having identified, located, and captured a man they regarded as
an enemy of the city, what were the police to do with him? The alter-
natives were few. A small number of those taken into custody each
year could be executed and these, of course, ceased forever to be a problem. Most prisoners, however, had done nothing to merit so harsh or
so satisfactory a fate; and it was these individuals who created difficulties, for, in dealing with them, authorities had but two imperfect devices: the power to confine and the power to exile.[70]

The first option, that of confinement, seems to have been the one
most favored by the lieutenants of police. Sitting in his capacity as
judge on May 25, 1759, at the special monthly session of the *police
extraordinaire*, Bertin pronounced sentence on forty-five women and
sixteen men. Faced with deciding between imprisonment and exile,
the lieutenant of police ordered the incarceration of thirty-three
women and all but one of the men.[71]

69. AN, AD-I 26, 120, 5. The hour for locking buildings was 8:00 P.M. during the
winter. Locks, however, could be picked and both inspectors and criminals carried the
necessary tools. See BO, MS 1424, pp. 73–74 and BA, MS 10136, fols. 185–88, on picking
locks and night patrols.

70. BO, MS 1424, p. 73. Lenoir reports that only twelve men were condemned to
death by the Châtelet in 1782 (*ibid.*, 119).

71. The most common penalty imposed by the lieutenants of police was, as we have

The place of confinement in each case was to be that large and complex institution known as the Hôpital Général. For the women this meant an element of the hôpital known as Salpêtrière on the southeastern edge of the city. Salpêtrière was the largest single section of the hôpital, housing close to 6,000 persons in 1737 and almost 7,000 by 1750. Reserved primarily for women (there were 227 elderly men living here with their wives), it was far more than a prison. Indeed, only about 15 percent of its inmates were prisoners, while the great majority were persons who, for reasons of age or infirmity, were unable to provide for themselves. These two groups, the prisoners and those the authorities called "the good poor," received different treatment and were housed in separate quarters, that containing the prisoners being known as *la maison de force* (literally, "the house of force") or more simply as "la force." Discipline here was, in Lenoir's words, "severe," and labor at spinning wheels or looms compulsory. Some inmates of the *maison de force*, confined in separate quarters and garbed in distinctive brown robes of coarse wool, knew they would remain where they were for the duration of their lives, but most women lived in uncertainty regarding the length of their confinement; this was rarely fixed by the lieutenant of police and depended instead on a prisoner's conduct after entering the hôpital.

Conditions at Salpêtrière, in the *maison de force* and elsewhere, were judged even by the authorities to be grim and inadequate. Above all the institution suffered from a lack of space. Many of the buildings that served as dormitories had makeshift buttresses projecting in all directions and were on the verge of collapse. Women living in these structures were, according to one report, literally risking their lives. But even the use of these sad and dangerous places did little to alleviate the overcrowding. Women slept in the corridors with as many as six individuals assigned at times to a single bed. Under such circumstances there was nothing to do but divide the night in half and sleep in groups of three.

It is no wonder that there were at least two uprisings in the *maison de force* at Salpêtrière in 1737 (during one of which 160 inmates escaped) and a third in February, 1739. Again in August, 1750, the

---

already seen, a fine, generally inflicted on persons guilty of some minor and routine infraction of regulations; here, however, I am concerned with the policy of police magistrates when dealing with those they judged not simply careless but, in some sense, genuinely dangerous, those they sentenced once or twice a month in a session of the *police extraordinaire*. See the sessions of May 25, 1759, in BN, MS JF 1322.

women confined there revolted and began trying to scale the thirty-foot wall that contained them. Inspector Poussot, who led the force sent to repress this rebellion, reported that upon his entry into the courtyard many women whom he had known began calling out to him: "Some asked to be hung, others to be shot . . . ; but they all insisted that there be an end [to their suffering]."[72]

At Bicêtre, which held men who were imprisoned in the Hôpital Général, the situation was much the same. The *maison de force* here contained four hundred men, or about 13 percent of a total population of three thousand; here, as at Salpêtrière, buildings were unrepaired, unsafe, and inadequate; here, too, there was impossible overcrowding and discontent. The image of Bicêtre, Lenoir contended, caused men more fear than the prospect of a sentence to the galleys.[73]

To the Hôpital Général—to Bicêtre and Salpêtrière—the lieutenant of police sent individuals who were poor and without social stature. Confinement in either institution carried great dishonor and was reserved primarily for prostitutes, thieves, vagabonds, and persons who had refused to comply with orders banishing them from Paris. Others whom the police judged dangerous received quarters elsewhere. Parisians of some prominence and those who had offended the censor were generally imprisoned in either the Bastille or Vincennes, both state prisons and both relatively comfortable. Vincennes was closed by the crown in 1784 upon the recommendation of the police, while the Bastille, though still in use after this date, never contained more than twelve prisoners during its last years.

The police sent many young men and women whose detainment they judged necessary not to an ordinary prison, whose impact they feared, but to one of two prominent religious establishments in the city. Young men were often sent at the request of their families and by order of the lieutenant of police to the monastery of Saint-Lazare on the northern edge of the city, just off the Rue Saint-Martin. Girls went to the convent of Sainte-Pélagie in the quarter of Place Maubert, where, like the boys at Saint-Lazare, they were made to pray, work, and study in the hope that they would learn the merits of obedience and the value of discipline.[74]

There were, of course, other prisons in Paris but most of these were

72. On those housed in Salpêtrière, on events and conditions there, see BN, MS JF 1322, fols. 157–73, 178–82; Mildmay, *Police of France*, 74; BA, MS 10136, fols. 514–15.
73. BN, MS JF 1322, fols. 179–80; BO, MS 1422, p. 94.
74. BO, MS 1422, pp. 86–91, 93.

attached to a particular jurisdiction or, like the Châtelet (Grand and Petit), Saint-Martin, and For l'Évêque, served primarily as detention centers for those awaiting a final disposition of their cases.

While making extensive use of Parisian prisons in their struggle against the enemies of order, some lieutenants of police recognized the inadequacies of these institutions. They were, it was clear, a financial burden on the state, a weight whose expenses inevitably exceeded whatever income authorities were able to derive from the forced labor of inmates. In addition, they could ordinarily be no more than a temporary expedient against crime and rebellion, for most of those the authorities ordered confined eventually went free and returned to the community to afflict it with new forms of misconduct. Far from being centers of rehabilitation, the prisons were, in Lenoir's words, "schools of vice" that eventually released a more dangerous person than they had received.[75]

In response to this last difficulty the Parisian police pressed to have a new prison constructed in the capital, one to which first offenders, debtors, and those guilty of very minor crimes could be sent. Believing that such an institution would further the reform of men rather than their corruption, both Sartine and Lenoir urged the government to provide the necessary funds. Finally, in 1780, Necker accepted the proposal and agreed to find money by which to realize it. The work of remodeling an old hôtel, the Hôtel de La Force in the quarter of Saint-Antoine, proceeded slowly; but in the closing years of the Old Regime, Paris acquired the new prison Sartine had envisioned—a prison that would, the police believed, return men to the city properly chastened rather than bitter and vengeful.[76]

Given the disadvantages of confinement—its impermanence, its cost, its tendency to corrupt—authorities, including the police, often sought to protect Paris not by incarcerating enemies but by banishing them. In the criminal court of the Châtelet, exile from the capital for periods of three to nine years was a penalty far more common than imprisonment, and the police, too, made common use of this device. Beggars and vagabonds arrested for the first time generally received their liberty if they agreed in writing to return to their native province. Once a month the lieutenant of police visited the *maisons de force* at

75. Lenoir to commissioners, October 4, 1774, in AN, Y 13728; see also BO, MS 1423, p. 424.
76. BO, MS 1422, pp. 95–96.

both Salpêtrière and Bicêtre to consult the wardens of these institutions and to determine which prisoners merited release. But again, the offers of freedom that followed such visits were frequently conditional on a written promise to quit Paris and never return. As a further effort to remove dangerous individuals from the capital, the lieutenant of police occasionally permitted military recruiters to enter Bicêtre and offer freedom to any man willing to serve abroad in his majesty's army.[77]

While many of those banished from the city managed eventually to return, exile had the advantage of being an inexpensive remedy to disorder; and if, once outside the city, a man did in fact remain elsewhere, Paris was free of the problems he had caused, not during an ephemeral period of confinement, but forever.

Statistics do not exist that would permit us to judge the effects of exile and the other techniques employed by the police to defend Paris. We cannot satisfactorily measure the incidence of crime before and after 1667 to determine whether the police proved a more adequate barrier against violence and theft than had the ancient walls of the city. Even if such measurement were possible and showed a diminution in urban crime following La Reynie's appointment, it would, nonetheless, be difficult to demonstrate a causal link between the two phenomena; for the quality of a society's police force does not, in the eyes of most social scientists, play a primary role in determining how much disorder and deviant conduct a community experiences. One might argue that their part in provisioning the city and their efforts to sustain the family and to control social values through censorship gave the police a greater impact on levels of disorder during the eighteenth century than many police forces have today; but, in the absence of figures showing a decline in criminality, such argument remains futile.

Whatever their real impact on security in the capital, the police did, during the eighteenth century, have an effect on the way Parisians perceived their city. In 1660, the poet and critic Nicolas Boileau-

77. Petrovitch, "Criminalité à Paris," 226–33. The lieutenant criminal and his aides appear to have imposed exile with twice the frequency they inflicted sentences of confinement and death. That exile suggested itself so often as a penalty is no doubt closely linked to the fact that a majority of defendants were outsiders, immigrants to Paris who had been born in the provinces and who, in the authorities' estimation, ought to return to them. Lenoir to Dupuy, April 28, 1779, in AN, Y 12830; Sartine to Count of Saint Florentin, January 24, 1762, in BA, MS 12686.

Despréaux was complaining that in comparison with Paris, the darkest, most sinister forest in France would be a welcome refuge from danger:

> Le bois le plus funeste et le moins fréquenté
> Est, au prix de Paris, un lieu de sûreté.

A hundred years later, men had come to view the capital as one of the few cities in Europe where a person need not be afraid, and Sébastien Mercier could write in the last decade of the Old Regime that "the streets of Paris are safe both night and day."[78] Facts and figures aside, Parisians believed themselves more secure in 1780 than they had a century before; and can one doubt the close tie between this perception —this abatement of fear—and the illuminated, carefully patrolled streets that the police had given eighteenth-century Paris?

---

78. Mercier, *Tableau de Paris*, I, 196. See also Petrovitch, "Criminalité à Paris," 220–21.

6

A Place
To Live

Near the center of Paris, on the northwestern corner of one of the city's
three or four busiest intersections, stood the Cemetery of the Innocents. Named for the children Herod had slain in his effort to kill Jesus,
this plot of ground contained the remnants of fifteen generations of
men and women—victims for the most part not of a ruthless monarch
but of a city that destroyed human beings more quickly than it could
produce them. Burials in the capital had for so long enjoyed an advantage over baptisms that Parisians could have found no more suitable
a monument for the heart of their city than the graveyard chance had
bequeathed them. Standing where it did, the Cemetery of the Innocents accorded death the central place it deserved in Paris; and while
affording rude commemoration to the hundreds of thousands of persons its earth had received and consumed since the twelfth century,
the cemetery served also as a mutely eloquent warning of the destiny
that awaited many who entered the capital.[1]

Conscious of the toll urban life took among residents of Paris, the
police worked to reduce this exaction. Since the creation of his office
in 1667, the lieutenant of police had borne responsibility for the
amelioration of life in the city as well as for the guarantee of public
order. It was his task to protect and preserve life not only from the
assassin and the armed thief, but from the entire range of its enemies:
from disease and natural disaster, from accident and fire, from hunger
and unwholesome food. By 1780 the police were devoting approximate-

1. Fire destroyed Parisian parish registers in 1871, but some of the yearly police reports based on these registers have survived (see AN, K 1020-21, nos. 126–27); figures for
births and deaths from 1670–1675, 1678–1684, and 1709–1789 may be found in *Recherches statistiques sur la ville de Paris et le département de la Seine* (2nd ed., 6 vols.;
Paris, 1826–60), II, table 53.

ly a quarter of their personnel and a fifth of their funds to this task.[2]
Only the labor of maintaining public order and providing security
against criminal activity consumed a greater share of their resources.
But in what forms was this commitment of men and money cast? How
did the police proceed in their attempt to prolong the lives of Parisians,
and can we gauge with what success they worked?

RELIEF

Partly to guarantee order in the city, but also partly as a humanitarian
gesture aimed at preserving life, the lieutenant of police dispensed
considerable quantities of relief to the hungry and the cold of Paris.
Through his hands passed the charity not only of the crown but that of
many private persons as well, persons who chose to have their dona-
tions administered by secular authority rather than the church. The
well-known hostess Madame Geoffrin, for example, turned over to
Sartine each year a fixed sum of money which she asked that he employ without mentioning her name for charitable purposes; and Lenoir
reports receiving similar contributions; from factory owners in the
Faubourg Saint-Marcel who donated wood for the poor during cold
winters, and from a relative who each year gave a tenth of his considerable revenues, asking that the money go to alleviate misfortune and
hunger.[3]

The funds available to the police, from both public and private
sources, were larger than ordinary accounts of expenditures suggest
and may, indeed, have justified Commissioner Lemaire's claim in 1770
that the lieutenant of police was the principal protector of the unfortunate in Paris. While Lenoir's budget for 1780 shows only 66,000
livres allocated for relief, this figure does not include the 300,000 livres
which the police received yearly from licensed gaming houses and
which, in large part, was disbursed as charity; nor does it encompass
the special funds available to the lieutenant of police during periods of
particular hardship, like the winter of 1783–1784 when he was able to
obtain from the crown almost 250,000 livres in aid for the poor. Between January and December, 1783, the police appear to have taken in
and dispensed more than a million livres in relief; and Lenoir asserts

2. See tables 2 and 8. The estimate for personnel includes those listed under "Service"
(except lighting) and under "Inspection" (except censors); the figure for expenditures is
that shown for "Public Services."
3. BO, MS 1422, p. 629; MS 1423, p. 181.

that the following year his agents counted twenty thousand persons receiving assistance from the police, either directly or by way of the church.[4]

This assistance took a variety of forms. To some it came as temporary employment and a small but regular wage. Throughout the eighteenth century the police hired men to help clean, clear, and light the city's streets, while women they engaged after 1780 in the tasks of spinning thread and working hemp. Under Sartine, they began permitting a fixed number of needy boys and young men to work nights as lantern-bearers, collecting fees from pedestrians who were willing to pay to have someone accompany them home.[5]

Aware that such positions existed, many Parisians turned to the police in times of crisis for help they could not find elsewhere. When, for example, severe cold forced an end to construction during January, 1784, large crowds of men began to gather outside the Hôtel de Police each morning, asking for work that would permit them to survive. The police took them on, Lenoir wrote in a dispatch to Versailles, as much to alleviate their desperate condition as to engage their help in making the streets serviceable.[6]

To those he was unable to employ during such periods of common hardship the lieutenant of police tried to distribute, through both his commissioners and the curés of the city's parishes, commodities essential to life. During the winter of 1783–1784, the poor received sizable quantities of rice, fish and coal; and two years later, one finds the police beginning as early as September to supply needy families with peat for fuel. At the same time Thiroux de Crosne ordered his commissioners to see that fires were kept alight in public squares and major intersections so that the least fortunate in the capital did not freeze to death on the streets as had only too often happened in previous years.[7]

In a city the size of Paris, there were those who, even during the best of times, required assistance but who, for a variety of reasons,

4. BO, MS 1422, pp. 690–91, 701, 703, 969; MS 1424, pp. 50–51; Lenoir to controller general, May [?], 1784, in AN, F-4 1017. In the provision of relief there was considerable collaboration between the police and the church, funds or food provided by the one often being distributed by the other. While parish curés might sometimes hand out wood or bread supplied by the police, police agents administered and dispensed money collected in the city's churches to assist victims of fire (see BN, MS JF 1324, fols. 12–138).

5. BO, MS 1422, pp. 643–44, 690–91. Funds to finance some of these forms of employment came from revenues the police collected from gaming houses.

6. BN, MS fr. n.a. 2775, fols. 40–41.

7. [?] to Gojard (chief subordinate of the controller general), January 4, 1784, and Crosne to Gojard, September 1, 1786, in AN, F-4 1017.

were unable to labor on the roads or in a spinning shop. Despite their incapacities many of these individuals turned to the police for assistance. Each month the lieutenant of police received a number of petitions from persons like Madame Goutière who contended in October, 1730, that she and her eleven children would starve unless Hérault granted her a modest pension. Though he could not provide financial assistance to all who sought it, the lieutenant of police did manage to help some. The widow Dubois, for example, who petitioned Marville regularly during the 1740s, received a monthly allowance of twelve livres—not a grand sum, but one which apparently made a world of difference to her.[8]

While the number of welfare payments they were able to make was probably small, the lieutenants of police did sometimes find other ways of assisting those in need. One family that addressed itself to Sartine for help came, he discovered, because the eldest son had joined the army, leaving his mother and younger siblings without food or the means to obtain it. In this case, a letter to the secretary of war obtained the young man's release and restored him to those whose survival seemed so clearly to depend on his presence.[9]

Many of the handicapped whom they were unable to aid directly, the police permitted to seek private charity on the city's streets. Though begging in Paris was formally illegal except when undertaken by the three hundred blind men and women who inhabited the hospices known as the Quinze-Vingts, the lieutenants of police tacitly permitted as many as three thousand other individuals to solicit alms. So long as these persons remained in the places police officers had assigned them, they were free to ask contributions from all who passed.[10]

It also appears appropriate to credit the police, and particularly Sartine, with the relief—the nourishment—given many of the city's foundlings. Every year in Paris thousands of mothers sought to divest themselves in one way or another of infants newly born to them. Some left their babies on the street or the step of a church; others wished the

8. Mme Goutière to Hérault, October 4, 1730, in BA, MS 10006; see, for example, "the Widow Dubois" to Feydeau de Marville, July, 1746, in BA, MS 10026.

9. In 1780, the police seem to have devoted 19,364 livres to welfare payments (BO, MS 1422, p. 971). Assuming, for the sake of a rough estimate, that all were the size of that received by the widow Dubois in 1746 (144 livres a year), the police would have been distributing financial relief to 134 persons. (This figure does not include former employees of the police or their families who, in 1780, were getting a total of 37,500 livres in pensions.) BO, MS 1423, p. 181.

10. BO, MS 1422, p. 691; Lenoir to commissioners, November 30, 1782, in AN, Y 12830.

separation to be temporary, lasting only as long as the child required milk from a woman's breast. But whether they wished to be rid of their offspring for good or only for several years, these women created a demand for wetnurses in the city; and this demand, the inability of Paris itself to provide such women in sufficient numbers, and the desperate need of many peasant families for currency with which to pay taxes, had all produced a tacit bargain between city and countryside—a bargain which merely lent a new dimension to their ancient exchange of money for nourishment.

Numbers of peasant women, each bearing a local priest's certification of her morals and marriage, arrived in the capital every week, most of them in carts led or driven by employees of the police known appropriately as "leaders" (meneurs). These men, numbering twenty in 1754, circulated throughout the small villages of the provinces surrounding Paris.[11] Natives of the areas in which they worked, it was their job to seek out women able and willing to feed a second or third child, to carry them and their suckling infants to Paris, and then to provide transport for the return. In addition, they visited all women in their area who were already caring for a child, carrying the woman's monthly wage and sometimes a message or clothing sent by the parents.

Within the city itself the police maintained four centers responsible for directing this traffic. A small staff waited at each of these locations to receive and shelter wetnurses newly arrived in Paris; and when these women had found a tiny client and departed, it was the job of this same staff to maintain correspondence with them. A royal declaration issued January 29, 1715, had initially granted the lieutenant of police authority over the women (known as recommandaresses) who had been lodging provincial wetnurses since the twelfth century; but twelve years passed before the police under Hérault collected these women into the four centers just mentioned, centers where their work as hostesses, correspondents, and accountants could be more readily observed and controlled. Dissatisfied with the women he found holding title of recommandaresse, Hérault replaced them in 1729 with new women upon whom he counted to improve both services and administration.[12]

11. Mildmay, Police of France, 80.
12. BN, MS fr. 8058, fol. 401; Peuchet, Mémoires, I, 282; Alfred Franklin, La Vie privée d'autrefois: Les Parisiens, XVIIᵉ–XVIIIᵉ siècle, ed. Arlette Farge (Paris, 1973), 82.

But the improvements Hérault envisioned apparently remained largely unrealized, and by 1765 the number of wetnurses arriving in Paris from the provinces was no longer sufficient to feed infants without maternal care. Too many women had found themselves poorly cared for during their stay in Paris and, above all, too many had found it impossible to collect the monthly fees due them once they took charge of a Parisian child and returned to their villages; and though it was individual parents, not the foundling homes, that had been defaulting on payments, the public institutions found themselves with infants they could not feed.[13]

Under the pressure of circumstance, the police worked at persuading goats to nourish the children, but the ewes collected for this duty found their charges every bit as distasteful as had the human beings who initially abandoned them on the streets. Some other way would have to be found to keep alive the foundlings, who, by this time, accounted for almost a third of the baptisms recorded each year in Paris. And so when it became clear that the experiment with animals was a failure, Sartine decided to reform the institutions provincial wetnurses were finding unsatisfactory. He ordered the four receiving centers Hérault had established closed and in their place created two new, specialized agencies. The first of these, known as the *bureau des recommandaresses* and located on the Rue Neuve Saint-Augustin, assumed the traditional functions of reception and lodging. Here, twelve hours a day, every day of the year, from 8:00 A.M. to 8:00 P.M., a staff of seven individuals under the direction of a mother and daughter named d'Hamecourt welcomed women brought into the city by the *meneurs* and examined the certificate their parish priests were supposed to have given them, a certificate attesting to each woman's moral rectitude. Judging these valid, members of the staff then proceeded to inscribe the names of the women in a register, saw that they were examined by a doctor, and provided them and their children with space in one of the dormitories attached to the office. In common rooms that also formed part of the facility, the new wetnurses stationed themselves daily and waited mutely to be approached by one of the Parisian mothers or fathers who had come to examine them. Monthly fees were negotiable but, once agreed upon, were inscribed in a register maintained by office staff.

13. BO, MS 1421, pp. 363–64 on this dilemma and the efforts of the police to resolve it.

Though parents paid the first month's wage directly to the wetnurse before she and they quit the *bureau de recommandaresses*, all further payments they made through the second agency Sartine had created, that known as the *direction*—or the *bureaux*—*des nourrices*. It was to this second office, as well, that parents went for important news about their offspring—to learn that they had discovered the great art of walking, that with words they were mastering the world around them, or—perhaps more likely—that far away they had died.

At the *bureaux des nourrices*, part of the staff of fifteen men corresponded with hundreds of priests who were asked to see that women in their parishes who were nursing children did not neglect them. Other personnel in the *bureaux* oversaw the financial accounts, making sure that wetnurses were paid regularly from a special fund even when parents had defaulted on their contracts. It was probably this agency, the *bureaux des nourrices*, that managed in the end to overcome the problem Sartine and Paris had faced in the mid-1760s. By seeing that no woman failed to receive her monthly wage and by taking on itself the legal burden of collecting from defaulters, the new institution managed to tempt more wetnurses into the city each year, enough to sustain—at least against hunger—thousands of new and fragile lives.

By the time the Old Regime entered its last decade, Sartine's administrative changes and those contributed by Lenoir had created a branch of the police employing roughly fifty persons: twenty-two of them office and medical staff, at least twenty engaged as *meneurs*, and a small, indeterminate number hired specifically to make periodic inspections of the homes in which, at any one time, something like nine thousand small Parisians were growing, doing their best to survive and merit a return to the great city.[14]

A LIMIT TO HAZARD

When the police spoke of making Paris secure for those who inhabited it, they intended more than an effort to sweep thieves and assailants from the streets. Encounter with angry or desperate men was but one of the risks that came with residence in the capital. There were other dangers far more ordinary. In a city as large and congested as eighteenth-century Paris, accident was a greater threat to life than crime. A single man's haste or lapse of attention might convert the

14. *Almanach royal, 1785*, 427; Mildmay, *Police of France*, 77–81; BO, MS 1424, pp. 148–50; MS 1421, p. 365.

simplest object or act into a source of danger. The building in which men lived, the fuel they used for warmth, the animals they depended on for food, for transport, and for companionship, even daily amusement—all could threaten life as well as serve and enhance it. To make Paris secure, to make it safe, the police sought, in a variety of ways, to reduce disregard and negligence in the city as well as malevolent assault.

One of their concerns was the quality of new construction and the condition of structures already standing. Since the creation of his office, the lieutenant of police had had the power to order repair or demolition of any building he judged hazardous to the public; but for many years the procedures by which he was to exercise this authority remained ambiguous and complex. By legal maneuvering a landlord could for long periods of time delay any remedy or reconstruction he had been commanded to undertake. Prompted no doubt by Hérault and by the report of some serious accident, the crown moved in July, 1729, to provide the police with a clear and unequivocal process for exacting repairs.

Henceforth, after noting a hazardous structure in their district, commissioners of police were to have the owner summoned before the next session of the Chambre de Police. If the proprietor failed to appear or to contest the complaint filed against him, the lieutenant of police ordered demolition or repairs to begin immediately. If, however, the owner denied that his property was unsafe, the magistrate appointed an expert—the police architect—to examine the structure and rule on its soundness. Should a proprietor fail to initiate immediately repairs ordered by the lieutenant of police, a police commissioner was empowered to hire whatever men were necessary to undertake them. Money for this work came initially from the receiver of police fines but was, of course, eventually collected from the reluctant owner. To further expedite matters, the declaration of 1729 provided that in the event of imminent danger, a commissioner did not have to wait for the weekly session of the Chambre de Police but could go immediately before the lieutenant of police in his *hôtel* to obtain an order of condemnation.[15]

If buildings could be dangerous, so too could their appurtenances. One day in August, 1772, a large sign some merchant had suspended out over his door to attract the attention of customers caught more

15. AN, AD-I 26, 120, 8.

than the eye of one young pedestrian when it fell on him. Learning that the boy had been seriously injured, Sartine acted to prevent any recurrence of such needless harm. Three days after the accident, commissioners throughout the city received orders obliging them to see that all signs in their districts were placed flat against the walls that supported them, not hung perpendicularly so as to project out into the street. Anyone slow in complying with this order Sartine wanted cited and promptly summoned before his court.[16]

During the 1780s Parisians began to experience a new danger linked to the construction industry. For centuries men had quarried stone in and around the city, heedless of the fact that they were slowly eviscerating Paris, undermining both its streets and the land on which its buildings stood. When in 1781 a road collapsed near Ménilmontant, killing a number of travelers, the city suddenly took alarm. Widespread panic prompted an investigation and a decision by the government to divest the *bureau des finances* of authority over the quarries. Finding that the bureau's inspections of these sites had been careless and inadequate, the crown hastily conferred responsibility for their proper maintenance jointly on the director general of buildings and the lieutenant of police. Immediately, agents of these two officials set to work to discover the extent of tunneling under the city and to see that old, poorly buttressed shafts were reopened and reinforced. The situation, they discovered, was particularly serious in the Faubourgs Saint-Jacques and Saint-Germain, where a number of lots were on the verge of collapse. Here, workers no sooner saved one structure than they discovered another in grave danger. For eight years—until the fall of the Old Regime—men labored to restore the city's foundation; and due, no doubt, to their efforts, Parisians experienced during this period no repetition of what had happened on the road to Ménilmontant.[17]

Few accidents in the capital were more common or, potentially, more serious than those involving fire. Though there were a number of major conflagrations during the eighteenth century—that of the Petit Pont, for example, in 1718 and particularly those at the Chambre des Comptes and Hôtel-Dieu in 1737—the police appear to have made considerable progress in limiting the destruction and death caused each year by fire. As early as 1670, La Reynie issued a series of regulations

16. Sartine to commissioners, August 28, 1772, in AN, Y 13728.
17. BO, MS 1421, pp. 607–608.

designed to reduce the incidence of fire in the city; and successive lieutenants of police periodically amplified and reiterated this initial ordinance. New versions of it appeared in 1706, 1726, 1735, and 1781. Each of these acts devoted considerable attention to prescribing the materials and procedures that could be used in the construction of chimneys; each obliged residents to see that their own chimneys were swept carefully and regularly. Hérault's ordinance of 1735 went on in twenty-one articles to forbid persons from smoking or carrying uncovered lights in any building containing wood, grain, or other combustibles. Merchants were not to leave hay on the street in front of their establishments, but to store it only in some closed and secure place. All those dealing in inflammable items were barred from doing business on days of public celebration, days when there were fireworks and widespread inebriation. In the event a fire did catch in some building, neighbors all along the street were obliged to open their doors to the police and to contribute whatever water they had available; at the same time, members of the building trades were required to obey immediately any summons from a commissioner of police and to lend whatever assistance he required in controlling a blaze.

Six years before issuing this lengthy ordinance, Hérault and the Parlement of Paris had cooperated to prohibit any further manufacture of fireworks or gunpowder in the capital. Upon recommendation from the lieutenant of police, the Parlement declared that all persons engaged in producing these items would have three months to abandon their present locations and establish themselves at a specified distance from the city. This decree, issued in April, 1729, was a major step toward eliminating the tragically recurrent explosions like that which dismembered five people on September 1, 1724, and initiated a blaze that burned out of control for ten hours.[18]

The labor to prevent fire required constant vigilance on the part of the police and a readiness to keep regulations abreast of both mercantile and technical innovation. In August, 1763, Sartine informed his commissioners that a number of women had begun selling torches to Parisians returning late from cabarets on the northwestern edge of the city. Many who bought these additional sources of light were so drunk that they could think of nothing better to do with them when they reached home than throw them aside. Because this carelessness and

18. BN, MS JF 1326, fols. 42–43, 61, 108–11, 255; AN, AD-I 22B, 8, 13.

Table 10 The Quartiers of Paris: Population and Services

The Quartiers (Ranked by population in 1714)	Estimated Population (1714)	% of Total Population	Rank by Superficies (Visual Estimates)		Commissioners		No. of Guardsmen (Guard & Gardes Françaises)		% of Guardsmen	
			1714	1789	1715	1789	1714	1770	1714	177[0]
1. Cité (I)	45,200	8.21	13	15	2	3	22	44	5.90	8.[ ]
2. Saint-Antoine (XV)	44,875	8.15	1	1	2	3	0	61	0	12
3. Saint-Martin (X)	43,500	7.90	5	7	3	3	17	32	4.56	6
4. Place Maubert (XVI)	42,675	7.75	2	2	2	2	66	74	17.69	14
5. Saint-Denis (IX)	40,475	7.35	8	10	3	3	50	22	13.40	4
6. Saint-Benoît (XVII)	34,550	6.28	9	6	2	2	66	22	17.69	4
7. Luxembourg (XIX)	33,025	6.00	4	4	3	3	86	27	23.06	5
8. Saint-Germain-des-Prés (XX)	30,375	5.52	3	3	2	3	33	66	8.85	13
9. Saint-André-des-Arts (XVIII)	27,500	5.00	12	12	3	2	0	5	0	1
10. Saint-Jacques-de-la-Boucherie (II)	25,450	4.62	19	19	2	2	0	0	0	0
11. Palais-Royal (V)	25,150	4.57	6	13	3	3	22	10	5.90	2
12. La Grève (XI)	24,500	4.45	15	17	2	2	0	32	0	6
13. Temple (XIV)	21,300	3.87	7	9	3	2	0	12	0	2
14. Montmartre (VI)	18,900	3.43	10	5	1	3	11	22	2.95	4
15. Louvre (IV)	18,800	3.42	16	8	2	2	0	42	0	8
16. Les Halles (VIII)	18,375	3.34	20	20	2	2	0	12	0	2
17. Saint-Paul (XII)	16,600	3.02	11	11	2	2	0	10	0	2
18. Sainte-Opportune (III)	16,000	2.91	18	18	2	2	0	0	0	0
19. Saint-Eustache (VII)	12,000	2.18	14	14	2	2	0	24	0	5
20. Sainte-Avoie (XIII)	11,175	2.03	17	16	2	2	0	0	0	0
TOTALS	550,425	100			45	48	373	517	100	100

SOURCES: *Almanach royal, 1715*, 192–95; *Almanach royal, 1789*, 394–96; BN, MS JF 1325, fol. 218; Lacaille, *Description de la ville*; Deharme, "Plan de Paris"; for sources on the guard in 1789, see Map 2.
NOTE: Estimates of population are based on multiplying the number of houses in each quarter (Lacaille in his

No. of Garbage Carts, 1714	% of Carts	No. of Lanterns, 1714	% of Lanterns	No. of Fire Pumps, 1716	% of Pumps	No. of Fire Stations, 1789	% of Fire Stations	No. of Fountains, 1763	% of Fountains
6	7.06	407	7.36	0	0	2	8	2	3.7
8	9.41	329	5.93	0	0	2	8	3	5.56
6	7.06	415	7.50	0	0	1	4	2	3.7
4	4.71	300	5.42	4	25	2	8	3	5.56
5	5.88	304	5.49	0	0	2	8	5	9.26
4	4.71	304	5.49	0	0	2	8	6	11.11
6	7.06	330	5.97	0	0	2	8	2	3.7
6	7.06	393	7.10	0	0	3	12	3	5.56
4	4.71	310	5.60	4	25	0	0	3	5.56
4	4.71	181	3.27	0	0	1	4	2	3.7
4	4.71	332	6.00	0	0	1	4	3	5.56
3	3.53	199	3.60	0	0	0	0	2	3.7
3	3.53	361	6.53	0	0	1	4	2	3.7
4	4.71	282	5.10	4	25	3	12	4	7.41
4	4.71	192	3.47	0	0	1	4	4	7.41
2	2.35	140	2.53	0	0	0	0	1	1.85
3	3.53	174	3.15	0	0	0	0	1	1.85
2	2.35	158	2.86	0	0	0	0	0	0
4	4.71	248	4.48	0	0	1	4	1	1.85
3	3.53	173	3.13	4	25	1	4	5	9.26
85	100	5522	100	16	100	25	100	54	100

Description de la ville supplies this data) by twenty-five (for a discussion of this figure, see Reinhard, *Paris pendant la révolution*, I, 32). Calculating twenty-five persons per house probably exaggerates the population of peripheral quarters and, in compensation, underestimates that of central districts.

stupidity had already caused several fires, Sartine ordered his agents to see that the enterprising torch salesmen be kept off the streets and relieved of their merchandise.[19]

Less than a year after Joseph Montgolfier managed to send a sheep, a chicken, and a duck 1500 feet into the air above Versailles and the physicist J. A. C. Charles traveled by air from Paris to Nesle, the lieutenant of police issued an ordinance banning any further unauthorized experimentation near the capital with "machines aérostatiques." A number of balloons, modeled on Montgolfier's and burning cheap brandy in the stoves they carried aloft, had been launched from the Tuileries Gardens only to descend in crowded districts of the city. Thus far, no one had been hurt and no fires set, but Lenoir was unwilling to take further chances. Balloonists who insisted on flying near the capital could henceforth count on facing a police agent and a fine of 500 livres when, at last, their craft settled back to earth.[20]

Police efforts to prevent the outbreak of fire must have saved the lives of some who would otherwise have perished; but lacking carefully kept data on the incidence of such accidents, this contention is obviously difficult to substantiate.[21] More tangible, more readily apparent to us than the impact of preventive measures, is the progress the police made in coping with fires once they had begun.

Prior to the eighteenth century, authorities in Paris, faced with the task of extinguishing fire, had relied on their power to summon and exact service from monks, army units, and all masons, carpenters, and roofers who dwelt in the city; they issued ordinances prescribing the maintenance of wells and the storage of tools—ladders, hammers, axes —throughout each quarter; they turned in the face of conflagration to the whole community for help. But on October 12, 1699, François Dupérier obtained a patent on a portable pump he had designed, and the situation began to change. Intending his new device as a weapon against fire, Dupérier produced thirteen replicas of it by 1705 and created a company of "guards" to transport them wherever they were needed. The new company seems to have floundered; but in 1716 the

19. Sartine to commissioners, April 24, 1763, in AN, Y 13728.
20. Isambert, Jourdan, and Decrusy, *Recueil des lois*, XVII, 403–404.
21. Mildmay, after spending three years in Paris, claimed that the terrible fires so common in London rarely occurred in the French capital, attributing this happy circumstance in part to "the houses and stair-cases being built with stone, and the chimneys and partition-walls erected, conformable to several ordonnances." *Police of France*, 93–94.

crown, recognizing its utility, intervened, ordering that 6,000 livres a year be spent to maintain a force of thirty-two men and sixteen pumps. Dupérier, responsible jointly to the prévôt des marchands and the lieutenant of police, remained at the head of the regenerated and enlarged company.

Letters patent of April 17, 1722, doubled the size of the new fire department, ordering Dupérier to construct seventeen more pumps and increase the number of men trained to use them to sixty. After an immediate initial payment of 40,000 livres to cover new equipment and new uniforms, the company was to receive 20,000 livres a year for ordinary expenses. Supervision of the force and its funds would no longer involve the prévôt des marchands but became wholly the responsibility of the lieutenant of police.

The company of sixty men (fifty-six active members and four reservists) was organized into eight brigades, seven of them based at monasteries and one at a boys' school. For their work the seven men who constituted each of these brigades received 100 livres a year. As the service they rendered did not consume all their time, members of the company had other vocations: curiously, twenty-three of them were master shoemakers (*cordonniers*) and another eleven were cobblers (*savetiers*); there were, in addition, small collections of locksmiths and tobacco merchants.

In 1767, Sartine appointed an extraordinarily able administrator named Morat to reorganize the fire department, which had changed little since 1722. Within three years Morat had raised the number of brigades to sixteen and had increased the size of the company as a whole to 160 men. The new administrator introduced a series of ranks and corresponding differentials in pay to stimulate diligence and courage. Between 1767 and 1771, he created sixteen permanently manned stations where Parisians could, at any hour, secure the assistance of a pump and men to operate it. Three at a time the men of each brigade served twenty-four-hour shifts in the new stations. For each day in the station there were two away from it, but the lodgings of all firemen, marked as they were by a sign and containing a small bell which could be rung from the street, were rarely sanctuaries from duty.

By 1770 Morat and his company of 160 men were receiving 73,000 livres a year from the funds of the police. In 1776 the sum allocated to them climbed to 78,000, shortly thereafter to 82,000, and finally, in December, 1785, to 116,000 livres. This increase in funds was accom-

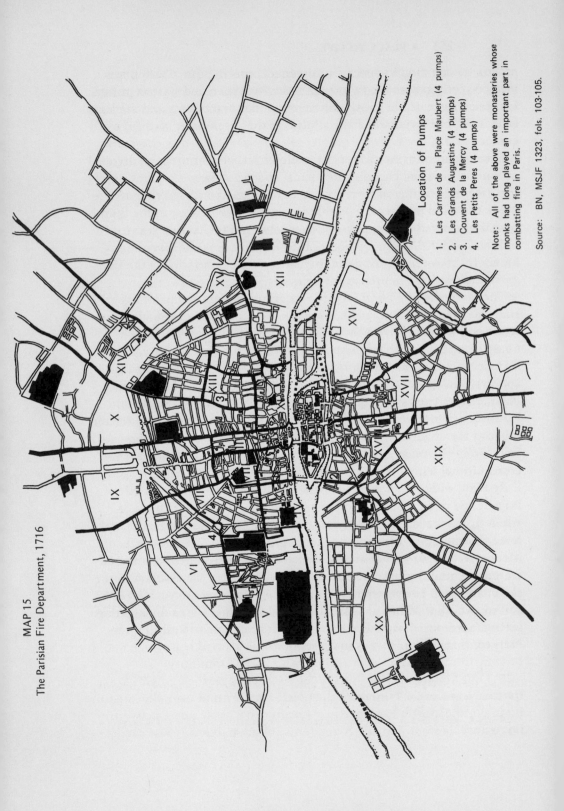

MAP 15
The Parisian Fire Department, 1716

Location of Pumps

1. Les Carmes de la Place Maubert (4 pumps)
2. Les Grands Augustins (4 pumps)
3. Couvent de la Mercy (4 pumps)
4. Les Petits Peres (4 pumps)

Note: All of the above were monasteries whose monks had long played an important part in combatting fire in Paris.

Source: BN, MSJF 1323, fols. 103-105.

panied, as one might expect, by augmentations in both size and services. Shortly before the Revolution, the Parisian fire department had become a force of 221 men, who together manned not sixteen stations as in 1770, but twenty-five. Of all the entities created or brought together to form the police of eighteenth-century Paris, this company was surely among the most remarkable in its development: an original unit of 32 men had become one of 221; an initial budget of 6,000 livres had grown until it stood, on the eve of revolution, at 116,000 livres.[22]

For the ordinary fireman (garde) this dramatic increase in the company's funds had meant a doubling of salary, from 100 livres a year in 1722 to 200 livres a year by 1770. Those constituting the relatively new hierarchy above him, of course, got more. Brigade commanders (brigadiers) received 400 livres, and their assistants earned the neat intermediary sum of 300 livres. Above the brigades were the company's staff officers: two adjutants earning 800 livres apiece, two sublieutenants each receiving 1,500 livres, and, immediately subordinate to Morat, a single lieutenant who drew 5,000 livres a year.

Despite its increase to 200 livres a year, the wage paid a fireman appears small when set beside that of most other employees of the police; nonetheless, as he looked back on his own administration, Lenoir recalled that "of all the men and soldiers working at and watching over the security of Paris, the firemen—this troop made up of so few—were the most remarkable in the city for their courage and incorruptible fidelity."[23]

By 1789, then, the police had built a force of over two hundred trained and dedicated men to fight fire in the city, a force that was seven times the size it had been when it was first formed in 1716, a force that functioned with a budget twenty times its original size. Moreover, an able administrator, Morat, had altered organization and technique, making his company not only larger but quicker and more skillful as well. Lenoir testifies to a new rapidity of response after 1767, and reports that Morat so reduced the fighting of fire to a science that intendants from all over France began sending their subordinates to Paris for instruction in its principles.[24]

22. BN, MS JF 1325, fols. 103–106, 113–16, 127; BO, MS 1421, pp. 601–602; MS 1424, pp. 107, 111; [?] to controller general, undated (but written shortly after October 29, 1786), and letters patent, December 11, 1785, both in AN, F-4 1017.
23. BO, MS 1421, p. 603.
24. Ibid., 601, 603. For Morat's standing orders of operation, see BO, MS 1424, pp. 110–11.

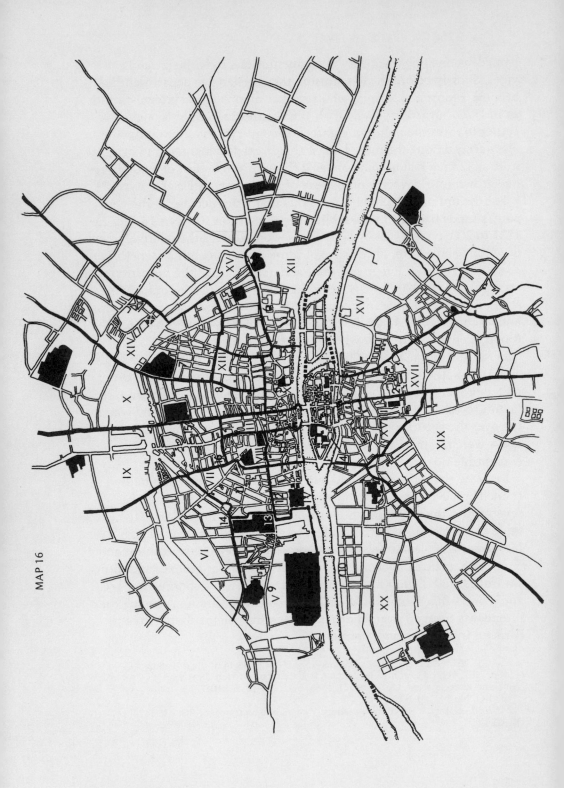

MAP 16

Map 16
THE PARISIAN FIRE DEPARTMENT, 1739

LOCATION OF PUMPS

1. The Carmelite friars of the Place Maubert
2. The Jesuits of the Rue Saint-Jacques
3. The archbishopric
4. The *hôtel* of the first president of the Parlement
5. The chapel of Saint-Esprit
6. The Jesuits of the Rue Saint-Antoine
7. The hospice of the Enfants Rouges
8. The *hôtel* of the lieutenant of police

9. The Capuchin friars
10. The coach station for Versailles
11. The General Post Office
12. The Oratorians
13. The Opera
14. The Bank
15. The hospital of the Trinity
16. The *Comédie-Italienne*

NOTE: There were two pumps at each of the above locations.
SOURCE: *Almanach royal, 1739,* 405–406.

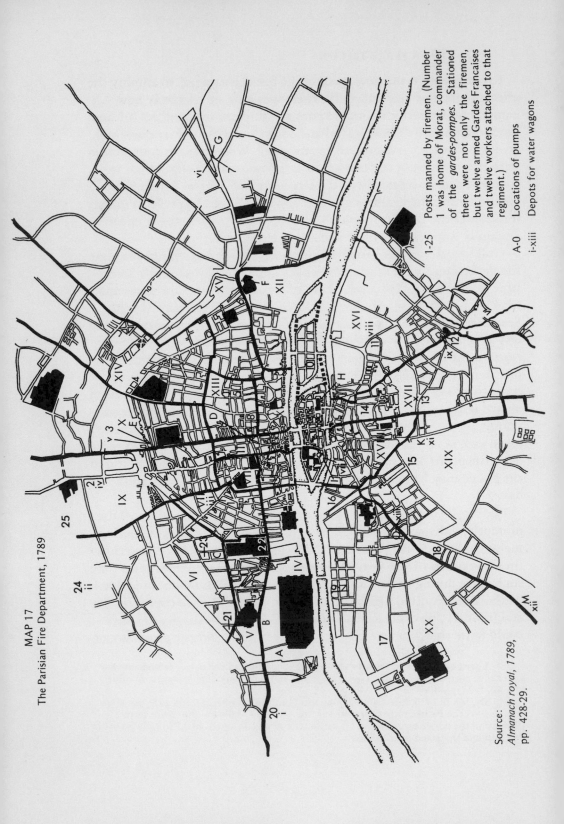

MAP 17
The Parisian Fire Department, 1789

Source:
Almanach royal, 1789,
pp. 428-29.

1-25   Posts manned by firemen. (Number 1 was home of Morat, commander of the *gardes-pompes*. Stationed there were not only the firemen, but twelve armed Gardes Francaises and twelve workers attached to that regiment.)

A-O   Locations of pumps

i-xiii   Depots for water wagons

To complement the new speed of the fire department, to amplify the effects of its new size and spirit, there was new, or relatively new, equipment. Dupérier's portable pumps—thirteen of them in 1705 and more than fifty by 1789—gave Parisians an extremely important tool, an advantage they had not before possessed. When used in conjunction with two or three of the more than thirty water carts that Morat introduced and scattered about the city after 1767—carts which held about four hundred gallons of water and which could be refilled in four minutes at the nearest fireplug—a pump could pour a steady effective stream of water on the flames of any blaze.[25]

Vital to realizing the benefits of new equipment and a more adequate fire department were apparent changes in public attitudes. For some time after the fire department had come into being in 1716, Parisians remained suspicious of official declarations that the service was free. Fearful of having to pay a charge for professional help, residents of the city generally tried to control fire themselves and, on occasion, even resisted the efforts of firemen to enter a building. In 1722 the fire department received only 77 calls for assistance from a population of more than half a million persons. But public fear of the new institution abated with each succeeding year as men witnessed its successes and permitted themselves to believe that they might enjoy this valuable assistance at no expense. The number of persons turning to the fire department for help increased to 107 in 1723; and by 1780, this arm of the police may have been receiving as many as six or seven calls a day.[26]

The results of this change were impressive. In learning to report fires promptly, Parisians prevented many minor accidents from becoming major conflagrations. Whereas records show an average of five serious fires a year from 1722 to 1724, Lenoir indicates that there was but one such blaze during the entire eleven years he was lieutenant of police. Authorities acquired a new confidence in their ability to cope with fire and limit its powers of destruction. By 1770 Commissioner Lemaire could write that "there is no fire, however violent, whose progress can-

25. A series of valves in the city's water mains permitted the police to concentrate water that normally fed public fountains in the series of pipes supplying the fireplugs. BO, MS 1424, pp. 106–107.

26. BN, MS JF 1325, fols. 247–56 (Dupérier's annual report); BO, MS 1421, pp. 602–603. In 1968 the Parisian fire department received 45,000 calls for assistance from a population the police estimated at six million, or what amounted to 3,750 calls for every five hundred thousand inhabitants.

not be quickly halted without its being necessary to demolish the structures that are in flames; on the contrary, they are saved in such a way that only the fireplace suffers any damage, other areas—and especially neighboring buildings which the fire has not yet reached when help arrives—being wholly preserved."[27]

Fire and unbuttressed quarry shafts were not the only hazards Parisians faced. There were many others, among them the animals that fed the city and transported its goods. During the eighteenth century most streets in Paris lacked the sanctuary that sidewalks have since come to afford pedestrians. In confined and busy passageways, residents had daily to brave encounter with horses and heavy wagons. Inevitably, there were collisions and consequent injury to the more vulnerable party. In an effort to diminish the harm done those on foot, police ordinances obliged wagon drivers to descend from their vehicles on entering the city and walk, reins in hand, at the head of their horses. The same regulations forbade those who rode horses or drove carriages from permitting their animals any speed greater than a walk.

The wall erected by the Farmers General during the 1780s created a new problem for pedestrians. Gates through this barrier had been so constructed as to force both carriages and those on foot into a common line of traffic. If the results were everywhere unfortunate, it was at Passy that the carelessly designed accesses to the city caused greatest difficulty. Here, on Sunday afternoons, the many carriages returning from Versailles had to pass amid large numbers of slightly inebriated companions making their way back from the inexpensive cabarets that lay outside the city's new customs wall. Prompted by warnings from a subordinate and by an accident in the fall of 1788, the lieutenant of police ordered the General Farms to reconstruct this gate so as to guarantee the safety of pedestrians. Such action is typical of a number of minor ameliorations which, considered together across a period of years, may have spared dozens of lives.

In addition to horses and the carriages or wagons they drew, a pedestrian had also to contend with herds of cattle brought into the city to be slaughtered and with an occasional pack of homeless dogs. Since at least 1725, police regulations had made it illegal for owners to let their pets run free at night, but only under Lenoir does it appear that the police made a serious effort to protect Parisians from stray dogs and the

27. BN, MS JF 1325, fols. 247–56; BO, MS 1421, pp. 602–603; MS 1424, p. 112.

rabies they sometimes carried. In May, 1784, Lenoir banned the further raising of dogs in both the capital and its faubourgs. Those who already owned animals might keep them, but only on condition that the pets remain indoors or, when outside, on a leash. To see that his order was obeyed, the lieutenant of police commissioned a number of men to patrol the city with muskets and shoot any dog they found wandering loose on its streets. Lenoir warned that attempts to interfere with these men and their work would bring a fine of 200 livres.

The police had also issued a series of regulations aimed at giving pedestrians a decent chance against frightened cattle. Butchers were to herd their animals only in the early hours of the morning, before the streets became crowded. At least two men—one ahead, one behind—were to accompany cattle on drives into and through the city. To prevent wounded animals from fleeing the slaughterhouse and racing madly through the streets—an event that was, it seems, all too common—workers were obliged to fetter each animal before it was killed and to see that all exits from the slaughterhouse were firmly closed.[28]

Any list of hazards in eighteenth-century Paris would have to include the Seine. Though the river nourished life in a variety of ways, it could also take it; and the police joined the *bureau de ville* in efforts to reduce the number of its victims. That periodic floods should not take the city by surprise, agents of these two authorities measured the river's height daily, kept track of rainfall, and watched for the warm winds out of the south and west that melted snow upstream and caused the Seine to rise. When the waters reached a certain height, the lieutenant of police and the prévôt des marchands ordered bridges and vulnerable, low-lying areas evacuated, offering protected space to refugees in which they might store furniture and other belongings. When the river had subsided and families could return to their houses and apartments, the police followed along urging residents to empty cellars and wells as quickly as possible in order to prevent the stagnant water left behind from becoming a source of disease.[29]

Much of the water consumed in Paris came from the Seine, being distributed by large numbers of street vendors who filled their pails at the river. Though the major sewer on the northern side of the Seine

28. Sartine to the commissioners, April 26, 1766, in AN, Y 13728; AN, 0-1 361, nos. 17–21; Peuchet, *Mémoires*, I, 277; police ordinance, May 21, 1784, in APP, DB 355; Isambert, Jourdan, and Decrusy, *Recueil des lois*, XXIX, 84–85.

29. BN, MS JF 1319, fols. 105–11; AN, K 1022, no. 157.

deposited its waste below the city, a small tributary on the south, the Bièvre, carried garbage, excrement, and industrial waste from the Faubourg Saint-Marcel into the river upstream, above the heavily populated areas of the capital; and all along its course through Paris, the Seine served residents as a repository for various forms of refuse and dirt.

Aware to some extent that this pollution was an undesirable and unhealthy presence in drinking water, the police made a crude effort to protect consumers by prescribing places along the river from which vendors might draw the water they sold. These were invariably points where the river ran free, points which lay as far as practical from sewer openings and the boats that served eighteenth-century Paris as laundries.

For those who drew a living from the river or found regular amusement there, each day brought the possibility of a miscalculation or a lapse of balance that could prove fatal. Until 1765, anyone who fell into the Seine stood little chance of surviving unless he was a strong swimmer and could save himself. By the terms of a peculiar ordinance, Parisians received a small fee for any corpse they fished out of the Seine and carried to the morgue. Under these circumstances, boatmen and bystanders were inclined to approach a victim of the river only when all struggle and other disheartening signs of life had ceased.

On September 7, 1765, Sartine acted to alter this situation. He wrote his commissioners:

> I am told that far from assisting persons who have fallen into the river, boatmen [les gens de Rivière] distance themselves and wait for the individual to drown in order to collect the small fee they receive for bodies taken from the river. Henceforth, I will see that those who save someone from drowning are rewarded. Please inform the boatmen in your quarter of this new policy. You are to give certificates which my office will honor to those who have assisted a drowning man, but give these—to prevent abuse—only when the Guard confirms an individual's story. Humanity suggested this idea to one of your colleagues, Mr. Thiot. I can only applaud his zeal and charity.[30]

If a man's chances of being pulled from the Seine improved during Sartine's administration, it was under Lenoir that the police joined the bureau de ville in promoting new methods for treating victims once

---

30. Sartine to commissioners, September 7, 1765, in AN, Y 13728.

they were laid ashore. To their credit, both authorities began late in the 1770s to discourage such popular forms of first aid as hanging a victim by his feet or rolling him about in a large barrel; instead, they urged residents to send immediately to the nearest guardpost for trained assistance.

Guardsmen, acting on the best medical advice available, learned under Lenoir to undress persons taken from the river and to keep them warm. They were taught as well to make use of the implements in medical kits stored after 1775 in each guardpost. Among these was a nozzle that was placed in the victim's mouth and used as a conduit through which to blow air into his lungs. There was, alas, also something known as the "machine fumigatoire," a device, I regret to say, for pumping tobacco smoke into a person's rectum. Following its invention late in the 1770s by an enterprising doctor named Pia, this redoubtable instrument became standard equipment not only in guardposts, but on all bridges of the city, and at fixed points along the quais. Both the *bureau de ville* and the police found it an impressive tool and were willing to argue that it had revived many persons who would, without its use, have perished.[31] Whatever the merits of Doctor Pia's invention, the other methods introduced by the police for treating the drowned were unquestionably an improvement on earlier forms of care. By 1780 persons taken from the river were no longer being battered to death in barrels or strung up to dry in the sun; instead, thanks to Lenoir and his colleague at the Hôtel de Ville, they were receiving both reasonable treatment for shock and at least a primitive form of artificial respiration.

PUBLIC HEALTH AND POLLUTION

It was not victims of the river alone who required protection from well-intentioned bystanders and the practitioners of popular medicine. The cost and the frequently apparent inadequacy of professional medical care led many of the injured and the ill in Paris to turn for help to untrained healers who claimed reassuring powers over disease and other forms of disability. While some of these claims were no doubt sincere and some perhaps even accurate, many were no more than an attempt to exploit fear and the credulity it so readily engenders; but

31. Lenoir to commissioners, September 30, 1775, in AN, Y 13728; BO, MS 1421, p. 368; AN, AD-I 26, 115, 3.

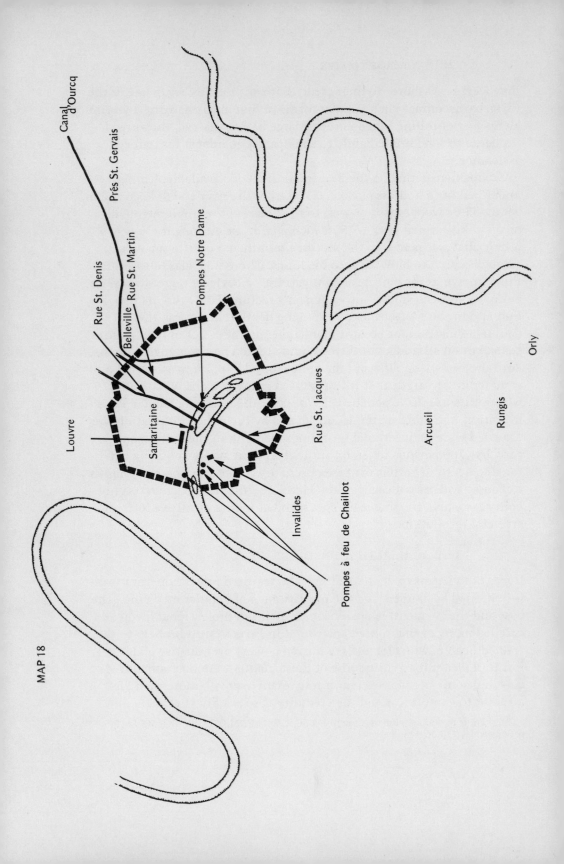

MAP 18

Canal d'Ourcq

Prés St. Gervais

Rue St. Denis

Rue St. Martin

Belleville

Pompes Notre Dame

Louvre

Samaritaine

Rue St. Jacques

Invalides

Pompes à feu de Chaillot

Arcueil

Rungis

Orly

Map 18
THE PARISIAN WATER SUPPLY, 1802

SOURCES OF WATER

1 Belleville (since the twelfth century)

2 Prés Saint-Gervais (since the fourteenth century)

3 Samaritaine (a pump on the Pont Neuf, built in 1608)

4 Arcueil and Rungis (an aqueduct, originally built by the Romans about 360, that carried water from these two sources to Paris; the structure was repaired under Marie de Medici, work being completed in 1624)

5 Pumps of Notre Dame (pumps on the Pont Notre Dame, constructed in 1670)

6 Steam pumps at Chaillot (three pumps built about 1785, supplying 11,625,000 gallons a day of water unfortunately drawn from below the city)

7 River Ourcq (a canal completed in 1802 diverted the water of this stream into the city; the project which supplied the city with an additional 21 million gallons of water had initially been suggested in 1676 by Riquet de Bon Repos)

SOURCES: Lacaille, *Description de la ville*; Deharme, "Plan de Paris"; BN, MS JF 1335, fols. 14–20.

MAP 19

Map 19

THE STORAGE AND DISTRIBUTION
OF WATER, 1763

SYMBOLS   TOTALS

f Fountain   54

● Well   21

■ Pump   5

R Reservoir   9

NOTE: The freedom many men treasured most—respite from the struggle to survive—depended less on the political system under which they lived than on more mundane circumstances, like the distance they found themselves from the nearest public fountain.
SOURCES: Lacaille, *Description de la ville*; Deharme, "Plan de Paris."

worse than the fraud these men and women practiced was the physical damage their secret remedies and clandestine procedures too often inflicted.

Under Louis XIV and for some time thereafter, the police issued ordinances forbidding this unlicensed practice of medicine and pursued violators wherever they could find them; but the results of these efforts were far from satisfactory. As late as the 1760s, Sartine was still asking the government for sufficient means "to diminish the number of this multitude of individuals—scourge on the people's health—who, by means of a certificate they have purchased or within the sanctuary of some privileged place, exercise, without right and without having been examined, a profession which requires long study coupled with true and certain understanding."[32]

During Sartine's administration the police appear to have come to terms with their failure and to have realized that their attack on charlatans was also an assault on popular medicine—an assault that could not succeed so long as professional care remained beyond the means of many Parisians. Abandoning efforts at repression, they sought instead to regulate the forms of amateur practice by issuing permits to all who agreed to submit themselves and their remedies to periodic inspection.

Sartine assigned an inspector of police to implement the new policy. Working first in conjunction with an established royal commission of doctors and druggists and, after 1778, with the Royal Society of Medicine, this inspector attempted to see that all remedies distributed in the capital were first examined and tested by competent professionals. To insure accountability he recorded the names of all whose products were approved and required that they keep him informed of any changes in address. Finally, in order to encourage compliance, he employed some whose medicines had been approved as informers, paying them to report others who had not submitted to examination or whose practice went beyond the recommendation and sale of potions.

Commissioner Lemaire contended that the new policy—the effort to regulate popular medicine rather than suppress it—had, by 1770, proven remarkably successful, leaving the poor access to beneficial remedies, while protecting them from those that might prove baneful.

32. While licensed doctors and surgeons could also do a patient more harm than good, their practice was at least open and founded on considerable cumulative experience. If we consider popular and professional treatment of the drowned, it would appear that, despite their shortcomings, the physicians of the eighteenth century were a better risk than their untrained competitors. BO, MS 1421, p. 366.

Lenoir, however, indicates much less satisfaction with the work of the police, suggesting that it was the Royal Society of Medicine rather than his own subordinates that began, after 1778, to reduce significantly the harm done by charlatans.[33]

While seeking to drive dangerous amateurs out of the city, the police worked during the last fifteen years of the Old Regime to promote improved practice and effective innovation among licensed physicians. Under Lenoir they established annual prizes for those contributing significant new ideas to the treatment of illness and disease. In 1782 one of these awards went to a Parisian doctor for his essay on rabies and the following year another was bestowed on a physician at the Hôtel-Dieu for what were described as great advances in reducing the incidence of puerperal fever among women who gave birth in that hospital. To encourage familiarity with the latter individual's methods, the police paid to have them carefully summarized, then published and distributed.[34]

Since the early 1730s, the lieutenants of police and other authorities had expressed concern over the spread of venereal disease in the capital. In 1735 members of the Assemblée de Police decided to erect a separate building at Bicêtre to house victims of this malady; and two years later they underwrote the costs of experimenting with a new treatment proposed by a provincial doctor named Charbonnier. More effective, however, than Charbonnier's technique, which involved the use of smoke, were the methods employed in a new hospital Lenoir established at Vaugirard in 1780. Here doctors sought to treat and save the many infants born each year with venereal disease and the wet-nurses who, unknowingly, contracted it from their charges. By administering a remedy (presumably mercury in some form) to the nurse, doctors hoped to communicate, in controlled and beneficial quantities, the same substance to the diseased child. Initially an experiment, the program appears to have had significant success. After two years of work and observation, the physicians involved claimed to have saved two-fifths of the infants and almost all of the wetnurses they had treated.[35]

Prostitutes, pregnant and sick, seem also to have judged the new in-

---

33. BO, MS 1424, pp. 94–98, 121.
34. BO, MS 1421, p. 378.
35. Entries for March 17, August 18, 1735, February 14, March 14, July 18, 1737, in BN, MS 11356; BO, MS 1421, pp. 365–66.

stitution a success, for they began appearing there voluntarily for treatment, gaining admission without charge on the condition that they agree to complete the program and, during its course, to nurse not only their own child but any other that might require milk. Shortly after its founding, the hospital at Vaugirard had become an indispensable addition to the older facilities at Bicêtre, facilities which were capable of treating only two hundred persons at a time and which had left many of the most innocent to die neglected on the street or in some private shelter.

At the same time they were supporting care for victims of venereal disease, the police paid the costs of a new treatment for epilepsy. Beginning in 1784, Lenoir furnished two doctors, a father and son named Le Dru, with over 17,000 livres a year for providing indigent epileptics with a new kind of electrical therapy that appeared to reduce the frequency and duration of their attacks. It was Lenoir who saw to it that guardposts in the city were provided with first-aid kits and stretchers; it was he who supplied curés in all rural villages sheltering Parisian infants with professionally prepared medicines and instructions on the care of childhood illnesses; and it was he who, with the approval of the government, began permitting inoculation against smallpox, despite the ban on this practice issued by the Parlement of Paris.[36]

But the efforts of the police to guarantee public health extended beyond their attention to the quality of medicine and medical practice available in the capital. In addition to controlling drugs dispensed by amateur healers and apothecaries, the police tried as well to see that food sold in the city was free of taint. Both commissioners and inspectors of police had orders to keep close watch over meat displayed in the butcher shops of their quarters, while the persistent sale of unwholesome mushrooms prompted the lieutenant of police in 1782 to forbid their storage overnight and to require that new supplies entering the city each day be carefully inspected. By banning the use of copper containers for the transport and storage of milk, Lenoir appears to have significantly reduced the number of persons succumbing to verdigris, a poisonous copper sulfate that had been an inevitable presence in much of the city's milk. According to one author, writing in 1788 or 1789, "We know that verdigris was distributed with milk and that this poison took a horrible toll among the population of Paris. It is to Mr.

36. BO, MS 1421, pp. 364, 367–69; Lenoir to the controller general, February 12, 1785, in AN, F-4 1017.

Lenoir that we owe this reform [the proscription of copper containers], which, however unimportant in appearance, is more valuable than all those which have no other object than a further increase in the espionage of the police."[37]

At least as important to the health of Parisians as these steps to guarantee the quality of food and medical care were earlier efforts to improve the collection and disposal of refuse that accumulated in the city —of the waste that nourished rats and served as breeding grounds for bacteria. Though it is easy enough to find men complaining throughout the eighteenth century that "Paris at this moment might rightly be considered the dirtiest city in the universe despite its opulence and magnificence," there is reason to believe that the capital was a cleaner city in 1789 than it had been at the turn of the century. One notes, for example, that while Hérault and Berryer had difficulty during the 1730s and 1740s dissuading important nobles from ordering the dung from their stables thrown into the streets, Lenoir's major concern by 1776 is the inveterate presence of simple dirt and mud. More objective evidence of improvement is the increase in resources devoted to cleaning the city, an increase that seems to have greatly outstripped the growth of Paris itself. Between 1718 and 1789, funds allocated for removing refuse more than doubled, and the number of carts performing this service grew from 85 to 130. What is more, the collection of waste, which had occurred but once a week in 1700, was, by 1770, undertaken daily.[38]

If there was a chorus of dissatisfaction with refuse removal in the last decade of the Old Regime, Lenoir claims (without denying that there were serious and regrettable shortcomings to the work a limited number of men could do) that many of these complaints reflected not the quality of this public service but rather a change in habit and individual perspective. In 1779, it seems, Doctor Tronchin, a man whose ideas and services were then much in vogue, published a series of recommendations on how persons might improve or maintain their health. Among the suggestions he offered was the counsel to walk

37. Sartine to commissioners, May 10, 1766, in AN, Y 13728; Le Moyne, *Dictionnaire de police*, II, 417; *Encyclopedie méthodique: Jurisprudence*, IX, 616.
38. AN, 0-1 360, no. 95; BN, MS JF 1319, fols. 64, 72, 87, 94–97; Lenoir to commissioners, November 12, 1776, in AN, Y 13728; BO, MS 1421, pp. 605–606. We know that the government spent a total of 300,000 livres between 1704 and 1720 on lighting, cleaning, and fire protection. If the percentage of this sum spent on cleaning was then roughly what it was in 1780 (37 percent), the amount spent on waste removal alone would have been about 111,000 livres. By 1780, the figure was 206,307 livres.

regularly, preferably early each morning. This advice, according to Lenoir, created a new fashion among "the elegant young men and ladies of Paris," who began appearing on the streets with the break of day, sometimes before the garbage carts had begun their rounds. Understandably, they were not pleased with the refuse and dirt they encountered at this hour; but the censure they so readily voiced points not to a city less clean than it had been, but rather to new expectations and standards of sanitation among a vocal part of the population.[39]

An essential complement to improvements in the collection of waste were the new arrangements made in 1758 for its disposal. Eighteenth-century Paris had come to possess three kinds of public dumps: one serving as repository for garbage collected on the streets; another as receptacle for human waste removed at night from the toilets (fosses d'aisances) that by law each building in the city had to contain; and a third as space into which builders might cast the rubble and stone that was banned from other dumping grounds. Once situated, the first two types of pits—those for garbage and for sewage—tended to remain where they were; for regularly, during the cooler months of each year, peasants in need of fertilizer dug from them a fourth of their contents, leaving behind new space for the refuse of Paris. While this arrangement spared municipal authorities the expense of periodically buying new sites, it also meant that there was no natural impetus to close down dumps that time and urban growth had brought within the city.

Many Parisians were living in unwelcome and unhealthy proximity to such areas when, in October, 1758, the Council of State ordered all refuse dumps closed and relocated outside populated districts. This order, though appearing over the name of the king and his council, was, in fact, the work of Henri Bertin, who also assumed responsibility for its execution. The lieutenant of police had begun his efforts to obtain such a decree early the same year. When in January the controller general rejected an initial request for support in the council, Bertin carried his case to the procureur general and the first president of the Parlement. With a report that contained a careful account of anticipated expenses and that urged the importance of his proposal to public health, Bertin sent the two men a covering note on February 8: "I am convinced," he said, "that if you will both speak to the controller

39. BO, MS 1421, p. 605.

general of this project as useful, you will obtain what I alone have been unable to." By October, as we have seen, the lieutenant of police had the decree he sought, and the work of relocation began. Five years later, Paris had freed itself from the bulk of its own malodorous and unsanitary waste.[40]

But this achievement, however important to the control of pests and disease, did not suddenly clear the polluted air of the great city. If the refuse dumps were gone, other sources of contamination remained. There were, above all, the tens of thousands of chimneys that poured smoke each day into the sky over Paris; but to these—common and apparently inevitable—residents of the capital seem to have given less attention than to local sources of pollution that were at once more offensive and less overwhelming in scope.

Each neighborhood had its own particular grievance—an artisan's shop, a depression in the earth where water collected and stood, a poorly tended cemetery. In an act of self-defense dated July 27, 1676, the Parlement of Paris ordered that all furnaces adjacent to its chambers in the Palais be immediately dismantled or destroyed. Smoke from these devices had grown intolerable on days when the wind was out of the north, distracting judges and making the conduct of patient argument and deliberation impossible. During the 1730s many of the children housed at Sainte-Pélagie in the quarter of Place Maubert were unable to contend with the billowing fumes from nearby potters' shops and, once they began experiencing severe chest pains, had to be transferred elsewhere.

In the Faubourg Saint-Marcel, it was artisans producing starch who provoked the loudest cries of protest. D'Argenson began receiving complaints from this district before he left office in 1718, and expressions of discontent continued under his successors. Believing that their commissioner of police had been bribed by the starchmakers and was furnishing his superior with false information, residents of the area at last joined together and addressed themselves directly to the lieutenant of police, René Hérault, and to the procureur general of the Parlement. In a lengthy petition accompanied by the testimony of a physician, they claimed that the water the starchmakers were releasing each day into the streets of the faubourg was so foul that the stench from it rotted meat and forced inhabitants to live behind windows and doors that

40. BN, MS JF 1321, fol. 129 bis, 133.

were always closed. Unless something was done, they warned, this noisome smell would, in time, provoke revolt and disorder in the faubourg.

A similar warning came from inhabitants of the quarter of Saint-Jacques-de-la-Boucherie, particularly those whose lodgings lay close to the river, between the Pont au Change and the Pont Nôtre-Dame. These individuals suffered from the concentration in their district of the city's *cuiseurs de tripes*, persons who prepared for lower-class consumption intestines and other animal parts unused by butchers. In pursuing their livelihood, the *cuiseurs* were obliged to perform two tasks that offended their neighbors. They had first to wash the entrails they had collected from a slaughterhouse, and this need took them to the Seine and to the arcades of the Quai de Gesvres. Residents complained that the continual presence of the *cuiseurs* on the quai made passage there extremely difficult, while further downstream those who operated the pump Samaritaine on the Pont au Change found the water they drew from the river befouled with sizable remnants of cattle, pigs, and sheep. Cows' heads kept drifting into their machine, clogging it, and causing repeated damage.

Still, it was the actual cooking of entrails that caused inhabitants of the district most pain. In a petition sent to Hérault in 1736, the neighbors of the *cuiseurs* contended that the fumes these men produced damaged not only fabric but metal as well. To protect themselves from harm, they said, they had to live in darkened rooms shut as tightly as possible against the polluted and dangerous air.[41]

Human industry was not the only source of local pollution in eighteenth-century Paris. There were as well the city's cemeteries, some of which, like the cemetery for criminals at Montfaucon, were overused and poorly maintained. Among these sad and unpleasant places, that which caused greatest concern and agitation was the Cemetery of the Innocents located in the quarter of Les Halles. One-third of the approximately sixty parishes in Paris, as well as the Hôtel-Dieu and the Châtelet, used this small site for the interment of their dead. Each year workers cast two thousand bodies—more than five a day—into the large open pits that served most who were carried here as the only grave they would ever have.[42]

41. BN, MS JF 1326, fol. 214; MS JF 1332, fols. 57–58, 97–98; MS JF 1333, fols. 78–109.
42. BN, MS JF 1317, fols. 48, 73–74, 104. Estimates of the number buried annually in the cemetery during the 1730s ranged between twelve hundred and two thousand.

While the majority of Parisians understandably did what they could to avoid this place, there were some who could not escape it. Enclosing the cemetery on three sides were rows of five- and six-story dwellings in which perhaps two thousand persons made their homes. For years these individuals had complained to the canons of Saint-Germain-l'Auxerrois, who owned and administered the cemetery, that the odors from it were becoming unbearable. By 1730 these complaints had become frequent, bitter, and sharply insistent. Still, nothing was done, and during several of the ensuing summers—that time of year when distasteful smells ripen into something intolerable—inhabitants of the area abandoned verbal protest and rioted in the streets.

Ironically, a report prepared for the Assemblée de Police in 1738 stated that putrefaction of exposed corpses was not the major cause of the cemetery's unbearable smell. The principal source was, it seems, excrement and urine that inhabitants of the surrounding buildings dumped from their windows onto the graveyard below. Though these structures had large common vats into which individual chamber pots were to be emptied, these facilities were, for some reason, often on the fifth floor; and many residents found the relative proximity of a window irresistible.

But whatever the source of their problem, the men and women who lived adjacent to the cemetery were profoundly worried about the stench that afflicted their lives. To appreciate the violence of their concern—a concern which had produced riots—one has to understand that polluted, malodorous air was, in the opinion of most eighteenth-century Parisians, something more than a nuisance, constituting rather a potent threat to health, an inevitable source of disease and—too often—of death. In their petition to Hérault, residents of the Faubourg Saint-Marcel had argued that the stench produced by starchmakers "could . . . cause contagious diseases, even the plague"; and opinions in the quarter of Saint-Jacques-de-la-Boucherie were similar. An investigator sent there in response to complaints about the preparation of tripe spoke with one woman who asserted that she had been in good health before abandoning her old neighborhood for lodgings near the river. The foul air of the new quarter was, she believed, slowly killing her; and the investigator, having approached one or two of the shops where entrails and animal parts were cooked, found her opinion highly credible. In the quarter of Les Halles, residents claimed to suffer frequently from blisters and fever that both they and the commissioner of police in the district, Laumonier, attributed to the Cemetery of the Innocents.[43]

While the smells Parisians feared may not themselves have increased the incidence of disease in a neighborhood, individual efforts to find refuge from polluted air may well have encouraged illness and contagion. By shutting themselves off behind tightly closed windows and doors, residents of the city were denying themselves the sanitary effects of sunlight and ventilation. Pollution may thus have become an indirect cause of disease, prompting residents to live in confined and darkened rooms, where pathogenic microorganisms might readily concentrate and multiply.

In any case, given the widespread conviction that foul odors did serious physical harm, it is hardly surprising that eighteenth-century Parisians were ready to riot over "corrupt" or "infected" air, a problem which, for them, was as serious as death itself. Nor is it surprising to find the police working in conjunction with other municipal authorities to ameliorate an evil that bore so directly on both public health and public order. Throughout the century, police and *bureau des finances* had enforced limitations on the height of new construction, believing that "the excessive height of buildings is not less prejudicial to the cleanliness of the air than to the safety of residents in a city so large and so populous." Though financial embarrassment delayed serious work until 1786, the police and the Hôtel de Ville had persuaded the crown as early as 1769 to order demolition of all buildings lining the city's bridges. Such action, they argued, was absolutely necessary, for it would not only contribute greatly to the appearance of the capital but was also "the only means of working effectively to bring about the cleanliness [and] the freer circulation of the air."[44]

While working to make Paris accessible to the passage of cleansing winds, the police attempted as well to banish from the capital the more offensive sources of pollution. By 1763 they had completed the relocation of refuse dumps and sewage pits outside the city. Within another decade Sartine had obliged the producers of tripe to close down their shops in the quarter of Saint-Jacques-de-la-Boucherie and to reestablish themselves on the Île des Cignes, south and west of the city's

---

43. BN, MS JF 1332, fol. 57; MS JF 1333, fols. 78–79; MS JF 1317, 147–48.
44. Isambert, Jourdan, and Decrusy, *Recueil des lois,* XXVII, 270–74; AN, 0-1 360, nos. 107–108.

heavily populated districts. On a smaller scale other lieutenants of police rendered a similar service. Hérault, for example, ordered an ink-
maker named Hoyau out of the quarter of Saint-Benoît in 1732, when
an investigation confirmed claims that his shop was emitting great
quantities of evil-smelling smoke.[45]

Though the police failed in their attempts during the eighteenth century to end the slaughter of livestock inside Paris, and though they
were unable to persuade the crown that the Hôtel-Dieu ought to be
moved out of the city, they did manage one last important success in
their campaign against pollution.[46] In 1784, Lenoir reports, the government at last decided to act as the police had so often counseled, agreeing to close and relocate all cemeteries remaining within the capital.[47]
Despite resistance from the church, the disagreeable labor of exhuma-
tion began, continuing through all but the hot and unsuitable months
of summer. Within three years, workers in the pay of the police had
carted south out of Paris the last, mingled remnants of the city's dead;
and by 1789, even the ancient, apparently indispensable Cemetery of
the Innocents was gone. In its place—on ground that had, in six centuries, consumed several times a hundred thousand lives—stood a
bustling market, filled with animation and the produce of distant
farms.

Each year in January or February, French monarchs received from
their lieutenant of police in Paris a report on the number of baptisms
and burials that had occurred in the capital during the preceding year.
During the first half of the eighteenth century, these documents contained little but grim information. Looking at them in 1749, one would
have noted that during the last thirty years there had been only 98 infants born to replace every 100 persons who died; and in the face of
such evidence, what could one conclude but that the city destroyed

45. BO, MS 1424, p. 155; BN, MS fr. 21732, fol. 207.

46. On police efforts to establish slaughterhouses beyond the city's limits—efforts
that continued for more than fifty years—see BN, MS JF 1334, fols. 8–178; on Lenoir's
recommendation that the Hôtel-Dieu be replaced by four smaller institutions on the
outskirts of the city—advice given on the grounds that "one does not bring into the
center of the city causes of that unhealthiness that one is trying to do away with"—see
BO, MS 1421, pp. 367–68.

47. BO, MS 1421, p. 369. Twenty years earlier, acting on his own authority, Sartine
had ordered the closing and relocation of the criminals' cemetery at Montfaucon which
was, he contended, almost as responsible for polluting the air as a nearby refuse dump
(BN, MS JF 1321, fols. 133–34).

human beings more quickly than it could replace them, that—for all
its vanity and power, for all its cruelty to outsiders—the capital was
demographically dependent on immigration from the farms and villages of France.

But in January, 1787, the police were able to report that births in
Paris had outnumbered deaths not only in 1786 but in a surprising
number of preceding years. During the last two decades of the Old
Regime, there were, in fact, two years in which births exceeded deaths
for every single year in which death prevailed; and in the same twenty
years, from 1769 to 1789, 103 children were born in the city for every
100 individuals who perished. Indeed, the favorable trend had begun
earlier. Since midcentury the ratio of births to deaths had been somewhat more than 101 to 100; and though the margin was slender, it appeared that life had gained a permanent advantage over death. Paris had
become capable of sustaining itself demographically and could henceforth, it seemed, survive without a steady influx of outsiders. While
noting this change, Lenoir was not sure he could explain it. Was it, he
asked himself, simply and wholly "the will of Providence," or did it
result, in part, from the labor of the police to make Paris a safer and
more habitable city? [48]

Recent work in historical demography suggests a tenuous answer to
Lenoir's question. Many demographers have argued that the surplus of
births over deaths experienced throughout Western Europe after 1750
was due not to an increase in the birthrate but rather to a decline in
mortality. Baptisms, they have contended, began consistently to outnumber burials—in Paris, presumably as elsewhere—not because
more women were bearing children (or because women were bearing
more children), but because fewer human beings were dying. For this
change, coming as it did in the latter half of the eighteenth century,
before most major advances in medical therapy, demographers have
found but one explanation that satisfies them: an amelioration of the
physical environment. By improving the conditions under which they

48. BO, MS 1421, pp. 369, 379; *Recherches statistique sur Paris*, II, table 53. It is
worth noting that not all historians are willing to accept the demographic data we have
at face value. See Louis Henry, "Le Volume de l'immigration à Paris de 1740 à 1792,"
Population, VI (1971), 1073–85. But Henry's argument that extant records exaggerate
births and underestimate deaths conveniently ignores circumstance and social practice
(e.g., the custom among Parisian women of going to the country to give birth) that
would have had precisely the opposite effect on the figures that have come down to us.

lived, men imposed new limits on the spread of infectious disease and thereby reduced significantly the incidence of their own mortality.[49]

In Paris, credit for many of these changes belongs to the police. Emergency relief, improved disposal of refuse and human waste, better ventilation, more careful control of vermin and other animal pests— such achievements were theirs, the work of men and not of Providence. Given these accomplishments, Lenoir might have been less hesitant in claiming for himself and his predecessors an important part in having made Paris in the last years of the Old Regime as capable of sustaining life as of destroying it.

49. Henry, "Population of France," 434; Thomas McKeown and R. G. Brown, "Medical Evidence Related to English Population Changes in the Eighteenth Century," in Glass and Eversley (eds.), *Population in History*, 300, 303–307.

7

The Rhythms of
Urban Life

Having surveyed the basic objectives of police activity between 1718 and 1789, one is inclined to ask to what extent this activity and the policies it embodied changed in response to new leadership and altered circumstance. We know, for example, that several months after he had succeeded Lenoir as lieutenant of police in August, 1785, Thiroux de Crosne drafted a memorandum to the controller general, asking additional funds for the operation of the police. Implicit in the financial detail of his request are both an assessment of the preceding administration and a statement of projected changes in policy. Paris, according to Crosne, required a larger number of inspectors responsible for sanitation (*inspecteurs de netoiement*) and additional employees charged with sweeping bridges, quays, and public squares. It needed, as well, an expanded network of paid informers and a more efficient apparatus for enforcing censorship. Clearly, the new lieutenant of police believed that two activities—the removal of waste and the gathering of intelligence—deserved more attention than his predecessor had given them.[1]

If, in a general sense, Crosne may be said to have continued previous efforts to guarantee order and improve life in the city, it is also clear that he intended a new emphasis on functions that had, he believed, been neglected. With a change in chief administrators, there were to come changes in the tactics the police employed and in the specific urban problems that preoccupied them. Concentration on relief as a means of assuring civil order was to yield, in part, to a more thorough search for the city's disaffected and, presumably, to new efforts at re-

1. Crosne to controller general, undated, in APP, DB 355.

278

pression. Public sanitation would take precedence over Lenoir's support of medical experimentation.

But Crosne's request to the controller general, while by no means a complete budget, affords what is unfortunately a rare view of the impact new leadership might have on the work of the police. It leaves the historian regretting the absence of other documents like it in the hand of Hérault or Berryer or Sartine—similar financial proposals that would permit straightforward and confident inference regarding the problems and priorities of each new administration. Without this kind of evidence, it is often difficult to perceive changes in the preoccupations of the police or, perceiving them, to be sure they are not retrospective distortions resulting from incomplete records or inadequate research.

If it is possible with some assurance to contrast Hérault's emphasis on espionage and order with the attention Sartine and Lenoir gave public services, and if Joseph d'Albert's appointment in May, 1775, portends an assault on the guilds of the city and hence a transitory departure from traditional economic policy, change in the concerns and activity of the police is a phenomenon less apparent than continuity.[2] Each new lieutenant of police spent much of the term that lay ahead of him reiterating the suggestions, the complaints, and the orders of his predecessors.

In asking the controller general for funds to increase the number of guardposts and fire stations in Paris, Crosne was echoing appeals that had been made intermittently for more than sixty years; and when Lenoir chastised his commissioners for their apparent reluctance to remain in their quarters and perform essential judicial functions, his rebuke differed little from those Sartine or Marville had delivered. In the sentences he handed down in court and in the ordinances he issued as an administrator, each lieutenant of police repeated the enjoinders of his predecessors. Dates change; here and there one article of a regulation disappears or another is added; but often the replication is perfect,

2. Between 1753 and 1780, the funds devoted to security (guard, maréchaussée, and lights) rose from 840,000 livres a year to 1,151,000 livres, an increase of 37 percent. During the same period, money spent on public services (fire department, garbage collection) increased by 50 percent, from 226,000 livres to 340,000. These figures suggest a new emphasis after 1750—and particularly under Sartine and Lenoir, whose administrations span most of this period—on service rather than security (see table 8). We have also seen that Sartine and Lenoir spent only a quarter of what Hérault had on informers who reported directly to the lieutenant of police.

down to the least significant phrase. A fire ordinance of 1781 closely
resembles one drafted in 1735, and this document is itself a reproduction of regulations appearing nine years earlier. The same might be said
of ordinances relating to security and a hundred other matters, those
produced under one lieutenant of police being frequently precise dupli-
cates of the acts issued by another.

For this continuity, for the great similarity among administrations,
there are several explanations. One lies in the character of the administrative staff serving the lieutenants of police. Many members of this
staff could measure their experience in decades, and such men were inclined to press new lieutenants of police to continue work and patterns
of their predecessors, work with which they were familiar and comfortable. Lenoir regarded these men as the proper conservators of police
policies and practices, suggesting that anyone who became lieutenant
of police had much to learn from them: "The head of the police should,
during the first part of his administration, realize that there is much to
learn from those associates and assistants with more experience than
he has had. . . . Far from resisting generally accepted principles, he
ought to follow them; and without at first hoping to do better, he
ought to continue the work of the preceding administration, if such a
course does not involve him in abuses or deficiencies that are too
salient."[3]

Financial embarrassment also contributed to the resemblance one
police administration bore to another. Without additional funds it was,
understandably, difficult for a new lieutenant of police to make significant changes in procedure or policy, even when he had gained the confidence to do so. Lenoir reports that many of the more important
projects he urged upon the government died because there was not
money to implement them, and the same fate probably awaited the
proposals Crosne submitted to the crown in 1785 or 1786.[4] Wanting
the means to do otherwise, new lieutenants of police frequently had no
choice but to continue along the course marked out by their predecessors.

The repetitive character of much that the police did derived, however, less from a chronic inadequacy of funds or the influence of a
conservative bureaucracy than from the fact that many of the city's

3. BO, MS 1423, p. 144.
4. BO, MS 1421, p. 611.

problems and needs were themselves rhythmic phenomena, linked to the regular alteration of the seasons and to the cycles of religious observance under the Old Regime. In determining the particular emphases of police activity, it is often more useful to know the month or day of the year than to have at hand a list of administrators and their terms in office.

Whatever the identity of the lieutenant of police, whatever his intentions, the recurrent celebration of certain Christian holidays gave an inevitable cadence to life in Paris and to the work of the police. There was, of course, the weekly repetition of Sunday and the concomitant ban on labor, commerce, and many forms of secular amusement. Once each week the police gave up their persistent efforts at compelling men to work and became instead advocates of idleness. If actual enforcement of the prohibitions against labor and diversion was generally less severe, less absolute, than that promised in published ordinances, it was nonetheless real, consuming much of the energy and attention of the police. On Sunday morning, while some officers patrolled the streets seeking to prevent all activity but the sale of foodstuffs, others stood watch in the city's churches to see that dress and behavior were appropriately respectful; and while tolerating many forms of commerce and amusement in the afternoon, the police continued patrols aimed at enforcing the proscription against physical labor.[5]

This same effort occupied the police during many of the annual holidays celebrated by the church, the only difference being that the ban on what Sartine called "servile work" was enforced with particular stringency, especially on the four holiest days of the year—Easter, Whitsunday, Christmas, and Epiphany. Some holidays, like Corpus Christi, brought additional obligations. This celebration, accompanied as it was by numerous processions throughout the city, obliged the police to spend much of the preceding week inspecting the routes that would be followed. Every year, late in May or at the beginning of June, the commissioners of police received orders to see that all obstacles were cleared from the paths the processions would take. They were also to inspect the cobblestone of the streets and notify the lieutenant of police of spots that required attention. Finally, they were to join the

5. Sartine to commissioners, November 23, 1763, July 22, 1764, August 1, 1765, June 1, 1768, in AN, Y 13728; BN, MS JF 1330, fols. 39, 50.

police architect in going over the temporary platforms erected for spectators, making sure that these structures would bear the weight of a crowd without accident.[6]

It is interesting to note that even the repair of roads in the city was to some extent a function of religious life and its rhythms. The timing of Easter, and hence the feast of Corpus Christi, determined when paving crews would begin to undo the damage of winter, and it was the choice of processional routes for this day that decided which streets would receive immediate care.

Of all the annual holidays, it was Easter—or rather the period of Lent preceding it—that had the greatest impact on the activity of the police. For forty days, police commissioners gave up their ordinary schedules and spent meal hours not at the table with their families but rather prowling about inns and restaurants, watching other people eat and seeing to it that no one but the sick and the pregnant indulged in the consumption of meat. During the remainder of the day, they and other agents of the police made sure in the course of their rounds that the city's butchers were properly idle, their shops empty and closed.[7]

Needless to say, this change in the dietary habits of Parisians altered the work of those responsible for provisioning the capital. Each year in December and January the lieutenant of police gave considerable time to finding the additional quantities of grain, vegetables, and fish that Parisians consumed during Lent. At the same time, he worried about the date of Easter, hoping it would not fall too early in the spring, before enough grass had appeared to fatten sufficiently the animals that the capital would again require after its long abstinence.[8]

It was not the church and its calendar of celebrations alone that gave form to the work of the police. There was also nature and the revolving passage of the seasons. Paris, like the farms and villages surrounding it, lived amidst this movement and felt, with the rest of France, its impact. Needs changed. Problems came and went and came again. With each succession of seasons, the police faced a partially new set of difficulties and tasks.

6. Sartine to commissioners, December 26, 1764, in AN, Y 13728; Lenoir, Crosne to Commissioner Gillet, June 7, 1781, June 11, 1783, June 9, 1786, in AN, Y 12830.

7. Sartine to Commissioner Cocquelin, February 13, 1773, Sartine, Lenoir, and Crosne to commissioners, numerous examples, the first dated February 9, 1774 and the last February 20, 1787, in AN, Y 13728.

8. BO, MS 1424, p. 138; BN, MS fr. n.a. 6765, fols. 203–20.

Summer and the open roads which carried many wealthy Parisians out of the city to their country homes also brought large numbers of strangers into the capital—tourists, businessmen, and others of uncertain purpose. We have figures for those arriving in one section of Paris, the Oratoire, during the spring and summer of 1791, and may presume a roughly similar pattern prior to the Revolution. In April, 70 visitors arrived to take up lodgings in this part of the city; in May there were 100; in June, 150; and in July, 300.[9]

Each individual arriving in the city demanded time and attention from the police. Simply examining the hotel registers, as inspectors of police were required to do, took four times as long in July as it had in April. Random nightly searches of boardinghouses and hotels consumed more time, since at each establishment a larger number of rooms were occupied and required inspection. As they were not inclined to accept at face value many of the explanations newcomers offered for their presence in Paris, inspectors found it necessary each summer to give many additional hours to the tedious surveillance of visitors.

Theft, always the principal crime in Paris, seems generally to have reached its apogee in August of each year, the same month it was at its peak in the countryside.[10] Those who have noted this phenomenon suggest that it may be linked to a decline in the employment of domestic servants during the summer. With many of its well-to-do inhabitants off at their country estates, Paris was presumably unable to hire and feed as many of those who sought domestic work as it could at other times of the year. Those left unemployed, the argument goes, were forced to steal in order to survive. A simpler explanation may lie in the sunshine and heat of August. It would have been during this time of year that sheets and the other textiles so often taken were left outside to dry or air; and it would also have been in the heat of late summer that Parisians made their other property more vulnerable by opening their windows in search of a cool breeze. But whatever the cause of the increase in theft during August, it would recurrently have placed an additional burden on the three inspectors responsible for most criminal investigations.

It was always during the warmest months of the year that the city's

9. Reinhard, *Paris pendant la révolution*, I, 39.
10. Petrovitch, "Criminalité à Paris," 209–11.

polluted air attracted most attention, both from the people and from
the police. In late May or early June of every year, the lieutenant of
police issued an ordinance obliging residents to wash the street in front
of their homes or shops twice each day. This work, to be done at six in
the morning and three in the afternoon, was essential, the ordinance
declared, to insure "the cleanliness of the air" in Paris. Still, each summer the lieutenant of police had to spend much of his Friday morning
in court fining those who had failed to attend to this task. Ordinary
forgetfulness or lassitude cost an individual five livres, while arrogant
defiance, like that evinced by a *procureur* of the Parlement named Des-
touches, might bring a penalty four times as great.[11]

At least once each summer the commissioners received a memorandum from the lieutenant of police urging them to pay special attention to the conduct of butchers. Sartine wrote his commissioners on
July 22, 1762, to remind them that the heat of the season required the
police to do all possible to prevent "corruption of the air." As part of
this effort, the commissioners were to inspect with special care and frequency the shops of butchers in their district, making sure that blood
did not collect in the streets outside and that the shops themselves
were kept free of excrement and rotting flesh.[12]

As summer approached its end, the police began their annual campaign against mendicancy, hoping to drive many of the city's vagabonds out into the countryside where they would be of use in the approaching harvest. Special directions went out to the inspectors and to
the guard late each August that all beggars, even most of those ordinarily tolerated, were to be rounded up and brought before a commissioner
of police. At the same time the commissioners received orders to set
aside all other tasks and to remain at home where they would be readily available to serve as judges "during those days set aside to execute
the ordinance regarding beggars."[13]

With the coming of fall, the attention of the police turned from pursuing mendicants to calculating the results of the recent harvest. Using
reports on the size of each crop, the lieutenant of police and his administrative staff could, to some extent, foresee eventual shortages and
begin preparations to cope with them. These same reports served the

11. Police ordinances from May and June, 1726–1775 and a police sentence, June 28,
1726, all in AN, AD-I 22B, 7; Lenoir to commissioners, June 4, 1781, in AN, Y 12830.
12. Sartine to commissioners, July 22, 1762, in AN, Y 13728; Lenoir to commissioners, August 21, 1778, in AN, Y 12830.
13. Crosne to commissioners, August 19, [?], in AN, Y 12830.

lieutenant of police in drafting a series of ordinances issued annually in the fall, ordinances in which he described the availability of a given item and proceeded then, in language that was forever the same, to establish the price at which that commodity might be sold.[14]

It had always been one of the principal objects of the police to keep the streets of Paris open, for the city's well-being depended on the ability of wagons and porters to make their way along these routes into thousands of apparently unimportant corners of the capital. Each season threatened this essential liberty of movement in its own peculiar way. Summer brought the proliferation of temporary commercial structures and their gradual encroachment on space allocated to traffic. Late in the autumn construction throughout the city came to an end and contractors, if not carefully watched, were inclined to store their building materials in the streets.[15]

Winter seems to have brought an accumulation of ice and frozen dirt that made transport particularly difficult. In a note to Commissioner Gillet dated December 27, 1780, Lenoir reminds his subordinate that the season makes it necessary to devote extraordinary care to keeping the streets clear. The commissioner is to "make his inspections every day, as often as possible" and to keep the lieutenant of police accurately informed regarding the condition of roads in his district of the city. Anxiously, the police waited for rain or a momentary thaw that would make it possible to remove accumulated debris. With the first sign of either, the lieutenant of police ordered his commissioners to summon residents outside to break the melting ice. Simultaneously, the crews responsible for collecting urban refuse were ordered to work. "Given the present thaw," Lenoir wrote on February 1, 1784, "I have ordered the agents and inspectors responsible for cleaning to station their most intelligent workers around the mouths of the large and small sewers and to get them to do everything possible to prevent them from clogging."[16]

There is a note of desperation in some of these orders, a hint that it would be disastrous to miss the chance afforded by each brief respite from the cold. For this tone of urgency, there was surely justification. Winter was an inevitable trial for the city, an ordeal of uncertain sever-

14. Cf. BN, MS JF 1316, fols. 128 and 135, for example.
15. Sartine to commissioners, November 26, 1766, in AN, Y 13728.
16. Lenoir to Commissioner Gillet, December 27, 1780, and February 1, 1784, Crosne to Commissioner Dupuy, January 6, 1786, in AN, Y 12830.

ity and duration. Its potential effect on the capital and on the work of
the police is, perhaps, best conveyed by a report Lenoir submitted to
the minister responsible for Paris on January 28, 1784. "The extreme
harshness of the season," he begins, "which has made itself felt continuously for six weeks increases both the needs of the police and their
anxiety regarding the maintenance of order and the supply of provisions." Little flour arrives, Lenoir points out, and farmers send produce
only because they badly need money. Transportation has become exceedingly difficult; a wagon that under normal circumstances would be
drawn by three horses and carry twenty-five sacks of flour now can
carry only twelve sacks and requires five or six horses to do so.

Of necessity, writes Lenoir, the cost of many items has risen; for,
were they denied the right to increase prices, merchants would bring
nothing into the city. As a consequence of the rising cost of flour, the
price of bread now stands at ten and a half sous for a four-pound loaf,
and it would be impossible and unfair to require bakers to sell it for
less. All construction has come to a halt, leaving many in the building trades without employment. These men appear daily outside the
Hôtel de Police, hoping to find work cleaning the streets; and Lenoir
takes them on as much to alleviate their desperate condition as to
profit from their help in clearing the roads.

Commodities of all kinds have become very scarce this season, continues Lenoir. The earth yields neither grass nor vegetable. Shipments
of supplies are late, obliging most residents to live off nothing more
than the dried vegetables and the cheese that were stored away in the
fall. This sad and distressing portrait, which unfortunately is only too
accurate, is made still grimmer at the moment by the heavy snow that
covers the ground. Mounds of snow, Lenoir has learned, prevent the
inhabitants of certain villages from even leaving their homes; and high
drifting piles of it obstruct the roads, causing Paris, too, both concrete
need and a sense of isolation.

The lieutenant of police is doing what he can, he reports, to mitigate
the ordeal. Lenoir has seen to it that large quantities of flour move regularly down the river, which—happily—remains open; and he hires as
many as he can of the unemployed who wait in the cold outside. But
more must be done. The police have already spent their last authorization of 20,000 livres in relief and require at least 25,000 livres more. It
will also be necessary, Lenoir argues, to open royal stores of rice, wood,

coal, and other commodities, either to the police or to the clergy, for distribution among the poor.[17]

If the winter of 1784 was particularly harsh, the principal problems it posed—those of unemployment in the construction industry and inadequate means of transport and supply—were recurrent. Whatever the year, the onset of winter obliged the police to devote a larger portion of their resources to relief and to roads. It also demanded that they increase expenditures on lighting, for light—candles and oil—was their principal weapon in combatting the armed robbery and murder that Parisians had long associated with the extended nights of December, January, and February. An anonymous report written in 1643 expresses the popular conception of winter as a time of hidden danger and violence: "The greatest disorder in Paris is to be encountered during the winter when, days being short, residents and visitors find it necessary to employ the first hours of the night to go about their errands. And it is then that most murders, robberies, and other brushes with danger occur. . . . And it is as much pages and lackeys who perpetrate these crimes as soldiers from the regiments of the Guards and cavaliers visiting from their garrisons."[18] By the second half of the eighteenth century, the success of the police in artificially lengthening winter days had altered this attitude and eliminated much of the fear that for so long had accompanied the approach of December.

If it was the violence of individuals that most concerned the police during the coldest months of the year, it was the anger and misconduct of crowds that began to preoccupy them with the coming of spring. March or April generally brought the first of a series of successive increases in the price of grain, as supplies stored from the last harvest began to disappear. With this progressive augmentation in the price of grain, which generally reached its peak in July, went a gradual rise in the price of bread and a consequent, growing sense of discontent among the city's poor. Aware of this cycle and of its danger, the lieutenant of police issued an ordinance each May prescribing measures that would facilitate the conservation of grain; and every spring he reiterated the need to inspect frequently all bakeries in the city, see-

17. BN, MS fr. n.a. 2775, fols. 40–41.
18. Cited in Petrovitch, "Criminalité à Paris," 219. The figures Petrovitch has collected suggest that, if assault was indeed more common in January than in June during the seventeenth century, this had ceased to be the case a hundred years later.

ing that none of them exceeded the controlled price on bread. Hoarding
again became an issue to which the police were forced to give attention; and it was often in April or May that specially commissioned
agents left Paris to buy abroad the quantities of grain or livestock that
could not some summers be found in France.[19]

But despite these efforts, the police were not always able to contain
popular discontent, as in May, 1775, when riots over the price of bread
forced Lenoir from office, or in April, 1789, when a crowd that had
earlier demanded reductions in the price of bread moved on to pillage a
number of food shops in the Faubourg Saint-Antoine and to sack the
home of an unpopular manufacturer. The danger of riot and the concern it evoked in the police continued on beyond the spring. It was,
after all, during the summer of 1725—before flour from the new harvest could reach Paris—that serious disturbances over the price of
bread compelled another lieutenant of police, d'Ombreval, to resign his
post.[20]

On August 29 of that year, the crown summoned its intendant at
Tours, René Hérault, to succeed d'Ombreval. The new lieutenant of
police, unfortunately, left no known record of the intentions he carried
with him from the Touraine to Paris: there is no financial request to
the controller general, no statement to his new subordinates on essential changes in policy. In our attempt to describe the effect of his succession on the Parisian police, we are left with rumors of enmity toward the Jansenists and with records of the relatively large sums he
devoted to domestic espionage. But we know, too, that it was late
summer when he assumed office, the time of year when it was still
necessary to attend with special care to the problems of air pollution,
theft, and mendicancy. Fall would soon be at hand and with it the annual recurrence of other problems and preoccupations. Whatever the
designs Hérault brought with him to the lieutenancy of police, he
learned—as would each of his successors—that Paris, like the land
upon which it had grown, passed regularly through an alternation of
needs, a repeated sequence of natural and cultural phenomena that de-

19. Ordinances of May 18, 1726, May 12, 1727, May 20, 1728, May 12, 1736, in AN,
H-2 1880 (6); Sartine to commissioners, April 21, 1774, Albert to commissioners, May
24, 1775, in AN, Y 13728; BN, MS fr. n.a. 6765, fols. 4–6.

20. BN, MS JF 1103, fol. 149; Rudé, Crowd in the French Revolution, 43; René
Louis de Voyer de Palmy d'Argenson, Journal et mémoires du marquis d'Argenson, ed.
E. J. B. Rathery (9 vols.; Paris, 1859–67), I, 54.

termined to a large extent the activity of both its residents and its
administrators.

During the decades that separate the death of Louis XIV and the Revolution, there appears to have been more continuity in the work of
the police than change; or, to put it another way, the change that did
occur seems to have been primarily cyclical, not linear. The alterna-
tions of day and night, the succession of the seasons, the recurrent
rituals of the church—it was these rather than the priorities of a new
administration that governed policy and the activity that embodied it.
With the exception of d'Albert's transitory dismemberment of the
guilds and the new attention Sartine and Lenoir gave public services,
repetition, not innovation characterized the operations of the police.

But to say that their activity changed little, or changed in accord
with recurrent patterns, is not to say that the police of Paris were in
1789 what they had been when the century began. Their work may
have remained largely constant, but the instrument by which that
work was accomplished had been dramatically transformed. If the
enormous range of police activity had been rather thoroughly plotted
during the reign of Louis XIV (in the initial edict that created the lieutenancy of police and during the tenure in this post of La Reynie and
d'Argenson), it was left to the eighteenth century to create an apparatus commensurate with the ambitions of the crown in Paris. The
change that is most visible and significant in the police of eighteenth-
century Paris is not change in their preoccupations or policy but
change in the nature of the organization through which they sought to
perform the myriad tasks expected of them.

The most obvious change this organization underwent was a change
in size. While the figures available for the early part of the eighteenth
century are not complete, it seems safe to say that the police force
that existed in Paris was at least several times larger in 1789 than it had
been in 1718; and this increase in size could only have meant an increase in the capacity of the police to carry out the duties assigned
them, assuming—as the evidence warrants—that the expansion of the
force as a whole was not accompanied by a considerable decline in
individual competence.

The growth that the police experienced during the eighteenth century was not a uniform process. Some elements of the force grew rapid-

ly; a few grew little or not at all; and one or two even diminished in size. Dramatic increase was most apparent in the forces of patrol, where a watch numbering 150 men in 1718 was absorbed by a new entity, the guard, that counted more than a thousand individuals in its ranks by 1789. This was an increase of something like 600 percent during a period when the city itself may have grown by only 9 percent, passing from a population of 550,000 to one of 600,000. As this section of the force responsible for deterrence increased, so, too, did other elements, particularly those engaged in inspection, services, and administration. There were 18 building and public works inspectors in 1789 and none when Louis XV's reign began; there were 25 employees at the Mont de Piété which itself had not existed in 1715; and there were all those who worked at managing the traffic in wetnurses, men and women who had not been affiliated with the police seventy-five years before. The fire department climbed from 32 men to 221, the number of refuse collectors increased by over 50 percent, and the administrative staff went from 8, or perhaps fewer, to 35. Only those units of the police concerned with investigation and the provision of justice failed to grow at a rate many times that of the city itself.

These increases in personnel were accompanied by a similar expansion in resources. Royal funds spent on police activities in Paris grew during our period from something like 500,000 livres to well over 2 million.[21] In the last years of Louis XIV's reign, the crown had spent less than 300,000 livres cleaning and lighting the streets of Paris; before revolution dislodged Louis XVI, the monarchy was devoting more than twice that sum to the same tasks. A fire department that had received 6,000 livres in 1716 (and nothing before that date) was getting nineteen times as much by 1785. And more money meant, in many cases, new supplies of equipment and new structures in which to house it: 85 garbage carts became 130; in place of 4 fire stations, there were 25, housing not 16 pumps but more than 50.

An augmented budget brought the police not only new quantities of equipment but also some improvements in the quality of the devices they employed. Most notable of these ameliorations was the oil-burning reflector lamp, which, under Sartine, replaced the old candle-

21. See table 8. To get the initial figure, which is a very crude estimate, I have added 200,000 livres (for the watch, the lieutenant of police, the commissioners, and the inspectors) to the known figure of 300,000 livres allocated for lights, the collection of refuse, and protection against fire.

bearing lantern. While furnishing the city with more light than had its predecessor, the new lamp required the attention and care of only half as many men. We have seen, too, that the police devised means for diverting supplies of water from fountains to fire hydrants scattered throughout the city, and that after 1770, under Morat, they brought into service some thirty mobile tanks capable of transporting large quantities of water wherever it was needed to feed the pumps Dupérier had introduced just as the century began.

More men, more money, new equipment—these were not the only changes the police experienced under Louis XV and Louis XVI. With the increase in resources and personnel had come a new professionalism. If there were many more policemen in Paris in 1789 than there had been seven decades earlier, it is also true that more of those who performed police functions were permanent employees who received remuneration for the work they did. Lamplighters were now paid for their labor rather than being coerced into this service without reward as had been the case prior to Sartine's reform of 1769. Fires ceased to be fought by whatever carpenters, masons, roofers, monks, and soldiers one could assemble and became, instead, the responsibility of proud, dedicated, trained men who gave more than a third of their time to protecting Paris against the kind of disaster London had experienced in the seventeenth century, men who drew at least two hundred livres a year for their work as fire fighters. By 1789 patrol of the city was no longer the responsibility of independent office-holders in the watch but had become the sole task of the salaried employees who constituted the guard. Part of the new professionalism apparent in the police of eighteenth-century Paris consisted, then, in the simple fact that many of those who performed what were judged to be police functions had come to rely on these activities, in whole or in part, for their income. The work they did had, by the 1780s, become their profession, the labor they did in order to survive.

But there is another sense in which the police became a more professional company after 1718. If, in an extended sense, a professional is one who has acquired particular competence in some activity by virtue of exclusive devotion, then many of those who served the lieutenant of police came increasingly to deserve this appellation as the eighteenth century progressed. Most commissioners and inspectors acquired specialized functions to which they were expected to give particular attention and in the performance of which they acquired uncommon expertise; employees responsible for wetnurses and their charges ceased trying to do all facets of their work and confined themselves primarily to a single domain—reception and care or correspondence and accounts; and a whole new corps of public inspectors came into being, each of whose members had a narrowly defined responsibility. While some of these individuals were on the watch for hazardous structures, others kept tabs on the condition of urban streets, and still others saw to it that the city's lamps functioned.

This specialization in activity is also apparent among the lieutenant of police's own administrative staff, where, after 1759, a single, omnicompetent secretariat became eight distinct offices, each with its own particular competence. And, in the development of these specialized administrative offices, there is some ground for arguing that the police became not simply a more professional company but a genuine bureaucracy as well, an institution largely controlled and run by its administrative bureaus. It was, after all, these bureaus that stored and dispensed the information, the empirical data necessary for making intelligent decisions about policy; and it was these bureaus that preserved the long lists of precedent upon which chief administrators often relied in choosing their own courses of action. As lieutenants of police came and went, those who worked in the bureaus stayed on, increasing their command of both essential information and precedent, gaining further prestige and stature. It was these bureaucrats who, in the latter half of the century, by means of a brief they had drafted, imposed on each new head of the police an initial definition of his duties; and it is no wonder given their accumulation of experience that, following each change in leadership, they continued for some time to mold the work of their new superior.

There is one final change in the nature of the Parisian police that requires attention. As the force grew in size and became a more professional unit, it also acquired a relatively stable institutional framework or form. It came to possess a structure, both physical and functional, that survived intact the passage of individuals. One aspect of this structure was concrete and tangible. During the course of the eighteenth century, the police rooted themselves in permanent locations, where, day after day, year after year, they and the services they offered could be located and utilized. Guardposts and fire stations, the general headquarters, and even, in one case or two, the offices of commissioners ceased to follow the whims and peregrinations of personnel. Individuals occupied a position on the force and then departed; but when they had gone, the police remained behind, fixed in the same spot, as a new individual stepped in to replace the old.

As the physical existence of the police began to acquire a durable structure, as their presence in the city assumed specific and permanent manifestations that residents could rely on, so too did the borders of their responsibility develop a new fixity; and this was true both for individual members of the force and for the institution as a whole. Commissioners ceased to be jacks of all trades, surrendering many of their tasks to others in order that they might concentrate on judicial functions and the specialized tasks, or departments, assigned them. The role of inspectors became more clearly that of investigators, and members of the administrative staff devoted themselves increasingly to a narrow and carefully delineated set of duties.

The collective responsibility of all these individuals was spelled out in the commission each new lieutenant of police received from the crown; for in this document the monarchy made known what work it expected of its principal representative in Paris and, hence, of all those who served him. Commissions existed, in theory, to give French kings flexibility in the delegation of authority, to permit them to confer and revoke power as changing circumstance and talent suggested. Given the nature of their posts, one would expect that, as royal commissioners, the lieutenants of police would not have had a constant set of duties, that instead these would have shifted and changed as one individual succeeded another in the post. But the available evidence indicates that, by the latter half of the eighteenth century, the commissions issued the lieutenants of police had become standardized. Those conferred on the last three men who filled this position grant the same powers and impose the same duties.[22] If the lines describing police responsibilities in Paris had sometimes shifted in the past, they had by the 1770s largely ceased to do so. A relatively durable structure of roles had emerged for the police to complement and fill the permanent bases they had erected for themselves in the city.

By 1789 the police force of France's capital was a larger and more professional unit than it was in 1718, a company that had at its disposal new quantities of resources, often improved equipment, and a more clearly delineated sense of its responsibilities. But what impact

22. BN, MS fr. 22063, fols. 191 (to Lenoir), 196 (to Albert), and 290 (to Crosne).

did these changes have on Paris, on the city the police had been created, in part, to serve? Did they, in any sense, make the capital itself a better place than it had been? Perhaps the fairest way to gauge their effect is in terms of that amelioration about which the police themselves cared most and which they worked hardest to achieve. Let us ask, then, whether the changes that occurred during the eighteenth century in the Parisian police made it possible for these agents of the crown to provide greater security in 1789 than they had been able to furnish when the century began.

It is undeniable that the police were a vastly more competent body in 1789 than they had been in 1718, but did this new competence permit them to afford Parisians greater safety from the ill will and desperation of their neighbors? That it did cannot perhaps be demonstrated incontrovertibly, though such a conclusion seems reasonable given the greatly enhanced powers of patrol and investigation the police enjoyed and given, too, the sense city dwellers expressed of new immunity from danger. And while Parisians were showing less concern about being stabbed or clubbed on the streets, they were, in fact, enjoying far more adequate protection against other forms of menace, against the impersonal forces that had always inhabited the city and never deigned to hide in the shadows before they took a life. Through improved and expanded efforts to control fire, hunger, disease, accident, and pollution, the police did limit the number of victims these enemies claimed, and thereby contributed significantly to making Paris a safer, more habitable place. Thanks in part to the police and the changes they underwent, a large European city that for so long had killed far more than it created became during the eighteenth century as much a place to live as to die.

But while the police had managed by 1789 to make individual Parisians more secure, they obviously were unable to do the same thing for the regime they served. In the spring and summer of 1789, the police became victims rather than masters of event; and the monarchy they were supposed to protect began its capitulation to the forces opposing it. Why this failure, given the enhanced abilities of the police and their success in guaranteeing individual security?

Whatever else might be said in response to this question—a question that could easily lead to a lengthy discussion of the Revolution and its causes—it is important to recall the obvious, to remember that the police functioned in a context that the will and energy of any individual or institution could refashion only in minor ways. Given the economic structure of the time, with its inherent limits on the production and transport of agricultural commodities, the police—whatever their size or competence—were bound at times to fail in furnishing Paris with adequate supplies of essential foodstuffs. Under the conditions that prevailed in the countryside of eighteenth-century France, there was virtually no way they could contain the individual desperation and public danger issuing from urban hunger. Nor were they able to stem the flow of disparaging commentary which, over the course of the century, undermined the allegiance many Parisians felt for the acts and, indeed, the forms of government. We have seen that the police did not greatly expand their efforts to detect criticism of the regime, whether spoken or written; but even if they had, it is unlikely they could have silenced the significant voices of discontent, given the support these enjoyed among the literate, politically powerful classes in the city. So long as these influential residents were unwilling to collaborate in censorship, so long as many of them openly flaunted proscribed opinions and conspired to protect their authors, no police force was going to be able to protect the crown from its detractors or end the erosion their persistent disparagement produced in support for the government.

By the 1780s the police of Paris were, indeed, a much larger, more efficient, and better equipped company than they had been in 1718; and many of the tasks they undertook, they performed with new efficacy. But there remained immutable limits to what they could achieve in eighteenth-century France, limits imposed by the agricultural techniques of the masses and the political convictions of the elite. Fire that destroys buildings and lives the Parisian police had gained the means to control; but against the flames that consume regimes, they found no tools. Before this form of conflagration they were impotent, unable to save the monarchy—or even themselves.

Appendix

The Fourteen Lieutenants of Police: Biographical Data

Gabriel Nicolas de La Reynie
1625–1709

Birthplace: Limoges
Father's position: Robe family
Wife's father's name: Garibal
Wife's father's position: Maître des requêtes, president of Grand Conseil
Date of marriage: 1668
Protectors: Duke d'Épernon, governor of Guienne
Early career: President of presidial court at Bordeaux, 1646
Maître des requêtes: 1661
Intendant: No
Lieutenant of police: March, 1667–1697
Age upon becoming lieutenant of police: 42
Conseiller d'état: 1680
Great offices of state: No
Other posts and honors: Active on Conseil d'État

Marc René de Voyer d'Argenson
1652–1721

Birthplace: Venice
Father's position: Count d'Argenson, ambassador to Venice
Wife's father's name: Lefevre de Caumartin
Wife's father's position: Maître des requêtes, conseiller d'etat
Date of marriage: 1693
Protectors: Pontchartrain (a relative of d'Argenson's wife)
Early career: Attorney, 1669; lieutenant general of *sénéchaussée* and presidial
  court of Angoulême, 1679; judge, *grand jours* at Poitiers, 1692; investigates
  usurpation of nobility, 1696
Maître des requêtes: 1694 or 1695
Intendant: No
Lieutenant of police: January 29, 1697–January 28, 1718

Age upon becoming lieutenant of police: 45
Conseiller d'état: 1709
Great offices of state: Keeper of the seals, 1718–1720
Other posts and honors: President, Conseil des Finances, 1718–1720; Conseil des Affairs du Dedans du Royaume, 1719–1720(?); becomes Marquis d'Argenson, Académie Française, 1718

Louis Charles de Machault d'Arnouville
1666–1750

Birthplace: ?
Father's position: Robe family
Wife's father's name: Millon
Wife's father's position: Maître des requêtes
Date of marriage: 1700
Protectors: ?
Early career: *Conseiller*, Grand Conseil, 1691; *conseiller*, Parlement of Paris
Maître des requêtes: 1694
Intendant: Of commerce
Lieutenant of police: February, 1718–January, 1720
Age upon becoming lieutenant of police: 52
Conseiller d'etat: 1720
Great offices of state: No
Other posts and honors: First president, Grand Conseil, 1740

Marc Pierre de Voyer d'Argenson
1696–1764

Birthplace: Paris
Father's position: Lieutenant of police; later keeper of the seals
Wife's father's name: Larcher
Wife's father's position: *Conseiller*, Parlement of Paris
Date of marriage: ?
Protectors: Father, Marc-René d'Argenson; Duke d'Orleans, both the regent and the regent's son
Early career: Attorney, Parlement of Paris, 1715; *avocat du roi*, Châtelet, 1718; *conseiller*, Parlement of Paris, 1719
Maître des requêtes: 1719
Intendant: Tours, June, 1720–March, 1722; Paris, 1740–1743
Lieutenant of police: January 30, 1720–June, 1720; March, 1722–January, 1724
Age upon becoming lieutenant of police: 24; 26
Conseiller d'etat: 1724
Great offices of state: Secretary of war, 1743–1757
Other posts and honors: Director of the Librairie, 1737–1738; president of the Grand Conseil, 1738–1740; superintendent of postal administration, 1743; Académie des Sciences, 1729; Académie des Inscriptions, 1749

Gabriel Taschereau de Baudry
1673–1753 or 1755

Birthplace: ?
Father's position: ?
Wife's father's name: ?
Wife's father's position: ?
Date of marriage: ?
Protectors: ?
Early career: ?
Maître des requêtes: 1711
Intendant: Of finance, 1722
Lieutenant of police: July, 1720–March, 1722
Age upon becoming lieutenant of police: 47
Conseiller d'etat: 1722
Great offices of state: No
Other posts and honors: ?

Nicolas Baptiste Ravot d'Ombreval
?–1729

Birthplace: ?
Father's position: *Avocat général* of *cour des aides*, Paris
Wife's father's name: ?
Wife's father's position: ?
Date of marriage: ?
Protectors: Marquise de Prie (d'Ombreval's cousin)
Early career: *Avocat du roi*, Châtelet; *avocat général, cour des aides*, Paris, 1705
Maître des requêtes: 1722
Intendant: Tours, 1725–1729
Lieutenant of police: January 31, 1724–August 29, 1725
Age upon becoming lieutenant of police: ?
Conseiller d'etat: ?
Great offices of state: No
Other posts and honors: ?

René Hérault
1691–1740

Birthplace: Rouen
Father's position: Wood merchant; later receiver general of the Domaines et Bois, Rouen
Wife's father's name: (1) ? (2) Moreau de Séchelles
Wife's father's position: (1) President, Grand Conseil (2) controller general
Date of marriage: ?
Protectors: Fathers-in-law

Early career: *Avocat du roi*, Châtelet, 1712; *procureur général*, Grand Conseil, 1718
Maître des requêtes: 1719
Intendant: Tours, 1722–1725; Paris, 1740
Lieutenant of police: August, 1725–January, 1740
Age upon becoming lieutenant of police: 34
Conseiller d'etat: 1730
Great offices of state: No
Other posts and honors: ?

Claude Henri Feydeau de Marville
1703(?)–1787(?)

Birthplace: ?
Father's position: Lieutenant, Gardes Françaises
Wife's father's name: Hérault
Wife's father's position: Lieutenant of police
Date of marriage: 1738
Protectors: Father-in-law; Prince of Conti
Early career: *Conseiller*, Parlement of Paris, 1726; president, Grand Conseil, 1738
Maître des requêtes: 1736
Intendant: No
Lieutenant of police: January 2, 1740–May 27, 1747
Age upon becoming lieutenant of police: ?
Conseiller d'etat: 1747
Great offices of state: No
Other posts and honors: Director general of the Economats, 1773; first president, Grand Conseil, 1748; becomes Count of Gien and Marquis of Dampierre; Conseil Royal des Finances, 1776

Nicolas René Berryer
1703–1762

Birthplace: Paris
Father's position: *Procureur général*, Grand Conseil
Wife's father's name: Fribois
Wife's father's position: Subfarmer; later Farmer General
Date of marriage: 1738
Protectors: Mme de Pompadour
Early career: *Avocat général* of the Requêtes de l'Hotel, 1728; *conseiller*, Parlement of Paris, 1731
Maître des requêtes: 1739
Intendant: Poitou, 1743–1747
Lieutenant of police: May, 1747–October 16, 1757
Age upon becoming lieutenant of police: 44
Conseiller d'etat: 1751

Great offices of state: Secretary of navy, 1758–1761; keeper of the seals, 1761–1762

Other posts and honors: Conseil des Dépêches, 1757

Henri Baptiste Bertin de Bellisle
1720–1792

Birthplace: Perigueux
Father's position: Count de Bourdeilles; maître des requêtes
Wife's father's name: ?
Wife's father's position: ?
Date of marriage: ?
Protectors: Mme de Pompadour
Early career: Attorney, Bordeaux, 1741; *conseiller*, Grand Conseil, 1741; president, Grand Conseil, 1749; *commissaire* for affair involving Mahé de la Bourdonnais
Maître des requêtes: 1745
Intendant: Roussillon, 1749–1753; Lyon, 1754–1757
Lieutenant of police: October 29, 1757–November 21, 1759
Age upon becoming lieutenant of police: 37
Conseiller d'etat: 1761
Great offices of state: Secretary of state for a specially created fifth department (mines, manufacture, commerce, archives, etc.), 1763–1780; controller general, 1759–1763
Other posts and honors: Becomes First Baron of Périgord; Académie des Sciences, 1763; Académie des Inscriptions, 1774

Antoine Gabriel de Sartine
1729–1801

Birthplace: Barcelona
Father's position: ?
Wife's father's name: Hardy du Plessis
Wife's father's position: ?
Date of marriage: ?
Protectors: Duchess of Phalans or, possibly, Phalaris, the latter a friend of the regent
Early career: *Conseiller*, Châtelet, 1751 or 1752; lieutenant criminal, Châtelet, 1755
Maître des requêtes: 1759
Intendant: No
Lieutenant of police: November or December, 1759–August 29, 1774
Age upon becoming lieutenant of police: 30
Conseiller d'etat: 1767
Great offices of state: Secretary of navy, 1774–1780
Other posts and honors: Becomes Count d'Alby

Jean Charles Pierre Lenoir
1732–1807

Birthplace: Paris
Father's position: *Lieutenant particulier*, Châtelet
Wife's father's name: (1) Montmorency-Laval (2) Plaissance
Wife's father's position: ?
Date of marriage: ?
Protectors: Sartine; Maurepas; Calonne
Early career: *Conseiller*, Châtelet, 1752; *lieutenant particulier*, Châtelet, 1754; lieutenant criminal, Châtelet, 1759; reporter of commission appointed to judge La Chalotais, 1770
Maître des requêtes: 1765
Intendant: Limoges, 1774 (appointed but did not serve)
Lieutenant of police: August, 1774–May, 1775; June, 1776–August, 1785
Age upon becoming lieutenant of police: 42; 43
Conseiller d'etat: 1775
Great offices of state: No
Other posts and honors: Royal librarian, 1783

Joseph François Raymond d'Albert
1721–1796

Birthplace: Ille-sur-Tet
Father's position: Provincial noble; bailli of Ille-sur-Tet
Wife's father's name: ?
Wife's father's position: ?
Date of marriage: ?
Protectors: Turgot; Bertin
Early career: Attorney, professor of law, Perpignan; *conseiller, conseil souverain*, Roussillon, 1759; *conseiller*, Parlement of Paris, 1764; commissioner of the Domaine
Maître des requêtes: 1775
Intendant: Of commerce, 1769–1775 (resigned 1770–1775 in support of Parlement)
Lieutenant of police: May, 1775–June, 1776
Age upon becoming lieutenant of police: 54
Conseiller d'etat: 1788
Great offices of state: No
Other posts and honors: ?

Louis Thiroux de Crosne
1736–1794

Birthplace: Paris
Father's position: President, *chambre des enquêtes*, Parlement of Paris
Wife's father's name: La Michodière
Wife's father's position: Prévôt des marchands; conseiller d'etat

Date of marriage: ?

Protectors: Vergennes (a relative); Breteuil

Early career: *Avocat du roi*, Châtelet; *conseiller*, Parlement of Paris; reviewed for Conseil d'État the decision of the *parlement* of Toulouse against Calas, 1763

Maître des requêtes: 1761

Intendant: Normandy, 1769–?; Lorraine, 1775–1785

Lieutenant of police: August, 1785–July 15 or 16, 1789

Age upon becoming lieutenant of police: 49

Conseiller d'etat: No

Great offices of state: No

Other posts and honors: ?

Note: Biographical information on some lieutenants of police is readily available, while data on others, like Baudry, is almost nonexistent. Much of the extant material is anecdotal and of little use for social, political, or administrative analysis. Amid that which remains one finds occasional disagreement regarding familial background and the dates of birth or death. Tenure in office is a matter over which there is more than occasional dispute. Little agreement exists regarding the precise period each of these men occupied the lieutenancy of police, and one sometimes finds confusion even over the order in which they served. Confronted with this conflicting testimony, one can proceed only by selecting that which appears most reasonable. In cases of dispute, I have preferred the testimony of the *Almanach royal* above all, that of the older manuscript sources to that of the biographical dictionaries, and the less anecdotal, modern *Dictionnaire de biographie française* to other such works.

The appendix I have compiled is as precise as I could make it, in order that mistakes, where they exist, may not remain masked and uncorrected. Error there is, I am sure, particularly regarding the periods of service as lieutenant of police, though this inaccuracy I believe in all cases to involve days or weeks rather than years. (For the suggestion that Sartine's protectress might have been the Duchess of Phalaris rather than Phalans, as I had interpreted the manuscript, and for information about his candidate that I could not find about mine, I am indebted to my friend and colleague, Jospeh Dicorcia.)

SOURCES: APP, EA 16, dossiers 1, 3–7, 9–13; BN, MS fr. 22153, fols. 3–7, 16–19, 20–21, 71; BN, MS fr. n.a. 1214, fols. 627–28; BN, MS JF 1416, fol. 30; BO, MS 1422, p. 740; *Almanach royal*, 1719; *Biographie universelle; Dictionnaire de biographie française;* François Aubert de la Chesnaye-Desbois and Badier, *Dictionnaire de la noblesse* (3rd ed., 19 vols.; Paris, 1863–77); Edme Théodore Bourg [Saint-Edme], *Biographie des lieutenans-généraux, ministres, directeurs-généraux, chargés d'arrondissemens, préfets de la police en France, et de ses principaux agens* (Paris, 1829).

Bibliography

During a single day in May, 1871, in an act of frustration and anger, the Communards at once greatly simplified and greatly complicated the work of anyone who wants to study the police of Paris prior to 1789. The fire they set that day at the Préfecture de Police, while illuminating the sky of Paris for hours, extinguished much of the light that might have shown on more than a century; for, along with the building, it was a significant part of the city's past that served as fuel for the fire.

Destroyed were approximately 6,000 registers and boxes, many of which contained hundreds of pages of information about the police and the city under the Old Regime. According to those who had cared for these materials and who were asked after the fall of the Commune to estimate the losses, the fire burned approximately 80 registers of royal orders to the lieutenants of police; 40 registers of these officials' correspondence with other authorities; 3,000 registers and another 3,000 boxes of data collected by the police on markets, prices, and provisions, on illicit meetings, public health, and all the other matters that fell within the extensive competence and responsibility of the lieutenant of police; 150 registers treating the frequent transfer of prisoners between Paris and the provinces; 16 boxes of plays in manuscript submitted to the police for censorship; 80 boxes of edicts, decrees, and ordinances affecting Paris issued by the Conseil d'État, the Parlement, and other authorities with power over the city; several boxes with material on the police's role in the construction of public monuments, markets, and other urban amenities; several more on the cemeteries of Paris; 2 boxes relating to the diamond necklace affair; and 300 boxes containing the dossiers of individuals detained by administrative order (the infamous *lettres de cachet*). Together the thousands of dossiers in

305

these 300 boxes constituted a vast and invaluable source for those interested in writing the social history of eighteenth-century Paris. Many of the folders, like that of Saint-Just, arrested in 1786, contained miniature portraits that the police had affixed, as they do photographs today, for purposes of future identification.

All of this is now beyond the reach of curiosity or discipline, without the power to haunt the consciences of historians who read slowly or find themselves too easily diverted by the pleasures of Paris. It is gone, and it is worth noting here that this is so in order to spare others who may study the police disappointment and, perhaps, some wasted labor. Today, there are in series A of the archives of the Préfecture de Police—the series specifically devoted to documents dating from the period prior to 1870—only eight boxes (AA 1–8) and thirty-three registers (AB 362–83, 396–406) that are of much interest to those curious about the police of the Old Regime. In burning the Préfecture de Police in 1871, the Communards reduced an overwhelming profusion of data to more than manageable size; but at the same time they condemned some of those interested in their city's past to hours and days of often fruitless hunting through tens of catalogues and hundreds of boxes scattered throughout Paris.

The wrath of the Communards is now more than a century old, but its power over the present survives. And it is frustrating to find what one can know about Paris, about its police, constrained by a sentiment that ought to be aged and feeble, sobering and mysterious to discover rage still at work when those in whom it seemed to live are gone.

An asterisk appears beside the works listed below that have proven most useful to this study. I have also taken the liberty of commenting briefly on some of the sources that follow.

Manuscript Sources

Archives Nationales

From Series AD (Administrative library: Rondonneau collection)
    Subseries AD-I (Administrative and political regime), nos. 18, 22A–28.
    Subseries AD-IX (Finances), no. 389.
From Series F (General administration of France):
    * Subseries F-4 (General accounts), nos. 1017, 1032.
      Important data on police expenditures, particularly for the 1780s.
    Subseries F-7 (Police affairs), nos. 3006, 4774.

With rare exceptions this subseries contains documents relevant to the revolutionary and postrevolutionary periods.

From Series G (Financial and special administrations):
Subseries G-7 (Controller general of finances), nos. 446–47, 1725–1728. Material here, including correspondence of Marc-René d'Argenson, pertains primarily to the period prior to 1718.

From Series H (Local administrations and miscellaneous accounts):
Subseries H-2 (*Bureau de Ville* of Paris: intendancy and *generalité* of Paris), nos. 1880(2)–1880(6) (chronological table); nos. 1880(7)–1880(15) (alphabetical table). Useful overview of regulations issued by a number of urban authorities between 1709 and 1744 and contained in the collection of Commissioner Dupré at the Bibliothèque Nationale.

Series K (Historical monuments), nos. 716, 1020–22. Includes useful memorandum by the keeper of the seals, Miromesnil, on the functions of the lieutenant of police.

From Series O (King's household and emperor's household):
Subseries O-1 (Ministry of the king's household and king's household), nos. 69, 354, 360, 361, 369, 395, 405, 417, 432, 480, 487, 499, 618. Contains valuable payrolls from mid-century and abundant evidence of police involvement in familial problems.

* Series Y (Châtelet of Paris and *prévôté* of the Île-de-France), nos. 9498–9500, 9510–11, 9515, 9530, 9532–39, 9620, 9625, 9641–44 (Chambre de Police); 10620–35 (registers of reports by the guard and the inspectors of police); 11810–11, 13018, 13163 (notebooks of the watch and guard); 12224–25, 12497 (commissioners' records); 12830, 13728 (letters written by the lieutenant of police); 17020, 17112, 17115, 17119–20 (a miscellany of declarations and ordinances). Essential data on the work of the guard and the commissioners; on the lieutenant of police in his capacity as judge and on his relationship to subordinates.

Archives de la Préfecture de Police

Series D (Powers and competence of the prefecture of police):
Subseries B, nos. 355–56.

Series E (Dossiers of individuals unassociated with any significant "affaire"):
Subseries A, no. 16, dossiers 1, 3–7, 9–13 (biographical information on the lieutenants of police).

Bibliothèque Nationale

* *Fonds français* (manuscripts in French), MSS nos. 6791, 6801; 8049–53 (part of the Dupré collection), 8057–60, 8085–90, 8092–94; 8118 (deliberations of Conseil de Police, 1666–1667); 11356 (minutes from the Assemblée de Police, 1728–1740); 11357–60 (reports of Commissioner Marais); 16847 (more material on the Conseil de Police of 1666–1667); 21641, 21732 (from Delamare's collection); 22062–63, 22096–98, 22100–101, 22114–16, 22122–24, 22151, 22153 (biographies of the lieutenants of police from La

Reynie to Berryer), 22175, 22177, 22191 (from the Collection Anisson-Duperron). Valuable material on the activities of numerous authorities in Paris and on the work of the police as censors. Particularly important is MS 11356, the minutes of the Assemblée de Police.

Nouvelles acquisitions françaises (new acquisitions in French), MSS nos. 1214, 1643, 1645, 1799, 2775, 3348 (this last MS contains a number of letters Malesherbes and Sartine exchanged).

* Collection Joly de Fleury, MSS nos. 450, 1103 (correspondence with Crosne); 1310–36 ("Assemblées de Police": not minutes but reports, petitions, and other papers relating to matters considered at meetings of the assemblée—to be used in conjunction with MS fr. 11356); 1415–16 (fol. 30 of 1416 contains biographical material on Lenoir), 1418–19, 2428.

Bibliothèque de l'Arsenal

* Archives of the Bastille (MSS 10001–12725), nos. 10006, 10015, 10021, 10025, 10029, 10136, 10145, 10249–50, 10252, 10282–83, 10293–94, 10321–22, 10879, 11232, 11660, 11732, 11746–47, 11751, 12399, 12436, 12686. Police records until 1775, though most materials date from the 1720s, 1730s and 1740s: incoming letters, dossiers on individuals, reports of agents, including the registers of several inspectors. A great quantity of essential data.

Bibliothèque de l'Institut

"État des baptêmes des mariages et des mortuaires de la ville et faubourgs de Paris." 2 vols. Contains figures on burials and baptisms by month and by parish for the years 1713–1788.

Bibliothèque Historique de la Ville de Paris

Cote provisoire (provisional classification), no. 4725. Previously numbered MS 29736, it is entitled "Affaires générales de la police et de l'hôtel de Paris en l'année 1753."

Nouvelles acquisitions (new acquisitions), MSS nos. 477 (MS by Lenoir), 481.

Bibliothèque Municipale d'Orléans

* MSS 1421–23. Entitled "Mémoires de J.-P. Lenoir," these are, in fact, primarily an assemblage of essays in various stages of completion on the character and activities of the Parisian police. Lenoir intended to publish a book on the subject and produced many drafts of the chapters that were to constitute it. Absolutely vital.

* MS 1424. Lenoir's manuscript copy of the "Mémoire sur l'administration de la police" that Commissioner Lemaire wrote in 1770. More useful than the copy Gazier published in 1879 because this one contains Lenoir's annotations and corrections. The starting point for all work on the prerevolutionary police.

309   BIBLIOGRAPHY

Printed Primary Sources

Académie Française. *Dictionnaire de l'Académie française.* 4th ed.; 2 vols. Lyon: Benoit, Duplain, Joseph Duplain, 1772.

Alletz, Pons Augustin [Le Sage]. *Le Géographe parisien, ou le conducteur chronologique et historique des rues de Paris.* 2 vols. Paris: Valleyre [etc.], 1769.

Almanach parisien. Paris: The Widow Duchesne, 1771.

Almanach royal. Paris: D'Houry [etc.], 1718–1789.

Alphand, Adolphe, ed. *Atlas des anciens plans de Paris.* 2 vols. Paris: Imprimerie Nationale, 1880.

Argenson, René Louis de Voyer de Palmy, marquis d'. *Journal et mémoires du marquis d'Argenson.* Edited by E. J. B. Rathery. 9 vols. Paris: Widow J. Renouard, 1859–1867.

Barbier, Edmond. *Chronique de la régence et du règne de Louis XV, 1718–63.* 8 vols. Paris: Charpentier, 1857.

————. *Journal d'un bourgeois de Paris sous le règne de Louis XV.* Paris: Union Générale d'Editions, 1963.

Boislisle, Arthur Michel de, ed. *Lettres de M. de Marville, lieutenant général de police, au ministre Maurepas, 1742–1747.* 3 vols. Paris: H. Champion, 1896–1905.

————. *Mémoire de la généralité de Paris.* Paris: Imprimerie nationale, 1881. Vol. I of what was to have been a multivolumed work entitled *Mémoires des intendants sur l'état des généralités dressés pour l'instruction du duc de Bourgogne.* No further titles appeared.

Boislisle, Arthur Michel de, and Pierre de Brotonne, eds. *Correspondance des controleurs généraux des finances avec les intendants des provinces, 1683–1715.* 3 vols. Paris: Imprimerie Nationale, 1874–1897.

Brice, Germain. *Description de la ville de Paris et de tout ce qu'elle contient de plus remarquable.* 7th ed.; 4 vols. Paris: François Fournier, 1717.

Chasles, François Jacques. *Dictionnaire universel chronologique et historique de justice, police et finances.* 3 vols. Paris: C. Robustel, 1725.

Cotgrave, Randle. *A dictionarie of the French and English Tongues.* Originally published in 1611. Columbia: University of South Carolina Press, 1950.

Delamare, Nicolas, and Le Clerc du Brillet. *Traité de la police.* 2nd ed., rev. 3 vols. Amsterdam: At the expense of the company, 1729. Delamare's surname is sometimes written "De Lamare," sometimes "De La Mare," and sometimes, as in the *National Union Catalogue,* "de Lamare," where the initial syllable is treated as a particule and the work is catalogued under "L."

Des Essarts. See Le Moyne.

Dictionnaire universel françois et latin, vulgairement appelé Dictionnaire de Trévoux. 7th ed.; 8 vols. Paris: By the Company of Associated Bookdealers, 1771.

Dugas de Bois-Saint-Just, Jean Louis Marie, marquis. *Paris, Versailles et les provinces au XVIIIᵉ siècle, anecdotes sur la vie privée de plusieurs minis-*

tres, évêques, magistrats célèbres, hommes de lettres et autres personnages connus sous les règnes de Louis XV et Louis XVI. 2 vols. Paris: Le Normant, 1809.

Dulaure, Jacques Antoine. Nouvelle description des environs de Paris. Paris: Lejay, 1786.

Encyclopédie, ou Dictionnaire raisonné des sciences, des arts et des métiers. 17 vols. Paris: Briasson [etc.], 1751–1765.

Encyclopédie méthodique: Finances. 3 vols. Paris: Panckouke, 1784–1787. Vols. 33–35 of the Encyclopédie méthodique. 199 vols. Paris: Panckoucke, 1782–1832.

Encyclopédie méthodique: Jurisprudence. 10 vols. Paris: Panckouke, 1782– 1791. Vols. 143–52 of the Encyclopédie méthodique. 199 vols. Paris: Panckouke, 1782–1832. The last two volumes of this work were done by the police archivist Jacques Peuchet and are sometimes listed separately as Encyclopédie méthodique: Police et municipalité.

Estienne, Robert. Dictionnaire françois-latin. Rev. ed. Paris: Robert Estienne, 1549.

Hurtaut, Pierre Nicolas, and Magny. Dictionnaire historique de la ville de Paris et de ses environs. 4 vols. Paris: Moutard, 1779.

Isambert, François, Athanase Jourdan, and Decrusy. Recueil général des anciennes lois françaises depuis l'an 420 jusqu'à la révolution de 1789. 29 vols. Paris: Belin-Le-Prieur, 1821–1833.

Lacaille, Jean de. Description de la ville et des faubourgs de Paris. Paris: Éditions Les Yeux Ouverts, 1967. Reproduction of a detailed map that appeared first in 1714.

Larchey, Loredan, ed. Documents inédits sur le règne de Louis XV; ou . . . le journal des inspecteurs de M. le lieutenant de police De Sartines. Brussels and Paris: Les Marchands de Nouveautés, 1863. Partial publication of MSS 11357–60 at the Bibliothèque Nationale.

Lemaire, Jean Charles. La Police de Paris en 1770. Edited by Augustin Gazier. Nogent-le-Rotrou: G. Daupeley, 1879. An edition of Lemaire's memoire (cf. BO, MS 1424) written in 1770 under order from Sartine and upon the request of the Empress Maria Theresa.

Le Moyne, Nicolas Toussaint [Des Essarts]. Dictionnaire universel de police. 7 vols. Paris: Moutard, 1786–1789. Last volume ends with word "Paumier."

Lenoir, Jean-Charles-Pierre, Détails sur quelques éstablissements de la ville de Paris demandé par S.M. la Reine de Hongrie. Paris: n.p., 1780.

Le Rouge, Georges-Louis. Les Curiosités de Paris, de Versailles, de Marly, de Vincennes, de S. Cloud, et des environs. 2 vols. Paris: Saugrain the elder, 1742.

Lescure, Mathurin Adolphe de, ed. Correspondance secrète inédité sur Louis XVI, Marie-Antoinette, la cour et la ville de 1777 à 1792. 2 vols. Paris: Plon, 1866.

Manuel, Pierre. La Police de Paris devoilée par l'un des administrateurs de 1789. 2 vols. Paris: J. B. Garnery, an II [1791?].

Mercier, Louis Sébastien. *Tableaux de Paris.* Rev. ed. 12 vols. Amsterdam: n.p., 1782–1788.

* Mildmay, William, Sir. *The Police of France.* London: E. Owen and T. Harrison, 1763.
Based on a stay of several years during the early 1750s. Valuable as both an introduction and for some of the detail it contains.

Necker, Jacques. *De l'administration des finances de la France.* 3 vols. n.p., 1784.

Peuchet, Jacques, ed. *Collection des lois, ordonnances et règlements de police depuis le XIIIᵉ siècle jusqu'à l'année 1818: Police moderne de 1667 à 1789.* 8 vols. Paris: n.p., 1818–1819.
The first part of this collection, treating the period from the thirteenth to the seventeenth century, never appeared; that which was printed ends with the year 1771.

————. *Mémoires tirés des archives de la police de Paris.* 6 vols. in 3. Paris: A. Levavasseur, 1838.
A fascinating and troubling source, which often reads much like one of Dumas's novels. At once incredible and persuasive, it may be the work of a police archivist who claimed to have evidence for all he recorded here; or it may, as is sometimes claimed, have come from the pen of Baron Etienne de Lamothe-Langon (1786–1864), a prefect of Toulouse under Napoleon, who gave up public life for letters following the Restauration and who proved very prolific in his new vocation, producing, among many other works, a novel entitled *Le Vampire ou la vierge de Hongrie.* To be enjoyed and used with care. Excerpts from the *Mémoires* were published by Gallimard in 1934 under the title *Les Secrets de la police, de Louis XIV à Louis Philippe.*

Piganiol de la Force, Jean Aymar. *Description historique de la ville de Paris et de ses environs.* 10 vols. Paris: Associated Bookdealers, 1765.

Ranconet, Aimar de. *Thresor de la langue françoise, tant ancienne que moderne.* Edited and enlarged by Jean Nicot. Paris: D. Douceur, 1606.

Raunié, Émile, ed. *Chansonnier historique du XVIIIᵉ siècle.* 10 vols. Paris: A. Quantin, 1879–1884. Largely satirical commentary on the characters and activities of most of the lieutenants of police. References to Marc-René d'Argenson and René Hérault are particularly numerous.

Richelet, Pierre. *Nouveau Dictionnaire françois.* Rev. ed. 2 vols. Rouen: n.p., 1719.

Salle, Jacques Antoine. *Traité des fonctions, droits et privilèges des commissaires au Châtelet de Paris.* 2 vols. Paris: P. A. Le Prieur, 1759.

Thiéry, Luc Vincent. *Guide des étrangers et voyageurs à Paris.* 2 vols. Paris: Hardouin et Gattey, 1787.

Secondary Sources

* Abbiateci, André, *et al. Crimes et criminalité en France 17ᵉ–18ᶜ siècle. Cahiers* of *Annales,* No. 33. Paris: A. Colin, 1971.

Antoine, Michel. "Les Comités des ministres sous le règne de Louis XV." *Revue historique de droit français et étranger.* 4th series. XXVIII (1951), 193–230.

———. *Le Conseil.du roi sous le règne de Louis XV.* Geneva: Droz, 1970.

———. *Le Fonds du conseil d'état du roi aux Archives Nationales.* Paris: Imprimerie Nationale, 1955.

Antoine, Michel, et al. *Guide des recherches dans les fonds judiciaires de l'ancien régime.* Paris: Imprimerie Nationale, 1958.

Ariès, Philippe. *Histoire des populations françaises et de leurs attitudes devant la vie depuis le XVIIIe siècle.* Paris: Seuil, 1971.

Babeau, Albert Arsene. *Paris en 1789.* Paris: Didot, 1892.

———. *La Ville sous l'ancien régime.* Paris: Didier and Co., 1880.

Barker, Ernest. *The Development of Public Services in Western Europe, 1660–1930.* Originally published in 1944. Hamden, Conn.: Archon Books, 1966.

Barroux, Marius. *Essai de bibliographie critique des généralités de l'histoire de Paris.* Paris: H. Champion, 1908. Very useful. Sections on atlases, eighteenth-century guides, administration, police, customs, amusements, statistics.

Baudrillart, Henri. *Pertes éprouvées par les bibliothèques de Paris pendant le siège par les Prussiens en 1870 et pendant la domination de la commune révolutionnaire en 1871.* 2nd ed., rev. Paris: L. Techener, 1872.

Bernard, Leon. *The Emerging City: Paris in the Age of Louis XIV.* Durham, N.C.: Duke University Press, 1970.

Biographie universelle, ancienne et moderne. 52 vols. and supplement. Paris: Michaud Bros., 1811–62.

Bloch, Camille. *L'Assistance et l'état en France à la veille de la révolution (1764–1790).* Paris: Picard, 1908.

Bluche, François. *Les Magistrats du parlement de Paris au XVIIIe siècle.* Besancon: Jacques et Demontrond, 1960.

Bonnassieux, Louis Marie. "Note sur l'ancienne police de Paris." *Bulletin de la Société de l'histoire de Paris et de l'Ile-de-France,* XXI (1894), 187–92.

Bosher, J. F. *French Finances 1770–1795: From Business to Bureaucracy.* Cambridge: Cambridge University Press, 1970.

Boucher, Louis. *La Salpêtrière; son histoire de 1656 à 1790, ses origines et son fonctionnement au XVIIe siècle.* Paris: A. Delahaye et Lecrosnier, 1883.

Bourde, André J. *Agronomie et agronomes en France au XVIIIe siècle.* 3 vols. Paris: S.E.V.P.E.N., 1967. Vol. 2, pp. 1079–95, contains a valuable account of Bertin's career.

Bourg, Edme Théodore [Saint-Edme]. *Biographie des lieutenans-généraux, ministres . . . , [et] préfets de police en France, et de ses principaux agens.* Paris: Théodore Edme Bourg, 1829. Contains the same anecdotes and information to be found in the *Biographie universelle.*

Buisson, Henry. *La Police, son histoire.* Vichy: n.p., 1949.

Cahen, Leon. *Le Grand Bureau des pauvres à Paris au milieu du XVIIIe siècle.* Paris: G. Bellais, 1904.

———. "Les Idées charitables à Paris au XVIIe et au XVIIIe siècles d'après les règlements des compagnies paroissiales." *Revue d'histoire moderne*, II (1900–1901), 5–32.

———. "La Population parisienne au milieu du XVIIIe siècle." *Revue de Paris*, V (1919), 146–70.

Carré, Henri Frédéric. *Le Règne de Louis XV*. Paris: Hachette, 1909. Vol. VIII, part 2 of Ernest Lavisse (ed.), *Histoire de France depuis les origines jusqu'à la révolution*. 9 vols. Paris: Hachette, 1900–1911.

Chagniot, Jean. "Le Guet et la garde de Paris à la fin de l'ancien régime." *Revue d'histoire moderne et contemporaine*, XX (1973), 58–71. A fine, carefully researched article. Easily the best piece of work to date on the watch and guard of Paris.

Chassaigne, Marc. *La Lieutenance générale de police de Paris*. Paris: A. Rousseau, 1906. Well-written thesis submitted to the Faculty of Law at the University of Paris. Relies almost exclusively on printed sources.

Chaussinand-Nogaret, Guy. *La Noblesse au XVIIIe siècle; de la féodalité aux lumières*. Paris: Hachette, 1976.

Chevalier, Louis. *Classes laborieuses et classes dangereuses à Paris pendant la premiére moitié du XIXe siècle*. Paris: Plon, 1958.

Cilleuls, Alfred des. "Les Recensements de la population en France avant 1830," in the *Compte rendu* of the Académie des Sciences Morales et Politiques, CLXII (1909), 783–94.

Clément, Pierre. *La Police sous Louis XIV*. Paris: Didier and Co., 1866.

Cobb, Richard. *The Police and the People*. New York: Oxford University Press, 1970.

Coussilan, Auguste A. [Jacques Hillairet]. *Dictionnaire historiques des rues de Paris*. 2 vols. Paris: Editions de Minuit, 1963. The first volume contains a useful introduction to a number of eighteenth-century Parisian institutions.

Coyecque, Ernest. *Inventaire de la Collection Anisson sur l'histoire de l'imprimerie et la librairie principalement à Paris*. 2 vols. Paris: Ernest Leroux, 1900. The Collection Anisson comprises MSS fr. 22061–193 at the Bibliothèque Nationale.

Darnton, Robert. "The Memoirs of Lenoir, Lieutenant de Police of Paris, 1774–1785." *English Historical Review*, LXXXV (1970), 532–59. Professor Darnton has reproduced here pp. 716–44 of MS 1422 at the Bibliothèque Municipale d'Orléans.

Dictionnaire de biographie française. Paris: Letouzey and Ané, 1933–.

Dictionnaire de Paris. Paris: Larousse, 1964.

Dollinger, Philippe, Philippe Wolff, and Simonne Guenée. *Bibliographie d'histoire des villes de France*. Paris: C. Klincksieck, 1967.

Dumas, François. *La Généralité de Tours au XVIIIe siècle; administration de l'intendant Du Cluzel (1766–1783)*. Paris: Hachette, 1894.

Dumolin, Maurice. "Notes sur les vieux guides de Paris." *Mémoires de la Société de l'histoire de Paris*. XLVII (1924), 209–85.

Égret, Jean. *Louis XV et l'opposition parlementaire*. Paris: A. Colin, 1970.

El Kordi, Mohammed. *Bayeux aux XVIIe et XVIIIe siècles: contribution à l'histoire urbaine de la France*. Paris: Mouton, 1970.

Ellul, Jacques. *Histoire des institutions de France.* Paris: Presses Universitaires de France, 1955.

Flammermont, Jules. *Remontrances du parlement de Paris au XVIIIᵉ siècle.* 3 vols. Paris: Imprimerie Nationale, 1888–1898.

Forges, Patricia Lemoyne de. "La Police dans la région parisienne" in Patricia and Jean Michel Lemoyne de Forges, *Aspects actuels de l'administration parisienne.* Work and Research of the University of Paris in Law, Economics, and the Social Sciences, Administrative Sciences Series, No. 3. Paris: Presses Universitaires de France, 1972.

Forster, Robert and Elborg, eds. *European Society in the Eighteenth Century.* New York: Harper & Row, 1969.

Fosseyeux, Marcel. "L'Assistance aux prisonniers à Paris sous l'ancien régime." *Mémoires de la Société de l'histoire de Paris,* XLVIII (1925), 110–29.

————. "Le Budget de la charité à Paris au XVIIIᵉ siècle." *Revue des études historiques,* LXXXV (1919), 253–64.

————. *L'Hôtel-Dieu de Paris au XVIIᵉ et XVIIIᵉ siècles.* Paris: Berger-Levrault, 1912.

Franklin, Alfred. *Dictionnaire historique des arts, métiers et professions exercés dans Paris depuis le XIIIᵉ siècle.* Paris: H. Welter, 1906.

————. *La Vie privée d'autrefois; les Parisiens, XVIIᵉ–XVIIIᵉ siècle.* Edited by Arlette Farge. Paris: Perrin, 1973.

Frégier, Honoré Antoine. *Histoire de l'administration de la police de Paris, depuis Philippe-Auguste juqu'aux états généraux de 1789.* 2 vols. Paris: Guillaumin, 1850.

Funck-Brentano, Frantz. *Archives de la Bastille.* Paris: E. Plon, Nourrit and Co., 1892–1895. Vol. 9 of Henry Martin (ed.), *Catalogue des manuscrits de la Bibliothèque de l'Arsenal.* 9 vols. Paris: E. Plon, Nourrit and Co., 1885–1899.

————. *Les Lettres de cachet à Paris, étude suivie d'une liste des prisonniers de la Bastille (1659–1789).* Paris: Imprimerie Nationale, 1903.

Furet, François, and Adeline Daumard. *Structures et relations sociales à Paris au XVIIIᵉ siècle.* Paris: A. Colin, 1961.

Gay, Jean-Louis. "L'Administration de la capitale entre 1770 et 1789." *Paris et l'Île-de-France. Mémoires.* VIII (1956), 299–370.

* Glass, David Victor, and David Edward Charles Eversley. *Population in History.* Chicago: Aldine Publishing Company, 1965. Most useful for my purposes were the articles by Bourgeois-Pichat, Goubert, Habakkuk, Helleiner, Henry, McKeown and Brown, and Meuvret.

Gruder, Vivian. *The Royal Provincial Intendants: A Governing Elite in Eighteenth-Century France.* Ithaca, N.Y.: Cornell University Press, 1968.

Hannaway, Caroline C. "Medicine, Public Welfare, and the State in Eighteenth-century France: The Société Royale de Médecine of Paris, 1776–1793." Ph.D. dissertation, Johns Hopkins University, 1974.

Henry, Louis. "Le Volume de l'immigration à Paris de 1740 à 1792." *Population,* VI (1971), 1073–85.

Hérault, Commandant. "L'Éclairage des rues de Paris à la fin du XVIIᵉ et au

XVIIIᵉ siècles." *Mémoires de la Société de l'histoire de Paris.* XLIII (1916), 129–265.

Herrmann-Mascard, Nicole. *La Censure des livres à Paris à la fin de l'ancien régime (1750–1789).* Paris: Presses Universitaires de France, 1968.

Kaplan, Steven L. *Bread, Politics, and Political Economy in the Reign of Louis XV.* 2 vols. The Hague: Martinus Nijhof, 1976.

Labrousse, Ernest, *et al. Des derniers temps de l'âge seigneurial aux préludes de l'âge industriel (1660–1789).* Paris: Presses Universitaires de France, 1970. Vol. 2 in *Histoire économique et sociale de France.* Edited by Ferdinand Braudel and Ernest Labrousse. Paris: Presses Universitaires de France, 1970–.

La Chesnaye-Desbois, Francois Aubert, and de Badier. *Dictionnaire de la noblesse, contentant les généalogies, l'histoire et la chronologie des familles noble de la France, l'explication de leurs armes et l'état des grandes terres du Royaume.* 3rd ed.; 19 vols. Paris: Schlesinger Bros., 1863–1877.

Lallemand, Léon. *Histoire de la charité.* 4 vols. Paris: A. Picard and Son, 1902–1912.

———. *Histoire des enfants abandonnés et délaissés.* Paris: A. Picard and Son, 1885.

Lavedan, Pierre. *Histoire de Paris.* "Que Sais-Je?" Series. Paris: Presses Universitaires de France, 1967.

———. *Histoire de l'urbanisme.* 3 vols. Paris: H. Laurens, 1926–1952.

———. *Histoire de l'urbanisme à Paris.* Paris: Association for the Publication of a History of Paris, distributed by Hachette, 1975.

Lazare, Louis, and Félix Lazare. *Dictionnaire administratif et historique des rues de Paris et de ses monuments.* Paris: F. Lazare, 1844.

Le Clerc, Marcel. *Histoire de la police.* "Que Sais-Je?" Series. Paris: Presses Universitaires de France, 1964.

Le Grand, Léon. "Les Papiers des secretaires d'état de la maison du roi et de la guerre et l'histoire de la ville et généralité de Paris." *Mémoires de la Société de l'histoire de Paris,* XLIX (1927), 31–43.

Lelarge, André. "Le Numérotage des maisons de Paris sous Louis XVI et pendant la révolution." *Bulletin de la Société de l'histoire de Paris et de l'Ile-de-France,* LX (1933), 63–68.

Lemaire, H. "Les Cimetières de Paris de 1760 à 1825." *Bulletin de la Société de l'histoire de Paris et de l'Ile-de-France,* LI (1924), 82–90.

Lemoigne, Yves. "Population and Provisions in Strasbourg in the Eighteenth Century," in *New Perspectives on the French Revolution.* Edited by Jeffrey Kaplow. New York: John Wiley and Sons, 1965.

Le Roux de Lincy, Antoine Victor. *Histoire de l'Hôtel de Ville de Paris.* Paris: J. B. Dumoulin, 1846.

Lespinasse, René de. *Les Métiers et corporations de la ville de Paris.* 3 vols. Paris: Imprimerie Nationale, 1896–1897.

Levasseur, Émile. *Histoire des classes ouvrières et de l'industrie avant 1789.* 2 vols. Paris: A. Rousseau, 1900–1901.

———. *La Population française.* 3 vols. Paris: A. Rousseau, 1889–1892.

Lot, Ferdinand. *Recherches sur la population et la superficie des cités remontant a l'époque gallo-romaine.* 2 vols. Paris: E. Champion, 1944–1946, 1950.

Marion, Marcel. *Dictionnaire des institutions de la France aux XVIIe et XVIIIe siècles.* Originally published in 1923. New York: Burt Franklin, 1968.

McCloy, Shelby T. *Government Assistance in Eighteenth-Century France.* Durham, N.C.: Duke University Press, 1946.

Meuvret, Jean. "Le Commerce des grains et des farines à Paris et les marchands parisiens à l'époque de Louis XIV." *Revue d'histoire moderne et contemporaine,* III (1956), 169–203.

Ministre des Travaux Publics, de l'Agriculture et du Commerce. *Territoire, population.* Paris: Imprimerie Royale, 1837. Vol. 2 of *Statistique de la France.* 1st series. 13 vols. Paris: Imprimerie Royale [etc.], 1835–1852.

Molinier, Auguste. *Inventaire sommaire de la collection Joly de Fleury.* Paris: A. Picard, 1881.

Mols, Roger. *Introduction à la démographie historique des villes d'Europe du XIVe au XVIIIe siècle.* 3 vols. Gembloux: J. Duculot, 1954–1956.

Monin, Hippolyte. *L'État de Paris en 1789.* Paris: D. Jouaust, 1889.

Montbas, Hughes, Vicomte de. *La Police parisienne sous Louis XVI.* Paris: Hachette, 1949.

Moreu Rey, Enric. *Un Barceloni a la cort de Maria-Antonieta: Sartine.* Barcelona: Editorial Selecta, 1955.

Mousnier, Roland. *État et société en France aux XVIIe et XVIIIe siècles.* "Les Cours de Sorbonne." Paris: Centre de Documentation Universitaire, 1969.

———. *Paris au XVIIe siècle.* Les Cours de Sorbonne. Paris: Centre de Documentation Universitaire, 1962.

———. *Les XVIe et XVIIe siècles; les progrès de la civilisation européenne et le déclin de l'orient, 1492–1715.* Paris: Presses Universitaires de France, 1954. Vol. 4 of *Histoire générale des civilisations.* Edited by Maurice Crouzet. 7 vols. Paris: Presses Universitaires de France, 1953–1957.

Mumford, Lewis. *The City in History: Its Origins, Its Transformations, and Its Prospects.* New York: Harcourt, Brace, and World, 1961.

Paultre, Christian. *De la répression de la mendicité et du vagabondage en France sous l'ancien régime.* Paris: Larose and Tenin, 1906. Based on MSS JF 1307–309 at the Bibliothèque Nationale.

Peronnet, Michel. "Police et réligion à la fin du XVIIIe siècles." *Annales historique de la révolution française,* XLII (1970), 375–97.

Pessard, Gustave. *Nouveau dictionnaire historique de Paris.* Paris: E. Rey, 1904.

Pillorget, René, and Jean de Viguerie. "Les Quartiers de Paris au XVIIe et XVIIIe siècles." *Revue d'histoire moderne et contemporaine,* XVII (1970), 253–77.

Poëte, Marcel. *Répertoire des sources manuscrites de l'histoire de Paris.* 3 vols. Paris: E. Leroux, 1915–1916.

———. *Une vie de cité; Paris, de sa naissance à nos jours.* 3 vols. Paris: A. Picard, 1924–1931.

Pronteau, Jeanne. *Les Numérotages de maisons de Paris du XVe siècle à nos* *jours.* City of Paris. Commission of Historical Works: Sub-commission of Contemporary Municipal History, No. 8. Paris: Imprimerie Municipale, 1966.

Quentin, Henri [Paul d'Estrée]. "Journal du lieutenant de police Feydeau de Marville." *Nouvelle Revue rétrospective*, VI (1897), 97–120, 169–216, 265–88.

———. "Origines du chansonnier de Maurepas." *Revue d'histoire littéraire de France*, III (1896), 332–45.

———. "Un policier homme de lettres, l'inspecteur Meusnier (1748–1757)." *Revue rétrospective*, n.s., XVII (1892), 217–76.

Raeff, Marc. "The Well-Ordered Police State and the Development of Modernity in Seventeenth and Eighteenth-Century Europe: An Attempt at a Comparative Approach." *American Historical Review*, LXXX (1975), 1221–43.

Raisson, Horace. *Histoire de la police de Paris.* Paris: Le Vasseur, 1844. Without references. Treats those who headed police rather than the police themselves.

[Fourier, Jean Baptiste, Baron]. *Recherches statistiques sur la ville de Paris et le département de la Seine.* 2nd ed.; 6 vols. Paris: Department of the Seine, 1826–1860.

Reinhard, Marcel. *Paris pendant la Révolution.* "Les Cours de Sorbonne." 2 vols. Paris: Centre de Documentation Universitaire, 1966.

Richet, Denis. *La France moderne: l'esprit des institutions.* Paris: Flammarion, 1973.

Roche, Daniel. "Aperçus sur la fortune et les revenues des princes de Condé à l'aube du XVIIIᵉ siècle." *Revue d'histoire moderne et contemporaine*, XIV (1967), 217–43.

Rudé, George. *The Crowd in the French Revolution.* New York: Oxford: Oxford University Press, 1967.

———. "La Taxation populaire de mai 1775 à Paris et dans la région parisienne." *Annales historiques de la révolution française*, XXVIII (1956), 236–59.

Saalman, Howard. *Medieval Cities.* New York: Braziller, 1968.

Saint-Germain, Jacques. *La Reynie et la police au grand siècle.* Paris: Hachette, 1962.

———. "D'Argenson, lieutenant-général de police sous Louis XIV." *Revue Littérature, Histoire, Arts et Sciences des Deux Mondes*, XIX (1966), 387–403.

Sars, Maxime, Comte de. *Le Noir, lieutenant de police (1732–1807).* Paris: Hachette, 1948. Makes no use of Lenoir's papers in Orléans.

Sée, Henri. *La France économique et sociale au XVIIIᵉ siècle.* Rev. bibliography. Paris: A. Colin, 1967.

Seigle, Joel David. "The Impact of Bureaucratization in France: Solidarity and Differentiation in the Royal Administration in the Second Half of the Eighteenth Century." Ph.D. dissertation, University of Chicago, 1973.

Sennett, Richard, ed. *Classic Essays on the Culture of Cities.* New York: Appleton-Century-Crofts, 1969.

Stead, John Philip. *The Police of Paris.* London: Staples Press Limited, 1957. Law enforcement in Paris from the time of Saint Louis to the 1950s. The eighteenth century gets fifteen pages.

Thuillat, Louis. *Gabriel Nicolas de La Reynie, premier lieutenant général de police de Paris.* Thesis, Faculty of Law, Poitiers. Limoges: Imprimerie Général, 1930.

Toutain, Jean Claude. *La Population de la France de 1700 à 1959. Cahiers* of the Institut de Science Economique Appliquée. Series AF (Quantitative History of the French Economy), no. 3. Paris: I.S.E.A., 1963.

Vallée, Léon. *Catalogue des plans de Paris et des cartes d'Île-de-France.* Paris: H. Champion, 1908.

Wilhelm, Jacques. *Paris au cours des siècles.* Paris: Hachette, 1961. This piece of work, done by a man who was chief curator of the Musée Carnavalet, is full of wonderful prints, drawings, and paintings. Very helpful in making eighteenth-century Paris concrete and tangible.

The World Almanac and Book of Facts, 1976. New York: Doubleday and Co., 1976.

Index

319